# ONE WEEK LOAN

# FROM HOUSE OF LORDS TO SUPREME COURT

2009 saw the centenary of the Society of Legal Scholars and the transition from the House of Lords to the new Supreme Court. The papers presented in this volume arise from a seminar organised jointly by the Society of Legal Scholars and University of Birmingham to celebrate and consider these historic events. The papers examine judicial reasoning and the interaction between judges, academics and the professions in their shared task of interpretative development of the law. The volume gathers leading authorities on the House of Lords in its judicial capacity together with academics whose specialisms lie in particular fields of law, including tort, human rights, restitution, European law and private international law. The relationship between judge and jurist is, therefore, investigated from a variety of perspectives and with reference to different jurisdictions. The aim of the volume is to reflect upon the jurisprudence of the House of Lords and to consider the prospects for judging in the new Supreme Court.

# From House of Lords to Supreme Court

## Judges, Jurists and the Process of Judging

Edited by

James Lee

·HART·
PUBLISHING

OXFORD AND PORTLAND, OREGON
2011

Published in the United Kingdom by Hart Publishing Ltd
16C Worcester Place, Oxford, OX1 2JW
Telephone: +44 (0) 1865 517530
Fax: +44 (0) 1865 510710
E-mail: mail@hartpub.co.uk
Website: http://www.hartpub.co.uk

Published in North America (US and Canada) by
Hart Publishing
c/o International Specialized Book Services
920 NE 58th Avenue, Suite 300
Portland, OR 97213-3786
USA
Tel: +1 503 287 3093 or toll-free: (1) 800 944 6190
Fax: +1 503 280 8832
E-mail: orders@isbs.com
Website: http://www.isbs.com

British Library Cataloguing in Publication Data
Data Available

ISBN: 978-1-84946-081-1

Typeset by Hope Services, Abingdon
Printed and bound in Great Britain by
CPI Antony Rowe Ltd, Chippenham, Wiltshire

# Acknowledgements

This collection comprises papers given at the Society of Legal Scholars Annual Seminar 2009, 'Judges and Jurists: Reflections on the House of Lords', which took place at the Law Society in November 2009. No collection of papers from a conference can hope to capture the subsequent frank and stimulating discussion amongst academics, practitioners and the judiciary. But the essays here accurately reflect the quality of the event, and pay tribute to the twin inspirations for the Seminar: the transition from the House of Lords to the new Supreme Court of the United Kingdom, and the Centenary of the Society of Legal Scholars.

I note my gratitude to all the chairs, speakers and delegates at the Seminar, many of whom supported the idea of the event from its very outset: I thank particularly Dame Mary Arden, Anthony Arnull, John Baldwin, John Blackie, Alexandra Braun, Adrian Briggs, Richard Clayton, Elizabeth Cooke, Brice Dickson, Sir Terence Etherton, David Feldman, Mary Ford, Sir Francis Jacobs, Andrew Le Sueur, Aileen Kavanagh, Hon Michael Kirby, David Miers, Alan Paterson, Lord Rodger of Earlsferry, Keith Stanton, Jenny Steele and Graham Virgo.

The Seminar could not have taken place without a generous grant from the Society of Legal Scholars from its Annual Seminar Series Competition, and I greatly appreciated the encouragement of several Presidents of the Society for the project: Sarah Worthington, Fiona Cownie and Nick Wikeley. The administrative assistance provided by Mel Scott, Sally Thomson, Clare de la Torre, Luke Price and Jonathan Laidlow was invaluable.

Finally, I should like to thank Richard Hart, Rachel Turner, Melanie Hamill, Jo Ledger and the rest of the team at Hart Publishing for their patience and efficiency.

James Lee
Birmingham
May 2010

# Contents

# Contributors

**Professor Anthony Arnull** is the Barber Professor of Jurisprudence at the University of Birmingham.

**Dr Alexandra Braun** is CUF Lecturer at the University of Oxford and Fellow and Tutor in Law at Lady Margaret Hall.

**Professor Adrian Briggs** is Professor of Private International Law at the University of Oxford, Fellow of St Edmund Hall, Oxford and a Barrister at Blackstone Chambers.

**Professor Elizabeth Cooke** is a Law Commissioner for England and Wales and Professor of Law at the University of Reading.

**Professor Brice Dickson** is Professor of International and Comparative Law at Queen's University Belfast.

**Dr Aileen Kavanagh** is Reader in Law at the University of Oxford and Fellow of St Edmund Hall.

**Hon Michael Kirby AC CMG** is a former Justice of the High Court of Australia.

**James Lee** is a Lecturer in Law at the University of Birmingham.

**Prof Alan Paterson OBE FRSE** is Professor of Law at the University of Strathclyde.

**Professor Keith Stanton** is Professor of Law at the University of Bristol.

**Professor Jenny Steele** is Professor of Law at the University of York.

**Professor Graham Virgo** is Professor of English Private Law at the University of Cambridge and Fellow of Downing College.

# Table of Cases

## CAYMAN ISLANDS

## EUROPEAN COURT OF HUMAN RIGHTS

## EUROPEAN UNION

## FRANCE

## GERMANY

## INDIA

ISLE OF MAN

UNITED KINGDOM

## UNITED STATES

# Table of Legislation

## INDIA

## INTERNATIONAL INSTRUMENTS

## UNITED KINGDOM

**Primary Legislation**

## Secondary Legislation

## UNITED STATES

# 1

# *Introduction*

JAMES LEE

O N 30 JULY 2009, the Appellate Committee of the House of Lords
delivered its final decisions. There was little fanfare after the last judicial
speech, which was delivered in *R (on the application of Purdy) v Director
of Public Prosecutions*[1] by Lord Neuberger of Abbotsbury, who has become
Master of the Rolls rather than become a Justice of the new Supreme Court of
the United Kingdom. After Lord Neuberger concurred in allowing the appeal,
Lord Phillips of Worth Matravers, then Senior Law Lord and now first President
of the Supreme Court, simply proclaimed: 'Here endeth our final judgments.'[2]
This collection provides, as did the Seminar, an opportunity to celebrate on their
Lordships' behalf, and to mark the inauguration of the new Supreme Court.

This collection originates in the Society of Legal Scholars Centenary Seminar,
which took place at the Law Society's Hall in November 2009. The Seminar
marked two events: the transition from the House of Lords to the Supreme Court
of the United Kingdom, and the culmination of the Society of Legal Scholars' year
of Centenary celebrations.

The first meeting of the nascent Society of Public Teachers of Law was on 15
December 1908 in the Council Room of the Law Society, where the co-founder of
the Society, Professor Edward Jenks, was Director of Legal Studies. The first Annual
Meeting of the Society was on 1 July 1909 in the same room. The relationship
between academic and practising lawyers has been a theme of the Society since its
inception. At that first Annual General Meeting, the Society's co-founder and first
President, Professor Goudy, explained the importance of its members:

> Upon us rests, in considerable measure, responsibility for the future competency of our
> judges and barristers and solicitors, and to some extent also of our legislators, statesmen
> and administrators... [F]uture reform of the laws, and consequent amelioration of the
> social and political conditions in this country, may largely depend upon the knowledge
> we impart to, and the ideas we instil into, the minds of our pupils.[3]

---

[1] *R (on the application of Purdy) v Director of Public Prosecutions* [2009] UKHL 45; [2009] 3 WLR
403.

[2] F Gibb, 'Historic last words that bring years of uncertainty and fear to an end' *Timesonline*, 30
July 2009 http://business.timesonline.co.uk/tol/business/law/article6733943.ece.

[3] Quoted by W Holdsworth, 'The Vocation of a Public Teacher of Law' (1925) 2 *Journal of the
Society of Public Teachers of Law* 1, 11.

So it was appropriate that our event, which gathered together judges, jurists and practitioners, was held at the Law Society.

There is another anniversary to note. The first volume of the *Journal of the Society of Public Teachers of Law* recorded the establishment of the Birmingham School of Law,[4] which represented an expansion both in the provision of public teaching of law, and in legal scholarship, to the provinces. The Seminar was organised under the auspices of the Birmingham Law School, which in 2008–09 celebrated its own anniversary, of 80 years since its foundation. The Holdsworth Club, the University of Birmingham's Law Society, is named in honour of Sir William Holdsworth, and is as old as the Law School. The Club has provided since the 1920s one of the leading annual platforms for extra-judicial comment, with the Presidential Addresses offering reflections on the nature of law, judges and jurists.[5]

From its very early days, the Society of Legal Scholars encouraged judicial interaction. Indeed, in 1932, the Society's Journal published Lord Atkin's 1931 lecture given at the Great Hall of King's College.[6] In that lecture, his Lordship made his first reference to the 'neighbour' principle,[7] some seven months before it would be enshrined in tort law by the majority decision of the House of Lords in *Donoghue v Stevenson*.[8] His Lordship went on to assert that '[there] is no doubt that one of the sources of the law is the criticism and the suggested improvements made from time to time by thoughtful writers and lecturers.'[9]

In *Donoghue* itself, Lord Buckmaster did not entirely agree: 'the work of living authors, however deservedly eminent, cannot be used as an authority, though the opinions they express may demand attention'.[10] Leap forward to 2009, and we find that in six out of the seven final decisions of the House, reference was made to academic literature.[11]

---

[4] C Grant Robinson, 'A Birmingham School of Law' (1924) *Journal of the Society of Public Teachers of Law* 22.

[5] A selection of Presidential Addresses from the Club's first 50 years was published in 1978: BW Harvey (ed) *The Lawyer and Justice* (London, Sweet & Maxwell, 1978).

[6] Lord Atkin, 'Law as an Educational Subject' (1932) *Journal of the Society of Public Teachers of Law* 27.

[7] Lord Atkin, 'Law as an Educational Subject' 30.

[8] *Donoghue v Stevenson* [1932] AC 562; argument was heard on 10 and 11 December 1931, while the judgments were delivered on 26 May 1932.

[9] Lord Atkin (n 6), 27.

[10] *Donoghue* (n 8) 567. See also N Duxbury, *Jurists and Judges: an essay on influence* (Oxford, Hart Publishing, 2001) 65.

[11] In addition to *Purdy* (n 1), those decisions were *Moore Stephens (a firm) v Stone Rolls Ltd* [2009] UKHL 39, [2009] 1 AC 1391, [2009] 1 WLR 1764; *Lexington Insurance Co v AGF Insurance Ltd* [2009] UKHL 40, [2009] 3 WLR 575; *Fisher v Brooker & Ors* [2009] UKHL 41; *R v C* [2009] UKHL 42, [2009] 1 WLR 1786; *Masri v Consolidated Contractors International Co SAL* [2009] UKHL 43, [2009] 3 WLR 385; and *Transport for London (London Underground) Ltd v Spirerose Ltd* [2009] UKHL 44, [2009] 1 WLR 1797. The 'odd one out' which did not mention academic writing was *R v C*, on the meaning of 'unable to communicate' in s 30(2)(b) of the Sexual Offences Act 2003. The speech of Baroness Hale does nevertheless make several references to Law Commission and Government Papers and Reports.

And, of course, often our judges are learned jurists in their own right: our keynote speakers at the Seminar, the Hon Michael Kirby and Lord Rodger of Earlsferry are pre-eminent examples, with their frequent contributions to leading journals. In 1950, Justice Felix Frankfurter of the United States Supreme Court, himself a former Harvard Law Professor, offered a toast to the Health of the Society at its Annual Dinner in Lincoln's Inn Hall. Justice Frankfurter mischievously said of Lord Wright that 'he practises the secret vice for a judge of being a scholar'.[12]

It would be misleading, however, to suggest that the modern partnership between judges and jurists is always a happy one. For instance, Lord Justice Munby, the new Chairman of the Law Commission, observed in a recent restitution case:

> [If] I may be permitted to say so, we need to be on our guard against over–refined analysis which may look all very well on the scholar's page but which may seem less convincing when exposed to 'the purifying ordeal of skilled argument on the specific facts of a contested case'.[13]

Thus, as TB Smith wryly remarked in his Presidential Address to the Society: 'Zeus asserted that it is for the judges to make the law, and for academics to accept judicial formulations without demur.'[14]

One of those who supported the idea of the Seminar in its early beginnings was Professor Sir Neil MacCormick, the Society's President in 1983–84, who died from cancer in April 2009. Yet he remained an inspiration for the event and its twin themes, and we offer this collection as a tribute to him. In one of his final seminal works, Sir Neil noted that:

> Judges in courts everywhere have become more explicit in their reflections about their reasoning and argumentation, and have joined issue with. . . scholars on many occasions. They continue, of course, to write and issue opinions on cases they decide, furnishing an astonishingly rich repository of practical argumentation at work.[15]

> It is sometimes said that [a typical] account of legal reasoning is skewed by the fact that it takes its evidence of the character of reasoning exclusively from judicial opinions in the higher appellate courts. Thus it is not representative of the real day-to-day business of the law. But . . . [for a study of legal argumentation] there is no better source material than the type of carefully considered arguments to be found in the opinions of judges in higher tribunals.[16]

---

[12] F Frankfurter, 'Toast to the Health of the Society' (1947–1951) 1 *Journal of the Society of Public Teachers of Law (New Series)* 363, 364.

[13] *Commerzbank Ag v Price-Jones* [2003] EWCA Civ 1663 [48] (as Munby J). It should be noted that the reference to 'the purifying ordeal of skilled argument' is a famous quote from *Cordell v Second Clanfield Properties Ltd* [1969] 2 Ch 9, 16, per Megarry J who often found his own textbook being cited to him in court: an occupational hazard for the judge-jurist.

[14] TB Smith, 'Authors and Authority' (1972–73) 12 *Journal of the Society of Public Teachers of Law (New Series)* 3, 7.

[15] N MacCormick, *Rhetoric and the Rule of Law* (Oxford, Oxford University Press, 2005) Preface, v.

[16] MacCormick, *Rhetoric and the Rule of Law* vi.

Taking its inspiration from MacCormick, this collection examines this 'rich repository', and deliberately focuses on the upper echelons of the judiciary. Top courts are, after all, distinctive. Frederick Pollock lamented the timidity of the dissenters in *Donoghue* in declining to go against the perceived wisdom of authority in tort cases from the lower courts: 'Parts of their opinions read as if they had forgotten that they were judging in a Court of last resort.'[17] Through their decisions, the House of Lords provided, and the new Supreme Court has, with its first year of judgments, begun to provide what Baroness Hale recently described as the 'grist to the advocates' and academics' mills'.[18]

More generally, we consider the legacy of the House of Lords and the prospects for the new Supreme Court. For that reason, the chapters here focus on the transitional state of affairs: the various essays reflect upon judges' judging and judging judges in the modern House of Lords. The issues were well captured by Lord Hope, then Second Senior Law Lord, who replied on behalf of their judicial Lordships to the tributes offered in a valedictory debate in the House of Lords and noted that 'what is really happening today is that the House is losing part of itself':[19]

> As a result of the way the appellate jurisdiction has been operated since 1876, when the Lords of Appeal in Ordinary were first admitted to the House's membership, the House of Lords has become a byword for judicial work of the highest quality. As a brand name it has been unsurpassed. The reputation of the whole House has been greatly enhanced by it, throughout the common-law world and beyond—so much so that the decision to end the appellate jurisdiction caused almost universal surprise overseas. Why give up something that seemed so valuable?[20]

It was with that international perspective that the Seminar opened, and this collection begins, with the keynote address of Hon Michael Kirby from the Seminar. His stimulating chapter, 'A Darwinian Reflection on Judicial Values and Appointments to Final National Courts', argues in favour of variety and evolution when it comes to judicial appointments to our highest courts,[21] drawing on his own experience as a judge in New South Wales and the High Court of Australia and the experiences of several other jurisdictions. In a companion chapter, 'From Appellate Committee to UK Supreme Court: Independence, Activism and Transparency', Dr Aileen Kavanagh seeks to challenge some of the assumptions underlying the move to the Supreme Court and also engages with Hon Michael Kirby's arguments. She questions whether the Justices will become more 'activist' in the wake of the transition, and makes a provocative but compelling argument as to whether increased transparency will necessarily translate into increased public confidence in the judiciary.

[17] F Pollock, 'The Snail in the Bottle and Thereafter' (1933) 49 *Law Quarterly Review* 22.
[18] *OBG v Allan* [2007] UKHL 21, [2008] AC 1, [303].
[19] Hansard HL col 1514 (21 July 2009).
[20] Hansard HL col 1514 (21 July 2009).
[21] Compare the view of Sandra Day-O'Connor, a former United States Supreme Court Justice, in 'Take Justice off the Ballot' *New York Times*, 21 May 2010 www.nytimes.com/2010/05/23/opinion/23oconnor.html.

In addition to the effect of the creation of the Supreme Court on our judges, it is instructive to consider whether there will be any impact on the attitude *towards* the Justices. As is apparent from the first two chapters, there will be a complex relationship between the judiciary and public opinion: although judges are unelected, it 'is wrong to stigmatise judicial decision-making as in some way undemocratic'.[22] That relationship is considered by Professor Elizabeth Cooke in 'Taking women's property seriously: Mrs Boland, the House of Lords, the Law Commission and the role of consensus'. Professor Cooke takes as her example the various responses to the famous decision of the House of Lords in *Williams & Glyn's Bank Ltd v Boland*.[23] By understanding the interaction of the various parties to law reform, so Professor Cooke argues, we can better appreciate the role of consensus in the development of the law. In my essay, '"Inconsiderate Alterations in our Laws": Legislative Reversal of Supreme Court Decisions', I seek to explore the interaction between our highest court and other branches of government through the phenomenon of legislative reversals. Taking two recent examples from private law, I examine legislative reactions to decisions of the House of Lords, which I criticise for the incoherence of their approach.

Next comes a series of chapters which assess the contribution of the House of Lords and the new Supreme Court to particular substantive areas of law, written by experts in their respective fields. In so doing, the authors examine the development of the law and also the role of jurists in contributing to it. Each chapter provides a valuable and innovative account of the relevant law.

A distinctive feature of the workload for modern top court is the number of appeals involving human rights.[24] In the light of that, Professor Jenny Steele looks at the impact of the Human Rights Act on tort law in '(Dis)owning the Convention in the Law of Tort'. Professor Steele, through a survey of the decisions of the House of Lords in the area, identifies the patterns in the outcomes of the appeals and argues that there has been greater continuity in the approach of their Lordships than might appear at first sight. For Professor Steele, two concerns have been important: first, the protection of public authorities from the threat of liability in tort; and secondly, the risk (perceived or real) of transferring the ability to determine the scope of the law of tort to the European Court of Human Rights in Strasbourg.

A similar (perhaps parochial) attitude to that second concern might arguably be discerned in some decisions in the context of European Law (if we substitute Luxembourg for Strasbourg). Indeed, as Professor Anthony Arnull observes in 'Keeping Their Heads Above Water? European Law in the House of Lords', the Supreme Court has already caused some controversy in one of its most

---

[22] *A v Secretary of State for the Home Department* [2004] UKHL 56, [2005] 2 AC 68 [43] (Lord Bingham).

[23] *Williams & Glyn's Bank Ltd v Boland* [1981] AC 487.

[24] See, for example, B Dickson, 'Judicial Activism in the House of Lords 1995–2007' in B Dickson (ed), *Judicial Activism in Common Law Supreme Courts* (Oxford, Oxford University Press, 2007), 379–85 and S Shah and T Poole, 'The Impact of the Human Rights Act on the House of Lords' [2009] *Public Law* 347.

high-profile cases so far, by declining to make a reference to the European Court of Justice in *Office of Fair Trading v Abbey National plc and Others*.[25] Professor Arnull respectfully takes the Justices to task for that refusal, but argues that it is consistent with the previous attitude of the House of Lords to such decisions. But he contrasts those cases with a more positive attitude of their Lordships to the role of European law in the wake of the *Factortame* litigation.[26]

The tension between the common law and Europe has been keenly felt in the field of private international law.[27] In his chapter, 'The development of principle by a final court of appeal in matters of private international (common) law', Professor Adrian Briggs persuasively offers the thesis that the recognition of foreign judgments depends upon whether the person against whom it is asserted 'lent himself to it'. Professor Briggs goes on to argue that the scope for the new Supreme Court to develop legal principle (surely one of its principal functions[28]) has been circumscribed in the context of the conflict of laws, which are increasingly regulated at the European level.

What, then, of the scope for the development of principle by the Supreme Court in other areas? The recognition of the principle of unjust enrichment is an excellent example of the fertile relationship between judges and jurists. In 'The Law of Unjust Enrichment in the House of Lords: Judging the Judges', Professor Graham Virgo traces the impact of the House of Lords on what is still a young principle through 10 leading cases since the seminal decision of *Lipkin Gorman v Karpnale*.[29] Although commending the willingness of their Lordships to engage with the academic literature, Professor Virgo argues that too often in the key recent decisions complexity of reasoning has taken the place of engagement with fundamental questions of theory and principle.[30]

Professor Keith Stanton's chapter examines the decisions of the House of Lords from almost exactly the same period as Professor Virgo. In 'Use of scholarship by the House of Lords in Tort cases', Stanton presents the results of a meticulous study of the reference to academic literature in tort decisions of the House of Lords since 1990. He distinguishes between the variety of possible references to academic material and argues that, while express references may be now more frequent than in Lord Buckmaster's time, the basic methodology of the judges has not transformed. But explicit engagement with the literature is now common in decisions of our top court, and it is clear that academics influence both the outcome of individual cases and the direction of the law on points of principle.

The arguments of these chapters on specialist areas of the law lead to broader questions about the interaction between judges and academics. Dr Alexandra Braun presents a comprehensive overview of the relationship between judges

---

[25] *Office of Fair Trading v Abbey National plc and Others* [2009] UKSC 6.

[26] Beginning with *R v Secretary of State, ex parte Factortame* [1991] 1 AC 603.

[27] As Professor Arnull recognises at fn 87 of his chapter.

[28] See Pollock (n 17).

[29] *Lipkin Gorman v Karpnale Ltd* [1991] AC 546.

[30] See also J Lee, 'Restitution from the Revenue: Exacting Principles from the Court Of Appeal' [2010] 18 *Restitution Law Review* 75.

and jurists in her chapter, 'Judges and Academics: Features of a Partnership'. With comparative reference to the situations in France, Italy and Germany, Dr Braun highlights the formal and informal opportunities for judges and jurists to influence one another. She concludes that the former distinction in the role of legal scholarship between England and other jurisdictions no longer stands. Indeed, some judges can now even rely on their own articles.[31]

As Dr Braun notes, the different uses and impact of academic literature raise questions both about the role of counsel and about how the Justices of Supreme Court approach decisions. The final two chapters of the collection are written by two of the leading authorities on the process of judging in our highest court: Professors Alan Paterson and Brice Dickson. Both essays examine the dynamics of the courtroom. In 'Does Advocacy matter in the Lords?', Professor Alan Paterson presents some of the findings of a series of interviews, building upon his pioneering work in *The Law Lords*.[32] His chapter offers fascinating and revealing insights into the contrasting views of judges and barristers on the role of advocacy. At its best, excellent advocacy may cause a judge to change their mind and may divide a court: Professor Brice Dickson considers split decisions in 'Close Calls in the House of Lords'. He argues that such decisions reveal serious divisions and tensions between members of the Appellate Committee. *Donoghue v Stevenson* was of course one of the most famous close calls. One of the most high-profile decisions in the first year of the Supreme Court produced a 'close call': there was a 5:4 split in the first nine-judge decision of the Supreme Court, *R (on the application of E) v Governing Body of JFS*.[33] Professor Dickson concludes by considering what lessons there may be for Supreme Court in the prevalence of such split decisions.

This introduction has endeavoured merely to adumbrate some of the themes which were discussed at the Seminar and which are explored in this collection. What emerges is that what the late Professor Peter Birks identified as a relationship of 'partnership', born of 'the necessity of sharing between judge and jurist the task of interpretative development of the law',[34] will continue to be an important feature of decision-making in the Supreme Court. It is hoped that the chapters amount to a fitting celebration of the passing of the Judicial House of Lords, the inauguration of the Supreme Court and the Centenary of the Society of Legal Scholars.

---

[31] See, for example, Lord Millett's use of his own article, 'The *Quistclose* Trust: Who Can Enforce It?' (1985) 101 *Law Quarterly Review* 269, in *Twinsectra v Yardley* [2002] UKHL 12, [2002] 2 AC 164 [80] and generally [77]–[103].

[32] A Paterson, *The Law Lords* (London, Macmillan, 1982).

[33] *R (on the application of E) v Governing Body of JFS* [2009] UKSC 15, [2010] 2 WLR 153. *Moore Stephens* (n 11) was the final 'close call' in the Appellate Committee.

[34] P Birks, 'The Academic and the Practitioner' (1998) 18 *Legal Studies* 397, 413.

# 2

# A Darwinian Reflection on Judicial Values and Appointments to Final National Courts*

## THE HON MICHAEL KIRBY

### I DARWINIAN ADAPTATION AND VARIATION

THE YEAR 2009 was notable in the United Kingdom for at least two events. For lawyers, it saw the commencement of a new national Supreme Court. For the wider world, it afforded an occasion to remember the bicentenary of the birth of the great scientist Charles Darwin, and the sesqui-centenary of the publication in 1859 of his work *The Origin of Species*.[1]

Chapter 4 of *Origin*[2] concerns 'Laws of Variation'. Darwin's proposition in that chapter was that living organisms survived and adapted to their environment by processes of variation by which they were modified, thus contributing to the 'innumerable complex co-adaptations of structure which we see throughout nature between various organic beings'. These laws of variation were essential to the survival of organisms and to their gradual evolution to fit them for the world in which they lived. This was a central pillar of Darwin's grand theory of evolution. That theory has proved important as an explanation of the natural world and all living things within it.

It was Darwin's thesis that helped challenge the simplistic notion of divine creation, based on untestable beliefs. He did so by a postulate premised on a rational understanding of the world and grounded in the scientific method. The theory has, in turn, resulted in a staggering collection of advances in knowledge.

---

* Revised and updated from a paper presented to the Annual Seminar of the Society of Legal Scholars, 5–6 November 2009, London.

[1] C Darwin, *The Origin of Species* (1859) (Great Books edition) RM Hutchins (ed), (Chicago, Encyclopaedia Britannica, 1952) 1.

[2] Darwin, *The Origin of Species* 65. Thus, Darwin presented the question whether thicker and better fur in north dwelling animals [in the Northern Hemisphere] was a consequence of a process of selection over generations or was influenced by the severe climate itself. An interaction of biological and environmental forces was postulated.

It had a profound impact on organised society. That impact continues to the present time.

My thesis is that Darwin's theory of variation has relevance, by analogy, to the living organism of the law. Specifically, it has relevance to the institutions of the law, by which binding rules are made. In all systems of law derived from the British Isles, the decisions of a final national court play a crucial part in defining the legal values of the nation and expressing the rules by which its people live together and co-exist with foreign nations and organisations.

A final national court plays a specially important role in helping its society to adapt to the ever-changing environment in which law operates. My proposition is that, to be successful, such an institution must, like all living physical organisms, adapt to the laws of variation. It must be able to reflect the variety of values that will permit it to adjust to changing times and needs. If this is correct, Darwin's thesis will have implications for the appointments of judges to courts, including to a final national court. Variety is essential to flourishing adaptation. Reproduction by identical or near identical cloning will endanger the capacity of the institution to cope with contemporary challenges, even perhaps to survive.

These conclusions have a Darwinian message to lawyers, to parliaments and to citizens about how they should go about appointing the judges to such important national institutions. Variety not sameness is the message that Darwin teaches. It is also the message that I propound.

## II  THE JUDICIAL SETTING

The creation of the Supreme Court of the United Kingdom[3] is, by any account, a most significant constitutional development. I can think of no other modern parliamentary democracy that would have effected such a significant change to one of its principal constitutional organs with such comparative speed and with relatively little public and professional debate.[4]

The change, symbolised by ceremonial events in which the Queen participated in October 2009, attracted some media attention. However, much of it was of the superficial 'infotainment' variety.[5] Several legal commentators predicted that the new court would exhibit a greater transparency than the Appellate Committee of the House of Lords that it replaced.[6] Others opined that the change was cosmetic and not an 'epoch-making event'. Still others expressed concern that the change might result in a drift away from quality in commercial judgments. However, they

---

[3]  Constitutional Reform Act 2005 Pt 3.

[4]  A Le Sueur, 'From Appellate Committee to Supreme Court: A Narrative' in L Blom-Cooper, B Dickson and G Drewry (eds), *The Judicial House of Lords 1987-2009* (Oxford, Oxford University Press, 2009) ('Blom-Cooper et al').

[5]  See eg the coverage of the brooch and hat worn by Baroness Hale of Lincoln at the opening of the new Supreme Court: *The Times* (London 2 October 2009).

[6]  E Fennell, 'More independence? Their Lordships have never hesitated to make their views clear in the past' *The Times* (London 1 October 2009).

consoled themselves with the thought that such cases were now often resolved in the City by arbitration rather than litigation.[7]

Desperate journalists, noticing the presence at the opening ceremonies of visitors from Commonwealth countries, the United States and Europe, sought to draw lessons from the record of Supreme Courts created in the other English-speaking countries, progeny of the British judiciary beyond the seas.[8] Justice Albie Sachs, then recently retired from the Constitutional Court of South Africa, suspected that the physical move of the Court's premises and the change of name would 'have little more than symbolic importance'.[9] However, he recognised that symbols matter. And that it would 'only be to the good if the concept of the independence of the judiciary is reinforced'.[10]

Amidst the froth and bubble, there was remarkably little public reflection on the comparatively modest process of consultation with the people of the United Kingdom that took place in the re-design, re-creation and re-establishment of their nation's apex court. In the United States of America, Australia, and most similar nations, any such change would have required huge public debate. In Australia, at least, it would have necessitated a constitutional referendum, few of which, in the history of the nation, have secured the double majority mandated by Australia's Constitution.[11]

The High Court of Australia bears its title quite possibly to reflect the relationship which the court was originally intended to enjoy (if that be the word) with their Lordships as members of the Judicial Committee of the Privy Council, and despite the earlier decision to name the highest court in Canada 'the Supreme Court of Canada', after the model of the Supreme Court of the United States.[12] However, even an attempt, at this stage, to 're-badge' the High Court of Australia would require a constitutional amendment. Its passage would be no sure thing, given the history of the Court under its current name and the natural inclination of Australians to conservatism before altering constitutional things so long settled. I mention these differences not out of criticism of what has occurred in the United Kingdom, but in order to contrast the comparative ease of securing constitutional alterations, large and small, in Britain, when compared with most other countries.

Amidst all the insignificant and desultory commentary on the new court, my eyes fell upon one statement that seemed to express an accurate prediction. It was attributed to the new President of the Supreme Court, Lord Phillips of Worth

---

[7] Fennell, 'More independence?'.

[8] D Pannick, 'The Supreme Court may have had a shambolic start but it's getting better all the time' *The Times* (London 1 October 2009).

[9] A Sachs, 'Nelson Mandela and Mahatma Gandhi were locked up in our court' *The Times* (London 1 October 2009).

[10] ibid

[11] Australian Constitution s 128 (a majority of the total electors voting, and the majority of the electors in a majority of the states).

[12] British North America Act 1867 (UK). See K Keith, 'The Interplay with the Judicial Committee of the Privy Council' in Blom-Cooper et al (n 4) 315 at 328 ff and RJ Sharpe, 'Canada', ibid, 350.

Matravers. He is recorded as saying that it is 'inevitable that there will be more interest in who is appointed to the Supreme Court and I am bound to say that is a perfectly legitimate state of affairs'.[13] He contrasted the attention to the selection procedure for the most recent appointee confirmed to the Supreme Court of the United States, Justice Sonia Sotomayor. By comparison, he pointed out three appointments in recent months of judges who would become members of the new Supreme Court of the United Kingdom had 'received no publicity whatsoever'.[14]

My purpose is not, of course, to urge that the United Kingdom, any more than Australia, Canada or other countries, should go down the track confirmation process for federal judges in the United States. I will suggest that their process is deeply flawed. The flaws affect not only the filling of positions and the gross delays that attend their consideration, but also the consequent caution imposed on the President by the process, in the hope of avoiding a filibuster in the United States Senate.[15]

My thesis is that appointees to a final national court necessarily bring with them values that influence their judicial decisions. That judging in such a court is not, and should not be, a purely mechanical or technical task. That appointing authorities have a legitimate interest in the values that a newly appointed judge will bring to such a court in his or her performance. That a range of backgrounds, interests and skills is important in the case of such appointees, more so even than in the appointment of judges to intermediate and trial courts. That the community that will be affected, indeed governed, by expressions of the law made by such judges therefore has a legitimate interest in knowing more about the values of potential appointees. And that the fiction that such judging is value-free, or value-neutral, is wearing thin and unlikely to last much longer. So that demands will increase for an appropriate democratic involvement in the appointment of such judges at the critical moment of their confirmation in office.

But what should that democratic component be? And how can it be introduced without importing overt and partisan politicisation into judicial institutions?

### III CREATION OF THE NEW SUPREME COURT

The opening of the new Supreme Court of the United Kingdom, in its redesigned building across Parliament Square, revived Australian memories of the action of

---

[13]   F Gibb, 'Supreme Court opens as fears raised of US-style selection of judges' *The Times* (London, 1 October 2009).

[14]   Gibb, 'Supreme Court'. The appointment to the Supreme Court of the United Kingdom in March 2010 of Lord Justice Dyson conformed to the previous tradition. It was announced by the Prime Minister in a press release of a few lines. The statement by the Supreme Court itself was likewise extremely short, with four lines describing solely the new appointee's previous judicial service. There was little public discussion. A consideration of the new Justice's remarks in a dissenting opinion in the Court of Appeal and in his article 'Some Thoughts on Judicial Deference' [2006] JR 103 might have been fruitful for an engaged media and society.

[15]   MA Fletcher, 'Obama criticised as too cautious, slow on judicial posts' *Washington Post* (Washington, 16 October 2009) A1, A20.

the great, great grandmother of the present Queen, Queen Victoria, in signifying her royal assent to the legislation that earlier gave birth to the Supreme Court of Canada (in 1867) and the High Court of Australia (in 1901). Continuity, not revolution, is the modern hallmark of British constitutional history.[16]

The termination of the arrangements by which the highest court of the United Kingdom comprised a committee of the House of Lords and was housed in a corridor of the Upper House of the United Kingdom Parliament, came about, apparently, with some gentle persuasion, reinforced by notions of judicial independence contained in the European Convention on Human Rights.[17] According to such notions, it was considered anachronistic and anomalous, in the twenty-first century, that a nation's highest court should be so closely, even physically, associated with the parliamentary chambers of the principal law-maker of the United Kingdom. The fact that no one alleged that the Law Lords were actually influenced by the legislative (or executive) law-makers working in the parliamentary buildings was beside the point. In the matter of judicial conduct, English law had long insisted that not only must the rules of integrity be observed; they must manifestly appear to be observed.[18]

Fifty years before the principle of the separation of the judicature was belatedly insisted upon in the United Kingdom, the High Court of Australia imposed a similar rule in the case of a 'court' of the Australian judicature. An early innovation of the Commonwealth of Australia was the adoption, in the Australian Constitution, of a provision envisaging laws for the conciliation and arbitration of interstate industrial disputes. This provision,[19] in turn, gave rise in 1904 to the creation of a new federal 'court' to perform the constitutional tasks: the Commonwealth Court of Conciliation and Arbitration. Successively, Justices of the High Court of Australia, and later other federal judges, served as presidential members of this important and distinctive national 'court'.

In 1956, however, in a dramatic decision, the High Court of Australia invalidated the federal legislation creating this 'court'.[20] It held that the language and structure of the Australian Constitution, providing for an independent judicature, as set out in a separate chapter (Chapter III), forbade the attempt of the Australian Parliament to confer on a court-like body not only powers to decide contested matters requiring the application of the law to facts as found, but also legislative-like powers to create entirely new legal norms in the form of awards for the settlement of industrial disputes.

In this way, the special Australian 'court' was declared constitutionally invalid. The result was a huge dislocation and much inconvenience. The immediate

---

[16] *cf* S Pincus, *1688, The First Modern Revolution* (New Haven, Yale, 2009).

[17] European Convention on Human Rights art 6.

[18] *R v Sussex Justices, ex p McCarthy* [1924] 1 KB 256, 259, where Lord Hewart CJ famously observed that 'justice should not only be done, but should manifestly and undoubtedly be seen to be done'. See *Johnson v Johnson* (2000) 201 CLR 488 [42].

[19] Australian Constitution s 51(xxxv). See now the decision of the High Court of Australia in *New South Wales v The Commonwealth* (*Work Choices Case*) (2006) 229 CLR 1.

[20] *R v Kirby ex p Boilermakers' Society of Australia* (1956) 94 CLR 254.

outcome was the enactment of new laws that created two bodies—a federal court to perform the court-like functions, and a federal tribunal (the Commonwealth Conciliation and Arbitration Commission) to perform non-court functions.[21]

The essential principle that was involved in the foregoing decision, and the steps that followed it, was that the judicial power must be conserved to judges serving in courts, properly so called, and properly so functioning. Upon the basis of that principle, there would be little doubt that an attempt today to place a federal court in Australia within a federal or state parliament, or allowing federal judges to be members of such a parliament and to participate there (however rarely) in the legislative process, would be struck down as incompatible with the Australian Constitution. It would be seen as inconsistent with the need to preserve the manifest independence and separation of the judiciary from the other branches of government.

Accordingly, to the extent that it was known in Australia, the move of the new Supreme Court of the United Kingdom to refurbished and separate premises outside the Palace of Westminster would have caused no special surprise. If there were any surprise, it would only have been that, for historical reasons, the move was so long in coming. In such matters, symbols count, although I concede that Australian symbols have, over time, sometimes themselves been confusing.

Until comparatively recently, the High Court of Australia regularly utilised state court buildings for its hearings. This was so both on circuits to outlying state capitals, and even in Melbourne and Sydney respectively where, successively until 1980, the seat of the High Court was first based. In 1980, in Canberra, Queen Elizabeth II opened the new building erected to house the High Court of Australia in its permanent home. Suitably enough, the opening ceremony was performed on the anniversary of the birth of Queen Victoria, 24 May 1980. That was a day that, in my youth, was celebrated throughout Australia, and elsewhere in the British Empire, as Empire Day. Those celebrations had continued long after the passing of the late Queen Empress.

Quaint historical anachronisms and temporary accommodations are therefore understandable to Australians, especially Australian lawyers.[22] But viewed with modern eyes, the notion of the highest judges of the United Kingdom daily rubbing shoulders with Members of Parliament and of the executive government looked increasingly alien to the essential principles that the British rulers themselves had

---

[21] Conciliation & Arbitration Act 1904 (Cth) s 6. The provision was inserted by amending Act No 44 of 1956 which followed the decision of the Privy Council affirming that of the High Court of Australia: *R v Kirby* (1957) 95 CLR 529.

[22] These were also addressed in the United States. Until October 1935, when the Supreme Court moved into its own building in Washington DC, it shared space with other governmental institutions. In the 1790s, it occupied the Lower House of the state legislature in New York. Thereafter it shifted to Philadelphia and in 1819 moved to Washington where, for 40 years, it was housed in a chamber of the unrestored Capitol building. In the late 1850s, the Court moved upstairs to the old Senate Chamber. It was for critical lack of space rather than separation of powers reasons that Chief Justice Taft in 1925 began lobbying for a separate building for the Court, under its exclusive control. See M Bloomfield, 'Buildings, Supreme Court' in KL Hall (ed), *The Oxford Companion for the Supreme Court of the United States* (New York, Oxford University Press, 1992) 99.

transplanted throughout their Empire. Central to their transplant was a judiciary at once professional, impartial and manifestly independent. In nearly 35 years as a judge in Australia, I was never subject to improper pressure or attempted corruption. That fact represents an Australian achievement. But the judicial model that it carries forward was the one inherited from the United Kingdom.

To mark the notable occasion of the creation and inauguration of a new national Supreme Court in one of the oldest polities on earth, to whose courts the High Court of Australia and the people of Australia owe a huge intellectual debt, I offer the present reflections. I accept that it may seem inappropriate for someone who was, until recently, a judge in the Australian legal system, to intrude ideas for the consideration of a largely United Kingdom audience. No one is in doubt that the new Supreme Court is, in a real sense, a continuation of the Appellate Committee of the House of Lords, indeed an evolution from it. In constituting the new court, great pains have been taken to maintain all of the already serving and available members of the House of Lords. Observing this rule was extremely wise, if Australian experience in the creation of new superior courts from old courts constitutes any guide.[23]

The hard-earned reputation for judicial excellence of the Appellate Committee of the House of Lords (and of its alter ego, the Judicial Committee of the Privy Council) has assured the new Supreme Court of the United Kingdom a beginning unequalled by any other recently established final national court of which I am aware. The only final court bearing an imperfect comparison was the Federal Court of India of 1935, which was replaced by the Supreme Court of India in 1950. The three other early Supreme Courts of the English-speaking common law tradition—the Supreme Court of the United States, the Supreme Court of Canada and the High Court of Australia—were created completely afresh. There was no equivalent lineage in their judicial membership to assure to the fledgling institutions a similar certainty of success. Just the same, any creation of a new final national court, with a distinct charter, new premises and some fresh personnel, inevitably raises hopes that, to some extent, a new start will be made and some new ideas adopted. New aspirations, appropriate to the occasion, will normally attend the creation of a new court.

The present is a time of remarkable social, economic and technological challenges for the law. The Imperial era, in which the House of Lords and its judges predominated in the exposition and application of the law for a quarter of humanity, is now well and truly over. The potential for the new Supreme Court of the United Kingdom to exert influence over other courts, in the many countries where the common law continues to flourish, will depend not on Imperial coercion but on the intellectual cogency of the new court's reasoning and the relevance of

---

[23] MD Kirby, 'Judicial Supersession: The Controversial Establishment of the New South Wales Court of Appeal' (2008) 30 *Sydney Law Review* 177. On the creation of the NSW Court of Appeal, the order of seniority of judges of the State Supreme Court was altered by the elevation of some of them to the new appellate court, so that they enjoyed a higher status and precedence than those formerly senior to them. The disruption that this caused lasted decades.

its opinions to the solution of like problems in other jurisdictions.[24] Still, there is a great potential for utility to others, in part because of the traditions of the past and in part because of the continued use of the English language and many features of English legal traditions throughout the world. These considerations are now reinforced by new links (such as the internet) that did not exist in the days of Empire.

At the centre of these reflections is the troublesome question concerning the appointment of judges to a final national court. So long as, in the United Kingdom, those judges were substantially hidden away in the Law Lords' corridor of the Palace of Westminster, they would be guaranteed a very high measure of anonymity from all but the cognoscenti in Britain and abroad. Now this has changed.

The Law Lords were not, of course, unknown to the judges and many lawyers in Australia, the Commonwealth and other English-speaking countries. Doubtless, in recent years, many of them will also have become known to Europe by reason of their engagement with continental lawyers, 30 years after Lord Denning described the 'incoming tide' of European influences on the law of the United Kingdom.[25] However, save for an occasional foray into the public consciousness of Britain—as when the *Spycatcher* judges were displayed upside down in a London tabloid—most of the final court judges, until now, have lived their lives without the public scrutiny ordinarily addressed in other lands to leaders of the legislative, executive and judicial branches of government. Their values and occasional idiosyncrasies, their particular modes of analysis and writing, and their special interests were often known to us who read their judicial opinions (until recently, still called their 'speeches'). However, for the general public and even for most persons serving in the other branches of the government of the United Kingdom, such elements of their personality, and anything more, would generally have constituted unexplored territory.

All of this may gradually change now that the Supreme Court of the United Kingdom has a distinctive face and home. Slowly but surely, the individuals who make up the leadership of the third branch of government of the United Kingdom will probably become known to the people they serve. Their decisional values are therefore likely to be much more openly displayed, analysed, evaluated and criticised. Endeavours in Britain to go on suggesting that final court judging is value-free are not likely to survive long as a greater realism invades the attention to the new court.[26] It is my thesis, like Lord Phillips, that these changes are inevitable. Being grounded in an appreciation of reality, the changes will generally be healthy. And they are likely to require the judges themselves to be more conscious of the values they bring to bear in their judicial decision-making.

---

[24] *cf* MD Kirby, 'Australia and New Zealand' in Blom-Cooper et al (n 4) 350; RJ Sharpe, 'Canada', ibid, 359; A Chaskalson, 'South Africa', ibid, 366.

[25] *HP Bulmer Ltd v J Bollinger SA* [1974] Ch 401, 418.

[26] See on this T Etherton, 'Liberty, the Archetype and Diversity: A Philosophy of Judging', Lecture to the Institute of Advanced Legal Studies, 9 July 2009, unpublished, ms 29–30.

It is also likely that increased public scrutiny will make the judges more aware of the values underpinning the opinions of their colleagues and of the court as an institution, including on the occasions when the judges disagree, either as to the disposition of an appeal or in their reasoning towards a common disposition.

Once it is appreciated that final courts, in particular, are obliged, by the nature of their functions, to analyse evidence and legal questions, and to solve disputes, in part by reference to considerations of legal principle and legal policy,[27] the notion that the judges are operating on a kind of automatic pilot of purely 'technical' law will almost certainly become untenable. The fiction that judging in a final court is value-free will then be exploded. The assumption that it does not matter greatly who is appointed to a judicial seat in a final court, so long as he or she has the 'merit' of high professional experience, is then dissolved. Suddenly it becomes clear that the appointments made to the final court are very important indeed for the shape of the nation's law. They are important because the values of the judges necessarily affect (and in some cases decide) judicial outcomes.

Select a judge with a general disposition to 'creative' approaches to the law, with an appreciation that mechanically applying old precedents may today produce unjust and awkward outcomes, and you will probably secure dispositions very different from those that tend to be favoured by a judge who is not inclined to legal creativity but is disposed simply to apply old precedents without too much worry about their unsuitability or inappropriateness. Appoint a legal 'liberal' and the outcomes, in terms of judicial dispositions, will tend to be different over time from those crafted by a legal 'conservative'. Install a person who has an interest in, and knowledge about, international human rights law and that judge's decisions are likely to be significantly different, over the long haul, from those of a lawyer who is generally sceptical about such 'new-fangled' (even 'European') notions, and possibly even a little hostile towards them. Elevate a judge whose background was originally in the Family Law Division (such as Lord Scarman) and it may be more likely that his or her values will be marginally different from those of a judge whose background was in large commercial or insolvency disputes (such as Lord Diplock). Appoint a judge who is a devoted adherent to church or other religious beliefs and it is likely that his or her decisions on bio-ethical questions, may be different from those of a non-believer or humanist.

None of the foregoing is inevitable, still less irreversible. People, even judges, change their positions over the course of their service which, in the case of final court judges, tends to have been comparatively long. Chief Justice Mason in Australia is a judge whose judicial values appeared to change mid-career, when he was elevated to be Chief Justice of the High Court of Australia. Of course, differences in judicial values do not necessary follow the lines of modern political parties (which, in recent times, tend anyway to be noted for their close similarities rather than differences over a wide range of subjects). The complete divorce of

---

[27] *Oceanic Sun Line Special Shipping Co Inc v Fay* (1988) 165 CLR 197, 252 (Deane J); *cf Northern Territory v Mengel* (1995) 185 CLR 307, 347.

the judiciary from party politics is one of the great legacies of the British judiciary to the world. No one is suggesting that this legacy is about to change or that it should do so. Nor am I suggesting that any of the foregoing judicial 'inclinations' are necessarily improper. Or that a good judge will not strive to be conscious of personal inclinations and to make appropriate adjustments of the mind in reaching judicial orders impartially and independently.

The fact remains, however, that there are deep-lying values that emerge in the performance by judges of their professional functions. They affect the way the judges see problems, and whether they see a problem at all. Inclinations are important to assessments. So are intuitions that play an inescapable part in any form of decision-making, including that by judges. If judges say that they have no sin of personal inclinations, born of their life's experience, they deceive themselves and the truth is not in them. Analysis of the decision-making of final courts by reference to mathematical scalograms that track decisional patterns over the years of judicial service, tend to confirm the impressionistic assessment of the cognoscenti. Few leading judges of our tradition can be classified by reference to the categories of party politics. But most can be catalogued by reference to other considerations such as background, inclinations, tendencies and professional and other experience.[28] To deny these truths is to fly in the face of informed professional assessment; as well as the more precise statistical analysis. It also contradicts, in my own case, a lifetime's experience spent observing, and participating in, the governmental function of appellate judging.

It is ironic that it is the step of the final court of the United Kingdom, in moving across Parliament Square to its new home, that will probably remove the court from the protective anonymity of the parliamentary corridor in which it hitherto operated. The irony derives from the fact that that corridor was in the very building where the examination of the values of everyone else was a daily obsession, not only of the occupants of the building themselves, but of the news media and many of the general public.

The important question thus posed is how far the shift will not only remove the cloak of anonymity, but expose the new court to the analysis of the values of its highest judges in a way that has not hitherto generally occurred in the United Kingdom, certainly at a popular or public level. Until now, such analysis was generally discouraged not only by situational considerations but also by doctrinal beliefs rooted in the traditional 'declaratory' function of the judiciary and the positivist, objective and linguistic analysis of the judiciary's performance. In the United Kingdom, these long-held verities are about to be exposed (as in other common law final courts) to the light of greater public attention and enhanced legal realism. As Lord Phillips has remarked, these developments are likely to

---

[28] AR Blackshield, 'Quantitative Analysis: The High Court of Australia 1964–1969' (1972) 3 *Lawasia* 1; *cf* F Kort, 'Predicting Supreme Court Decisions Mathematically' (1957) 51 *American Political Science Review* 1; G Schubert, 'Judicial Attitudes and Policy-making in the Dixon Court' (1969) 7 *Osgoode Hall Law Journal* 1; A Tyree, 'The Geometry of Case Law' (1977) 4 *Victoria University of Wellington Law Review* 403.

be healthy ones. But they have also great significance for the choice of persons to serve on the final court and thus the process by which that choice is made and given effect.

## IV  ESTABLISHMENT OF THE HIGH COURT OF AUSTRALIA

Some of the foregoing themes about values in the law (and the special importance of judicial appointments in a final court) can be illustrated by turning back to the establishment of the High Court of Australia in 1903.

Although the Australian Constitution of 1901 envisaged the court as 'a Federal Supreme Court' and as the primary repository of 'the judicial power of the Commonwealth',[29] detailed provision for the operation of the court and for the appointment of the Justices was not enacted until 1903.[30] Federal legislation[31] subsequently provided that the court would be described as a 'superior court of record [that] consists of the Chief Justice and two [later six] other Justices'.[32]

In the appointment of new Justices, provision is also now made for the Federal Attorney-General, before any appointment of a Justice to a vacant office, to consult with the Attorneys-General of the states in relation to the appointment.[33] That provision was not enacted until 1979. Although it has resulted in a pool of inter-governmental nominees and was designed to assuage state criticisms of repeated interpretations of the Constitution by the High Court inimical to state powers, the process of 'consultation' in Australia (unlike in India)[34] means just that. The states provide nominees. There is no obligation for the Commonwealth to limit appointments to those nominated, much less to accept any of the nominees. My own appointment to the High Court of Australia in 1996 followed my nomination by the Attorney-General for New South Wales. I was then serving as President of the Court of Appeal of that state. But not all Justices in recent years were nominated by a state government.

State perceptions of the inclination of the High Court judges to interpret the Constitution in a way most favourable to the expansion of federal legislative powers go back to the early days. Yet at the very beginning, the view of that matter taken by the original appointees to the High Court of Australia was not without nuance. The three original Justices were the Chief Justice, Sir Samuel

---

[29]  Australian Constitution s 71.
[30]  Judiciary Act 1903 (Cth).
[31]  High Court of Australia Act 1979 (Cth).
[32]  ibid s 5.
[33]  ibid s 6.
[34]  The Supreme Court of India is established by the Constitution of India art 124. Judges of the Supreme Court are to be appointed by the President 'after consultation with such of the judges of the Supreme Court and of the High Courts of the States as the President may deem necessary'. The word 'consultation' has been given a meaning obliging it to be effective and implying an exchange of views after examining the merits of appointments. It does not necessarily connote concurrence but it comes very close. See *SP Gupta v Union of India* AIR 1982 SC 149; *Union of India v Sankalchand Seth* AIR 1977 SC 2328.

Griffith (then Chief Justice of Queensland), Mr Justice Edmund Barton (first Prime Minister of Australia) and Mr Justice Richard O'Connor. Each had played a part in the constitutional conventions in the 1890s that led to the adoption of the Australian Constitution. Each was a fine and ambitious lawyer. Each had seen himself as a potential Chief Justice. Yet, once the new national court was created, they all worked closely together. They appeared conscious of the historical function that they were performing as the initial expositors of the law in Australia, especially the written constitutional law.

Because of similarities between provisions in the Australian and United States constitutions, the original Justices in the High Court initially followed American constitutional doctrines on federal questions, including those of inter-governmental immunities and reserved state powers.[35] In effect, from a reading of the Constitution as a whole, they concluded that it was intended to preserve and maintain a kind of balance between federal and sub-national powers. Such a view would perhaps now be explained in terms of two interpretive principles that have come to the fore in recent decades in the construction of legislation more generally: a *purposive* construction, aimed at upholding the overall objective of the law, and a *contextual* construction, aimed at subjecting particular provisions to the overall structure and object of the document.

The harmony of the original Justices of the High Court of Australia is evident from the fact that they lunched together daily and formed a strong social and professional bond. However, in 1906, the appointment of two additional Justices, each a fine lawyer with less conservative legal views, shattered the calm of the new court. If ever it was necessary to demonstrate the importance of appointments to the values of a final national court, that lesson was quickly drawn to notice in Australia when Justice Isaac Isaacs and Justice Henry B Higgins took their seats. Isaacs, in particular, was no less brilliant than Griffith and even more ambitious. He was destined to become Chief Justice and the first Australian-born Governor-General. He had a great mastery of the law. And he differed fundamentally in his approach to the construction of the federal Constitution.

With the support of Higgins, Isaacs immediately began propounding a doctrine that would eventually prevail in 1920 in the *Engineers Case*.[36] According to this doctrine, if a relevant legislative power was granted by the Constitution to the Federal Parliament, the words of the grant were to be given their natural and ordinary meaning, and the paramountcy of federal law was to be upheld. There was to be no implied limitation upon such a meaning by reason of the federal character of the constitutional document in which the grant of power appeared. This was a rule of literalism which was much favoured by common law courts in statutory construction generally for most of the twentieth century. In constitutional adjudication in Australia (but not more generally), it continues to prevail.

---

[35] These doctrines were derived from *McCulloch v Maryland* 17 US 316 (1819). See *Deakin v Webb* (1904) 1 CLR 585; *Baxter v Commissioners of Taxation* (NSW) (1907) 4 CLR 1087.
[36] *Amalgamated Society of Engineers v Adelaide Steamship Co Ltd* (*Engineers Case*) (1920) 28 CLR 129.

In practical terms, this approach has meant the continuous expansion of the powers of the federal government and parliament. At the end of my service on the High Court, when a radical outcome of this approach effectively expunged a century of painstaking judicial elaboration of the federal industrial relations power,[37] I drew attention to the dichotomy that had evolved between the *contextual* interpretation of most legislation and the *literalist* interpretation of the Australian Constitution.[38] The shockwaves of the nationalistic and non-federal approaches of Isaacs and Higgins are felt in Australia to this day.

It is vital to appreciate that neither the position of the original Justices of the High Court of Australia nor that of Isaacs and Higgins was unarguable, illicit, improper, wrongly motivated or so-called 'activist'. Each is a legitimate and fully argued approach to the judicial task in hand. Each has had highly intelligent supporters in and outside the High Court. Each reflects a different spectrum of values and perceptions about the text and objectives of the Australian Constitution. Each is sincerely held by capable and independent judges. However, because these values have profound consequences for the outcome of cases (not to say for the distribution of governmental powers within the nation), the appointment of judges having such differing views is of legitimate interest to the governmental appointing authorities and to the people of the nation who will be affected by the decisions made by such judges.

According to Chief Justice Mason, writing on the Griffith Court that ushered in the earliest operations of the High Court of Australia:

> With the advent of Isaacs and Higgins, Griffith's dominating influence began its steady decline. The decline gathered pace with the death of O'Connor in 1912, his replacement by Gavan Duffy and the appointment of Powers and Rich as additional Justices in 1913. . . . Isaacs' knowledge of the law was just as comprehensive as Griffith's. Isaacs was an outstanding constitutional and equity lawyer whose influence has continued to the present day. He was just as determined and as energetic as Griffith had been. He was a prolific judgment writer; his judgments were encyclopaedic but prolix. The days of friendly concurrences were a thing of the past.[39]

Lest it be thought that the United Kingdom, with its different constitutional arrangements, is free from the potential for such a clash of values, it is necessary to reflect upon both the similarities and differences between the situation in Britain today and that of Australia after 1903.

The tradition of Austinian positivism has always been stronger in the judicial tradition of Britain. The absence of a single national written constitution with judicial powers of legislative disallowance has fostered an approach to judging that is generally more modest in its conception and technical or verbal in its exposition. Perhaps the very presence of the highest court within the parliamentary building enhanced a felt need on the part of the judges to limit

---

[37] *New South Wales v The Commonwealth (Work Choices Case)* (2006) 229 CLR 1.
[38] ibid [557] (Kirby J).
[39] AF Mason, 'Griffith Court' in T Blackshield, M Coper and G Williams (eds), *The Oxford Companion to the High Court of Australia* (Melbourne, Oxford University Press, 2001) 314.

the assertions of judicial power and to carve out a governmental role that was distinctively different and non-legislative.

However, the books on the shelves of judicial chambers daily demonstrated the fact that centuries of judicial creativity had preceded the appointments of all of the present judicial incumbents. Where else did the common law of England, come from if not from judicial predecessors? To deny the creative element in the judicial function in such a pragmatic and effective legal system was impossible in the face of ever-present reality. Perhaps its very creativity obliged a kind of fiction or sleight-of-hand to quieten the fears of a democratic people that unelected judges enjoyed too much power. Yet creative power they certainly enjoyed. Not only in the exposition (or 'declaration') of the common law, but also in the elaboration of ambiguities in legislation. And, over the centuries, some of that legislation certainly counts as 'constitutional' in character. It may not be in a single comprehensive document. But it exists.

In the exposition of the *common law*, there are many familiar instances of the creative role that now devolves on the Supreme Court of the United Kingdom. Take as an example the string of decisions in the English courts on the so-called 'wrongful birth' cases,[40] culminating in that of the House of Lords in *McFarlane v Tayside Health Board*.[41] To a very large extent, the problem presented to the courts was itself an outcome of the application of new medical technology. Lawyers might pretend that the rulings in the individual cases followed logically and inevitably from earlier decisional authority. However, no one could seriously suggest that the outcomes were exclusively a technical or purely verbal exercise for which a lifetime in commercial or insolvency law was the best preparation for a high judicial decision-maker.

Such a background might certainly be proof of intelligence, professional application, ability to perform legal analysis and a capacity for hard work. But these are not the only values that are called upon in litigation of such a kind; nor are they confined to commercial litigators. We discovered this in Australia when substantially the same problems came before the High Court of Australia in *Cattanach v Melchior*.[42] In that case, the High Court was divided four Justices to three.[43] The Australian decision is somewhat more forthcoming than the English one, I suggest, about the underlying policy choices faced by the law and the moral dilemmas presented by a decision in such a case, although some such discussions are present in the English decisions and in those of Canada, New Zealand, South Africa and continental Europe, to which reference was made in *Cattanach*.[44]

---

[40]    *Thake v Maurice* [1986] QB 644, leave to appeal to the House of Lords refused. See also *Gold v Haringey Health Authority* [1988] QB 481, 484; *Allen v Bloomsbury Health Authority* [1993] 1 All ER 651, 662.

[41]    *McFarlane v Tayside Health Board* [2000] 2 AC 59.

[42]    *Cattanach v Melchior* (2003) 215 CLR 1.

[43]    McHugh, Gummow, Kirby and Callinan JJ; Gleeson CJ, Hayne and Heydon JJ dissenting.

[44]    *Cattanach* (n 42) 50–51.

Even sharper have been the divisions between the judges addressing medical professional liability in the so-called 'wrongful life' cases.[45] The majority of the High Court of Australia on this occasion, rejected the existence of a cause of action asserted by a child profoundly injured by blindness, deafness and mental retardation occasioned by a repeatedly undiagnosed condition of foetal rubella.[46] The majority of the Court denied recovery on the basis that it was not logically possible for it to be asserted, on behalf of the child, that he should not have been born at all. Adapting the words of Professor Peter Cane, my own view was that 'the plaintiff . . . is surely not complaining that he was born, simpliciter, but that because of the circumstances under which he was born his lot in life is a disadvantaged one'.[47]

In the United Kingdom, the Congenital Disabilities (Civil Liability) Act 1976 (UK) expressly prohibited 'wrongful life' actions.[48] That Act had been drafted following recommendations of the Law Commission.[49] The values expressed in the Act reflected the same thinking as the English Court of Appeal expressed in the supervening case of *McKay v Essex Area Health Authority*.[50] In other jurisdictions, the preponderance of decisional law has followed roughly the same analysis, although not without occasional contrary views.[51] So far as the basic principles of tort law are concerned (and the evaluation of issues raised by relevant considerations of legal principle and legal policy),[52] respectfully I remain unconvinced. But this is beside the present point. The cases show that differing views can legitimately exist, and do exist, amongst the judges faced with such problems.

Useful insights can often be found from the study of judicial reasoning in other places. However, in the end, a final national court must reach its own conclusions on subjects involving the content of domestic common law. They must do so by reference not only to legal authority (which will not formally bind the final court to a conclusion), but also by reference to legal principle and policy. These considerations enliven an evaluative exercise which is stronger and more convincing if it is transparent in its performance. In *Harriton*, I put it this way:

> [J]ust as parliaments have their functions in our governance and law-making, so have the courts. The courts develop the common law in a principled way. They give reasons for what they do. They constantly strive for the attainment of consistency with established legal principles as well as justice in the individual case. . . . The appellant's life exists. It will continue to exist. No-one suggests otherwise. The question is who should pay for the suffering, loss and damage that flow from the respondent's carelessness. That is why the proper label for the appellant's action, if one is needed, is 'wrongful suffering'. The ordinary principles of negligence law sustain a decision in the

---

[45]  *Harriton v Stephens* (2006) 226 CLR 52.

[46]  Gleeson CJ, Gummow, Callinan, Heydon and Crennan JJ; Kirby J dissenting.

[47]  P Cane, 'Injuries to Unborn Children' (1977) 51 ALJ 704, 719. See *Harriton* (n 45) [10].

[48]  s 1(2)(b).

[49]  Law Commission of England and Wales, 'Report on Injuries to Unborn Children' (Law Com No 60, Cmnd 5709, 1974) 45–54.

[50]  *McKay v Essex Area Health Authority* [1982] 1 QB 1166.

[51]  See *Harriton* (n 45) [53]–[73].

[52]  ibid, [110] ff.

appellant's favour. None of the propounded reasons of legal principle or legal policy suggest a different outcome.[53]

Once again, at least at the level of a final court and in the absence of legislation, it is unconvincing to present such an issue as resolved by past judicial reasoning. Because of the procedures of leave or special leave, cases will rarely reach a final national court if there is a long and clear line of decisional authority standing in the way. The very nature of the court's jurisdiction is such that it must normally evaluate more than earlier judicial utterances. Once it starts to do this, it enters into the contestable territory of legal principle and policy. In the resolution of such questions, the values of the final national judges are incontestably influential. Sometimes they are controlling. And that is why those who appoint the judges and those whom the judges serve, have a legitimate interest in the values that may affect their judicial reasoning.

Apart from the common law, judicial values can also influence the outcome in contested cases of statutory interpretation. There could be few clearer illustrations of this proposition than in the divided decision of the House of Lords in *Fitzpatrick v Sterling Housing Association Ltd*.[54] There, the majority held that a person was capable of being a member of the 'family' of his same-sex partner for the purposes of the Rent Act 1977. The decision was reached over a strong dissenting opinion that laid emphasis upon the history of the Rent Act and how it would have been understood at the time of the enactment of the applicable provisions (and still more the provisions upon which they were earlier based, dating back to the early decades of the twentieth century).

A clash was thus presented in *Fitzpatrick* between a legal value that insisted on a literal interpretation of the words of the legislation as parliament 'intended' those words to apply when they first became law, and the value of reading such statutory words so that they would apply in contemporaneous social circumstances where, by other legislation and human rights provisions, discriminatory, unequal and prejudicial interpretations of the law, contrary to the rights and interests of minorities, have generally been discouraged.

The extent to which this clash of values has continued in the United Kingdom can be seen in *Mendoza v Ghaidan*.[55] In that case, the English Court of Appeal held that the survivor of a same-sex couple, who could succeed to a statutory tenancy, could be a 'spouse' under the Rent Act. In each of these cases, the United Kingdom courts declined to follow the earlier decision of the European Commission of Human Rights in the case of *S v United Kingdom*.[56] That decision had refused to extend the concept of 'family life' to include a same-sex relationship. Lord Slynn of Hadley, on this point, said specifically:

---

[53]   ibid [154].

[54]   *Fitzpatrick v Sterling Housing Association Ltd* [2001] 1 AC 27, 34. See A Lester et al (eds), *Human Rights Law & Practice*, 3rd edn (London, LexisNexis, 2009) 401 [4.8.48].

[55]   *Mendoza v Ghaidan* [2003] Ch 380 aff'd on appeal by the House of Lords in *Ghaidan v Godin-Mendoza* [2004] UKHL 30, [2004] 3 WLR 113.

[56]   *S v United Kingdom* (1986) 47 DR 274.

Leaving aside the fact these [Strasbourg] cases are still at an early stage of development of the law and that attitudes may change as to what is acceptable throughout Europe, I do not consider that these decisions impinge upon the decision which your Lordships have to take.[57]

If ever there was a clash of legal values and of genuinely contestable principles towards the proper approach to the meaning of beneficial legislation, it can be seen in the majority and dissenting opinions in the House of Lords in *Fitzpatrick*. It is not necessary to dig into the psychological well-springs of the respective Law Lords. Nor is it appropriate to evaluate their respective life journeys, religious inclinations or perceptions about human rights. Enough has been shown to indicate that the task of statutory interpretation, like that of 'declaring' the common law, is not mechanical. It cannot be performed (at least in a final national court) with no aids other than past cases and a dictionary or two. Individual judicial values affect outcomes. That is why values are significant for judicial appointments.

Increasingly, in the coming years this truth will be realised. It will be realised by the appointing officers in the executive government who have the all but last (formal) say under most constitutional arrangements about judicial appointments. But it will also influence the process of consultation and selection that is put in place for the making of such appointments.

Under the traditional (reformed) British model for the appointment of judges, including those of final courts, the last word conventionally belonged to the executive government chosen to reflect the majority in Parliament. Some (including in the judiciary and legal profession) have found this a defective arrangement. The critics fear purely political appointees. On the other hand, there remain strong arguments in support of the theory and practice that lies behind the appointment of judges by persons elected by the people.

The provision for a democratic element to be included in the appointment of judges, with their law-making role, has a doctrinal and political, as well as an historical, justification. Such an appointment provides a constitutional symmetry to the power, typically assigned to parliaments operating throughout the Commonwealth of Nations, to remove superior court judges on the grounds of proved incapacity or misconduct.[58] Both the appointment and removal of such judges are constitutionally important steps, comparatively rare, at once personal and public and having significance for the governance of a democratic polity.

Combined with the strong tradition of apoliticism (in Australia, including absence of contact with politicians and also with unelected officials) between the coming in and going out of the judges, the foregoing arrangements must be said to have worked well, on the whole, over a very long time. They recognise constitutional realities. They assure a democratic and even political role in the appointment of judges. And when the significance of judicial values is understood, that

---

[57] *Fitzpatrick* (n 54), 39–40.
[58] See eg Australian Constitution s 72; and Indian Constitution s 124(4).

political element has, in my view, been justified. Over time, it has tended, at least in Australia, to ensure a measure of diversity in the values of those appointed to high judicial office. It has attracted scrutiny of judicial appointments in the media, academic and 'professional' discourse. It has also provided a corrective to an exclusively professional judgment on appointments by involving consideration of the long-term deployment of individual decisional values, not just technical or linguistic skills.

In common law countries, the most radical alternative to this British model has evolved in the United States of America. In that country, under differing procedures, most state judges are either elected to office or are subject to electoral confirmation or recall, which involves a far more active democratic participation in the selection, appointment and retention processes. Switzerland is the only other country that has procedures for judicial election. Few legal observers in Commonwealth countries would favour such a process. It subjects candidates to direct pressures that may be inconsistent with the independent and impartial performance of their judicial functions. Those features represent the hallmark of a judiciary conforming to universal standards of human rights.[59]

The somewhat less radical provisions of the United States federal Constitution also introduced a democratic element in the appointment of federal judges, in the form of the constitutional requirement that federal judges must be nominated by the President but appointed 'with the Advice and Consent of the Senate'.[60] Historically, about 20 per cent of candidates nominated by the President to the Supreme Court of the United States have not been confirmed. The Senate is advised on such confirmations by the powerful Judiciary Committee. In recent times, a serious logjam has arisen, delaying the appointment of federal judges in a way that was clearly not envisaged by those who drafted the constitutional article.[61]

To Commonwealth eyes, however, this is only one of the defects of the United States federal provision. Whilst recognising the high importance of appointees and of their values for the discharge of their office, the confirmation procedure has tended to subject candidates to questions that lie at the heart of their future judicial performance. It has exposed them to substantial political pressure to participate in 'coaching' by representatives of the President, with a resulting potential to diminish the judicial office by needlessly involving its members, or potential members, in controversies defined by political and partisan perspectives.[62]

A measure of what can happen in this respect may be seen in the process involving Justice Sonia Sotomayor on her appointment to the Supreme Court of the United States in 2009. Prior to her appointment, in part as a result of talks or

---

[59] Universal Declaration of Human Rights arts 10-11, International Covenant on Civil & Political Rights art 14; European Convention on Human Rights art 6.1 ('Right to a fair trial'). See Lester, *Human Rights Law & Practice* (n 54) 324 [4.6.55].

[60] United States Constitution art II.

[61] *Washington Post* (Washington, 16 October 2009) A1, A20.

[62] See L Eisgruber, *The Next Justice: Repairing the Supreme Court Appointments Process* (Princeton, Princeton University Press, 2007).

papers she had delivered, three points of view were attributed to her from which she felt obliged to retreat during questioning in the confirmation hearings: (1) that her judicial decisions might sometimes be affected by her life's experience as a Latina who grew up in disadvantaged circumstances; (2) that it would be sensible for the Supreme Court sometimes to inform itself on decisions of other national courts considering common issues of comparative or international law; and (3) that, in construing the Constitution of the United States of America, the Supreme Court has functions that include re-considering past authority and developing old precedents.[63] The disclaimer or severe qualification of these three very sensible views, which would largely be uncontroversial (or at least fully debatable) in Commonwealth countries accustomed to greater realism and comparativism, evidences the danger of subjecting judicial candidates to such intense political pressures, in the appointment process. It illustrates the corrupting tendency of political partisanship to reduce the judicial candidate to the standards of the infotainment world of modern media and politics.

The previous Canadian government indicated that future candidates for appointment to the Supreme Court of Canada would be introduced to a committee of the Canadian Parliament and subjected to some form of questioning. However, no constitutional requirement obliging 'advice and consent' has been introduced into the Canadian Constitution. So far, despite the value-laden provisions of the Canadian Charter of Rights and Freedoms, the appointments procedure has been much more restrained. Its future development remains uncertain.

In South Africa, a procedure for appointment to the higher courts has involved facilities for application and nomination, town hall meetings with opportunities for public questioning of candidates; and the submission by an appointments authority of names of appointable candidates from whom the President must select the judge to be appointed. These procedures were considered necessary to alter the composition of the judiciary in South Africa, inherited from the previous apartheid years in that country. The achievements of the Constitutional Court of South Africa, in establishing its reputation and credentials in such a relatively short period, appears to vindicate the success of this model, as it operates in that country.

In India, under British rule, the judges of the higher courts were all appointed at the discretion of the Crown.[64] Under the Government of India Act 1935, there were no express provisions for 'consultations' on appointments to the Federal Court of India, although, as a matter of courtesy and convention, these were often doubtless made. With effect from January 1950, the Constitution of India

[63] J De Mint, 'Two Views of the Constitution and Supreme Court Nominations' *Washington Examiner* (Washington, 21 May 2009). See also 'A Steady Rise, Punctuated by Doubts' *Washington Post* (Washington, 12 July 2009); DS Broder, 'Battle Lines—For Another Day' *Washington Post* (Washington, 16 July 2009); NA Lewis, 'Old Confirmation Wars Fuelling Some Critics Now' *New York Times* (New York, 26 June 2009); and DM Herszenhorn, 'Court Nominee Criticized for Relying on Foreign Law' *New York Times* (New York, 26 June 2009).

[64] AP Datar, *Commentary on the Constitution of India*, 2nd edn (Nagpur, Wadhwa & Co, 2007) Vol 1, 769.

created a Supreme Court, whose judges were to be 'appointed by the President by warrant under his hand and seal after consultation with such of the judges of the Supreme Court and of the High Court in the states as the President may deem necessary for the purpose'. There was a proviso to this article that, 'in the case of appointment of a Judge other than the Chief Justice, the Chief Justice of India shall always be consulted'.[65]

In a series of decisions of the Supreme Court, this requirement of 'consultation' has been elaborated. In *SP Gupta v Union of India*,[66] it was concluded that 'consultation' connoted discussion and serious consideration; but without the necessity of concurrence. In part, because of the supersession of judges during the Emergency of 1975–77, a stricter view of the obligation was taken in *Supreme Court Advocates-On-Record Association v Union of India*.[67] There, a majority of the Court concluded that the 'consultation' was binding on the Executive so that, effectively, the judges had the last say on any proposed appointment. Reliance was placed on the imperative language of the duty to secure the opinion of the Chief Justice. This provision was contrasted with others in the Constitution providing for 'consultation'.

This decision has proved controversial and has led to revised procedures following a still further decision of the Supreme Court.[68] Suggestions have been made for an express amendment to the Indian Constitution to ensure that 'the finest talent [is] recruited to the judicial service'.[69] However, the expansive interpretation of the requirement of 'consultation' remains controversial. It has been strongly criticised by a distinguished retired judge of the Supreme Court as amounting to 'a mighty seizure of power' by which the judges have 'wrested authority . . . from the top Executive to themselves, by a stroke of adjudicatory self-enthronement'.[70] Those who defend the more recent rulings of the Supreme Court of India on this issue generally do so by reference to the peculiar needs of the Indian judiciary to be protected from the perceived defects of the political process.

In Australia, the procedures for judicial appointment have, so far, not formally challenged the ultimate repository of the appointments power. It belongs, in the traditional British way, to the executive government of the Commonwealth or the states or territories concerned. Nevertheless, within the past decade, procedures for advertising judicial vacancies and inviting applications and nominations have spread from the lower courts (where they began) to some superior courts, including State Supreme Courts and the Federal Court of Australia. The present

---

[65] Indian Constitution art 124(2).

[66] *SP Gupta v Union of India* AIR 1982 SC 149, paras 88, 997, 1101, 1013-5, 1026, per Venkataramaiah J.

[67] *Supreme Court Advocates-On-Record Association v Union of India* AIR 1994 SC 268.

[68] *Re President's Reference* AIR 1998 SC 16, (1998) 7 SCC 739.

[69] See eg India, National Commission to Review the Working of the Constitution; see also India, Law Commission, 121st report (1987).

[70] VR Krishna Iyer, 'Judiciary: A Reform Agenda' in *Constitutional Miscellany*, 2nd edn (Lucknow, Eastern Books, 2003) 27.

Federal Attorney-General (Mr Robert McClelland) has appointed a non-statutory committee to advise him on appointments. The committee presently comprises three judges or former judges (Chief Justice FG Brennan of the High Court; the Chief Justice of the relevant federal court; and Justice Jane Mathews, formerly of the Federal and Supreme Courts) and an official from the federal Attorney-General's Department. The committee's reports, which are confidential, are advisory only.

In a recent series of appointments to the Federal Court of Australia, it has been suggested that the government ultimately decided to go beyond the recommended nominees to ensure that the consideration of gender was given a higher weight than, seemingly, the committee had done. Under the foregoing procedure, there is no infusion of viewpoints or opinions about shortlisted nominees from the general population or from civic, professional or other groups.[71]

As stated, in the case of the High Court of Australia, legislation requires a non-binding consultation to take place with the Attorneys-General of the states of Australia. However, appointment is reserved, under the Constitution, to the Federal Executive Council which advises the Governor-General as the representative of the Queen. That Council comprises, relevantly, politicians who are also members of the Federal cabinet. In effect, because of the recognised legal, constitutional and political significance of appointees to the final national court in Australia, the ultimate decision is made by the Federal cabinet. It has before it recommendations from the Attorney-General. However, according to well substantiated reports in Australia, many a name has gone into cabinet with the support of the Minister, but, if the proposed appointee does not have the support of the Prime Minister and of senior Ministers, it is unlikely to get up.[72]

In this respect, Australian appointments to the final national court continue to observe the realism of past British constitutional practice. The politicians get but one chance to influence the values of the court, and this at the moment of appointment (or at the almost never used moment of removal). They recognise that the selection is extremely significant both for constitutional and other decision-making. They know that big 'mistakes' have been made in the past in the assessment of the values of appointees. They also know that, once appointed, the time for any direct political influence on the judge has passed.

In the United Kingdom, the selection procedure for the new Supreme Court is established by the Constitutional Reform Act 2005 (UK). It involves a panel of five persons, chaired by the President of the Supreme Court, presently Lord Phillips. The panel includes the Deputy President of the Supreme Court (presently Lord Hope of Craighead) and three other members, each nominated by the respective judicial appointments bodies of England and Wales, Scotland and Northern

---

[71] Attorney-General Robert McClelland, 'Announcement: Federal Court Appointments', Media Release, 23 October 2009.

[72] See 'Appointments that might have been. . .' in T Blackshield, M Coper and G Williams, *The Oxford Companion of the High Court of Australia* (Melbourne, Oxford University Press, 2001) 23–27.

Ireland. These nominees need not be judges or lawyers.[73] However, at the time of writing, one other nominee (for Scotland) is a judge. Thus, a majority of the five comprises serving judges. The selection procedure has been described in the media as 'convoluted'. It does not finally involve any direct political or parliamentary participation like that in the United States. Nor is there any direct involvement of citizens or civil society organisations. It is still a largely secret process which does not enjoy the muted political legitimacy that was provided by the former long-standing and traditional role of the Lord Chancellor in *selecting* judges of the higher courts, with the advice of his officials and consultations (but not direct decisional involvement) with the senior judiciary.

Commenting on the process adopted in the United Kingdom, Lord Pannick QC agreed that 'people would start to take more interest in who the judges were and how they were appointed because of the new visibility of [the Supreme Court]'.[74] To like effect, Professor Kate Malleson of the University of London (Queen Mary College) reportedly said that 'the trend generally towards openness and public knowledge' would ensure that the new Supreme Court could not function with anonymity. As its cases attract more attention, so would the composition of the court and so, it was suggested, would its 'lack of diversity'.[75]

From the context, it seems unlikely that Professor Malleson was referring solely to the fact that only one of the 12 Supreme Court Justices is a woman (Baroness Hale of Richmond) and all but one (Lord Kerr of Tonaghmore) has a background that includes a degree from either Oxford or Cambridge University. From time to time, there have been similar comments in Australia about the comparative lack of diversity in the professional practice, of most of the nation's final court judges. As in Canada, however, the gender imbalance of the final court in Australia is much less visible (in Australia three of seven are women, in Canada four of nine, including the Chief Justice, the Rt Hon Beverley McLachlin; in New Zealand, the Chief Justice is a woman, the Rt Hon Dame Sian Elias).

Two insightful comments on the new arrangements in the United Kingdom should be included. They are made by senior office holders in remarks offered on my original paper. I will not attribute them. From other communications, I believe that they are not isolated opinions. They reflect my own views.[76] The first wrote:

> I am like you . . . concerned about the extent to which the present system of appellate appointments has come under judicial control, without (at present) any reviewing process, with very real risks of unconscious cloning and with the Lord Chancellor retaining (in reality, despite the CR Act's elaborate provisions) no residual possibility of intervening. Another feature that you may not have noted is that retiring presidents/ deputy presidents get to sit on the appointments commissions which appoint those who are going to succeed them and to fill the extra place needed on the Court. That

---

[73] Constitutional Reform Act 2005 (UK) ss 26–28.
[74] F Gibb, *The Times* (London, 1 October 2009).
[75] ibid.
[76] Letters on file with the author, dated respectively 16 November 2009 and 11 January 2010.

seems quite wrong. Before the CR Act, the understanding was that retiring judges were not even consulted!

The other wrote:

> [T]he presence of the UK's two most senior judges on the panel will inevitably have a crucial effect on the decision making. It seems inconceivable that any lay member will be able to challenge successfully the views expressed by those judges as to any deficiency in legal expertise in a particular area in the Supreme Court required to be filled, and the views expressed by those judges as to the judicial and legal expertise of the applicants and the standing in which those applicants are held by their judicial colleagues. Moreover, there are inevitably personal associations between those judges and judicial applicants which members of the public and their elected representatives might consider undermine the integrity of the process, such as membership of the same Inn, or of the same club, or the formation of a close professional, and, possibly as a result, personal association over the years. Moreover, the President and Deputy President will inevitably feel an obligation to the other members of the Supreme Court, each one of whom is a statutory consultee. That itself raises questions about the professional and personal associations, such as I have described, between each of those persons and applicants. In those circumstances, the appointment panel looks, to my mind, badly balanced. I very much doubt whether it is capable of delivering the necessary diversity to which you refer . . .

Professional and media speculation about greater public attention in the United Kingdom to judicial appointments to the new Supreme Court, and to its decisions and values, appears to be wishful thinking, rather than an institutionally guaranteed likelihood.

## V  CONCLUSIONS

From the foregoing considerations concerning the importance of values (involving the ascertainment of relevant legal authority, legal principle .and legal policy) in final national courts of appeal, the following conclusions may be drawn:

1.  Judges in final national courts, even more than trial judges and judges in intermediate appellate courts, have very large responsibilities for the interpretation of constitutional and equivalent provisions (in the United Kingdom, the Human Rights Act 1998, for example); for the construction of important but ambiguous legislation; and for the ascertainment and 'declaration' of the evolving common law.

2.  The performance of the foregoing tasks, particularly at the level of a final national court, is rarely a purely technical or mechanical function, devoid of value judgments on the part of the decision-makers. In awareness about, and identification and resolution of, such issues, it is highly desirable that the judges of such courts should be conscious, and transparent, about their own processes of reasoning. They should identify and elaborate any general

consideration of legal principle and policy to which they have regard. They should not ignore, or disguise, such considerations by pretending that complex and novel legal questions can all be resolved by reference solely to considerations of legislative texts and past legal authority.

3.   Appreciation of these features of judicial reasoning, especially in a final national court, will have a number of practical consequences for the organisation of the court and for the performance of its functions. Such consequences may include: (a) provisions for the facility of intervention and the presentation of submissions by amici curiae in appropriate cases;[77] (b) facilitation of advocacy by the parties addressed not simply to past decisional authority but also to the broader considerations of principle and policy presented by an appeal; and (c) facilitation of the provision of judicial decisions of other final and appellate or equivalent courts and tribunals which may have addressed like questions, and in doing so, may have provided useful materials for reasoning by analogy and (where appropriate) for pursuing a course of consistency in the elaboration of international law.[78]

4.   For the tasks that are committed to final national courts, a range of professional and personal skills on the part of the judges appointed to serve is essential. As the business of such courts increasingly extends far beyond the resolution of commercial litigation, skills in, and awareness of, other disciplines beyond contract, maritime, taxation, equity and insolvency law is critical. Moreover, the appointment of judges of different sex, background, life experiences and professional engagement becomes imperative. The notion that a narrow range of educational, professional and intellectual attributes is sufficient for the discharge of the 'technical functions' of the court, should be firmly rejected by the government, parliament and by the courts and legal profession themselves. As the mechanical (or declaratory) conception of the judicial function gives way to greater realism about that function, the result is obviously a need to address more closely the criteria and procedures of judicial appointment.

5.   Once the foregoing is acknowledged, it demonstrates the wisdom of retaining a distinct role for the elected government in the appointment of judges, especially judges of appellate courts, and particularly judges of a final national court. One can safely delegate to unelected officials the selection of other officials whose functions are wholly, or mainly, technical. However, that is not the character of the functions performed today by a judge of a final national court. Inescapably, such a judge must resolve substantial 'leeways for choice'.[79] In the theory of popular accountability for such appointments

---

[77] cf *Levy v Victoria* (1997) 189 CLR 579, 600–04 (Brennan CJ); 650–52 (Kirby J).

[78] *Povey v Qantas Airways Ltd* (2005) 223 CLR 189, applying *Air France v Saks* 470 US 392 (1985) and considering *Sidhu v British Airways plc* [1997] AC 430 (concerning the meaning of 'accident' in art 17 of the Warsaw Convention on Civil Aviation in its application to deep venous thrombosis).

[79] J Stone, *Social Dimensions of Law and Justice* (Sydney, Maitland, 1977) 649, applying K Llewellyn, 'The Normative, The Legal, and The Law-Jobs: The Problem of Juristic Method' (1940) 49 *Yale Law Journal* 1355.

in a representative democracy, it is highly desirable (if not essential) to have more than a purely nominal or informal or restricted link to the elected government and parliament. The input of governments that change over time, and which are accountable to parliament, into the appointment of such judges, not only affords democratic legitimacy to the appointees. It also tends to secure, over time, the variety of changing values that are also reflected in the changing compositions of parliaments and governments. This is not to politicise the judiciary along purely partisan lines. It is simply to recognise the reality that strongly differing views are often held in society about the kinds of value judgments which such judges are called upon to perform.

6.  The type of politicisation of judicial appointments now seen both in federal and state courts in the United States of America seems unsuitable to the judicial tradition of Britain, which is itself reflected and observed in most Commonwealth countries and certainly in Australia. No one suggests the adoption of elections or political confirmation of the American variety. To our eyes, these procedures go too far and have too many faults. By the same token, the effective assignment of (most) judicial appointments to bodies operating wholly or substantially within an established legal culture is equally defective. Without disrespect to the very distinguished judges and other officials presently participating in such procedures, theirs is not the only (or even the main) voice that should be heard. To replace judicial appointment by elected politicians effectively by a system of judicial appointments selected by present or past judges is not only to sever the important link of democratic legitimacy for our judiciary. In the process, it risks the effective imposition of an overly narrow perspective about what really matters in judicial performance. It runs the particular risk of limiting the input of information and assessments concerning the very wide range of values and qualities that are essential to the judges of a final national court, once appointed.

7.  The foregoing conclusions do not require a total return to the former appointments system whereby persons were exclusively 'given the nod' in a mysterious and secret process undertaken by politicians advised by Departments, judges, and other officials. The introduction of opportunities for nomination of, and application by, candidates is desirable. So may be a facility for some kind of appropriate interview process. Nevertheless, the danger of a judicial dominance of the appointments of future judges is obvious. The risk in such procedure is that there may be insufficient questioning of present values and an excessively deferential attitude to the established professional values and culture. That danger is far greater than the supposed danger of purely political appointments, given the strong democratic inhibitions upon the appointing ministers to avoid public criticism on that ground. Those who wish to build an effective final national court will infuse its personnel with elements of variety and a questioning

inclination. All living creatures and their institutions thrive best where they exhibit diversity.[80]

The foregoing analysis suggests that the appointments procedures in the United Kingdom, Canada and Australia represent a work-in-progress so far as the final national courts are concerned. We need to avoid the Scylla of partisan American politics, whilst navigating around the Charybdis of new systems that effectively, if not formally, amount to judges appointing judges.

The guiding principle for the future should be the retention of a healthy democratic element at the moment of every judicial appointment; but with inbuilt procedures and diverse voices to assure against the selection of unappointable or purely political and unqualified candidates.

If we have not yet arrived at a universally acceptable model for the selection of such important and long-serving public office holders, we have at least begun the journey to a more transparent system. One important key to a successful system must lie in a recognition of the values that judges apply in their decisions and the high desirability, in elected democracies, that those who make value judgments should secure real, and not just nominal, authority from the ultimate source of power in every nation: the people.

The wisdom of the politicians may be that they will be more aware of the need for observance of the laws of variation of which Darwin wrote so long ago. In his bicentenary year, we should not forget the lessons of that great British scientist for the precious institutions of the law and the need for those institutions to resist turning judicial appointments over, effectively, to a perpetual professional elite.

[80] *cf* CR Sunstein, *Why Societies Need Dissent* (Cambridge, Massachusetts, Harvard University Press, 2006) 166.

# 3

# From Appellate Committee to United Kingdom Supreme Court: Independence, Activism and Transparency

AILEEN KAVANAGH*

## I INDEPENDENCE: APPEARANCES AND REALITY

ON 1 OCTOBER 2009, the highest court in the United Kingdom ceased to be the Appellate Committee of the House of Lords and became the Supreme Court of the United Kingdom. The Act which establishes the new Supreme Court (the Constitutional Reform Act 2005) reaffirms the traditional constitutional principles of the rule of law and judicial independence.[1] Indeed, it emphasises that there is a duty on 'the Lord Chancellor and other Ministers of the Crown and those with responsibility for matters relating to the judiciary or otherwise to the administration of justice' to 'uphold the continued independence of the judiciary'.[2] But apart from reaffirming traditional principles, has the new Supreme Court been given powers not possessed by the Appellate Committee? It seems not. The jurisdiction of the Supreme Court is very similar to that of its predecessor, with the exception that it will hear devolution issues formerly heard by the Judicial Committee of the Privy Council.[3] The 2005 Act does not make any changes to the existing leave requirements for appeals to the top court. Nor does it give the new court any radically new powers. It will perform basically the same function as the Appellate Committee of the House of Lords.

* I would like to thank all the participants at the *Judges and Jurists* Conference in London in November 2009 for helpful feedback on this paper.

[1] s 1 of the Constitutional Reform Act 2005 (hereafter 'CRA') provides: 'This Act does not adversely affect the existing constitutional principle of the rule of law.'

[2] CRA s 3(1).

[3] *The Supreme Court of the United Kingdom, Practice Direction 10*, available at www.supreme court.gov.uk/docs/pd10.pdf. In one recent Supreme Court devolution case, the Supreme Court was split 3:2, with Lords Hope and Rodger, the two Scots Justices, on opposing sides: *Martin v Her Majesty's Advocate* [2010] UKSC 10.

So what was the purpose of the constitutional reform? One of its main aims was to remove the perceived constitutional anomaly that the highest court of appeal in the UK was situated within one of the chambers of Parliament.[4] There was a fear that this might create confusion (both here and abroad) about the independent status of the judiciary in the UK, or might create the misleading impression that the UK's highest court operated 'under the shadow of the legislature'.[5] The desirability of having a court which was clearly independent from the legislature seemed to go hand in hand with the need to rectify another glaring anomaly in the UK's constitutional structure, namely, the fact that the Lord Chancellor was simultaneously a member of the legislature, executive and judiciary. This anomaly was also rectified by the CRA 2005.[6]

In the Government's Consultation Paper on a Supreme Court for the United Kingdom, much emphasis was placed on bringing the appearance of judicial independence in line with reality. The Government was keen to clarify that although the time had come to establish a new court, 'no criticism is intended of the way in which the members of [the Appellate Committee] have discharged their functions.'[7] However, in light of changes in public expectations, it was necessary to make judicial independence from the other branches of government crystal clear. The following statements from the Consultation Paper give a flavour of the Government's thinking on this issue:

> The considerable growth of judicial review in recent years has inevitably brought the judges more into the political eye. It is essential that our systems do all that they can to minimise the danger that judges decisions could be *perceived* to be politically motivated. The Human Rights Act 1998, itself the product of a changing climate of opinion, has made people more sensitive to the issues and more aware of the anomaly of the position whereby the highest court of appeal is situated within one of the chambers of parliament.[8]
>
> ... the fact that the Law Lords is a Committee of the House of Lords can raise issues about the *appearance of independence* from the legislature.[9]

The Constitutional Reform Act 2005 takes these appearances seriously, and rightly so. The new court no longer carries the name of the second chamber in Parliament but is clearly a 'Supreme Court'. The judges are no longer 'their Lordships' but rather 'Justices of the Supreme Court'.[10] Of crucial importance to the appearance of independence is the fact that the judges' chambers are no

---

[4] Department for Constitutional Affairs, *Constitutional Reform: A Supreme Court for the United Kingdom*, Consultation Paper 11/03, July 2003 [3]. For a detailed narrative of the political background to the constitutional reform, see A Le Sueur, 'From Appellate Committee to Supreme Court: a Narrative' in L Blom-Cooper et al (eds), *The Judicial House of Lords 1876–2009* (Oxford, OUP, 2009).

[5] Consultation Paper (n 4) [5].

[6] CRA s 3.

[7] Consultation Paper (n 4) [5].

[8] ibid [2].

[9] ibid [3].

[10] CRA 2005 s 23(6).

longer located along the corridors of the Houses of Parliament, but have been moved to their own building across Parliament Square.[11]

Together with the geographic move, the Supreme Court has a new website which provides clear information on current and future cases, links to judgments of the court and press releases on recent cases.[12] Justice Albie Sachs of the South African Supreme Court commented that 'any leading public institution in an open and democratic society should be able to pass the tour guide test, that is, to have its principal role explainable in a few clear and understandable sentences'.[13] The new Supreme Court of the United Kingdom now seems to meet (or at least aspires to meet) this test. Its website explains that:

> the Supreme Court has been established to achieve a complete separation between the United Kingdom's senior Judges and the Upper House of Parliament, emphasising the independence of the Law Lords and increasing the transparency between Parliament and the courts.[14]

It also provides brief biographies of the Justices of the new Supreme Court outlining their educational background and legal qualifications. The website contemplates and welcomes visits by the public to the court and shows a willingness to facilitate educational events for law students. It even announces the opening of the Supreme Court cafe and shop which boasts 'a range of gifts and products linked to the Supreme Court'.[15] There is no doubt that the new Supreme Court is more accessible and open to the public than its predecessor. As Jack Straw commented at the Supreme Court opening ceremony, 'no longer will the highest court in the land be hidden at the end of a corridor in the House of Lords, but instead members of the public will be able to walk in off the street to see for themselves the work of our senior judiciary'.[16] But the British public need not actually tread on the new Supreme Court carpet[17] to view the Supreme Court in action. Some of its proceedings will be televised, so that the public can see how the court operates from the comfort of their own home.[18]

Are these facts meaningless trivia about a new tourist destination in London or, alternatively, are they constitutionally significant details about the role of

---

[11]   The Supreme Court now resides in the refurbished Middlesex Guildhall on London's Parliament Square, opposite the Houses of Parliament and alongside Westminster Abbey and the Treasury.

[12]   www.supremecourt.gov.uk.

[13]   Justice Albie Sachs, 'Nelson Mandela and Mahatma Gandhi were locked up in our court', *Timesonline*, 1 October 2009.

[14]   www.supremecourt.gov.uk/about/significance-to-the-uk.html.

[15]   www.supremecourt.gov.uk/visiting/shop.html.

[16]   'Jack Straw: Supreme Court opening is major milestone for government's constitutional reform', 16 October 2009: www.justice.gov.uk/news/newsrelease161009a.html.

[17]   The pop-art carpet for the new Supreme Court was designed by Sir Peter Blake (whose previous work includes the design of the Beatles' album 'Sergeant Pepper's Lonely Hearts Club Band') and it incorporates symbols representing the four nations of the United Kingdom. There is also a floral Supreme Court emblem and a Supreme Court poem, written by the Poet Laureate Andrew Motion, see http://www.supremecourt.gov.uk/visiting/art-at-the-court.html.

[18]   See I Caplin, 'Television cameras in the Supreme Court will press all the right buttons' *Timesonline*, 15 October 2009.

an important institution in Britain's changing Constitution? I think the answer is closer to the latter. No public lawyer should be disdainful about the role of appearance in the administration of justice. We all know that justice must not only be done, but be seen to be done.[19] The physical move of the court to its own building and the changed nomenclature are important in this regard. They highlight the institutional separation of the courts from the legislature and emphasise that the courts are not, and should not be, subservient to the legislature.[20]

Of course, the establishment of a new Supreme Court of the United Kingdom does not *make* the judges of the highest court in the land independent, because they were already independent. But it does make them more *visibly* independent and, as Justice Sachs commented, 'it can only be to the good if the concept of the independence of the judiciary is reinforced'.[21] That the judges of the new Supreme Court will no longer be referred to as 'their Lordships' but simply as 'Justices' is also an important symbolic change. It emphasises that judges are public servants whose role is to decide disputes brought by citizens and administer justice in a fair and even-handed way. A less superior and more humble public image of the judiciary is conveyed.

Although the Constitutional Reform Act 2005 does not give the new Supreme Court any significantly new powers, it is nonetheless a useful and welcome piece of constitutional spring-cleaning. It clarifies the constitutional importance of judicial independence in the British Constitution. It lays the court open for all to see. The establishment of the new Supreme Court means that the judges themselves, the issues they decide and the procedures of the court are more transparent to the public than heretofore. These seemingly cosmetic changes have important symbolic and constitutional implications.

In this chapter, I want to pursue two further issues. The first is whether the change from Appellate Committee to Supreme Court will have a significant impact on judicial reasoning—in particular, whether it will make the court more 'activist' and more willing to challenge the elected branches of government than heretofore. The second question concerns the issue of the transparency of the judiciary and the extent to which the moral and political views of the judiciary should be known to the public. It will explore whether greater transparency about judicial reasoning is likely to enhance public confidence in the judiciary. Though it is an extremely important issue, my chapter will not deal with the process of judicial appointments under the Judicial Appointments Commission established by the CRA.

---

[19] *Secretary of State for the Home Department v AF (No 3)* [2009] UKHL 28, [2009] 3 WLR 74 [63].

[20] See the chapter by James Lee in this collection.

[21] Sachs, 'Nelson Mandela and Mahatma Gandhi' (n 13); see also E Fennell, 'More Independent? Their Lordships have never hesitated to make their views clear in the past', *Timesonline*, 1 October 2009.

II  WILL THE NEW SUPREME COURT BE MORE 'ACTIVIST'?

It was perhaps inevitable that when the new Supreme Court was established, questions would be raised (and indeed fears voiced) that the new court might become a bolder and more activist court. In a BBC radio programme on the subject of the new Supreme Court,[22] Lord Falconer, the former Lord Chancellor, seemed to view such a development in a positive light: 'the Supreme Court will be bolder in vindicating both the freedoms of individuals and, coupled with that, be more willing to take on the executive'.[23] Many of the senior judiciary were extremely doubtful that the new Supreme Court would hand down more activist decisions. The former senior Law Lord (Lord Bingham) and the current President of the Supreme Court (Lord Phillips) were both of the view that the move from Appellate Committee to Supreme Court would not make the Supreme Court justices more assertive or interventionist than their predecessors. There is no question, said Lord Bingham on a BBC radio programme, of the judges getting 'a rush of blood to the head'[24] or 'throwing their weight around'.[25]

In order to assess whether judges will become more activist, we need to first be clear about what is meant by 'judicial activism'. When a judge or a court is described as 'activist', many people understand that description as a term of abuse. It is a slogan used to suggest that judges are being inappropriately creative, arrogating to themselves powers they do not or should not have and overstepping the constitutional boundary of their role.[26] On this understanding, 'judicial activism' is equated with illegitimate judicial decision-making where the illegitimacy is due to excessive or arbitrary judicial creativity. Sometimes it is suggested that any form of judicial creativity amounts to inappropriate 'judicial activism' in this sense. The judges' job, we are told, is simply to apply the law, not to develop or make new law.

As Lord Bingham commented extra-judicially, 'this is a view which has few, if any, adherents today'.[27] Most people who understand the nature of judicial decision-making are aware that judges develop the law and indeed make new law. When adjudicating common law disputes, the courts necessarily develop and make new laws through their precedents.[28] Moreover, when the courts interpret unclear statutory provisions, judges necessarily exercise a creative role

---

[22] J Rozenberg, 'Top Dogs: Britain's New Supreme Court', BBC Radio Documentary broadcast by BBC Radio 4 on 8 September 2009; see also J Rozenberg, 'Fear over UK Supreme Court impact' 8 September 2009, news.bbc.co.uk/1/hi/uk/8237855.stm.

[23] Rozenberg, 'Top Dogs: Britain's New Supreme Court' (n 22).

[24] ibid, transcript, 6.

[25] ibid, transcript, 6.

[26] See WW Justice, 'Two Faces of Judicial Activism' in D O'Brien (ed), *Judges on Judging—Views from the Bench* (Chatham, Chatham House, 1997) 302; T Campbell, 'Judicial Activism—Justice or Treason?' (2001–04) 10 *Otago Law Review* 307, 311; JD Heydon, 'Judicial Activism and the Death of the Rule of Law' (2004) 10 *Otago Law Review* 493.

[27] T Bingham, *The Rule of Law* (London, Allen Lane, 2010) 45.

[28] ibid.

by elaborating, supplementing, modifying and developing statutory meaning.[29] Some judicial creativity is a necessary and unavoidable part of judicial decision-making. It is also desirable because it allows the courts to develop the law in line with changes in society and gives them some flexibility in arriving at the most just outcome in the individual case.[30]

So, the extreme view that judges should never make new law need not detain us here. More pertinent for our purposes is the more modest and realistic view which accepts that judicial creativity is a matter of degree. The central question then concerns the point at which acceptable development of the law shades into an illegitimate form of adjudication. For the purposes of this paper, I will take 'judicial activism' to refer to the extent to which the courts are willing to change and develop the law, as well as the courts' sense of when and why it is appropriate to do so. By contrast, judicial restraint refers to a judicial disposition to conserve existing law, refraining from pursuing a more developmental or creative approach to adjudication.[31]

It should be noted that in public law adjudication the question of judicial activism has an explicitly relational aspect vis-a-vis the legislature and executive because there, the courts have the power to review or scrutinise a legislative decision (ie primary legislation) or an executive decision for compliance with a range of legal standards. Thus, in public law adjudication, judicial activism governs the extent to which, or the intensity with which, the courts are willing to scrutinise a legislative or executive decision and the justification advanced in support of that decision. For this reason, many commentators define judicial activism in terms of the willingness of the courts to challenge or interfere with the decisions made by the elected branches of government.[32]

We now have a clearer idea of what we mean by judicial activism. It refers to the extent to which the courts are willing to be creative in their adjudicative function (ie their willingness to develop the law and make new law) but also their willingness to stand up to the executive and the legislature, holding them firmly to constitutional principles rather than deferring to them in a supine way. So, judicial activism has two dimensions. The first relates to judicial creativity. The second refers to the courts' relationship with the other branches of government. Both dimensions engage judges' views about the extent and limits

---

[29] R Cross, *Statutory Interpretation* (London, Butterworths, 1995) 49, 93. Perhaps one of the most dramatic and eye-catching instances of this judicial creativity is provided by the 'transformative' interpretations licensed by s 3 of the Human Rights Act, see generally A Kavanagh, *Constitutional Review under the UK Human Rights Act* (Cambridge, Cambridge University Press, 2009).

[30] See Kavanagh, *Constitutional Review* (n 29) 31ff; S Sedley, 'Distinction and Diversity: Law and the LSE' in R Rawlings (ed) *Law, Society and Economy: Centenary Essays for the London School of Economics and Political Science 1895–1995* (Oxford, Clarendon Press, 1997) 322; Justice Kirby, 'Judicial Activism? A Riposte to the Counter-Reformation' (2005–07) 11 *Otago Law Review* 1.

[31] A Kavanagh, 'Judicial Restraint in the Pursuit of Justice' (2010) 60 *University of Toronto Law Journal* 23, 24–25; J Daley, 'Defining Judicial Restraint', in T Campbell and J Goldsworthy (eds), *Judicial Power, Democracy and Legal Positivism* (Aldershot, Ashgate, 2000).

[32] J Waldron, 'Compared to what? Judicial activism and New Zealand's Parliament' (2005) *New Zealand Law Journal* 441.

of their institutional role vis-à-vis the other two branches of government, and the constitutional propriety of a judicial decision in a particular case.

Will the transfer of jurisdiction from the Appellate Committee to the Supreme Court and the move across Parliament Square lead the Justices to be more activist and creative, more willing to stand firm against the Executive and Legislature and more interventionist with respect to the policies set by them? Will the constitutional status associated with being the Supreme Court of the United Kingdom embolden judges to flex their muscles more than they did before?

Whilst the CRA 2005 brings about a significant and welcome constitutional reform, I do not think that the change from Appellate Committee to Supreme Court will, in itself, make the court inclined to be more 'activist'.[33] There are a number of reasons for this view. The first point to bear in mind is that the CRA 2005 does not give the Supreme Court any new powers. Nor does it grant it a substantially different jurisdiction from that exercised by the Appellate Committee. Whilst it is significant in constitutional terms to formally separate the judiciary from the legislature, the reform is largely clarificatory of the existing legal position. Secondly, we should be wary of simply assuming, without further reflection, that the new Supreme Court will have a newly enhanced constitutional status simply because it is a 'Supreme Court'. In my view, the Constitutional Reform Act merely clarifies its existing status as the highest appellate court. Although the Constitutional Reform Act gives the court a more visibly independent role, with a more clearly defined constitutional status together with different nomenclature, the judges are still the same people doing the same job and, crucially, operating under the same constraints.[34]

Such constraints include the fact that judges do not get to choose which issues to adjudicate, but rather have to address those issues that come before them through the vagaries of litigation. In general, judges are neither entitled nor equipped to reform the law in a root-and-branch fashion, but rather, they are empowered to make small incremental changes in the law which take effect within the broader legislative framework set by Parliament. Judges are bound to consider and sometimes follow past precedent. They must reflect on the existing legislative framework and ensure that their decision will not be fundamentally at odds with that framework or cause too much legal discordance within it. Moreover, judges are aware that the efficacy of their decisions is dependent, to some extent, on securing the support and respect of the Government. The courts

---

[33] This view is also shared by D Pannick, 'The Supreme Court may have had a shambolic start but its getting better all the time', *The Times* London, 1 October 2009). In a series of seminars about the UK Supreme Court held under the Chatham House Rule at Queen Mary University of London in November 2008, most judicial participants were of the view that merely calling the UK's top level court 'a Supreme Court' and moving it outside Parliament, would not result in the new court being more activist than the House of Lords. See A Le Sueur, 'A Report on Six Seminars About the UK Supreme Court', Queen Mary University of London, School of Law Legal Studies Research Paper No 1/2008, ssrn.com/abstract=1324749, 53–58.

[34] Baroness Hale, 'A Supreme Court for the United Kingdom?' (2004) 24 *Legal Studies* 36, 41.

have to rely on Government and/or Parliament to implement their decisions.[35] All these constraints which beset the judicial law-making role are just as pertinent after the enactment of the CRA 2005 as they were before.

There are multiple factors which lead judges to be more or less activist in particular cases, none of which will be significantly altered by the shift from Appellate Committee to Supreme Court. Consider judicial creativity under the Human Rights Act 1998. Elsewhere, I have argued that the willingness of the courts to be more or less creative or interventionist when adjudicating under the HRA was a deeply contextual issue depending on a judicial evaluation of all the relevant facts of the individual case.[36] Therefore, it was not possible to fix or pre-determine the degree of creativity or intervention in advance.

So what are the factors which led the courts to be more or less activist in a particular case under the HRA? They fall into three broad categories: relative expertise, law-making competence and institutional legitimacy.[37] We can take each one in turn. The amount of *expertise* judges possess on a particular issue is often an important factor determining the willingness of the courts to be creative or interventionist in any particular case. If, for example, judges were reviewing the Government's decision that a particular counterterrorist policy is necessary in light of the public emergency threatening the life of the nation, the court would have to ask themselves whether they had sufficient expertise and information (including the relevant intelligence information) on which to review that question in a robust and probing way. In general, the less information or expertise the courts possess, the more restrained or deferential they tend to be, and rightly so.

Another factor bearing upon the degree of judicial creativity appropriate in any particular case concerns the extent to which the incremental law-making powers of the courts are appropriate to the resolution of the particular issue before them. If radical root-and-branch reform of an entire area of law is required, that will be a more appropriate job for Parliament. If incremental and piecemeal reform involving the re-interpretation of one statutory provision can rectify the rights violation at issue in that case, without creating undue uncertainty in the law or excessive discordance with other legislative provisions, then the courts are better placed to carry out the required reform.[38]

Another factor concerns relative *democratic legitimacy*.[39] There may be some issues on which the courts have sufficient expertise and they are confident that the requisite reform could be carried out by judicial interpretation, but judges

---

[35] For an examination of the various constraints which beset judicial decision-making, see A Kavanagh, 'The Elusive Divide between Interpretation and Legislation' (2004) 24 *Oxford Journal of Legal Studies* 259, 270–73, 279–82.

[36] Kavanagh, *Constitutional Review* (n 29) 169–76, 201–09.

[37] ibid 182–97.

[38] See Kavanagh, 'The Elusive Divide between Interpretation and Legislation' (n 35); M Hunt, 'Sovereignty's Blight: Why Contemporary Public Law needs a Doctrine of Due Deference' in N Bamforth and P Leyland (eds), *Public Law in a Multi-Layered Constitution* (Oxford, Hart, 2003), 337.

[39] Kavanagh, *Constitutional Review* (n 29) 190–97.

nonetheless exercise some restraint because they believe that it would be more appropriate if the required law-reform was carried out by Parliament because of its democratic legitimacy. Not only are MPs popularly elected, drawing some of their legitimacy from that fact,[40] Parliament also has various tools at its disposal (which the courts do not) to ensure that a particular law reform attracts general popular support. Parliamentary bodies can canvass public opinion, consult interest groups, launch television campaigns, contribute to public education etc. Thus, in a decision concerning a child support scheme which treated homosexual and heterosexual partners differently, Lord Mance observed that in times of changing social conditions and attitudes, there are issues:

> in relation to which Parliament and the democratically elected government should be recognized as enjoying a limited margin of discretion, regarding the stage of development of social attitudes, when and how fast to act, how far consultation was required and what form any appropriate legislative changes should take.[41]

Here, Lord Mance is exercising some judicial restraint, not on grounds of limited expertise or law-making competence, but rather because his Lordship believed that Parliament is the most appropriate institution to carry out the required law-reform in a way which seems legitimate and maximises public support for it.[42]

Other factors determining the appropriateness of judicial creativity or intervention under the HRA are the severity of the claimed rights violation, the nature of the right involved and the importance of the countervailing public interest at stake. Also of relevance is the extent to which the courts can predict that their creativity would have good rather than bad consequences and indeed, the likelihood that the legislature or executive would be willing or able to rectify the alleged rights violation if the court did not step in to remedy it.[43] Moreover, if we think of periods of increased activism in the courts before the enactment of the HRA, we can see that they can come about in response to broader political developments and need not be caused by any formal constitutional changes. The way in which the British judiciary developed the grounds of judicial review so assertively in the 1990s was in no small part due to the fact that the Conservative Government at that time met with no meaningful opposition in Parliament.[44] So the willingness or ability of the courts to be more activist or interventionist is responsive to all of these factors and involves a careful and sometimes difficult judgment about their relevance, weight and combined import in the circumstances of a particular case.

---

[40] D Feldman, 'Human Rights, Terrorism and Risk: The Role of Politicians and Judges' [2006] *Public Law* 364.

[41] *M v Secretary of State for Work and Pensions* [2006] UKHL 11, [2006] 2 AC 91 [153].

[42] This case is discussed in Kavanagh, *Constitutional Review* (n 29) 193–94.

[43] For more detailed examination of the judicial choice between ss 3 and 4 HRA, see Kavanagh, *Constitutional Review* (n 29) 118–44.

[44] D Woodhouse, 'The Constitutional and Political Implications of a United Kingdom Supreme Court' (2004) 24 *Legal Studies* 134, 144–45.

Viewed in this light, one can see that the mere fact that the Appellate Committee is now called the Supreme Court and is formally and clearly independent of the second chamber of Parliament will not supplant this close contextual analysis. The necessity to evaluate and balance all these factors in the circumstances of the individual case is just as pressing now as it ever was. The fact that we now have a Supreme Court will not *determine* the constitutionally appropriate degree of judicial restraint. But will it be one more factor which judges will take into account in making that assessment? And, more importantly, could it be a crucial factor which might tip the balance in favour of judicial creativity in the circumstances of an individual case? It is hard to imagine such a case. Had the Constitutional Reform Act given the new Supreme Court new powers such as, for instance, the power to strike down legislation, or if it had vested in them a radically new jurisdiction, it might be possible to imagine such a scenario. But given that the nature of the reform is clarificatory of the existing legal position, it is difficult to see how their new guise as Justices of the Supreme Court would tip the balance in favour of a more activist or interventionist outcome.

This is not to deny that the general constitutional landscape in which judicial decisions take place has an impact on judges' sense of their own legitimacy and this, in turn, can influence the judicial belief that they can be more assertive vis-à-vis the elected branches of government. Significant constitutional reforms can of course give rise to gradual changes in judicial culture. Arguably, the HRA 1998 is just one such reform. The HRA has brought about significant changes in the constitutional landscape which have in turn led to an increased judicial willingness to stand up to the Executive or legislature.[45] But even here, it is instructive to be clear about the exact cause and extent of the constitutional change brought about by the HRA.

The reason why the HRA undoubtedly led to a change in judicial reasoning is that it gave the courts new jurisdiction to review primary legislation for compliance with a codified set of rights. This jurisdiction, combined with the new interpretive powers which accompanied them,[46] gave judges a sense of legitimacy in their new reviewing role. In cases where the courts might have otherwise decided to preserve the status quo, the HRA gave the courts the powers and therefore the legitimacy to be more creative when interpreting statutes in order to arrive at a rights-compatible outcome.[47] The HRA was one of the causes of a 'constitutional shift'[48] towards a more rights-orientated and interventionist form of constitutional adjudication.[49]

---

[45] A Kavanagh, 'Constitutionalism, Counter-terrorism and the Courts: Changes in the British Constitutional Landscape' (forthcoming).

[46] With respect to primary legislation, the most notable powers are the interpretive power under s 3 HRA and the declaratory power under s 4 HRA.

[47] An interesting case study in this regard is to compare the HRA case of *Ghaidan v Mendoza* [2004] UKHL 30, [2004] 3 WLR 113 and the pre-HRA case of *Fitzpatrick v Sterling Housing Association Ltd* [2001] 1 AC 27 on the same issue: see Kavanagh, *Constitutional Review* (n 29) 108–14.

[48] Sedley LJ in *Redmond-Bate v DPP* [2000] HRLR 249 [13].

[49] Kavanagh, 'Constitutionalism, Counter-terrorism and the Courts' (n 45).

But we should be careful not to exaggerate the nature of the shift. After all, the HRA did not lead to cavalier judicial creativity or unrestrained activism across the board. Post-HRA, the courts have stressed that a degree of deference was often appropriate, for instance in situations where the courts lacked sufficient expertise or law-making competence, or in cases where superior democratic legitimacy would enhance the effectiveness of the particular reform.[50] The adoption of review for proportionality has not led to wholesale 'merits review' for human rights cases.[51]

The point of this excursus into the issue of activism or restraint under the HRA is threefold. The first is to highlight the inevitably contextual nature of the judicial determination about the appropriate degree of creativity in any particular case. There is no constitutional reform which will eliminate the need for judges to make that determination on a case-by-case basis. The second is to show that whilst statutes of such constitutional importance as the HRA or the CRA can indeed change the constitutional landscape within which judges make their decisions and, further, that these changes can influence the degree of activism, we should beware of exaggerating the extent of those changes. The courts in the UK have always had a supervisory or constitutional review function, carried out largely through reliance on the constitutional presumptions of statutory interpretation.[52] In my view, one of the most significant effects of the enactment of the HRA was merely to make this constitutional function more visible. Third, when one compares the degree of change in the judicial role brought about by the HRA with that brought about by the CRA, one can indeed become more realistic and less alarmist about the prospect of the new Supreme Court getting what Lord Bingham described as 'a rush of blood to the head'. Even when implementing the HRA, the British judiciary remained sensitive to the limits of their constitutional role, or did not cast them aside with abandon. If the HRA did not bring about an inappropriately activist or politicised judiciary, it seems unlikely that the CRA will lead to this apocryphal scenario.

Finally, it is worth viewing the CRA in the context of the whole package of reforms that were introduced by the last Labour Government. One of the most significant constitutional developments has been a gradual move in the direction of a more clearly demarcated separation of powers.[53] One significant impetus towards this change has been the legal requirements set by art 6 of the European Convention on Human Rights concerning the right to a fair trial. It is also worth noting that the HRA case law arising under art

---

[50] Kavanagh, *Constitutional Review* (n 29) 167ff.

[51] ibid 237–41.

[52] For an account of the constitutional significance of presumptions of statutory interpretation, see D Keir and F Lawson, *Cases in Constitutional Law* (Oxford, Clarendon Press, 1979) 3; Cross, *Statutory Interpretation* (n 29) 166; T Endicott, 'Constitutional Logic' (2003) 53 *University of Toronto Law Journal* 201, 203; Kavanagh, *Constitutional Review* (n 29) 97–8.

[53] A Tomkins, 'The Rule of Law in Blair's Britain' (2007) 26 *University of Queensland Law Journal* 255.

6 has had a particular focus on the separation between executive and judicial functions.[54]

Indeed, it could be argued that the Constitutional Reform Act 2005 emanates from those general concerns arising from art 6, albeit here addressing the boundary between legislative and judicial functions. As the Government stated in its Consultation Paper on the establishment of a new Supreme Court:

> the Human Rights Act, specifically in relation to article 6 of the European Convention on Human Rights, now requires a stricter view to be taken not only of anything which might undermine the independence or impartiality of the judicial tribunal, but even of anything which might appear to do so.[55]

So, in addressing this worry about increased judicial activism in the new Supreme Court, we need to be careful about establishing the exact source of the constitutional change, as well as to be more precise about the correct causal connection between the constitutional reform and its impact on judicial reasoning. If the Constitutional Reform Act merely draws out the legal implications of art 6 ECHR, then the original source of any increase in activism is to be found in the European Convention, not in the CRA itself. This point also serves to highlight the difficulty of establishing a correct causal connection between the nomenclature and physical location of the new court and a move towards a predicted increase in the activism of the court. Taken in isolation, it seems unlikely that the shift from Appellate Committee to Supreme Court could bring about such a momentous change.

## III TRANSPARENCY

The final theme I wish to address concerns the value placed on increasing the *transparency* of the new Court in the political rhetoric surrounding the CRA 2005. The Consultation Paper on the new Supreme Court stated that:

> [The establishment of a new Supreme Court of the United Kingdom] is part of [the Government's] continuing drive to modernise the Constitution and public services. The intention is that the new court will put the relationship between the executive, the legislature and the judiciary on a modern footing, which takes account of people's expectations about the *independence and transparency* of the judicial system.[56]

But what might such increased transparency entail? Both before and after the CRA 2005, judges of the highest court are required to give public justifications for their decisions through the publication of detailed, written judgments which reveal the reasons for their decisions.[57] This in turn enables those decisions to be

---

[54] See *R (Anderson) v Secretary of State for the Home Department* [2002] UKHL 46, [2002] 3 WLR 1800; *R v Secretary of State for the Environment, Transport and the Regions ex p Alconbury* [2001] UKHL 23, [2003] 2 AC 295.

[55] Consultation Paper (n 4) [3].

[56] ibid [1].

[57] A Le Sueur, 'Developing Mechanisms of Accountability in the UK' (2004) 24 *Legal Studies* 73, 89.

subject to legal analysis as well as public scrutiny and critique. No one would doubt the importance and value of these basic requirements of open justice.[58] Although the CRA makes no substantive changes to these requirements, it reaffirms their value.

However, as we saw earlier, the CRA 2005 promotes enhanced transparency of the new Supreme Court in other ways, most notably through greater ease of access for members of the public to watch cases, television broadcasts of hearings, publication of press summaries about pending and decided cases, and better access to information related to the Supreme Court on its website.[59] By providing summaries of the cases and compiling news items for press release, the Supreme Court can contribute to greater public awareness and understanding of the work it does and the decisions it makes, including contributing to more informed media coverage of complex legal issues.[60]

Beyond these forms of enhanced public accessibility, is any further transparency required? When the Supreme Court was opened in October 2009, many commentators observed that the increased visibility of the Supreme Court would mean that the ideological beliefs of individual judges would be subject to greater public scrutiny.[61] The new President of the Supreme Court (Lord Phillips of Worth Matravers) was reported as saying that it is 'inevitable that there will be more interest in who is appointed to the Supreme Court and I am bound to say that that is a perfectly legitimate state of affairs'.[62] Others have suggested that we should use the opportunity provided by the establishment of the UK Supreme Court to be more transparent about who the individual judges are, including being more open about judges' backgrounds and their moral and ideological views.[63]

In this volume, Justice Kirby (formerly of the Australian High Court) advances the thesis that since members of the Supreme Court 'necessarily bring with them values that influence their judicial decisions', it follows that the community that is affected by their decisions 'has a legitimate interest in knowing more about the values of potential appointees [to the court]'.[64] Since judges' values inevitably affect judicial outcomes, the public necessarily has an interest in knowing what

---

[58] *R (Binyam Mohamed) v Secretary of State for Foreign and Commonwealth Affairs* [2010] EWCA Civ 65; *Secretary of State for the Home Department v AF (No 3)* [2009] UKHL 28, [2009] 3 WLR 74 [88].

[59] Pannick, 'The Supreme Court' (n 33).

[60] A Le Sueur recommended that the new Supreme Court should provide some officially produced 'executive summary' of cases in order to enhance accountability of the court: Le Sueur, 'Developing Mechanisms of Accountability in the UK' (n 57) 91.

[61] See, eg, Woodhouse, 'The Constitutional and Political Implications of a United Kingdom Supreme Court' (n 44) 143.

[62] See F Gibb, 'Supreme Court opens as fears raised of UK-style selection of judges', *Timesonline*, 1 October 2009, http://business.timesonline.co.uk/tol/business/law/article6855925.ece.

[63] M Kirby, 'A Darwinian Reflection on Values and Appointments to Final National Courts', this volume.

[64] ibid 12; see also Woodhouse, 'The Constitutional and Political Implications of a United Kingdom Supreme Court' (n 44) 151.

these values are.[65] We should engage in a public education programme about the nature of judicial decision-making, highlighting the way in which it is value-based rather than a dry mechanical exercise, showing that deciding what the law often involves making difficult decisions about the vexed moral questions of our day, revealing to the public that judges are human beings whose life experiences inevitably influence the way in which they make decisions.[66] Enhanced transparency about the nature of judicial reasoning (in particular the fact that it is value-based) would make people more realistic about what the judicial system can achieve and enhance public confidence in the outcomes it delivers. This view is shared by some academics in the UK who believe that 'independence and transparency are essential characteristics if public confidence in the judiciary is to be maintained'.[67] It is also supported by some journalists who believe that judges of the Supreme Court will inevitably become more familiar figures in the public arena[68] and that 'this can only be good for public life'.[69]

In what remains of this chapter, I want to question some of these conclusions. In particular, I want to question the belief that increased transparency about judges' moral views and background will necessarily lead to greater public confidence in the administration of justice, or whether it might in fact undermine such confidence. It goes without saying that public confidence in the judicial system is of critical importance to the functioning of the legal system and indeed to the observance of the rule of law.[70] Therefore, we need to pay keen attention to factors which might either increase or diminish it.

The argument under scrutiny here has the following form:

1. Judges make important decisions on our behalf and those decisions depend in part on the judges' moral and ideological beliefs.
2. Therefore, we need to know what those moral views and beliefs are. We need to make them transparent.
3. Public knowledge of those beliefs and an enhanced awareness of the role they play in judicial decision-making will enhance public confidence in the judiciary and the administration of justice more generally.

I should clarify at the very outset that I support the first proposition without hesitation. Many of the issues which judges have to decide are at bottom moral

---

[65] Kirby, 'A Darwinian Reflection on Values and Appointments to Final National Courts', this volume 24–25.

[66] ibid; R Dworkin, 'Justice Sotomayor: The Unjust Hearings' *New York Review of Books* (New York 24 September 2009) 37–41.

[67] Woodhouse, 'The Constitutional and Political Implications of a United Kingdom Supreme Court' (n 44) 135; Dworkin, 'Justice Sotomayor: The Unjust Hearings' (n 66) 37.

[68] Editorial, 'Supreme Court: Britain's October Revolution', *The Guardian* (Manchester 1 October 2009); Frances Gibb, 'Supreme Court opens as fears raised of UK-style selection of judges' http://business.timesonline.co.uk/tol/business/law/article6855925.ece.

[69] M Kettle, 'It took 142 years, but at last Bagehot has got his way' *The Guardian* (Manchester 31 July 2009) 31.

[70] Lord Woolf, 'Should the Media and the Judiciary be on Speaking Terms?' in *The Pursuit of Justice* (Oxford, OUP, 2008), 154; Lord Woolf, 'Judicial Independence not Judicial Isolation' in *The Pursuit of Justice* (Oxford, OUP, 2008).

or political questions and judges cannot adjudicate them without engaging their own moral views.[71] This is especially true in the highest court of the judicial hierarchy where judges have to decide large questions of legal principle which are important in the public interest. The problems arise with respect to the second and third propositions and whether they necessarily follow from the initial premise in proposition 1. Should we make judges' moral and ideological beliefs more transparent, more central to public debate? And if we place them under the spotlight, will this lead to enhanced public confidence in the judiciary? I am not so sure.[72]

As a preliminary matter, it is worth noting that the British public do not seem keen to acquire this kind of information about the Justices of the Supreme Court. One notable feature of the move from Appellate Committee to Supreme Court in October 2009 was that it occurred without much public debate or indeed public interest.[73] Although one newspaper headline described the opening of the Supreme Court as 'Britain's October Revolution',[74] it was one in which hardly anyone outside of the legal elite was concerned to participate. So perhaps we should be sceptical about the common assumption that UK judges will 'inevitably' be subject to more public scrutiny now that there is a Supreme Court.[75] The court may well be more accessible and visible, but it may also be that the British public is not interested in looking. Of course, this empirical point about the apparent lack of public interest in the new Supreme Court does not dispose of the various normative questions about the value of enhanced transparency. Perhaps the public *ought* to be more interested in these issues. If so, then we would do well to consider the pros and cons of moving in the direction of enhanced transparency about who the Justices of the Supreme Court are and what their moral beliefs are.[76]

I want to suggest four possible reasons why increased transparency about judges' moral and ideological beliefs may undermine (rather than enhance) public trust and confidence in the judiciary.[77] The first concerns the danger that it would fuel fears about the subjectivity and potential arbitrariness of judicial decision-making. Justice Kirby has suggested that if the public understood more about

---

[71] See Kavanagh, 'The Elusive Divide' (n 35) 265ff.

[72] My reservations are partly inspired by O O'Neill, *A Question of Trust: The BBC Reith Lectures 2002* (Cambridge, Cambridge University Press, 2002).

[73] See J Rozenberg, 'Britain's new Supreme Court: Why has a fundamental change in the constitution been so little reported and debated?' available at www.entertainment.timesonline.co.uk/tol/arts_and_entertainment/the_tls/article68184.ece; Kettle, 'It took 142 years' (n 69).

[74] *The Guardian* (n 68).

[75] It may be part of the more general phenomenon that the British people are generally lacking in interest about their Constitution and constitutional reforms, see V Bogdanor, *The New British Constitution* (Oxford, Oxford University Press, 1999) 10.

[76] The focus of my discussion is on the issue of transparency about judges' moral, ethical and ideological beliefs. It has nothing to say about the transparency of the procedures of the court or the way in which judges are chosen to sit on particular cases etc. For discussion of this issue, see R Clayton, 'Decision-making in the Supreme Court: new approaches and new opportunities' [2009] *Public Law* 682.

[77] See generally 'Trust and Transparency' in O'Neill, *A Question of Trust* (n 72).

the moral and value-based nature of judicial reasoning, they would have more confidence in it and be more assured about the true nature of those decisions.[78] The enemy, according to Justice Kirby, is the outdated declaratory theory of law, which sets up as an ideal the classic image of the judge mechanically applying the law to the facts of an individual case. Once people realise that this image is a myth, a mere shibboleth, they will have a greater understanding of how judges make decisions and therefore be more confident that those decisions are reasonable.

However, much more threatening to a proper understanding of the nature of the judicial role, in my view, is the belief that judicial decisions are purely a matter of the predilections, prejudices and preconceived ideas of individual judges who are out of touch with how 'real people' live. This is the view fed to the British public by the tabloid press. If judges become public figures and their backgrounds and views are a matter of public knowledge and concern, then this is more likely to pander to that view, rather than dislodge it. Of course, the identity, educational and professional background of the Justices of the Supreme Court is not secret information. Those details are now available on the Supreme Court website and were in the public domain prior to the opening of the Supreme Court.[79] The issue here is whether judges should become public figures such that their lives, including their values and beliefs, are placed under a more probing public spotlight. There is a danger that doing this would generate more fear than it would allay.

The second point is that being more transparent about judges' moral views may in fact lead to greater secrecy about those views, and greater concealment of the role they play in judicial decision-making.[80] Paradoxical though it may seem, it is aptly illustrated by the nomination hearings for judges to the US Supreme Court. The US system of public hearings is motivated by a concern to have optimal public transparency about judicial appointments. It is based on a belief that there is an important public interest in revealing and scrutinising the moral and ideological beliefs of each nominee. For this reason, judges are interrogated about their views on abortion, discrimination, gay marriage as well as their 'judicial philosophy' on how the US Constitution should be interpreted.[81]

But as the recent nomination hearings for Justice Sotomayor demonstrated, the glare of enhanced transparency provided by these hearings can sometimes lead judges to conceal their moral views on particular issues (including their views about appropriate judicial methodology) and to distance themselves from previously

---

[78] Kirby, 'A Darwinian Reflection on Values and Appointments to Final National Courts', this volume, 33–34.

[79] Brief profiles of many judges are available in *Who's Who?* and are now available on the new Supreme Court's website at www.supremecourt.gov.uk/about/biographies.html.

[80] For the view that greater openness and transparency can in fact lead to secrecy and concealment, see O'Neill, *A Question of Trust* (n 72) 68.

[81] See generally L Epstein and J Segal, *Advice and Consent: The Politics of Judicial Appointments* (Oxford, Oxford University Press, 2005); Dworkin, 'Justice Sotomayor: The Unjust Hearings' (n 66) 38.

expressed moral views, however plausible or justifiable.[82] Moreover, rather than being a candid and open declaration of judges' real or actual moral beliefs, it is widely known that nominees to the US Supreme Court are in fact coached on how to present those views in a way which will secure nomination.[83] Therefore, it is not surprising that the picture of the moral views of a particular judge presented at the nomination hearing, does not translate directly into the judicial decisions. Many US Presidents have been surprised and indeed disappointed to discover that their preferred Supreme Court judge does not in fact toe the ideological line which was presented at their nomination.[84] Therefore, the Senate hearings for Supreme Court nominations do not always deliver on their promise of actually revealing the true moral views of the judicial nominees. Moreover, there is no evidence that subjecting nominees to this procedure enhances public trust in the judges of the US Supreme Court. This provides just one amongst many examples where the 'demands for universal transparency are likely to encourage evasions, hypocrisies and half-truths'.[85]

Even in the British system, it is well-known that a judge who has 'publicly expressed his opinions too vigorously may not be seen as impartial if he is required to adjudicate upon the issues about which he has commented in the media'.[86] In recent times, judges have recused themselves if they have revealed publicly their moral/political views on an issue which has to be decided before the court.[87] It follows that if judges' moral and political views are generally well-known and placed under the public spotlight for all to see, it may lead to a situation where either they have to recuse themselves in many more cases or, alternatively, attempt to conceal their moral/political positions so that this can be avoided.

There is another source of reservation about putting judges' moral and ideological beliefs under the public and media spotlight. This concerns the problem of undifferentiated information.[88] In the BBC Reith Lectures 2002 on the role of trust in public life, Onora O'Neill pointed out that the popular mantras about demands for openness and transparency have meant that we now have

---

[82] See Kirby, 'A Darwinian Reflection on Values and Appointments to Final National Courts', this volume, 26–27; Dworkin, 'Justice Sotomayor: The Unjust Hearings' (n 66) 38.

[83] See Dworkin, 'Justice Sotomayor: The Unjust Hearings' (n 66) 37, who claims that Justice Sotomayor was 'well advised' to conceal various aspects of judicial decision-making; see also L Eisgruber, *The Next Justice: Repairing the Supreme Court Appointments Process* (Princeton, Princeton University Press, 2007); and generally Epstein and Segal, *Advice and Consent* (n 81).

[84] Epstein and Segal, *Advice and Consent* (n 81) 121ff.

[85] O'Neill, *A Question of Trust* (n 72) 68. In her lectures on the role of trust in public life, she noticed that the contemporary demand placed on public institutions to be more transparent may in fact lead those institutions to underplay or conceal sensitive information. She points out that the requirements under the Freedom of Information Act may in fact lead head teachers and employers to write blandly uninformative reports and references for employees, precisely because they know that these documents are no longer secret but can be publicly available ibid 73ff.

[86] Lord Woolf, 'Should the Media and the Judiciary be on Speaking Terms?' (n 70) 155.

[87] The most famous recent example of this is that of Lord Steyn who refrained from sitting on *A and Others v Secretary of State for the Home Department* [2004] UKHL 56, [2005] 2 AC 68 (known as the 'Belmarsh prison' case) since he had recently published critical extra-judicial comments on Guantanamo Bay.

[88] O'Neill, *A Question of Trust* (n 72).

more publicly available information than we ever did before about all public institutions.[89] But, she argues, this has not in fact led to increased public trust and confidence in those institutions. One of the reasons is that increasing transparency can produce a flood of unsorted information and indeed misinformation that causes confusion rather than clarification.[90] Given that we are fed conflicting information, some of it false, some of it coming from untrustworthy sources in the media, enhanced transparency does not necessarily lead to enhanced trust.

These worries can also be applied to the prospect of increased transparency of the moral, political and ideological foundations of judicial decision-making at the highest level. Without a legal education, it is very difficult to process the strands of information which may be exposed in such a transparency exercise. If one emphasises to the public that judicial decisions are dependent on the background, intuitions, life experiences and moral views of individual judges, there is a danger of fuelling fears about the subjectivity of judicial decision-making, rather than enhancing confidence in it. Such facts are easily misunderstood. They are easily swamped in a barrage of information which is undifferentiated, and the credibility and source of the information may be difficult to verify. Simply making more information available about the moral foundations of judicial decisions, without being able to explore these issues against the backdrop of first-hand knowledge of how judicial decisions are made, may well be more dangerous than the current relative anonymity in which judges in the UK make their decisions.

Of course, the problem of undifferentiated information is exacerbated when one combines it with the problem of inaccurate, deliberately misleading or sensationalist reporting of legal issues. Much reporting of legal issues in the UK is accurate and responsible, but not all of it is. On controversial issues with a strong moral and/or political dimension (eg those involving the criminal law and sentencing), irresponsible reporting gives a misleading and confused picture of the sentencing process. Writing extra-judicially, Lord Woolf observed that 'the inaccuracy of the reporting of [sentencing] is preventing an open debate. An open public debate is a pre-condition for sensible sentencing'.[91] Here is another example where increased focus and attention on a topic does not necessarily lead to open or meaningful debate.

We have to take the risk of inaccurate reporting seriously when we consider the potential value of making judges' moral and political views 'more transparent'. The 'corrosive reporting of the tabloid press'[92] is a factor which has to be taken into account when considering whether it is desirable to make public figures of judges. Regular misreporting of legal issues may in fact be extremely damaging to the public's confidence in the legal system.[93] It can obfuscate more than it can enlighten. In fact, the Government recognised that misreporting of the

---

[89]   ibid 65.
[90]   ibid.
[91]   Lord Woolf, 'Should the Media and the Judiciary be on Speaking Terms?' (n 70) 156.
[92]   Lord Woolf, 'Current Challenges in Judging' (n 70) 206.
[93]   Lord Woolf, 'Should the Media and the Judiciary be on Speaking Terms?' (n 70) 158.

case law under the HRA has done much to undermine public confidence in the HRA.[94]

Finally, there is the worry that putting judges' moral and ideological beliefs in the public spotlight will in fact create some perverse incentives.[95] As noted above, it may paradoxically lead judges to be more secretive and circumspect about their backgrounds and their moral views. More worryingly, it may have a negative impact on judicial decision-making concerning highly sensitive moral, political and ethical issues. Typically, cases concerning bio-ethical issues attract considerable media attention.[96] Occasionally, that media attention of such cases includes some coverage of the individual judges' moral and religious background.[97] But if judges are public figures whose life, background and moral views are subject to the full glare of public scrutiny, then this may create incentives to decide these issues in a more cautious way then might otherwise have been the case.[98]

These four reasons do not provide a knock-down argument against enhancing the transparency about judges' individual moral, political and ethical beliefs, but they provide us with reasons not to be sanguine about the consequences of enhancing such transparency. They cast doubt on the widely held assumption that more information and public scrutiny of judges' backgrounds and moral views would enhance public confidence in the judiciary and their administration of justice. They urge us not to accept the mantra of 'openness and transparency' at face value and to approach the Government's rhetoric on this issue with a degree of scepticism. Enhanced transparency about judges' moral and political views requires careful handling. It may not achieve the aims often claimed for it.

It is easy for this warning about the need for caution in relation to enhanced transparency of judicial views to be misunderstood. It may give rise to a sense of

---

[94] See Department of Constitutional Affairs, 'Review of the Implementation of the Human Rights Act' (July 2006) for an account of the various myths and misperceptions about the HRA as a result of misreporting of how the HRA functions. Lord Falconer observed that these misperceptions have 'undoubtedly had an accumulative and corrosive effect upon public confidence both in the Human Rights Act and in the European Convention on Human Rights itself'; see Introduction by the Lord Chancellor (Lord Falconer) at www.justice.gov.uk/docs/full_review.pdf 5. For comment on the tabloid coverage of the coming into force of the HRA, see Lord Steyn, 'The New Legal Landscape' (2000) *European Human Rights Law Review* 549, 552.

[95] For an examination of the way in which enhanced transparency can create perverse incentives, see O'Neill, *A Question of Trust* (n 72) 50–55.

[96] Woodhouse, 'The Constitutional and Political Implications of a United Kingdom Supreme Court' (n 44) 144.

[97] ibid.

[98] Onora O'Neill documents how greater transparency by Government about how public institutions work can create such perverse incentives. Examples include how meeting the constant demand to keep records and provide information, including the demand to meet various Government 'targets' and performance indicators, can damage the work carried out by teachers, police officers, university lecturers and can distort the proper aims of professional practice: O'Neill, *A Question of Trust* (n 72) 49–50. She also points out how performance indicators can have a deep effect on professional and institutional behaviour: 'Thus, if a certain A-level board offers easier exams in a subject, schools have a reason to choose that syllabus even if it is educationally inferior. If waiting lists can be reduced faster by concentrating on certain medical procedures, hospitals have reason to do so, even if medical priorities differ. Perverse incentives are real incentives' ibid 55.

unease that I am seeking a return to the days when judges never communicated with the media or made public addresses so that their views on matters of public importance were largely unknown.[99] I should clarify that I am not suggesting that the judiciary should be a secret institution shrouded in mystery. Enhancing public awareness of the work of the judiciary is a good thing. The courts are an important public institution and, as such, they must make their practices, procedures and the reasons for their decisions publicly accessible. In order to enhance public understanding of its decisions, it is to be welcomed that the new Supreme Court now provides official summaries of its case-law and compiles press releases about cases of public interest. Such transparency and public accessibility are to be valued.[100] They will hopefully minimise the risk of inaccurate or misleading reporting mentioned above.

My point is simply that whilst transparency and accountability of the judiciary are desirable, 'they may not be the unconditional goods they are fashionably supposed to be'.[101] We should be careful to ensure that the *type* of transparency we pursue is appropriate to the task of shedding meaningful light on judicial decision-making and actually improving public understanding.[102] We need 'intelligent accountability'[103] rather than undiscriminating openness and transparency on issues which can in fact distort a proper understanding of the judicial role. It is by no means a foregone conclusion that optimal openness and transparency about every aspect of judicial decision-making (including the moral and political values which underpin them) will automatically lead to greater public trust in the courts and the administration of justice.

## IV CONCLUSION

The establishment of the Supreme Court of the United Kingdom is a constitutional landmark for the United Kingdom. Its establishment may simply be a consequence of earlier constitutional developments such as the HRA and indeed art 6 ECHR. Its overall effect is to emphasise the independence of the highest court of this country, to give added clarity about its constitutional reviewing role and to dissipate confusion that judges are both literally and metaphorically 'in the shadows of the legislature'. Furthermore, the Supreme Court's website, which enhances public awareness of the work of the highest court together with a press

---

[99] Lord Woolf, 'Should the Media and the Judiciary be on Speaking Terms?' (n 70) 156–67.

[100] Joseph Raz argues that the courts are subject to the principle of the public accountability of public actions which directs 'not only that courts should take their decisions for cogent reasons and that they should avoid irrelevant reasons, but also that as far as possible the fact that no irrelevant considerations affecting the decision should be publicly visible': see J Raz, 'On the Authority and Interpretation of Constitutions' in L Alexander (ed), *Constitutionalism: Philosophical Foundations* (Cambridge, Cambridge University Press, 1998) 190.

[101] O'Neill, *A Question of Trust* (n 72) 70.

[102] Le Sueur, 'Developing Mechanisms of Accountability in the UK' (n 57) 74.

[103] ibid 58ff.

office to assist the press in accurate and responsible reporting of its cases, is also a welcome development.

Whilst these facts are welcome, and indeed constitutionally significant, the argument of this paper is that they will have no radical or direct impact on the substance of the case law decided by the new Supreme Court. In particular, I have suggested that it will not, in itself, lead to more activist or indeed more deferential decisions. The degree of activism is subject to a multiplicity of factors which would not be displaced or substantially changed by the move from Appellate Committee to Supreme Court.

But we should bear in mind that if the new Supreme Court makes a decision which is perceived to be creative or bold,[104] the judicial rhetoric may go either way. On the one hand, if judges may feel that their new nomenclature and geographic location places a greater spotlight on them, they may then be motivated to downplay their creative role or indeed to make any link between their creativity and the fact that they are Supreme Court of the United Kingdom. Such downplaying of their creative role was the route adopted by many members of the senior judiciary just as the HRA was enacted.[105] Precisely because they were given new powers which might lead them to make creative decisions in the public and political eye, the judiciary tended (both in the case law and extra-judicially) to emphasise that they are nonetheless aware of their proper place in the constitutional scheme of things and were aware that restraint and deference are sometimes appropriate.[106] Alternatively, in a future bold decision, the Supreme Court might support a creative or interventionist decision with the fact that it is now the Supreme Court of the United Kingdom which is constitutionally entitled to review with intensity the actions of the elected branches of government. But we should know better than to simply deduce from this kind of judicial rhetoric a direct or dramatic causal link between the creativity (or indeed lack thereof) and the move from Appellate Committee to Supreme Court. Judicial rhetoric can often conceal the true nature of the reasoning process at work in the judicial decision.[107]

Finally, whilst I do not expect that the opening of the Supreme Court of the United Kingdom will bring about a substantial or radical change in judicial reasoning, it may well have a significant impact on the study of constitutional law in the UK and the way in which we understand the subject. Taken together with the other constitutional reforms in the last decade, there has been a shift towards a clearer separation of powers.[108] Perhaps this will lead to more scholarship on this important doctrine and will enable students to see more clearly that UK constitutional law does indeed rely on some version of that doctrine.

---

[104] An example since the Supreme Court's inauguration might be the decision in favour of the respondent banks in *Office of Fair Trading v Abbey National plc & Ors* [2009] UKSC 6, [2009] 3 WLR 1215.

[105] Examples of such judicial statements are provided in Kavanagh, *Constitutional Review* (n 29) 197.

[106] Lord Woolf, 'Should the Media and the Judiciary be on Speaking Terms?' (n 70) 199–200.

[107] J Raz, 'Legal Principles and the Limits of the Law" (1972) 81 *Yale Law Journal* 823, 849ff.

[108] Tomkins, 'The Rule of Law in Blair's Britain' (n 53).

# 4

# Taking Women's Property Seriously: Mrs Boland, the House of Lords, the Law Commission and the Role of Consensus

ELIZABETH COOKE*

## I INTRODUCTION

I N 1982, IN the House of Lords, the then Lord Chancellor, Lord Hailsham said that 'law reform is either by consent or not at all'.[1] That is sometimes true, and this paper looks at one pivotal case in order to examine the relationship between the judicial House of Lords and consensus in law reform.

When I was asked to give this paper, I started from a rather different angle. I felt that the obvious response to a celebration of the judicial House of Lords, by a Law Commissioner, might be to compare those two institutions and their effectiveness in law reform. This rather obvious wheeze instantly throws up a number of equally obvious points of comparison. The Law Commission was instituted to carry out law reform; the Judicial Committee of the House of Lords was not. The Law Commission can produce Bills; the House of Lords can decide only the point before it. The Law Commission is dependent upon the will of the government of the day to implement its recommendations, whereas the House of Lords creates instant law. I shall be referring to all those points in the course of this discussion. But the one on which I want to focus is equally obvious, and at first sight rather alarming. The Law Commission consults and works through consensus, insofar as that can be achieved. But decisions of the judicial House of Lords, and of its successor the Supreme Court, inevitably do not emanate from consultation. And it is that contrast, and its implications, that led my paper in the direction it has taken.

---

* I am writing in my personal capacity, and nothing I say is to be taken as the view of the Law Commission. I am grateful to my colleague Matthew Jolley for reading and commenting on an earlier draft of this chapter, but all the views and mistakes are my own.
[1] Hansard HL, col 437 (15 December 1982); the remark was made in the course of the debate on the Law Commission's Boland Report, cols 639–64.

Consultation is a part of modern legislation and regulation. Not a Land Registration rule changes but the Rules Committee consults upon it. Not a school dinner menu is overhauled but a questionnaire is found deep in a child's book bag, usually too creased to be filled in. We are constantly asked to take part in what the constitutional theorists call 'deliberative democracy',[2] involving not votes but voices. It ensures that we are all able to have a say, and is supposed to give us at least a chance to influence policy.[3] That in turn legitimises, or is supposed to legitimise, the decisions of the legislature and the regulatory bodies.

We are all a little sceptical, at times.[4] This paper does not seek to evaluate different consultation processes. Rather, I take as read the existence of consultation as a vital part in the democracy we have developed, a counterweight to the power exercised by a government with a majority in Parliament.

The Law Commission prides itself on unusually thorough consultation. Not a list of questions, but a thorough discussion of the law and its background and the options; not a creasable booklet, but a substantial volume. Our consultation on 'Easements, Covenants and Profits à Prendre' in 2008[5]—admittedly one of our longer efforts—ran to some 300 pages; the responses run to over 750 pages. Consultation is at the heart of what we do; consensus is one of our few weapons in the battle (as it sometimes is) to get our recommendations implemented. If we go out on a limb, and recommend change that is not, broadly, acceptable to our respondents, our recommendations have very little hope of passing into law.

By contrast, consultation and consent is not part of the judicial House of Lords' law-making process.[6] The casual observer might well suppose, in view of this, that the Law Commission produces consensus-based, democratic law reform and our highest court does not. But of course that is not the case.

Both the House of Lords and the Law Commission have a complex relationship to public opinion, consensus and consent. In order to explore that relationship, I have chosen to look at the decision in *Williams & Glyn's Bank Ltd v Boland*[7] (hereinafter '*Boland*'). It stands out in my mind as a useful focus for this issue because it is an instance where the House of Lords made a decision and the Law Commission was at once asked to respond. So both bodies had to tackle the same question. The casual observer might regard this as a single and quite

---

[2]  See, eg J Habermas, *Between Facts and Norms. Contributions to a Discourse Theory of Law and Democracy* (Boston, MIT, 1997).

[3]  The Government's Code of Practice on Consultation can be found at www.berr.gov.uk/files/file47158.pdf. Its Criterion 1 states: 'Formal consultation should take place at a stage when there is scope to influence the policy outcome.'

[4]  Only too often we feel like the audience for the Vogon captain's message to earth, just before demolition, in Douglas Adams' *The Hitch-hikers' Guide to the Galaxy* (London, Pan Books Ltd, 1979): 'There's no point acting all surprised about it. All the planning charts and demolition orders have been on display in your local planning department in Alpha Centauri for fifty of your Earth years, so you've had plenty of time to lodge a formal complaint and it's far too late to start making a fuss now.'

[5]  Law Com No 186.

[6]  I use the present tense because I have not yet got out of the habit of speaking of the judicial House of Lords in the present tense. And of course these remarks apply equally to the Supreme Court.

[7]  *Williams & Glyn's Bank Ltd v Boland* [1981] AC 487.

dramatic issue. He might also conclude that the House of Lords got it right whereas the Law Commission got it wrong, since the House of Lords' decision has stood the test of time whereas the Law Commission's recommendations were never implemented. The reality is more complex. Neither was entirely right or wrong; each was part of a longer process. Neither was able fully to reflect public consensus; each was part of a process by which a number of different bodies— commercial and academic communities as well as the general public—eventually reached a consensus, of sorts, on more than one difficult issue.

## II  MRS BOLAND'S CASE

The story is well-known. Mr and Mrs Boland's home was purchased, in 1969, in Mr Boland's sole name, as was not particularly unusual at the time (although it was no longer the norm). Mrs Boland did not know that the house had not been purchased jointly, as had their previous home. It was not disputed that Mrs Boland contributed substantially to the purchase price and thereby had a half-share in the house. Mr Boland ran a building business, and some time after the purchase he organised a business loan on the security of the house, without telling Mrs Boland. As in all good land law stories, he defaulted on the repayments, and the bank sought possession. Mrs Boland refused to move. Her defence to the possession proceedings was that she had an equitable interest in the house, because of her contribution to its purchase, and that her interest overrode the bank's mortgage by virtue of s 70(1)(g) of the Land Registration Act 1925.[8]

It was agreed by all concerned that Mrs Boland had an interest under a trust, of which Mr Boland was the trustee. But what was not agreed was whether her interest was overriding under s 70(1)(g); to be such an interest, it had to be an interest 'substituting in reference to land' and, said the bank, it was not. The house was held on a trust for sale arising automatically under the 1925 legislation by virtue of the equitable co-ownership; and the implication of a trust *for sale* was that the interest was financial only. Mrs Boland's interest was in the proceeds of sale, insofar as any ended up in Mr Boland's hands.

So said the textbooks of the time. Doubts had been expressed.[9] The Law Commission in its Third Report on Family Property[10] expressed the view that it was 'very doubtful' that such a right might be an overriding interest, and that 'decided cases and legal argument leave the question in some doubt'.[11] They went on to say: 'In our view no beneficial interest under a trust for sale . . . should amount to an overriding interest, whether it belongs to a wife or to anyone else.'[12]

---

[8] The corresponding provision today, only slightly amended, is sch 3 para 2 to the Land Registration Act 2002.

[9] See for example SNL Palk, 'First registration of title—just what does it do?' [1974] *The Conveyancer* 236.

[10] Law Com No 86, 1978.

[11] ibid 1.253(b).

[12] ibid 1.333.

The Court of Appeal, and then the House of Lords, responded to Mrs Boland by declaring that orthodoxy to be outdated and implausible. Judgments given in both courts rejected the idea that a wife was not in 'actual occupation', and that she did not have an interest 'subsisting in reference to the land'.[13] Lord Denning said in the Court of Appeal:

> Most wives now are joint owners of the matrimonial home—in law or in equity—with their husbands. They go out to work just as their husbands do. Their earnings go to build up the home just as much as their husband's earnings. Visit the home and you will find that she is in personal occupation of it just as much as he is. She eats there and sleeps there just as he does. She is in control of all that goes on there—just as much as he. In no respect whatever does the nature of her occupation differ from his. If he is a sailor away for months at a time, she is in actual occupation. If he deserts her, she is in actual occupation. These instances all show that 'actual occupation' is matter of fact, not matter of law. It need not be single. Two partners in a business can be in actual occupation. It does not depend on title. A squatter is often in actual occupation.[14]

And as Lord Wilberforce put it in the House of Lords:

> to describe the interests of spouses in a house jointly bought to be lived in as a matrimonial home as merely an interest in proceeds of sale, or rents and profits until sale, is just a little unreal.[15]

Both these points, together with the substantive outcome that they enabled, ring so obviously true that today's law students wonder why they needed to be said.

To say that the reaction of the lending institutions to this decision was pandemonium is only a slight overstatement. Fifteen or so years earlier, an unacceptable decision of the House of Lords in relation to the rights of a married woman in her home was met by instant legislation: the Matrimonial Homes Act 1967,[16] which gave spouses who did not own or co-own the family home the right to enforce their right of occupation against a purchaser, provided that it was registered. On this occasion the reaction was less of a knee-jerk, and the problem—as it was perceived—was referred to the Law Commission. That may have been because the problem was much more of a choice between the devil and the deep blue sea; no government would have been particularly keen either to offend the lending institutions by upholding the decision, or to outrage women by reversing it.[17]

---

[13] There was also the need to dispose of the provision in s 3(xv)(a) of the Land Registration Act 1925 that defines as a minor interest (and therefore not overriding) an interest under a trust for sale 'capable of being overridden by the trustees for sale'. For 'overridden', today we would more naturally say 'overreached'. 'Capable' generically, or in this case? In this case, said both appeal courts, the right was not capable of being overreached because there was only one trustee of the legal estate and so the requirements for overreaching were not met.

[14] *Williams & Glyn's Bank Ltd v Boland* [1979] Ch 312 (CA) 332.

[15] *Boland* (HL) (n 7) 507.

[16] The corresponding provision today in s 30 of the Family Law Act 1996.

[17] As Lord Scarman said in the House of Lords debate on the Boland Report (n 1): '[I]t was because of the need to achieve a balance between justice to the wife and justice to the purchaser and lender that the noble and learned Lord the Lord Chancellor referred the Boland question to the Law Commission.'

### III THE LAW COMMISSION'S PROJECT

The Law Commission had already done an immense amount of work on family property. Its Working Paper on Family Property Law in 1971[18] was a lengthy exploration of property rights in the matrimonial home, household goods, inheritance, family provision and European-style community of property.[19] That was followed by the First Report on Family Property in 1973,[20] setting out recommendations which were worked out, with a draft Bill, in detail in the Third Report on Family Property, in 1978.[21] The Report recommended the automatic co-ownership of spouses in the matrimonial home. At the time when the *Boland* decision was made, that Bill had already been introduced into the House of Lords. Indeed, the immediate consequence of *Boland* for the Law Commission was that one provision of the Bill became problematic, since clause 24 stated:

> *For the removal of doubt* it is hereby declared that the rights capable of being overriding interests under section 70(1)(g) of the Land Registration Act 1925 . . . do not include . . . in the case of land held on trust for sale, interests or powers which are under the Law of Property Act 1925 capable of being overridden by the trustees for sale.[22]

So the receipt of a reference to investigate and respond to the *Boland* decision was timely since, at least to a limited extent, the Law Commission had to respond to it in any event by amending its own Bill. But it also threw a large spanner in the works of the legal structure that the Commission had been creating, because the Commission had worked on the basis that a right must be registered, in order to bind a purchaser; the Commission had so far regarded as unacceptable the prospect of a spouse's interest binding a purchaser despite being unregistered. The House of Lords had now pronounced firmly against the Commission's principle. So the Law Commission had to decide, not only what to do about *Boland*, but also whether to re-think its own conclusions.

On this occasion the Law Commission did not publish a formal Consultation Paper. Instead, it conducted a consultation by correspondence with the financial institutions. Those that replied did so in various terms, but most were gloomy, speaking of the additional expense, risk and inconvenience that would be brought about by the decision. The idea was even floated that the only safe way to complete the purchase of a house with the aid of the mortgage would be for the mortgagee's solicitor to preside over completion of the purchase on site at the property. At the same time, over the period of the Commission's consultation, there began to be a few inklings that maybe things were not too bad.

[18] Working Paper No 42.
[19] As to which, see text to n 43.
[20] Law Com No 52.
[21] Law Com No 86.
[22] Emphasis added. Note that the ambiguity exploited in the *Boland* decision would have been thereby perpetuated, because it was assumed that 'capable' meant 'generically capable if there are two trustees'.

The Law Commission finally reported its conclusions in 1982, in a Report entitled 'Property Law: the Implications of *Williams & Glyn's Bank Ltd v Boland*' (hereinafter 'the Boland Report').[23] Its conclusions were threefold.[24]

First, it held firm the line that it was simply unacceptable to have equitable interests able to bind purchasers without being registered. Legislation must therefore provide that equitable interests under trusts could not be overriding interests but must be registered in order to bind a purchaser.

Secondly, however, whilst it was felt acceptable to deprive spouses of protection unless they registered their interests—regardless of how unlikely such registration might be—it was also felt that a spouse who held a registered equitable interest in the family home should also have the right to prevent any disposition being entered into without his or her consent (or a court order). This is particularly interesting, since such a consent provision is a feature of almost all European jurisdictions; but it attaches to spouses as such, not merely to those who co-own the family home.[25] But not only did the Law Commission take the view that the right must be registered; it also felt that it was an unacceptable infringement upon the status of ownership for a non-owning spouse to have such control.

And from there it moved to the third point, which was to reiterate its recommendation that all spouses should be co-owners of the matrimonial home. In other words, the requirement of registration was seen as another reason, ultimately, to give spouses an automatic half-share in the family home. The Report therefore presented these three recommendations as a package,[26] embodying protection for spouses—better, it was contended, than that given in *Boland* because it resolved the question of what the wife's share, if any, actually was—as well as protection for lenders.

## IV  THE SEQUEL TO THE PROJECT

We all know what happened next: nothing. The Law Commission's co-ownership Bill had had to be withdrawn pending the outcome of discussions about *Boland*, and it was never reintroduced. This was partly due to lack of Parliamentary time; and it was partly due to unease about the Commission's proposals. The Boland Report was the subject of debate in the House of Lords after its publication, and of the maiden speech of Lord Templeman, whose judgment at first instance in *Boland* had been so dramatically reversed. The misgivings voiced in that debate are illuminating because of their focus on public consensus and the differing views expressed about where that consensus lay. The Lord Chancellor observed:

---

[23]  Law Com No 115.

[24]  ibid 121.

[25]  E Cooke, A Barlow, T Callus, *Community of Property: a regime for England and Wales?* (London, The Nuffield Foundation, 2006) ch 5, 42.

[26]  Lord Scarman, in the House of Lords debate referred to earlier (n 1), said it was a 'highly intelligent package deal'.

The noble Lord, Lord McGregor of Durris, talked about social justice and what the people want. He seemed to think, as did the noble and learned Lord, Lord Denning, that what the people want is the co-ownership bill. I must tell them both absolutely flatly that they could not sit for a week in the Lord Chancellor's office and believe that. . . .the great and decisive change in the mood of the public with which my office is concerned is the extreme dissastisfaction and concern with the laws about matters ancillary to divorce.

Meanwhile, the building societies coped. The waiver system was developed,[27] no one got embarrassed about the enquiries made, no one took to carrying out completions on site. As Lord Hailsham went on to observe in the 1982 debate:

[The *Boland* decision] has been part of our law for over a year now, and . . . in fact conveyancers have come to terms with it—and come to terms with it fairly well. Contrary to their predictions, the world has not come to an end. . .

And in the face of that coping, the urgent need to respond to *Boland* slipped away. Co-ownership is so widespread that the original *Boland* problem rarely occurs. But in any event, a standard enquiry is sent out in the course of every conveyancing transaction, asking who is in occupation of the property and requiring anyone whose occupation is disclosed to sign a waiver of any rights they may have in favour of the purchaser. Where the *Boland* problem does occur, subsequent case law has cut down the range of cases in which the decision can cause embarrassment to the lending institutions (see below). For the remaining very few cases in which the interests of a modern-day Mrs Boland might prevail over a purchaser, the waiver form seems to do the trick. There must be instances where the borrower fails to pass these on to occupiers, or fills them in fraudulently, or so we might suppose; but I am not aware of any reported cases.[28]

So what happened here? The House of Lords' decision still stands today, although, as we shall see, its significance has been narrowed down considerably. But their Lordships' acknowledgement of the place of women in society, and their shrewd assessment of the virtue of a protection for women that depended upon registration, still ring true. Indeed, they are so much in tune with the way most of us think about these issues now that the major difficulty in teaching the *Boland* decision is to explain to students why it actually had to be decided, so obvious to them are its conclusion.

But the Law Commission, too, was in tune with public opinion. It had commissioned a public opinion survey in 1971, and its recommendations for co-ownership were supported by the views expressed by a representative sample of the public.[29] In that survey it asked the question:

---

[27] It was, after all, something the lending institutions should have been doing all along—in view of the wording of s 70(1)(g)—and many had already been doing so.

[28] The lender's only remedy would be against the borrower in these circumstances, as it was in *Boland* itself.

[29] See para 22 ff of the First Report, Law Com No 52.

> Some people say that the home and its contents should legally be jointly owned by the husband and wife irrespective of who paid for it. Do you agree or disagree?

91 per cent of husbands and 94 per cent of wives in a random sample of the population agreed. Lord Hailsham's insistence that what really troubled the public was not joint ownership but divorce was, on one level, true—that was certainly what made people angry enough to write to him. But on another level he was wrong; he gave greater weight, in his assessment of the views of the majority, to a self-selecting sample than to a representative, quantitatively significant sample—simply a basic mistake about social science. The Law Commission was right—and it knew it was right, because it did the research—about the convictions of the vast majority about equality and about the desirability of co-ownership. The *Boland Report* itself did not achieve its objective; but the work on co-ownership did bear fruit, in a form different from the co-ownership Bill, much later, as we shall see.

I suggest that only by looking at what happened later can we see what was really happening in *Boland*. History proved the judicial House of Lords, and indeed the Lords in Parliament, right on the narrow point of the uselessness of protection for women that depended on registration. But when we take a longer view, we find that both the Law Commission and the judicial House of Lords were part of a bigger process and were both closely involved in the processes of consultation and expression of public opinion.

### V  THE BIGGER PICTURE

We can get a better view of the roles that both the judicial House of Lords and the Law Commission can play in the processes of deliberative democracy if we step back a little and see the *Boland* decision as one stitch in a number of different tapestries, and Mrs Boland's story as a stepping-stone on a number of different paths.

### A  Defining the limits of *Boland*

One such path led towards the refinement of the *Boland* decision itself. This is an inevitable outcome of our system of precedent; a decision has a ratio, and only later cases can really determine how broad that ratio is. So one major decision is likely to be followed by a series of satellite cases determining its extent.

Today, the holder of an equitable interest in actual occupation of the property does still have an overriding interest that will bind a purchaser, but only if he or she is not a child;[30] only if the purchaser did not deal with two trustees of the

---

[30] *Hypo-Mortgage Services Ltd v Robinson* [1997] 2 FCR 422; they occupy the family home, it was said (at 426, in language reminiscent of the pre-*Boland* dicta about wives) 'as shadows of the occupation of their parents'.

legal estate, because we now know that overreaching trumps overriding;[31] only if the mortgage was neither entered into simultaneously with the purchase of the house,[32] nor a re-mortgage that replaced an acquisition mortgage.[33] Mrs Boland still wins, but the range of people who can benefit from her victory has been rendered remarkably narrow.

These are all court decisions made by judges without consultation. But it is unrealistic not to see them as a reaction to the post-*Boland* panic and a reflection of the view that lenders must not be put under further pressure. This is not about preferring moneyed might to the individual; it is far more a response to the concern that further risk to lenders might make domestic mortgage lending unreasonably expensive and therefore home ownership impracticable for the majority.

That social concern was a strong one and is reflected in the choices made by the judges in these subsequent cases. For example, the conclusion in *Flegg*[34] that overreaching trumps overriding is not an inevitable one. Views differ as to whether or not the Court of Appeal was forced to the conclusion it reached; my own view is that it was not. There are, of course, different ways to read the legislation. It probably does not get us anywhere to note that it seems that Benjamin Cherry (who was primarily responsible for the design and drafting of the 1925 legislation) once guessed at the opposite result.[35]

So there was no consultation involved in reaching these decisions; but there are far more minds and voices involved in them than those of the judges alone.

## B Towards the Trusts of Land and Appointment of Trustees Act 1996

The architecture of the 1925 legislation was a long time in its evolution.[36] One of the most challenging aspects of its drafting was the puzzle over what to do about multiple interests in land. The reformers took two decisions that we tend to take for granted, but without which most of the common law world still manages perfectly happily today.

One is that a trust arises by operation of law in all instances of co-ownership. The idea is to create a stable holding for the legal estate, vested invariably in one person or in joint tenants, so that ownership tends towards unity. Behind the scenes, equitable ownership could diversify freely, without troubling a purchaser. The model was apt for the commercial world of the nineteenth century when

---

[31] *City of London Building Society v Flegg* [1988] AC 54.

[32] Because we know, following *Abbey National Building Society v Cann* [1991] AC 56, that there is no *scintilla temporis* in which the actual occupation can take effect.

[33] *Equity & Law Home Loans Ltd v Prestridge* [1992] 1 WLR 137.

[34] *Flegg* (n 31).

[35] The 1925 edition of *Wolstenhome and Cherry's Conveyancing Statutes*, by BL Cherry, J Chadwick and JRP Maxwell (London, Stevens and Sons, 1925)) mentions s 70(1)(g) as a potential protection for equitable interests in the context of overreaching.

[36] See S Anderson, *Lawyers and the Making of English Land Law 1832–1940* (Oxford, Clarendon Press, 1992) and A Offer, *Property and Politics 1870–1914* (Cambridge, Cambridge University Press, 1981).

mortgaging or subdividing an interest under a trust was not such a strange thing to do as it is today. The idea that a trust is the *only* way to manage joint ownership is obviously nonsense, since almost no other jurisdiction in the world does this. But it was a powerful, flexible and original idea.

The other such decision (which my generation of law students found perfectly normal and that today's find almost incomprehensible) was that the implied trust arising in cases of ordinary joint ownership should be a trust for sale. The 1925 reformers adopted the trust for sale for concurrent joint ownership with a view to its use in the context of inheritance or business, where sale was a reasonable outcome. That it should become the norm for the joint ownership of husband and wife in the family home probably never crossed Benjamin Cherry's mind,[37] because *of course* the family home, insofar as owner-occupation was normal or achievable at the time (ie only really for the rich) at the time, would be vested in the husband.

By the late 1970s the trust for sale had started to look like an ill-fitting frock, with the sleeves too long, the skirt too short, etc. It fitted in places, but it was the wrong garment for the vesting of the family home. Its implications were no longer obvious. Stephen Cretney wrote a note in 1971 in the *Modern Law Review* interrogating its implications, and argued that the beneficiary's interest might be conceived of in a different way—as being in land or in money—in different contexts.[38] That shift from money to land was completed in *Boland*.

The decision in *Boland* that the equitable joint owner's interest was *in the land* was incompatible with the doctrine of conversion, and sounded the death-knell for the trust for sale. It took some time for the end to come. But the Law Commission's Report on Trusts of Land,[39] published in 1989, was implemented in the form of the Trusts of Land and Appointment of Trustees Act 1996, known as ToLATA. Just like the decision in *Boland* itself, s 1(1)(a) of ToLATA is today so blindingly obvious to students that it is quite hard to explain:

> 'trust of land' means (subject to subsection (3)) any trust of property which consists of or includes land.

And it is that obviousness, the complete comfortableness of the substitution of the trust of land for the trust for sale, that demonstrates that while consensus did not precede the House of Lords' decision in *Boland*, it certainly followed it.

## C  Towards the Land Registration Act 2002

It is not fanciful, I think, to see the Boland experience as a stepping-stone on the path towards the Land Registration Act 2002.

---

[37] Benjamin Cherry was, in large measure, the architect of the 1925 legislation, although of course it was also the project of decades of thought from the 1830s onwards.

[38] S Cretney, 'A technical and tricky matter' [1971] 34 *Modern Law Review* 441.

[39] Law Com No 181.

The new registration statute reflected a principled view of the role of registration,[40] and the Law Commission's conviction (expressed in the Boland Report) that a widening of the scope of unregistered interests as a hazard to purchasers was inconsistent with the idea of registration. Consistently with that view, the 2002 Act trimmed back, so far as was possible, the range of overriding interests, getting rid of some and prescribing that others would wither after 10 years from implementation.[41] And the successor to s 70(1)(g) itself is narrower than its predecessor, closing down yet another question arising from the *Boland*-type cases, namely: what if the 'actual occupation' is not obvious? The statute now prescribes that if the actual occupation is not obvious on reasonable inspection, the purchaser is not bound.[42] Mrs Boland still wins today, but only if her presence is obvious on reasonable inspection.

The Land Registration Act 2002 emanated from a joint project between the Law Commission and HM Land Registry, from consultation, from impact assessment, and from Parliamentary debate. It was lawyer's law, but it emerged from the full panoply of the processes of deliberative democracy.[43]

## D  The Road to Community of Property

Nor is it fanciful to see the *Boland* decision as a step on the very long road to the House of Lords' further, and overwhelmingly successfully decision, in *White v White*.[44]

To see how that happened, we have to go back to 1882 and the Married Women's Property Acts. They are the landmark that established the right of married women to own property,[45] a reform that benefited the wealthy but did nothing at all for the housewife. For reasons that are not now easy to discover, the nineteenth-century reformers seem to have paid no regard to the wisdom of the European community of property systems which ordained—and still do today—that marriage is a property-owning partnership which endows each spouse with a half-share in the matrimonial property, so that the housewife is not left destitute by her devotion to the family.

Why that wisdom was neglected we do not know. Sir Jocelyn Simon's call for it to be incorporated into our law in the 1960s was not heeded by Parliament, despite his unforgettable metaphor:

---

[40] Law Commission, 'Land Registration for the Twenty-first Century: a Conveyancing Revolution' (Law Com No 271) [1.10]: 'It will be the fact of registration and registration alone that confers title. This is entirely in accordance with the fundamental principle of a conclusive register which underpins the Bill.'

[41] Land Registration Act 2002 s 117.

[42] Land Registration Act 2002 sch 3 para 2(c)(i). Similar reasoning underlies the cutting back of the scope of the overriding interest for easements: sch 3 para 3.

[43] That is not to say that everyone, or even a majority of the public, agrees with it—most would surely have no opinion; the point is about process.

[44] *White v White* [2001] 1 AC 596.

[45] They had gained the right to keep their earnings in 1856.

> The cock bird can feather his nest precisely because he does not have to spend all his time sitting on it.[46]

It was hoped and demanded that the 1969 divorce reforms would institute a system of equal division,[47] so as to bring about at least deferred community of property.[48] As we all know, the provisions of the Matrimonial Causes Act 1973 were so open-textured that the courts were free to interpret them restrictively, so that when Mrs White sought financial provision in 1996 following her divorce from the husband with whom she had farmed for over 30 years, she recovered less than she would have been awarded had she sued for dissolution of the business partnership.

We also all know the ending of Mrs White's story: a new principle for ancillary relief, the 'yardstick of equality' and the explosion of the jurisprudence of 'reasonable needs' in ancillary relief. This was a court decision: but it can be seen as the outcome of consultative processes that went on for decades. The 1960s debates; the Law Commission's massive programme of work on family property in the 1970s; the public opinion survey that lay behind and legitimised that work; the academic commentary that kept up the pressure for change; the work of the Equal Opportunities Commission and of feminist movements, and so on.

What was Mrs Boland's place in this journey? The Boland Report placed her firmly in the midst of the debate about the property consequences of marriage by insisting that any watering down of the *Boland* decision must only be enacted alongside the proposal for automatic joint ownership of the family home. But perhaps more important than that was the change in the way we looked at women's property rights as a result of *Boland*. Mrs Boland was discovered to have rights *in the land*. In other words, her right was the *same sort of right* as her husband's. The *Boland* decision asserted equality in a very technical sense, which as discussed, led to the technical revolution of ToLATA; but it also chimed with a broader move towards equality. The conclusion that Mrs Boland had a right in the land rather than in money put her in the same relationship to her home as was her husband. She started as a shadow, in *Caunce v Caunce*;[49] she becomes, following *Boland*, a home-owner in her own right.

## VI  TOWARDS REFORM, TOWARDS CONSENSUS

The House of Lords is not constrained by the need to consult, but it *is* constrained by the ability to decide only the point before it. By changing, and nailing down,

---

[46] Sir Jocelyn Simon, 'With all my Worldly Goods. . .', Holdsworth Club lecture, University of Birmingham, 20 March 1964, 14.

[47] The aspirations, and their frustration, are discussed in S Cretney *Family Law in the Twentieth Century* (Oxford, Oxford University Press, 2003) ch 3.

[48] Some European jurisdictions have adopted this in preference to the immediate community system. The result is that the spouses own separate property during marriage, but that on divorce, bankruptcy or death their property is pooled and shared equally.

[49] *Caunce v Caunce* [1969] 1 All ER 722.

just one point of law at a time it can effectively force the rest of the world to pivot around it and work out what to do next. It is not preceded by consultation, but it forces collective thought following its decisions.

And so it was following *Boland*. We can trace a number of streams of collective decisions that followed from the House of Lords' pinning down just one point and thereby raising some consequential questions and compelling some further problem-solving. The *Boland* decision set some new hares running, but also provided direction for hares that were already on the move; in doing so, it blended with the work of the Law Commission and led us on towards some truly consensus-based decisions.

To some extent those processes can be seen at work in the decisions of the courts themselves as they work out the extent and the limits of the ratio of the leading decision. We have seen that the decisions that followed *Boland* went a long way to reassure lenders and to damp down the panic that followed *Boland*; and we have noted that there was a major public interest in these decisions as a way of keeping mortgage finance affordable.

But more obviously consensus-based are the major destinations reached after decades of debate, in which the *Boland* decision was just one of many forces moving the law forwards. The trust of land, the modern concept of registration, and the principle of equal division of marital property can all be seen as destinations on a journey and as conclusions reached collectively after much discussion and consultation. The decision in *White v White* was, again, on its face a decision taken by an unelected body that does not consult. But it is more realistic to view it as the outcome of years of Law Commission work, years of debate, and years of academic analysis. The public opinion survey carried out by the Law Commission in the early 1970s can be seen, I suggest, to have borne fruit in the *White* decision.

This is not a unique experience even in property law. The most recent example in the property law field is perhaps the decision in *Stack v Dowden*,[50] which has been followed by extensive consultation by the Land Registry in order to establish just what to do about the idea that it is the Land Registry's job to force people to declare trusts.[51]

I am very far from claiming that it always works like this. Sometimes the courts, lower and higher, are not so well in tune with other developments and with the processes of consensus.[52] James Lee, in the following chapter in this collection, presents a far less rosy picture, drawing our attention and concern to those cases

---

[50] *Stack v Dowden* [2007] UKHL 17, [2007] 2 AC 432.

[51] ibid [52] (Baroness Hale). Certainly there is something to said for it being *somebody's* job to do so. The Land Registry's dilemma here is that knowledge of how the equitable interests are arranged is precisely not the registrar's concern: Land Registration Act 2002 s 78: 'The registrar shall not be affected with notice of a trust.'

[52] There have been instances where the House of Lords has made a decision that seems to be out of tune. Rather than pivoting around it, the response of the lower courts and of other stakeholders is to marginalise the decision as far as possible: *Bruton v London Quadrant Housing Trust* [2000] 1 AC 406 may be such a one.

where a decision of the House of Lords has been stamped upon by the legislature without due regard for coherence.[53]

I am suggesting only that when all goes well, the House of Lords is naturally part of a larger, and truly democratic, process. *Boland* was a part, and perhaps a relatively small part, of several bigger legal developments whose conclusions now seem very obvious and ring very true, despite the length and difficulty of the path by which they were reached.

After the Law Commission's Boland Report was published, Mrs Boland was reported to have said:

> It's a wonderful thing to know that if this law goes through no woman will have to go through what I went through.[54]

That hope was disappointed. There was no revolution. The *Boland* decision, and the Boland Report that followed it, were each a move in a long chess game, a stitch in a tapestry, that led eventually to a position that lenders find comfortable, a revision of our concept of joint ownership trusts, a development of our view of registration, and a realistic concept of the effect of marriage upon property rights. Consensus happened, but it took time; no one step along the journey, and no single institution, can be judged in isolation.

---

[53] J Lee, '"Inconsiderate Alterations in Our Laws": Legislative Reversal of Supreme Court Decisions', this volume.

[54] *Daily Mail* (London, 20 August 1982).

# 5

# 'Inconsiderate Alterations in our Laws': Legislative Reversal of Supreme Court Decisions

JAMES LEE*

## I INTRODUCTION

The mischiefs that have arisen to the public from inconsiderate alterations in our laws, are too obvious to be called in question; and how far they have been owing to the defective education of our senators, is a point well worthy the public attention.

The common law of England has fared like other venerable edifices of antiquity, which rash and unexperienced workmen have ventured to new-dress and refine, with all the rage of modern improvement. Hence frequently it's symmetry has been destroyed, it's proportions distorted, and it's majestic simplicity exchanged for specious embellishments and fantastic novelties.[1]

S O SAID THE great jurist William Blackstone, writing in the first volume of his *Commentaries* in 1765.[2] It is the purpose of this essay to use two such incidents of legislative mischief to examine the prospects for judging in the new Supreme Court and the relationship between the judiciary and the other branches of government.

* I am very grateful to those who attended the Society of Legal Scholars Annual Seminar, and to my colleague Mr Graham Gee, for helpful comments on this paper. Some of the views on the Compensation Act presented here were submitted as evidence to the Constitution Committee of the House of Lords Inquiry into Emergency Legislation. Any errors are my own.

[1] W Blackstone, *Commentaries on the Laws of England: Volume 1 Of the Rights of Persons* (1765), (Facsimile of the First Edition, Chicago and London, University of Chicago Press, 1979) 10 [*sic*].

[2] A more recent passage highly reminiscent of Blackstone's observation comes from Sir Kenneth Keith in 'Philosophies of Law Reform' (1991) 7 *Otago Law Review* 363, 363–64: 'Too often hasty and partial glimpses have misled those introducing change. Some of you will recall all too clearly the various enactments relating to tertiary education introduced in 1989 and 1990: the fragmentation of the executive and parliamentary process meant that for some time no one—including Ministers and their advisers as well as those who were to be affected by the legislation and who wished to make submissions on it—could see the whole edifice. It did not exist. That was bad law making, and although in the end much of the mischief (actual and potential) was undone, time and money were wasted and goodwill damaged. And not all of the mischief has yet been undone. The resulting legislation is unnecessarily difficult.'

Here, we shall consider the legislative and executive responses to two recent decisions of the House of Lords, and consider their implications for the new Supreme Court. The first decision is *Barker v Corus*,[3] a case concerning causation and proportionate recovery, decided on 3 May 2006. Section 3 of the Compensation Act 2006 was inserted into the Compensation Bill at a late stage to address the effect of this decision on claims by victims of asbestos-related mesothelioma, and the Act received the Royal Assent on 25 July 2006. Secondly, *Rothwell v Chemical and Insulating Co Ltd*,[4] which was a decision principally on whether pleural plaques could constitute actionable damage in the tort of negligence. Though involving English appeals, the decision was pre-emptively reversed by the Scottish Parliament through the Damages (Asbestos-related Conditions) (Scotland) Act 2009. The Westminster Government and the Northern Ireland Executive both consulted as to whether to legislate in response to *Rothwell*: the former decided not to legislate,[5] while the latter suggested that it would recommend a change in the law.[6]

The phenomenon of legislative reversal illuminates the interplay of the new Supreme Court and Parliament, and of the common law and legislation. Before the Court's inauguration, there was speculation as to whether the Supreme Court Justices would be 'arrogating to themselves greater power than they have at the moment',[7] perhaps such as striking down legislation.[8] Would the new Supreme Court get its '*Marbury v Madison*[9] moment'?[10]

One of the final decisions of the Judicial House of Lords, *Transport for London (London Underground Ltd) v Spirerose Ltd*,[11] a case on compulsory purchase and statutory interpretation, saw their Lordships emphasise the limits of the judicial role. So we have Lord Walker noting: 'Parliament has enacted a statutory code of some complexity . . . For the Court to try to correct the code in accordance with its perception of what is fair would amount to judicial legislation.'[12] Similarly, Lord Collins of Mapesbury accepted

---

[3] *Barker v Corus* [2006] UKHL 20, [2006] 2 AC 572, [2006] 2 WLR 1027.

[4] *Rothwell v Chemical and Insulating Co Ltd* [2007] UKHL 39, [2008] 1 AC 281, [2007] 3 WLR 877, [2007] 4 All ER 1047.

[5] 'Pleural plaques: Jack Straw statement': www.justice.gov.uk/news/announcement250210a. htm.

[6] 'Dodds recommends law change for pleural plaques compensation': www.northernireland.gov. uk/news-dfp-290609-dodds-recommends-law.

[7] 'Top Dogs: Britain's New Supreme Court', BBC Radio 4, 8 September 2009, 8 pm.

[8] For a compelling argument that Parliamentary sovereignty at least requires some reconsideration, see S Lakin, 'Debunking the idea of parliamentary sovereignty: the controlling factor of legality in the British constitution' (2008) 28 *Oxford Journal of Legal Studies* 709. Cf M Gordon, 'The conceptual foundations of parliamentary sovereignty: reconsidering Jennings and Wade' [2009] *Public Law* 519.

[9] *Marbury v Madison* 5 US 137 (1803).

[10] T Poole, 'The reformation of English administrative law' (2009) 68 *Cambridge Law Journal* 142, 160.

[11] *Transport for London (London Underground Ltd) v Spirerose Ltd* [2009] UKHL 44.

[12] ibid [41].

TfL's fundamental point that it is not the role of the court to re-write legislation by adding additional assumptions of planning permission... There is a difference between legitimate purposive construction and impermissible judicial legislation.[13]

These statements aside, we shall have to wait to see whether their Lordships experienced a Damascene conversion on the symbolic walk across Parliament Square. I shall argue that equally important questions arise from looking at the counterpoint situation of the reversal of Supreme Court decisions. We can learn from the continuing interaction of 'the tectonic forces of judiciary, government and Parliament'.[14] As the late Professor Sir Neil MacCormick recognised, 'much of what is written both about the Rule of Law and about legal reasoning takes for granted the forum of adjudication. But that of legislation matters scarcely less.'[15]

Examining interventions in private law preserves a valuable perspective, in the contrast to the traditional focus on public law and human rights. In an important article on tort law reform,[16] Professor Peter Cane has argued that '[o]ther things being equal, we should prefer statute law to common law'[17] and that 'in general, political processes of law-making should be preferred [to] judicial processes'.[18] I shall argue that, at the very least, legislative reversals of particular private law decisions are not preferable to judicial development of the law. It must be stressed that plausible arguments could have been made in favour of the opposite outcome, as the dissents in each of the cases show. However, the legislators did not, in the main, make or rely upon those arguments. Why not?

Blackstone lamented the 'defective education of our senators'. The separation of our highest court from the legislature will have an obvious impact in that serving Justices will no longer be members of the legislature.[19] Section 137(3) of the Constitutional Reform Act 2005 provides that 'A member of the House of Lords is, while he holds any disqualifying judicial office, disqualified for sitting or voting in— (a) the House of Lords, (b) a committee of that House, or (c) a joint committee of both Houses.' In principle, therefore, those members of the Supreme Court appointed prior to its inauguration, who still received peerages, will be able to return upon their retirement. Other members of the House of Lords holding judicial office are also disqualified from sitting while serving:[20]

---

[13] ibid [131].

[14] AW Bradley, 'Relations between Executive, Judiciary and Parliament: an evolving saga?' [2008] *Public Law* 470, 489. Bradley takes up the 'tectonic plates' analogy which was suggested but declined by Dame Mary Arden in 'Judicial Independence and Parliaments' in K Ziegler, D Baranger and AW Bradley (eds), *Constitutionalism and the Role of Parliaments* (Oxford, Hart Publishing, 2007).

[15] N MacCormick, *Rhetoric and the Rule of Law* (Oxford, Oxford University Press, 2005) 7.

[16] P Cane, 'Taking Disagreement Seriously: Courts, Legislatures and the Reform of Tort Law' (2005) 25 *Oxford Journal of Legal Studies* 393.

[17] ibid 394.

[18] ibid (abstract) 393.

[19] See D Pannick, ' "Better that a horse should have a voice in the House [of Lords] than that a judge should" (Jeremy Bentham): replacing the Law Lords by a Supreme Court' [2009] *Public Law* 723.

[20] s 137(4) of Constitutional Reform Act 2005 adopts the meaning of 'disqualifying judicial office' provided by (a) Pt 1 of sch 1 to the House of Commons Disqualification Act 1975, or (b) Pt 1 of sch 1 to the Northern Ireland Assembly Disqualification Act 1975. This includes judges of the Court of Appeal of England and Wales, the Court of Session and the Court of Appeal in Northern Ireland.

Lord Neuberger MR is therefore presently disqualified, even though he did not follow his colleagues from the Appellate Committee to the Supreme Court.[21] Nor will future Justices necessarily be appointed to the Upper Chamber.[22] Thus, Sir John Dyson, who became the twelfth Justice of the Court on 13 April 2010, does not have a peerage.

It is not my purpose here to examine the role played by Law Lords in the legislative process of the House of Lords, not least because that subject has been very well covered by Lord Hope in an article in the *Law Quarterly Review*.[23] Lord Hope, it should be noted, was one of the Law Lords who, in 2003, believed that 'on pragmatic grounds, the proposed change [to the new Supreme Court] is unnecessary and will be harmful.'[24] It is certainly the case that their Lordships' absence will reduce the legal expertise on which Parliament as a whole is able to draw when passing legislation,[25] and it is clear that Parliamentarians will miss them.[26]

The focus here is on legislative reversal of judicial decisions, but it will also be necessary to acknowledge the opposite phenomenon of 'legislative affirmation', which was referred to by Lord Walker of Gestingthorpe in the *Spirerose* case.[27] Sections 1 and 2 of the Compensation Act 2006, s 3 of which is scrutinised below, may be seen to be an example of such affirmation. Nicholas McBride has described the sections as clearly 'drafted by the Ministry for Stating the Bleedin' Obvious and enacted in order that the Government could claim to be doing something about the UK's burgeoning "compensation culture". Neither section has any effect whatsoever on the current law, which already acknowledges the points made in each section.'[28]

The same, however, cannot be said of the two episodes considered below. In each case of purported reversal, it is not even clear to what extent the legislature

---

[21] One of the recent appointees to the Supreme Court, Lord Clarke of Stone-cum-Ebony, was given a peerage in recognition of his work as Master of the Rolls, not by virtue of his appointment to our highest court. It appears that this practice of offering a peerage to the Master of Rolls will be unaffected by the Act (www.number10.gov.uk/Page19005), although such peers would not be entitled to sit in the House while still presiding over the Civil Division of the Court of Appeal.

[22] Lord Bach, the Under-Secretary of State in the Ministry of Justice, stated that he could not assure Lord Pannick to the contrary: Hansard HL cols 1375–77 (20 July 2009).

[23] D Hope, 'Voices from the Past: The Law Lords' Contribution to the Legislative Process' (2007) 123 *Law Quarterly Review* 547.

[24] 'The Law Lords' response to the Government's Consultation Paper on Constitutional reform: a Supreme Court for the United Kingdom' (27 October 2003), www.parliament.uk/documents/upload/JudicialSCR071103.pdf.

[25] Although s 137(5) of the 2005 Act does allow for a disqualified member of the House of Lords to receive a writ of summons.

[26] See the valedictory debate in the House of Lords, Hansard HL cols 1507–17 (21 July 2009).

[27] *Spirerose* (n 11) [18], quoting Lord Nicholls of Birkenhead in *Waters & Ors v Welsh Development Agency* [2004] UKHL 19 [28]: both were referring to the 'affirmation' of the approach of Fletcher Moulton LJ in *Re Lucas and Chesterfield Gas and Water Board* [1909] 1 KB 16 to r 3 of s 2 of the Acquisition of Land (Assessment of Compensation) Act 1919.

[28] Website update to N McBride and R Bagshaw, *Tort Law* (Harlow, Pearson Longman, 2001): http://media.pearsoncmg.com/intl/ema/ema_uk_he_mcbride_tortlaw_3/legislation/compensation_act_2006.doc.

was successful in doing so. In one of our examples, we may soon have the Justices' views on the issue, as the Supreme Court has, at the time of writing, granted permission to appeal in a case involving s 3 of the Compensation Act.[29] While not wishing to be quite as strident in my criticism as Blackstone, I shall endeavour to demonstrate that there are significant difficulties with the approaches to the decisions.

## II  THE IMPORTANCE OF BEING COHERENT

A perennial question for legal theorists is whether we should expect our judges to be philosophers.[30] But what should we ask of our legislators in terms of jurisprudence?

Normally, we expect Parliament to legislate generally, while the courts deal with individual disputes. What if, as we shall see here, Parliament chooses to legislate about rights in a particular type of claim? Such a choice may give rise to questions of competence. As Ronald Dworkin has noted:

> I cannot imagine what argument might be thought to show that legislative decisions about rights are inherently more likely to be correct than judicial decisions . . . the technique of examining a claim of right for speculative consistency is a technique far more developed in judges than in legislators or in the bulk of the citizens who elect legislators.[31]

In *Law's Empire*,[32] Dworkin famously sought to demonstrate how judges should go about the business of judging. But he also offered an argument about the business of legislating, relying upon 'the principle of integrity in legislation, which asks those who create law by legislation to keep that law coherent in principle.'[33] This principle is a third ideal, in addition to, and different from, justice and fairness. Dworkin considers that the principle is most clearly demonstrated by what he calls 'checkerboard solutions', 'laws that treat similar accidents or occasions of racial discrimination differently on arbitrary grounds.'[34] He offers two hypothetical examples of such laws: an abortion statute and another concerning accident liability. Dworkin postulates that a parliament might choose to legislate that there should be strict liability on the manufacturers of automobiles, but

---

[29] Permission to appeal from the decision of the Court of Appeal in *Sienkiewicz v Greif (UK) Ltd* [2009] EWCA Civ 1159, [2010] 2 WLR 951 was granted on 4 March 2010: www.supremecourt.gov.uk/docs/pta-1002-1003.pdf. On the same day, permission was also granted to appeal in a related case on material contribution to risk, *Willmore v Knowsley MBC* [2009] EWCA Civ 1211.

[30] See, eg, CL Eisgruber, 'Should Constitutional Judges Be Philosophers?' in S Hershovitz (ed), *Exploring Law's Empire* (Oxford, Oxford University Press, 2006).

[31] R Dworkin, 'Political Judges and the Rule of Law' in *A Matter of Principle* (Oxford, Oxford University Press, 1985) 24.

[32] R Dworkin, *Law's Empire* (London, Fontana Press, 1986).

[33] Dworkin, *Law's Empire* (n 32) 167. For an eloquent argument about the duties incumbent upon legislatures, see J Waldron, 'Legislating with Integrity' 72 (2003–04) *Fordham Law Review* 373.

[34] Dworkin, *Law's Empire* (n 32) 179.

not on those of washing machines. So, from the outset, Dworkin is interested in private law as well as constitutional cases.

The value of legislative integrity has been challenged, recently in particular by Andrei Marmor[35] and Dale Smith.[36] In his essay, Marmor identifies what he takes to be the 'three main causes for the failure of legislative integrity':[37] first, division of legislative power (particularly in but not limited to the American federalist context).[38] In an age of devolution, such incoherence may be increasingly common. The other causes which Marmor considers are 'logrolling and compromise'[39] and 'partisan realignment and continuity of law'.[40] None of these directly addresses the incoherence which may result from the swift reversal of judicial decisions.

I shall not enter here fully into the debate on legislative integrity, nor is it necessary to argue that the legislature should not be allowed, as MacCormick, who had himself been a legislator,[41] put it, to have the 'last word':[42] 'Judicial precedents that are found unsatisfactory under democratic scrutiny can be corrected for the future (though only very exceptionally in a retrospective manner) by new legislation.'[43] What I do aim to show is that a failure to offer reasonable arguments inevitably undermines the coherence of the law when Parliament intervenes to reverse a specific judicial decision. If there are any situations in which legislative integrity is required, it is in cases such as these.

## III  DIALOGUE, HUMAN RIGHTS AND LEGISLATIVE REVERSALS

By using examples from private law, we shall draw out some interesting themes in recent work in constitutional theory. What literature there is on legislative reversals tends to consider the public law and human rights sphere. In such cases, the dynamics are different: an article in *Public Law* 20 years ago referred to the 'government's predeliction for the legislative reversal, including retrospective reversal, of "defeats" it has suffered at the hands of the judiciary in judicial review cases and in tribunals (especially in the social security field)'.[44] The nature of legislative reversal will vary depending on the context, as will the motivation. For example, Roach has surveyed 'the legislative attempts to reverse pro-accused

---

[35] 'Should We Value Legislative Integrity?' in RW Bauman and T Kahana (eds), *The Least Examined Branch: The Role of Legislatures in the Constitutional State* (Cambridge, Cambridge University Press, 2006).

[36] 'The Many Faces of Political Integrity', in *Exploring Law's Empire* (n 30).

[37] ibid 135.

[38] ibid.

[39] ibid 136.

[40] ibid 137.

[41] As a Member of the European Parliament for Scotland from 1999 to 2004.

[42] N MacCormick, *Institutions of Law: An Essay in Legal Theory* (Oxford, Oxford University Press, 2008) 202.

[43] ibid. MacCormick's observation is however made while offering a coherence-based approach to legal reasoning.

[44] P MacAuslan, 'Administrative justice—a necessary report?' [1988] *Public Law* 402, 407.

Supreme Court constitutional decisions in Canada and the United States'.[45] That is not so in the two examples which we shall consider: indeed, there were even some suggestions in Parliament that the Government had instigated the litigation in one of the cases.[46] Regardless of the truth of that suggestion, it is certain that, in the asbestos-related cases, the Government is a very likely defendant,[47] and so, as both decisions of the House of Lords went in favour of defendants, they cannot be classified as 'defeats'.

In the public law/human rights context, there will often be a swift legislative response to deal with a challenge in a decision. Some may be classified as 'emergencies': for example, if imminent trials are jeopardised.[48] Others may be a response to a declaration of incompatibility issued under s 4 of the Human Rights Act 1998 (although such a declaration does not of course affect the validity of the initial legislation),[49] using the powers to take remedial action afforded by s 10 of the Act. In other jurisdictions, different constitutional requirements may compel the legislation to be reconsidered.[50] Private law cases offer a different dimension.

There is, it must be noted, a significant overlap between human rights jurisprudence and private law,[51] and instances of legislative reversal have been the subject of several challenges. Without pretending to be comprehensive, there are broadly two possible lines of argument. First, the European Court of Human Rights has held that claims may be a 'possession', and therefore protected by art 1 of Protocol 1. A subsequent reversal of the law must therefore be legitimate and

---

[45] K Roach, 'Dialogue or defiance: legislative reversals of Supreme Court decisions in Canada and the United States' (2006) 4 *International Journal of Constitutional Law* 347.

[46] On *Barker*, see the testy exchange between Oliver Heald MP (Con) and the Minister, Bridget Prentice MP (Hansard HC cols 41–42 (17 July 2006) and the general debate later at cols 50–52. At col 51, Mr Heald observed: 'Ministers suggested in meetings that this was all to do with the insurance industry, but in fact the industry funded none of the cases that went to the House of Lords under the *Barker v Corus* umbrella: the Government funded two of the cases and one was funded privately. Those test cases were pursued because a lot of former Government employees, who worked in the Ministry of Defence and other Departments, were exposed to asbestos. This will be expensive for the Government in the long term, and I guess that they were attempting to ensure a smaller bill than they might otherwise have.

There must have been a moment—I imagine that it occurred in the Department for Constitutional Affairs—when someone suddenly said, "What have we done?" It was at that point that the decision was made to reverse this, and to do so quickly. I welcome that.'

[47] For a very recent asbestosis case, where two Government departments were liable, see *Young v The Advocate General For Scotland* [2009] CSOH 102A. The three first instance decisions in favour of the actionability of pleural plaques were all claims by former workers in naval dockyards: *Church v Ministry of Defence* (1984) 134 NLJ 623 and *Patterson v Ministry of Defence* [1987] CLY 1194 from the Chatham dockyard; and *Sykes v Ministry of Defence*, *The Times* (London 23 March 1984) from Portsmouth.

[48] See the Criminal Evidence (Witness Anonymity) Act 2008, enacted as a legislative response a month after the decision of the House of Lords in *R v Davis* [2008] UKHL 36, [2008] 1 AC 1128: 'Editorial' [2008] *Criminal Law Review* 749.

[49] s 4(6) of the Human Rights Act 1998.

[50] See generally Roach, 'Dialogue or defiance' (n 45).

[51] See J Steele, '(Dis)owning the Convention in the Law of Tort' in this volume.

proportionate.[52] In a pair of recent decisions,[53] the ECtHR considered the French legislative response to the decision in *Perruche*,[54] a claim for the 'wrongful life' of a disabled child. The defendant doctors' negligence had caused the baby's birth, as otherwise he would have been aborted. Weir has perceptively analysed 'the legislative reaction to the *Perruche* decision and the ensuing *brouhaha*',[55] and so I shall not do so here. In *Draon* and *Maurice*, the Court assessed the 'law *anti-Perruche*'[56] stating that 'the legislature is not in principle precluded in civil matters from intervening to alter the current legal position through a statute which is immediately applicable',[57] but compensation must be paid in recognition of the lost value of the claim, which is essentially an asset.

The second type of challenge focuses on art 6, which provides that a claimant is entitled to a fair hearing in determination of their civil rights by an independent and impartial tribunal established by law. Such an argument was unsuccessful before the House of Lords in *Matthews v Ministry of Defence*,[58] a claim for pleural plaques of the ilk which will be examined here. Some cases will combine both these challenges, as in one of the cases below.[59]

A current theme in constitutional theory, borrowed from across the Atlantic,[60] is that of dialogue between the courts and the legislature. The dialogue approach fits best a constitutional review framework which provides for the interaction between the courts, legislature and the executive, such as the Canadian Charter of Rights and Freedoms. Hickman has produced a valuable account of how such dialogue may be conceived under the Human Rights Act, recognising the 'distinct and valuable judicial role in determining substantive questions of rights while emphasising the relationship between courts and other branches.'[61] Such a theory is by no means uncontroversial. But might it be a helpful metaphor for understanding the processes when the legislative reversal of a private law decision of the Supreme Court is attempted?

Before embarking on the substance of the study here, we may offer a succinct example of dialogue in action. Although it must be conceded that judicial pleas

---

[52] A Du Bois-Pedain, 'On being dispossessed of a head of claim in a pending case' (2006) 65 *Cambridge Law Journal* 257.

[53] *Draon v France* [GC] (Application no 1513/03) (2006) 42 EHRR 40; *Maurice v France* [GC], (Application no 11810/03) (2006) 42 EHRR 40; judgments of 6 October 2005.

[54] Cour de Cassation, Ass Plén, 17 November 2000, Bull Ass Plén, no 9. Professor Cane takes wrongful birth type claims as one of his examples in his argument in favour of legislative processes: Cane, 'Taking Disagreement Seriously' (n 16).

[55] T Weir, 'The unwanted child' (2002) 6 *Edinburgh Law Review* 244, 245.

[56] ibid 250.

[57] *Maurice* (n 53), para 89.

[58] *Matthews v Ministry of Defence* [2003] UKHL 4, [2003] 2 WLR 435, [2003] 1 AC 1163. See T Hickman, 'The "uncertain shadow": throwing light on the right to a court under Article 6(1) ECHR' [2004] *Public Law* 122.

[59] *AXA General Insurance Ltd, Re Application for Judicial Review of the Damages (Asbestos-Related Conditions) (Scotland) Act* [2010] CSOH 2, 2010 SLT 179, considered below (n 144).

[60] See, eg, PW Hogg and AA Bushell, 'The Charter Dialogue Between Courts and Legislatures (or Perhaps the Charter of Rights Isn't Such a Bad Thing after All)' (1997) 35 *Osgoode Hall Law Journal* 75.

[61] T Hickman, 'Constitutional dialogue, constitutional theories and the Human Rights Act 1998' [2005] *Public Law* 306, 317.

for legislative action in private law often go unheeded, particularly with regard to Law Commission reforms,[62] sometimes Parliament does prove itself to be responsive to particular appellate decisions. In *Chapman v Chapman*,[63] the House of Lords declined to afford itself an ordinary jurisdiction to consent to the variation of trusts on behalf of those unable to do so.[64] Lord Simonds LC spoke for the House when he said: 'It is for the legislature . . . to determine whether there should be a change in the law and what that change should be.'[65] Parliament responded to this invitation with the short Variation of Trusts Act 1958. The Act was happily received by the courts, who noted that it conferred 'a very wide and, indeed, revolutionary discretion'[66] and that it granted the courts a 'very useful jurisdiction'.[67] Indeed, the Chapman trustees were subsequently successful with an application under the 1958 Act.[68]

*Chapman* illustrates the possibility of dialogue: the judiciary deny that they have a power; Parliament decides that they should; the courts then apply the new law. At this stage, judges have to interpret the statute using traditional methods of construction. They may do so literally or purposively, offering narrow or broad interpretations, which may give the law a different meaning from that envisaged by the legislature. Thus we have dialogue, as 'judicial decisions and legislation might be part of a continuing process, adjusted by the judges or by government as a response to each other'[69] and the courts make the most of their ability 'to bring principle to bear on legislative projects and advance principled goals in collaboration with Parliament.'[70]

But both sides must engage: in the cases which we shall examine here, we find not so much dialogue as legislative monologue and judicial soliloquy.


## IV CAUSATION: *BARKER V CORUS*


To succeed in a claim for negligence, a claimant must prove that the defendant breached a duty of care which they owed to the claimant and that that breach caused the claimant actionable harm. The claimant is able to establish factual

[62] As to which, see section VIII below.
[63] *Chapman v Chapman* [1954] AC 429.
[64] Most commonly, by reason of infancy or because a potential beneficiary had yet to be born. Traditionally, restrictive categories of conversion, salvage or emergency, compromise or maintenance applied: see, eg, *Re New* [1901] 2 Ch 534, 545.
[65] *Chapman* (n 63) 444. In full, 'We are as little justified in saying that a court has a certain jurisdiction, merely because we think it ought to have it, as we should be in declaring that the substantive law is something different from what it has always been declared to be, merely because we think it ought to be so. It is even possible that we are not wiser than our ancestors. It is for the legislature, which does not rest under that disability, to determine whether there should be a change in the law and what that change should be.'
[66] *Re Steed's WT* [1960] Ch 407, 420 (Lord Evershed MR).
[67] *Re T's Settlement* [1964] Ch 158, 162 (Wilberforce J).
[68] *Chapman v Chapman (No 2)* [1959] 1 WLR 372, [1959] 2 All ER 48 (Note).
[69] R Cranston, 'What do courts do?' (1986) 5 *Civil Justice Quarterly* 123, 142.
[70] Hickman, 'Constitutional dialogue' (n 61) 322.

causation if they can prove that, but for the defendant's breach, they would not have suffered the damage. In *Fairchild v Glenhaven Funeral Services*,[71] the House of Lords unanimously (but with individual reasoning) recognised an exception to the need for a claimant to prove 'but for' causation where they were unable to do so because of an 'evidential gap', building on the authority of *McGhee v National Coal Board*.[72] The question facing the House was expressed by Lord Bingham, then Senior Law Lord, thus:

> A and B owed C a duty to protect C against a risk of a particular and very serious kind. They failed to perform that duty. As a result the risk eventuated and C suffered the very harm against which it was the duty of A and B to protect him. Had there been only one tortfeasor, C would have been entitled to recover, but because the duty owed to him was broken by two tortfeasors and not only one, he is held to be entitled to recover against neither, because of his inability to prove what is scientifically unprovable.[73]

Both *Fairchild* and *Barker v Corus*[74] concerned this general situation in the context of asbestos-related mesothelioma. The claimant or deceased had been exposed to asbestos while working for more than one employer, each of whom was in breach of duty to their employees, but only one of the employers was still available to be sued. Mesothelioma is an indivisible rather than cumulative injury, and so it was not the case that each defendant had directly contributed to the injury itself,[75] as would be the case with asbestosis.[76] Due to the limitations of scientific knowledge about mesothelioma, it was not possible to determine the source of the causative asbestos.[77] Therefore the claimant could not prove that, but for any given employer's negligence, the injury would not have occurred. As a result, they could not satisfy the ordinary principles of factual causation to succeed in their claim. In *Fairchild*, the House held that, in such cases, the claimant should be allowed to 'jump the evidentiary gap' and the defendant could be held liable on the basis of material contribution to risk of harm.

When deciding *Fairchild*, the House did not determine the extent of liability under the exception, but it was assumed that liability was *in solidum*, ie that the defendant was liable for the full extent of the harm. However, in *Barker*, a majority of four Law Lords held that damages should be proportionate in accordance with the risk created by the individual defendant, Lord Rodger strongly dissenting. Of the panel who sat in *Barker*, two, Lord Hoffmann and Lord Rodger, had sat in *Fairchild*, and they vehemently disagreed about the scope of the exception. As

---

[71] *Fairchild v Glenhaven Funeral Services* [2002] UKHL 22, [2003] 1 AC 32.

[72] *McGhee v National Coal Board* 1973 SC (HL) 37 (Ct Sess), [1973] 1 WLR 1, [1972] 3 All ER 1008 (HL(Sc)).

[73] *Fairchild* (n 71) [9].

[74] *Barker v Corus* [2006] UKHL 20; [2006] 2 AC 572.

[75] Although it is possible with some indivisible injuries for a court to find that a defendant has made a material contribution to it: *Bailey v Ministry of Defence* [2008] EWCA Civ 883, [2009] 1 WLR 1052; J Lee, 'Causation in negligence: another fine mess' (2008) 24 *Professional Negligence* 194.

[76] See, eg, *Holtby v Brigham & Cowan (Hull) Ltd* [2000] EWCA Civ 111.

[77] It should be noted that the 'single fibre' theory of the aetiology of mesothelioma is, according to Smith LJ, no longer in favour: *Sienkiewicz* (n 29), [16].

to reasoning, by a bare majority, the House conceived the 'damage' as being the creation of the risk, rather than the mesothelioma (Baroness Hale concurred in the result, but adopted Lord Rodger's analysis on this point[78]).

There is open debate amongst tort lawyers as to the merits of the decision in *Barker*, and of the line of cases which have been labelled 'mesothelioma jurisprudence'.[79] Some academics endorse the approach of the majority,[80] arguing that 'although there may well exist strong arguments in favour of maintaining the rule against apportionment where causation can be established on an orthodox basis, it is perfectly reasonable to argue for a modification of that rule where the causal criteria have themselves been altered'.[81] For my part, I have argued elsewhere that the relationship between *Fairchild* and *Barker* is troublesome: that, 'on the *Barker* interpretation, one is left to wonder what the point of *Fairchild* was. The rough justice of liability under *Fairchild* is not so much smoothed as undercut.'[82] The 'risk as damage' approach taken by the majority in *Barker* may be seen to be problematic, as the mere contribution to risk is not usually recoverable as damage.

## V 'SYMMETRY DESTROYED'? LEGISLATIVE RESPONSE TO *BARKER*

### A Immediate Response

A consideration of the Hansard debates in the wake of *Barker* is instructive when reflecting upon the legislative intervention, as it reveals that the desire to reverse what was felt to be an injustice caused Parliament to act without full regard to the consequences for the coherence of the law.[83]

The then Government was not pleased with the *Barker* decision. The Minister for Employment and Welfare Reform (Mr Jim Murphy) observed:

> The Government and I are as disappointed with the *Barker* judgment as hon. Members are, not only because it adds further uncertainty and difficulty, and puts a further burden on those who have been diagnosed, but because it will lead to unfairness in how compensation is provided and offered. . . The Government find that utterly unacceptable.[84]

---

[78] *Barker* (n 74) [120].

[79] *Employers' Liability Policy 'Trigger' Litigation* [2008] EWHC 2692 (QB) [47]–[58] (Burton J).

[80] See the work of my colleague Sarah Green, 'Winner Takes All' (2004) 120 *Law Quarterly Review* 566 (on the Court of Appeal decision in *Barker*); 'The Risk Pricing Principle: A Pragmatic Approach to Causation and Apportionment of Damages' 4 (2005) *Law, Probability and Risk* 159. See also A Kramer, 'Smoothing the rough justice of the *Fairchild* principle' (2006) 122 *Law Quarterly Review* 547.

[81] Green, 'Winner Takes All' (n 80) 568.

[82] J Lee, 'Fidelity in interpretation: Lord Hoffmann and the Adventure of the Empty House' (2008) 28 *Legal Studies* 1, 12.

[83] An archive of the legislative history of the Act can be found on the former Department for Constitutional Affairs website, www.dca.gov.uk/legist/compensation.htm.

[84] Hansard HC col 213WH (13 June 2006).

The response of many MPs to the decision in *Barker* was condemnatory and emotive: the decision was described as 'appalling',[85] 'outrageous and wholly unacceptable'.[86] We may take a selection of observations from the Hansard reports of the Commons debates and a Westminster Hall debate as an illustration of the strength of feeling:

> The *Barker* judgment has no legitimacy, and a change in that respect is needed very urgently.[87]
>
> The *Barker* ruling is a disgrace to the House. Trade unions and their legal services teams should be able to work through us in this House to overturn that disgraceful decision taken in the other place.[88]
>
> [On] 3 May the House of Lords gave a judgment that would slash the amount of compensation that is paid to workers dying of asbestos-induced mesothelioma.[89]
>
> My hon. Friend listed professional bodies, voluntary organisations, relatives, families and so on. Does he know any other three people, apart from the three Law Lords, who agree with the decision?[90]
>
> If we do nothing else as legislators, we should protect those vulnerable people who are suffering as a result of the Law Lords' decision—I sometimes wonder what planet they are on when they make such decisions, which are seriously offensive to people who are suffering from that terrible disease.[91]

Although MPs are entitled to say what they like in Parliament, these are very strong words about a decision of the Appellate Committee of the House of Lords. To describe one of the House's decisions as having 'no legitimacy' is a bold and potentially damaging claim. That said, it must be conceded that some MPs offered more balanced assessments: 'The lawyers and the judiciary have wrestled, rightly and valiantly, with complex and difficult law, but it has created despair for the families whom we represent.'[92] Similarly, Mr Tim Boswell urged that it was necessary to 'look at the underlying legal concepts and, at the same time, confront the facts concerning the individuals and their families with this terrible disease.'[93]

## B  Compensation Act 2006

Following the debates and severe backbench pressure, a new clause was inserted into the Compensation Bill then before Parliament. This provision sought to

---

[85]  Judy Mallaber (Amber Valley) (Lab) (question to the Prime Minister): Hansard HC col 245 (7 June 2006).

[86]  Ian Stewart (Eccles) (Lab): Hansard HC col 200WH (13 June 2006).

[87]  Tony Lloyd (Manchester Central) (Lab): Hansard HC col 454 (8 June 2006).

[88]  Mr David Anderson (Blaydon) (Lab): Hansard HC col 498 (8 June 2006).

[89]  Jim Sheridan (Paisley and Renfrewshire, North) (Lab): Hansard HC col 192WH (13 June 2006)..

[90]  Jim Devine (Livingston) (Lab): Hansard HC col 194WH (13 June 2006). It is not clear to which three of their Lordships Mr Devine is referring.

[91]  Jim Sheridan: Hansard HC col 195WH (13 June 2006).

[92]  Michael Wills (North Swindon) (Lab): Hansard HC col 203WH (and generally cols 202–04WH) (13 June 2006).

[93]  Hansard HC col 208WH (and generally cols 208WH–211WH) (13 June 2006).

reverse *Barker*. But the Government and Parliament were unduly focused on the particular problems faced by mesothelioma victims, without regard to the wider scope of the exception to causation principles seen in the cases of *Fairchild* and *Barker*. The short title of the Act names one of its purposes as 'to make provision about damages for mesothelioma'. Subsections 3(1) and (2) make clear that the provision is further limited to asbestos-related mesothelioma. Incongruously, Part 1 of the Act, in which s 3 is located, is entitled 'Standard of Care', yet the section deals with causation (this is, of course, a result of the section being introduced at a late stage).

Section 3 of the Act provides (so far as material):

(1) This section applies where—

    (a)    a person ("the responsible person") has negligently or in breach of statutory duty caused or permitted another person ("the victim") to be exposed to asbestos,

    (b)    the victim has contracted mesothelioma as a result of exposure to asbestos,

    (c)    because of the nature of mesothelioma and the state of medical science, it is not possible to determine with certainty whether it was the exposure mentioned in paragraph (a) or another exposure which caused the victim to become ill, and

    (d)    the responsible person is liable in tort, by virtue of the exposure mentioned in paragraph (a), in connection with damage caused to the victim by the disease (whether by reason of having materially increased a risk or for any other reason).

(2) The responsible person shall be liable—

    (a)    in respect of the whole of the damage caused to the victim by the disease (irrespective of whether the victim was also exposed to asbestos—

        (i)    other than by the responsible person, whether or not in circumstances in which another person has liability in tort, or

        (ii)    by the responsible person in circumstances in which he has no liability in tort), and

    (b)    jointly and severally with any other responsible person.

Section 16(3) provides that 'Section 3 shall be treated as having always had effect', but s 16(4) provides that the section does not apply to claims settled or determined prior to 3 May 2006 (the date of the decision in *Barker*). This limitation is because the section aims to restore the pre-*Barker* assumption that liability under *Fairchild* was for the full extent of the damages, and so does not need to apply to cases prior to *Barker*. Thus the section applies retrospectively to all cases decided or settled between the decision in *Barker* and the enactment of the legislation.

Judicial interpretations of the section have been limited to the context of mesothelioma claims, and so to speak of 'reversing'[94] *Barker* may be accurate.

---

[94] Silber J in *Rice v Secretary of State for Business Enterprise & Regulatory Reform & Anor* [2008] EWHC 3216 (QB) [162]: 'Mr Kent accepts the argument that because Mr Rice's condition of

However, there is a difficulty. The Act only applies to applications of the *Fairchild* principle in asbestos-related mesothelioma cases, whereas, although that was the factual matrix of the claims in *Fairchild* and *Barker*, the exception is expressly not limited to such cases. Indeed, one of the key points in Lord Hoffmann's speech in *Barker* is the recantation of his view in *Fairchild* that the exception could only apply where there was a single causative agent:

> . . .In my opinion it is an essential condition for the operation of the exception that the impossibility of proving that the defendant caused the damage arises out of the existence of another potential causative agent which operated in the same way.[95]

This means that *Barker* must still apply to similar non-asbestos cases, producing an unsatisfactory inconsistency in approach. The focus throughout the Commons and Lords debates was on asbestos-related mesothelioma. Yet mesothelioma may be caused by other things, but the Act would not apply to claims in such contexts, let alone claims arising under the *Fairchild* exception in very different situations. How, then, are we to interpret the common law in the future? It might be argued that, since '[one] assumes that Parliament knows the law',[96] then, if Parliament only wished to prevent the effect of *Barker* in a particular situation in which it would apply, so be it.

But this position is far from satisfactory: we might expect such a legislative affirmation to be more explicit. At no point in the debates was the more general application of *Barker* even adverted to, let alone seriously considered. If the opposition was to the introduction of liability proportionate to contribution to risk where a defendant is liable under *Fairchild*, it is not easy to see why that should be limited to asbestos-related mesothelioma claims. Although the problem has no doubt been raised often in examination questions and academic articles, it is a genuine issue, as recognised by Foskett J, in a thorough judicial consideration of recent authorities on causation:[97] '[*Barker*] was reversed in relation to mesothelioma by virtue of section 3 of the Compensation Act 2006. But the issue remains as to the extent to which the decision could have an impact on analogous cases.'[98]

The Court of Appeal has considered s 3 in *Sienkiewicz v Greif (UK) Ltd*,[99] which concerned a woman who had developed asbestos-related mesothelioma, but had been exposed to asbestos both in her employment and in the general atmosphere.

---

mesothelioma was indivisible, the decision in *Fairchild* . . . provides a special rule whereby each tortfeasor, who is responsible for materially increasing the risk, is treated as having caused the disease. In addition, section 3 of the Compensation Act 2006 (which reverses *Barker* . . .), provides that each tortfeasor is liable in full subject to any right of contribution from any other.'

[95]  *Barker* (n 74) [24].

[96]  Lord Reid in *Rookes v Barnard* [1964] AC 1129, 1174.

[97]  *AB v Ministry of Defence* [2009] EWHC 1225 (QB) [223]–[237].

[98]  ibid [226]. In *Sienkiewicz* (n 29), Lord Clarke of Stone-cum-Ebony noted at [46] that '[whether] the principles applicable in such a case are applicable in other [non-asbestos related mesothelioma] types of case must be left for decision on a case by case basis.'

[99]  *Sienkiewicz* (n 29). Judgment in that case was handed down on 6 November 2009, the day on which this essay was presented at the SLS Seminar.

The difficulty under consideration here was not therefore directly in issue. But Smith LJ did identify some of the incoherence, accepting that 'Parliament did not apply its mind to the possibility that, at some future time, the common law might be declared differently'[100] from how it was in *Fairchild* and *Barker*. The argument here is broader: that Parliament did not apply its mind to the nature, or coherence, of the common law.

The *Fairchild* exception is based on justice and policy considerations, and those considerations should apply wherever the facts justify it. As I have written elsewhere: 'The irony here is that the law has now been rendered even more incoherent than it was in *Barker*, as the general approach to liability, of risk as damage, is untouched by the Act. We have a statutory exception to a common law exception.'[101]

The clear tension between Parliament and the judiciary in such cases is illustrated by the attempts by some MPs, emboldened by the apparent success of s 3, to introduce legislation concerning pleural plaques, which the Court of Appeal had held did not constitute actionable damage.[102] The Government declined to support an amendment, because the House of Lords was to hear the appeal:

> **Bridget Prentice:** I do not believe that it is right for the Government to pre-empt the Law Lords' consideration of those cases by legislating in that way at this time.
>
> **Chris Bryant:** But if the judges get it wrong, which they seem to do quite often, what legislative remedy would be available in the fairly near future?
>
> **Bridget Prentice:** I hope that, with the debates going on here and in the other place and with the careful consideration of the judges, they do not get it wrong.[103]

This is intemperate talk. It is implicit that if the judges do 'get it wrong', a legislative reversal will be swift. It should be recognised that Parliament did have the benefit of helpful insights from David Howarth MP (a Liberal Democrat and a legal academic from the University of Cambridge) and Lord Goodhart (an eminent barrister), but their focus was, understandably, on other issues which were in danger of being overlooked. David Howarth pointed out that any 'reversal' of *Barker* had to consider the second question decided in the case, as to whether *Fairchild* could apply where the claimant himself was responsible for some of the exposure to asbestos.[104] Lord Goodhart was concerned with the retrospectivity in the Bill, but was satisfied that it was justified in the exceptional circumstances.[105]

---

[100] *Sienkiewicz* (n 29) [34]. It is not necessary to consider the point here, but both Smith LJ and Lord Clarke ([18] and [55] respectively) state that the claims under the *Fairchild/Barker* exception are a 'new tort' of increasing the risk of injury, which is controversial: see K Amirthalingam, 'Causation, risk and damage' (2010) 126 *Law Quarterly Review* 162.

[101] J Lee, 'Fidelity in interpretation' (n 82) 12–13.

[102] *Rothwell v Chemical & Insulating Co Ltd & Anor* [2006] EWCA Civ 27, [2006] 4 All ER 1161 ('*Rothwell* (CA)' hereafter).

[103] Bridget Prentice and Chris Bryant: Hansard HC col 49 (17 July 2006). In the *AXA* case (n 144), Lord Emslie observed that '[certain] wayward observations are no doubt to be found' in the Scottish Parliament debates on the Lords' decision in *Rothwell*.

[104] Hansard HC col 43 (17 July 2006). This point is addressed by s 3(2)(i) and s 3(3)(b) of the Compensation Act.

[105] Hansard HC cols 1319–20 (19 July 2006).

His Lordship also made a crucial point, making clear that the House of Lords was entitled to reach the decision which it did in *Barker*: 'It would be incorrect to say that the decision in *Barker v Corus* was wrong. In a sense, no decision of the Appellate Committee of your Lordships' House can be wrong; its members declare the law, and the law, as declared by them, is the law.'[106] Yet even with these important interventions from learned lawyers, there was no mention of the broader causation issues. Instead, we had a former Lord Chancellor hoping that 'legal jargon would in no way deprive those who worked in [the shipbuilding industry] of their undoubted rights.'[107]

It may be that the approach of the legislators here is indicative of a general attitude towards judicial decisions, that it is only the outcome of the case that matters. But each of the cases under examination saw detailed judgments provided by their Lordships, and their reasons matter. As I have argued elsewhere, to treat a decision as a slogan or one-liner is to miss the point,[108] and the provision of concurring opinions is an important feature of the common law tradition.[109] If this point is not appreciated by those who legislate, there are two negative consequences: it will be to the detriment of the coherence of the law, and it will not even achieve the goal of 'reversing' the decision.

We shall close this section by quoting from Lord Hunt of Wirral, who spoke for the Opposition in the House of Lords debate on the amended Compensation Bill:

> I have to say—in sorrow, not anger—that these past few days have not seen the parliamentary process in its best light. A judicial decision of the House's Appellate Committee was made in May; an amendment to overturn it first appeared on the Order Paper last Friday; it was then debated and adopted in another place on Monday; just two days later, here we are debating it in the expectation that it will receive Royal Assent in a matter of days. I fully accept the urgency of this matter—this disease will not indulge us in our deliberations and every day more people are struck down—but it might have been better for the Government to have spent the summer preparing a comprehensive Bill to overhaul the system in a holistic, coherent fashion rather than unbalancing the Bill in this way. . . We are legislating in haste. Let us hope that we do not repent at leisure.[110]

## VI THE ESSENCE OF DAMAGE: *ROTHWELL V CHEMICAL AND INSULATING CO*

It has so far been argued that, while born of noble intentions, s 3 of the Compensation Act represents an unwise Parliamentary incursion into private

---

[106] Hansard HC col 1319 (19 July 2006).

[107] Lord Mackay of Clashfern: Hansard HC col 1322 (19 July 2006).

[108] J Lee, 'Causation in negligence: another fine mess' (2008) 24 *Professional Negligence* 194, 196; J Lee, 'A Defence of Concurring Speeches' [2009] *Public Law* 305, 324.

[109] Lee, 'A Defence of Concurring Speeches' (n 108).

[110] Lord Hunt of Wirral: Hansard HC cols 1318–19 (19 July 2006). The timeline is detailed above at text to n 3.

law. The next example will develop the analysis of such interventions, because it sees a divergence in legislative responses to a decision of the House of Lords.

As was mentioned above, during the Parliamentary debates over *Barker*, some MPs sought to legislate concerning pleural plaques in response to the decision of the Court of Appeal in *Rothwell*.[111] The Government declined to pre-empt the decision of the House of Lords. In *Rothwell v Chemical and Insulating Co Ltd*,[112] the House confirmed the result reached by the Court of Appeal. Their Lordships' approach, however, differed markedly from that of the Court of Appeal, and so we must briefly consider the reasoning of the Lords Justices.

To sue in negligence, a claimant must prove that he has suffered actionable damage. In the *Rothwell* appeals, the common factor was that the claimants had developed pleural plaques as a result of exposure to asbestos. Such plaques are 'localised areas of pleural thickening with well demarcated edges',[113] which in fewer than 1 per cent of cases produce any symptoms. The claimants' argument on appeal was that, although 'the development of pleural plaques is insufficiently significant, of itself, to constitute damage upon which a claim in negligence can be founded',[114] when such plaques were 'aggregated' with the risk of future disease (as a result of the prior exposure to asbestos) and associated anxiety, they ought to succeed. By a majority, the Court of Appeal held that this argument could not succeed, because the 'three heads of claim . . . individually could not found a cause of action',[115] and so the claimants could not conjure actionable damage by adding them together. In addition, the majority in the Court of Appeal (Lord Phillips CJ and Longmore LJ) were expressly persuaded that 'there are a number of reasons of policy why it is undesirable that the development of pleural plaques should give rise to a cause of action',[116] such as the encouragement of litigation, which might not be in the best interests of the claimant.

Smith LJ dissented. Her Ladyship disapproved of the majority's approach to the question of aggregation:

> [T]he majority has concluded that the question can and should be determined by policy considerations. I do not agree and consider that the question can and should be answered by the application of established legal principle to a new factual situation.[117]

Such a demand for principle over policy is distinctly Dworkinian,[118] although Smith LJ stated that she disagreed with the majority on the policy considerations

---

[111] *Rothwell* (CA) (n 102).

[112] *Rothwell v Chemical and Insulating Co Ltd* [2007] UKHL 39 ('*Rothwell* (HL)' hereafter).

[113] *Rothwell* (CA) (n 102) [10].

[114] *Rothwell* (CA) (n 102) [23].

[115] *Rothwell* (CA) (n 102) [68].

[116] *Rothwell* (CA) (n 102) [67].

[117] *Rothwell* (CA) (n 102) [112]. This is certainly the most natural interpretation of the majority's view, but it may not be what was intended. It may be that their Lordships only invoked policy because they thought that principle was clearly against allowing the claim: 'Nor can we see any justification for departing from logic or legal principle in the specific case of asbestos induced pleural plaques.' *Rothwell* (CA) (n 102) [68].

[118] J Lee, 'Fidelity in interpretation' (n 82) 4.

in any case.[119] Smith LJ's principled reasoning focused on the risk of future illness: the development of pleural plaques completes a cause of action because, by then the claimant 'was already subject to appreciable risks of other serious conditions arising from the same wrongful act.'[120]

The claimants appealed to the House of Lords.[121] Their Lordships dismissed the appeals, on the basis explained by Lord Rodger:

> Taken by themselves . . . the plaques are benign and asymptomatic. So, even assuming that the plaques could constitute a relevant 'injury' to the claimants' bodies, they do not cause them any material damage and so do not give rise to a cause of action.[122]

But it is worth observing that several of their Lordships sympathised with Smith LJ's disapproval of the majority's emphasis on policy. Lord Hoffmann, who may or may not be a Dworkinian,[123] referred to those policy arguments and confessed

> that some of these seemed to me rather speculative and I am inclined to agree with Smith LJ who said in her dissenting judgment . . . that 'the question can and should be answered by the application of established legal principle to a new factual situation'. But I respectfully disagree with Smith LJ about that principle. . .[124]

The claims therefore failed. Following their Lordships' decision, many of the same MPs who were active in the Compensation Act debates sought its reversal through statute, relying on the precedent set by the Compensation Act.


## VII 'SPECIOUS EMBELLISHMENT'? LEGISLATIVE RESPONSE TO *ROTHWELL*

### A  Holyrood: The Low Road?

Seven weeks after the Lords' decision in *Rothwell*, the Scottish Government announced its intention to legislate to ensure that those who had developed asbestos-related pleural plaques would continue to be able to recover in Scotland.[125] Significantly, reliance was placed on the passage of the Compensation Bill.[126] It is important that emergency legislation to reverse specific decisions of our highest court, now the Supreme Court, does not become the norm: the invocation of the

---

[119]  *Rothwell* (CA) (n 102) [136]–[146].

[120]  *Rothwell* (CA) (n 102) [135].

[121]  On the decision generally, see G Turton, 'Defining Damage in the House of Lords' (2008) 71 *Modern Law Review* 1009.

[122]  *Rothwell* (HL) (n 112) [88].

[123]  J Lee, 'Fidelity in interpretation' (n 82).

[124]  *Rothwell* (HL) (n 112) [17]. Similarly, Lord Hope observed, [50]: 'I am not attracted by the other reasons of policy that led the majority in the Court of Appeal to the conclusion that it was undesirable that the development of pleural plaques should give rise to a cause of action'.

[125]  'Asbestos claims bill planned', 29 November 2007: www.scotland.gov.uk/News/Releases/2007/11/29102156.

[126]  See, eg, Frank Maguire, Scottish Parliament Justice Committee, Official Report col 1083 (2 September 2008).

2006 Act as a precedent demonstrates that legislative incursions prove to be self-perpetuating. Any such interventions are, and must be, exceptional.

Dr Martin Hogg, one of the leading British authorities on causation and damages, provided a frankly devastating critique of the proposals, a developed version of which has since been published in *Scots Law Times*.[127] Hogg concluded that the Bill's passage would be a 'regrettable development', most importantly because it would 'solidify an impression increasingly given that politicians are in too great a hurry to interfere with a settled and sensible common law which has demonstrated its utility, good sense and justice over a great many years.'[128]

During the Justice Committee stage of the Bill, Hogg was called to give oral evidence. In a valiant attempt to contribute to the process of law reform, he argued:

> Doing things a little bit at a time is not, in my opinion, a coherent way of reforming the law. . . [Only to consider asbestos-related pleural plaques] would mean tinkering with well-established rules about when someone has suffered a personal injury . . . [P]icking out one condition, for no apparent reason as far as I can see—apart from its producing the greatest number of cases—does not give a good impression on the international stage.[129]

This evidence was not sympathetically received. Shortly after Hogg was thanked, Frank Maguire, a lawyer who has acted for victims of asbestos exposure in Scotland, gave evidence. He classified Hogg as being 'very much in the judicial supremacy area, which says, "Let judges get on with it. Do not interfere with them, whatever conclusions they come up with"'.[130] This is a canny argument, as members of a devolved government and legislature are understandably sensitive to any suggestion that their powers should be limited. But in truth, it is not simply a question of legislative power: just because the Scottish Parliament *can* legislate in response to a particular decision, does not mean that it ought to do so. Respecting the principle of legislative integrity requires value to be given to coherence. If asking for a coherent approach is taken to be anti-democratic, then what is an academic or lawyer to do?

We may draw an analogy with the former position of the Lords of Appeal in Ordinary during legislative debates in the House. In his article on the role of the Law Lords in Parliament, Lord Hope quotes[131] Viscount Sumner's opening to his speech during the second reading debate on Lord Gorell's Law of Libel Amendment Bill in March 1927:

> My Lords, it is a little difficult to know how your Lordships would like a Bill of this kind to be treated in debate. This is a Bill to alter in a material respect the Common Law of this country. Which do your Lordships think is the better course to pursue:

---

[127] M Hogg, 'Asbestos related conditions and the idea of damage in the law of delict' (2008) 31 *Scots Law Times* 207.

[128] ibid 212.

[129] Scottish Parliament Justice Committee, Official Report col 1072 (2 September 2008).

[130] ibid col 1083.

[131] Hope, 'Voices from the Past' (n 23) 554.

that those members of your Lordships' House who bear the somewhat invidious title of Law Lords should regard themselves as called upon to advise your Lordships to the best of their ability on such subject, or that they should recognise that law lectures are more appropriate to some other place than your Lordships' House?

Are, then, those qualified to give 'law lectures' during the passage of legislation forever to be viewed with disfavour? Are arguments for coherence when material alterations to the common law are contemplated merely to be viewed as the Canute-like rantings of judicial supremacists? Perhaps. The Scottish Parliament pressed ahead with the legislation and enacted the Damages (Asbestos-related Conditions) (Scotland) Act 2009. The Act provides, so far as material, as follows:

**1   Pleural plaques**

(1)   Asbestos-related pleural plaques are a personal injury which is not negligible.

(2)   Accordingly, they constitute actionable harm for the purposes of an action of damages for personal injuries.

(3)   Any rule of law the effect of which is that asbestos-related pleural plaques do not constitute actionable harm ceases to apply to the extent it has that effect.

(4)   But nothing in this section otherwise affects any enactment or rule of law which determines whether and in what circumstances a person may be liable in damages in respect of personal injuries.

**2   Pleural thickening and asbestosis**

(1)   For the avoidance of doubt, a condition mentioned in subsection (2) which has not caused and is not causing impairment of a person's physical condition is a personal injury which is not negligible.

(2)   Those conditions are—

(a)   asbestos-related pleural thickening; and

(b)   asbestosis.

(3)   Accordingly, such a condition constitutes actionable harm for the purposes of an action of damages for personal injuries.

(4)   Any rule of law the effect of which is that such a condition does not constitute actionable harm ceases to apply to the extent it has that effect.

(5)   But nothing in this section otherwise affects any enactment or rule of law which determines whether and in what circumstances a person may be liable in damages in respect of personal injuries.

. . .

**4   Commencement and retrospective effect**

(1)   This Act (other than this subsection and section 5) comes into force on such day as the Scottish Ministers may, by order made by statutory instrument, appoint.

(2)   Sections 1 and 2 are to be treated for all purposes as having always had effect.

(3)   But those sections have no effect in relation to—

(a)   a claim which is settled before the date on which subsection (2) comes into force (whether or not legal proceedings in relation to the claim have been commenced); or

(b)   legal proceedings which are determined before that date.

We see here the perpetually ironic draftsman's phrase, 'For the avoidance of doubt'. Has the decision in *Rothwell* been reversed? There is not quite the same confusion as was seen with the Compensation Act. Through ss 1(4) and 2(5), it is clear that the Act is not to affect any other aspect of the law of delict: the only intended alteration is that, notwithstanding the general position, pleural plaques and related thickening are to be viewed as an actionable injury.

Is this a checkerboard solution? Yes: the exception is one of policy, not principle. It is the same as Dworkin's example of singling out automobile manufacturers. Where the claimant has suffered an asymptomatic and non-external change, there is a statutory regime imposing liability on those defendants if the exposure was to asbestos, when they would not be liable if they had exposed the claimant to a different noxious substance. Hogg offers a list of such possible substances,[132] and concludes that 'there is nothing which makes asbestos special, save that it may have a more vociferous lobby pressing for a right to compensation.'[133] Thus, that asbestos gives rise to horrific diseases and that there are several prominent advocacy groups, including trade unions, who fight on behalf of victims of such exposure, provides an explanation for the distinction: it does not provide a justification. Lobbyists do not only work on behalf of the sick: the defendant-friendly reversal of the *Perruche* decision mentioned earlier was the result of 'fierce political lobbying by medical insurers'.[134] For Dworkin, this characteristic demonstrates that legislators are 'not institutionally better placed to decide questions about rights than judges are'[135] because 'in [some] cases legislators are subject to pressures that judges are not, and this must count as a reason for supposing that, at least in such cases, judges are more likely to reach sound conclusions about rights.'[136]

If there were any judicial indignation at the reversal by the Damages (Asbestos-related Conditions) (Scotland) Act, the Scottish courts soon had the opportunity to retaliate. In *Re Application for Judicial Review (Asbestos-Related Conditions) (Scotland) Act 2009*,[137] various insurance companies brought a petition for judicial review before Lord Glennie, on the grounds that the Act was 'outwith the legislative competence of the Scottish Parliament on the grounds of its incompatibility with certain Convention rights'.[138] The petitioners sought an interim interdict to prevent the Scottish Ministers from bringing the Act into force before the validity of the Act could be determined at a hearing. Lord Glennie noted that '*Rothwell* was perceived as having changed the law

---

[132] Hogg, 'Asbestos related conditions' (n 127) 210–11: 'coal dust is productive of coalworkers' pneumoconiosis, or "black lung" disease as it is sometimes called, silica dust of silicosis, bauxite dust of bauxite fibrosis, beryllium dust of berylliosis, cotton dust of byssinosis, and a mixture of silica and iron of silicosiderosis, among others.'

[133] ibid.

[134] KA Warner, 'Wrongful life goes down under' (2007) 123 *Law Quarterly Review* 209.

[135] Dworkin, 'Political Judges and the Rule of Law' (n 31) 25.

[136] ibid.

[137] *Re Application for Judicial Review (Asbestos-Related Conditions) (Scotland) Act 2009* [2009] CSOH 57.

[138] ibid [1].

and deprived a large number of claimants and potential claimants of their (*ex hypothesi* justifiable) right to compensation. Whether or not this is an accurate characterisation of the decision in *Rothwell* is beside the point.'[139] (Or exactly the point, depending.)

The petitioners, represented by the Dean of the Faculty of Advocates, argued that 'These cases, or at least this issue in these cases, are being decided not by an independent and impartial tribunal established by law, as was required by Article 6 of the Convention, but by legislative fiat.'[140] His Lordship concluded that the petitioners had a prima facie arguable case on this point. However, Lord Glennie accepted the submission of Mr Dewar QC, counsel for Scottish Ministers, that 'it was always within the competence of the Scottish Parliament to alter the Scottish law of delict. I accept this, insofar as the Act has prospective effect.'[141] Given that the petitioners were asking the court to 'call a temporary halt to the democratic process',[142] his Lordship did not believe that the challenge appeared to be sufficiently strong to 'overcome the court's reluctance to interfere with the acts of a democratically elected body'.[143] Therefore an interim interdict was not granted and the Scottish Ministers were able to bring the Act into force.

Scottish Parliamentarians will also be heartened that, when the proceedings reached the Outer House,[144] Lord Emslie held that the petitions had to be dismissed. He held that the insurers could not invoke art 6, as they were not parties to pending disputes.[145] Nor could the claimants invoke art 1 of the First Protocol, as the non-actionability of pleural plaques, classified as an 'immunity', was not a property right within the ECHR jurisprudence.[146] Even if he had held that these rights were engaged, his Lordship would have held

> [with] the greatest of respect to their Lordships, [that] there is nothing intrinsically unreasonable or outrageous about legislation which seeks to alter or reverse the effects of a judicial ruling at any level.[147]

The argument in this chapter is not that there *is* 'anything *intrinsically* unreasonable or outrageous' in legislative reversals. It is more nuanced than that: it is that respect for coherence and legislative integrity leads to better and more effective legislation. An illustration of the consequences of the two interventions considered here emerges from *AXA*. Lord Emslie's view of the 2009 Act was that, '[by] removing a medico-legal barrier, it allows affected individuals to assert a delictual cause of action against negligent former employers. It does

---

[139]  ibid [7].
[140]  ibid [11].
[141]  ibid [12].
[142]  ibid [19].
[143]  ibid [19]–[20].
[144]  *AXA General Insurance Ltd* (n 59). The other, difficult, public law challenges in the case, which also failed, need not be considered here: see T Mullen, 'The *AXA Insurance* case: challenging Acts of the Scottish Parliament for irrationality' [2010] *Scots Law Times* 39.
[145]  *AXA General Insurance Ltd* (n 59) [163].
[146]  ibid [191].
[147]  ibid [206].

not otherwise bear to affect the outcome of any claim.'[148] We should therefore note that the Scots Act does not purport to say anything about causation. Section 3 of the Compensation Act extends to Scotland.[149] It may well be that, where a claim is brought against one of several former employers for pleural plaques, and the claimant has to rely on *Fairchild*, the claim may be limited to proportionate recovery under *Barker*, which, as noted earlier, was only partially reversed by the 2006 Act. So, again, the absence of a coherent approach may leave a significant lacuna.

## B Westminster: The High Road?

Andrew Dismore, a Labour MP, introduced a private Member's Bill at Westminster, the Damages (Asbestos-Related Conditions) Bill, closely modelled on the Scots legislation, although the Bill omitted the 'not negligible' provision, beginning 'Asbestos-related pleural plaques are a personal injury which constitute actionable damage'.[150] In a debate on the Bill, Mr Dismore described the House's decision in *Rothwell* as 'weird and wonderful', and again invoked the Compensation Act precedent.[151] With the calling of the 2010 General Election, the 2009–10 session of Parliament prorogued and the Bill will thus make no further progress.

The Bill did not have the support of the UK Government. Instead, the Government's response to *Rothwell* was rather more circumspect. Indeed, the Secretary of State for Justice and Lord Chancellor stated that it ought not to follow that, merely because the Scots had legislated, so should the English: 'it is the essence of devolution that different decisions can be made. It would be very curious indeed if the result of devolution was that each jurisdiction had to follow the decisions of the other.'[152] In 2008, a consultation paper was produced by the Ministry of Justice, expressing the provisional view that a legislative reaction to *Rothwell* would not be appropriate. This position was eventually confirmed by the Secretary of State in March 2010,[153] in a short statement affirming the Labour Government's position, albeit announcing a 'Limited extra-statutory scheme' making ex gratia payments of £5,000 to those who had begun claims for pleural plaques prior to the Lords' decision in *Rothwell*. Given the brevity of that statement, reliance here will be placed on the arguments for the Government's view in the consultation paper.

---

[148] ibid [196].

[149] s 3(6).

[150] The Bill is available here: www.publications.parliament.uk/pa/ld200809/ldbills/072/09072.i-i.html.

[151] Hansard HC col 561 (16 October 2009).

[152] Hansard HC col 742 (21 July 2009), although during the debate on Andrew Dismore's Bill, Bridget Prentice MP, the relevant Minister, seemed to suggest that the Northern Irish position may have complicated the Government's attempts to formulate a response: Hansard HC col 563 (16 October 2009).

[153] Jack Straw statement (n 5).

One of the reasons was the unanimity of the House in *Rothwell*. If that is a threshold criterion, then there is a danger that it may have an insidious effect on judicial practice: whether a judge dissents or not should not be influenced by the prospect of inviting a legislative reversal of a majority decision of the highest court in the land. In *Barker*, Lord Rodger was the lone dissentient in the outcome. But unanimity as to result is not the same as univocality.[154] What is the relevance of Lady Justice Smith's dissent in the Court of Appeal, to which Lord Hope paid tribute,[155] although he disagreed with her reasoning?[156] For that matter, what of concurring opinions?[157]

Another argument offered by the Government against reversing *Rothwell* was the intricacy of the question of actionability of damage for the law of negligence. The issues involved in the claims are indeed complex: *Rothwell* has since been cited in several English decisions which have nothing to do with asbestos exposure. In *Pegasus Management Holdings v Ernst & Young*,[158] *Rothwell* was cited as authority for the proposition that 'the mere fact that a risk of loss existed was not itself a loss' (albeit that Lewison J doubted its utility on the facts of the professional negligence before him). Another case in which *Rothwell* was cited is *D Pride & Partners v Institute for Animal Health*[159] a case concerning claims by farmers for damages for the losses they alleged that they had suffered as a result of the tortious conduct of defendants which caused a leak of live foot-and-mouth disease virus. None of the claimants' livestock had been culled: the defendants disputed the claimants' right to claim for the loss of condition of the cows, and prayed *Rothwell* in aid for their argument.[160] Tugendhat J accepted that the majority of their claims were for pure economic loss and held that they had no reasonable prospect of success.[161]

Just as with *Barker* above, the attempt to 'reverse' the decision is imprecise: the focus is upon the application of the law to the facts of the instant decision, without sufficient regard to the fact that the decision establishes (or reiterates) matters of legal principle which have further implications beyond the question of whether a particular claim succeeds. However, it has been argued that there was complexity in the issues relating to causation and the actionability of 'risk as damage' raised by *Barker*, which have wider implications than were appreciated during the passage of the Compensation Act.

It was noted above that the Government hoped that their Lordships in *Rothwell* would not 'get it wrong', and so they did not wish to pre-empt the decision. But such a position is utterly inappropriate: it is akin to Dionysius ordering the

---

[154] See generally, J Lee, 'Fidelity in interpretation' (n 82).

[155] *Rothwell* (HL) (n 112) [48] (Lord Hope of Craighead).

[156] Brenda Barrett notes that, though in disagreement, 'their Lordships deemed it necessary expressly to address [Smith LJ's] reasoning': [2009] *Journal of Business Law* 229, 240.

[157] J Lee, 'A Defence of Concurring Speeches' (n 108).

[158] *Pegasus Management Holdings SCA v Ernst & Young* [2008] EWHC 2720 (Ch) [99].

[159] *D Pride & Partners (a firm) & Ors v Institute for Animal Health* [2009] EWHC 685 (QB).

[160] ibid [59].

[161] ibid [127].

shining sword to be suspended above the head of Damocles in order to teach him a lesson. It is unwise and constitutionally dangerous for the threat of a legislative reversal to be in the minds of the judiciary when they are deciding cases.

We have adverted throughout this paper to the problem of checkerboard statutes. If we now revisit the case of *Chapman*,[162] we can place some pieces onto our checkerboard. In *Chapman*, Lord Morton of Henryton observed that if the Chancery judges were inclined to authorise variations 'the way would be open for a most undignified game of chess between the Chancery Division and the legislature.' His Lordship continued:

> The alteration of one settlement for the purposes of avoiding taxation already imposed might well be followed by scores of successful applications for a similar purpose by beneficiaries under other settlements. The legislature might then counter this move by imposing fresh taxation upon the settlements as thus altered. The beneficiaries would then troop back to the Chancery Division . . . So the game might go on, if the judges of the Chancery Division had the power which the appellants claim for them, and if they thought it right to make the first move.[163]

## VIII 'ALL THE RAGE OF MODERN IMPROVEMENT'? CONSEQUENCES FOR LAW REFORM

The objection here has been to 'inconsiderate alterations in our laws'. In neither of the episodes above did Parliament have the benefit of a Report from the Law Commission, the provision of which might be thought to offer hope for more considerate alterations. What, however, does this survey suggest for the future of law reform in the age of the Supreme Court?

Anyone involved in the law will recognise the truth in Jonathan Morgan's observation that the 'lack of time in the legislative timetable for law reform is notorious: even Law Commission reports regularly gather dust, despite being ready for off-the-shelf implementation.'[164] Let us take an example from the field of negligence claims for psychiatric harm.

In the 1990s, the House of Lords considered claims for psychiatric harm in several cases. In *Alcock v Chief Constable of South Yorkshire Police*,[165] the claimants were relatives of those who died in the Hillsborough stadium disaster. The House of Lords unanimously adopted restrictive criteria which severely limited the ability of relatives such as the claimants to recover. In a subsequent decision,[166] the Court of Appeal held that police officers, qua their status as

---

[162] *Chapman* (n 63).

[163] *Chapman* (n 63), 468. Lord Templeman invoked the same game in the public law context in *R v Secretary of State for the Environment ex p Nottinghamshire CC* [1986] AC 240, 267: 'Judicial review is not just a move in an interminable chess tournament'. See S Lee, 'Understanding judicial review as a game of chess' (1986) 102 *Law Quarterly Review* 493.

[164] J Morgan, 'Policy reasoning in tort law: the courts, the Law Commission and the critics' (2009) 125 *Law Quarterly Review* 215, 220.

[165] *Alcock v Chief Constable of South Yorkshire Police* [1992] 1 AC 310, [1991] 3 WLR 1057.

[166] *Frost v Chief Constable of South Yorkshire Police* [1998] QB 254, [1997] 3 WLR 1194.

rescuers, could recover for psychiatric harm as a result of witnessing the disaster. The contrast between the failure of the families and the success of the individual police officers, when the disaster had been caused by the police's negligence, drew adverse headlines[167] and an Early Day Motion in Parliament.[168] The Law Commission produced a report[169] proposing reforms, but shortly afterwards the case was appealed to the Lords. In *White v Chief Constable of South Yorkshire Police*,[170] the House of Lords by a bare majority allowed the appeals. Both the majority and minority[171] paid tribute to the Law Commission's report.

Having surveyed the area, Lord Steyn concluded that there were 'no refined analytical tools which will enable the courts to draw lines by way of compromise solution in a way which is coherent and morally defensible. It must be left to Parliament to undertake the task of radical law reform.'[172] Lord Hoffmann was another member of the majority, who declined to

> enter further into the merits of the various proposals for reform because neither of the radical solutions, or indeed the Law Commission solution, is open to your Lordships. It is too late to go back on the control mechanisms as stated in the *Alcock* case [1992] 1 AC 310. Until there is legislative change, the courts must live with them and any judicial developments must take them into account.[173]

So the highest court in the land expressly pointed to Parliament, drawing a line under judicial development of the law. But, in reversing the Court of Appeal's unpopular decision, any political capital to be made out of reforming the law disappeared. Psychiatric harm was also an issue in *Grieves v Everard*, one of the conjoined appeals in *Rothwell*. Mr Grieves's anxiety (at being told that he had a significant risk of developing an asbestos-related disease) had developed into clinical depression. His claim failed. Lord Hope invoked *White's* 'cautionary advice'[174] about changing the law in the area, notwithstanding the non-implementation of the Law Commission's report in the intervening period.

---

[167] See the Law Commission's Report (n 169) 1, fn 1 and 2, fn 5: 'An editorial, "Putting safety first—at last", published in *The Guardian* on 5 June 1996 suggested that the relatives of Hillsborough victims had every reason to feel affronted following substantial out-of-court settlements in favour of police who entered the affected pens, when the relatives had received only "paltry sums" or nothing at all.'

[168] ibid, 2, fn 6, referring to EDM 121 1996/1997.

[169] Law Commission, 'Liability for Psychiatric Illness' (Law Com No 249, 1998).

[170] *White v Chief Constable of South Yorkshire Police* [1998] 3 WLR 1509; [1999] 2 AC 455.

[171] ibid [1999] 2 AC 455, 469 (Lord Goff).

[172] ibid 500. In full: 'In my view the only sensible general strategy for the courts is to say thus far and no further. The only prudent course is to treat the pragmatic categories as reflected in authoritative decisions such as *Alcock* and *Page v Smith* as settled for the time being but by and large to leave any expansion or development in this corner of the law to Parliament. In reality there are no refined analytical tools which will enable the courts to draw lines by way of compromise solution in a way which is coherent and morally defensible. It must be left to Parliament to undertake the task of radical law reform.'

[173] ibid 504.

[174] *Rothwell* (HL) (n 112) [54]. For further consideration of the state of the law on psychiatric harm, see J Lee, 'The fertile imagination of the common law: *Yearworth v North Bristol NHS Trust*' (2009) 17 *Torts Law Journal* 130.

The Government eventually offered a reply, a decade later, to the Law Commission's Report, first in a Department for Constitutional Affairs Consultation Paper,[175] and then a final response from the Ministry of Justice:

> The arguments in this complex and sensitive area are finely balanced. On balance the Government continues to take the view that it is preferable for the courts to have the flexibility to continue to develop the law rather than attempt to impose a statutory solution.[176]

It is not clear why the Government hesitated here but not elsewhere: I have attempted to show above that legislative reversals of judicial decisions may often be seen as 'complex and sensitive', with finely balanced arguments either side.

In another of the latter decisions of the House of Lords,[177] Baroness Hale reflected: 'My experience at the Law Commission has shown me how difficult it is to achieve flexible and nuanced reform to a rule of the common law by way of legislation.'[178] Given such difficulty, both in the initial proposition of reform and then seeking its implementation, it is possible that the Justices of the Supreme Court might adopt a more proactive stance to the reform of the law if they think that no legislative assistance will be forthcoming. The appropriate approach has been the subject of recent disagreement amongst their Lordships. In *Stack v Dowden*,[179] a majority of the House of Lords decided to develop the law applying to the proprietary rights of unmarried cohabitants, notwithstanding the imminent publication of the Law Commission's final report on the consequences of relationship breakdown.[180] Lord Walker, for the majority, took the view that, since a previous decision of the House of Lords,

> the law has moved on, and your Lordships should move it a little more in the same direction, while bearing in mind that the Law Commission may soon come forward with proposals which, if enacted by Parliament, may recast the law in this area.[181]

Lord Neuberger, though agreeing on the outcome of the case, disagreed with the majority's reasoning, and on the appropriateness of developing the law in anticipation of the Commission's Report. Furthermore, his Lordship suggested that different arguments are suitable for the courts as opposed to the legislature, and that the issue was one of institutional competence. In its Discussion Paper, the Law Commission concluded that it was impossible to draw up a scheme 'which can operate fairly and evenly across the diversity of domestic circumstances which are now to be encountered'.[182] Lord Neuberger viewed this statement as:

---

[175] Department for Constitutional Affairs, 'The Law of Damages' (CP(R) 9/07), paras 82–83.

[176] Ministry of Justice, 'The Law of Damages: Response to consultation' (CP(R) 9/07) 51.

[177] *Chartbrook Ltd v Persimmon Homes Ltd* [2009] UKHL 38, [2009] 1 AC 1101.

[178] ibid [99].

[179] *Stack v Dowden* [2007] UKHL 17, [2007] 2 AC 432, [2007] 2 WLR 831, [2007] 2 All ER 929.

[180] Law Commission, 'Cohabitation: The Financial Consequences of Relationship Breakdown' (Law Com No 307, 2007).

[181] [2007] UKHL 17 [26]. See also [47]–[48] (Baroness Hale).

[182] Law Commission, 'Sharing Homes: a Discussion Paper' (July 2002) para 1.31

a warning shot against the courts (as opposed to the legislature) refashioning the law. All the more so bearing in mind that. . . the Law Commission may soon make specific proposals for change in this area. In other words, the Law Commission's analysis may well justify the legislature changing the law in this field, but it does not support similar intervention by the courts, other than for the purpose of clarification and simplification.[183]

When the Law Commission did publish its report, it managed to take into account the House of Lords' decision, and concluded that the need for statutory intervention remained:[184]

Like all cases in this field, *Stack v Dowden* dealt with a particular set of facts, applying and developing general principles of property and trust law. The case is far from offering, and does not purport to offer, a comprehensive solution to the hardships that can arise for cohabitants on separation.[185]

On this view, the fact that the courts can only proceed incrementally on the basis of the facts before the court limits their ability to reform the law in the necessary way. In fact, the majority's approach in *Stack* was to establish a general rule (a presumption of equal beneficial ownership) and then find that the instant decision was an exception to it (the beneficial interest was divided 65:35 in favour of Ms Dowden).

With such thoughts in mind, it is a significant coincidence that, immediately after the Third Reading of the Damages (Asbestos-Related Conditions) Bill 2008–09, another Bill had its report stage on the floor of the Commons: the Bill which became the Law Commission Act 2009.[186] This short Act, described as 'small but perfectly formed',[187] has inserted two amended sections into the Law Commission Act 1965, governing the relationship between Government and the Law Commission. The Bill was a private Member's Bill, introduced by Lord Lloyd of Berwick, a former Law Lord who continues to be very active in the House's debates, in order 'to hold the Government to account in relation to the important subject of law reform'.[188]

Sir Kenneth Keith has diagnosed that often in the process of law reform, the right question is not asked: 'too narrow a question is likely to lead to a wilderness of single instances in the statute book, governed by no clear principle, threatening established values and producing apparently arbitrary results.'[189] I have argued that when statute follows a particular decision, Parliament ought to intervene

---

[183]    *Stack* (n 179) [104]–[105].

[184]    Law Commission, 'Cohabitation' (n 180) para 2.12 ff.

[185]    ibid para 2.14.

[186]    16 October 2009.

[187]    Emily Thornberry MP in the House of Commons Public Bill Committee, Column 10, 8 July 2009.

[188]    House of Lords 24 Apr 2009: Column 1735. The late Lord Kingsland put it more bluntly: 'In effect, the Government have got to put up or shut up about Law Commission proposals.' Pursuant to the Act, the Law Commission and the Lord Chancellor have agreed a Protocol governing their relationship: www.lawcom.gov.uk/docs/lc321_web.pdf.

[189]    Keith (n 2) 364.

in a way which pursues, rather than forsakes, coherence. The examples above show that in the area of law reform, the 'dialogue' does not always work. In the psychiatric harm context, all sides seem to be expecting the other to act. On cohabitation, there is a rush to act first. In both areas, the chess-game ends in stalemate.

## IX CONCLUSIONS

In the *Fairchild* decision, Lord Nicholls cautioned that '[to] be acceptable the law must be coherent. It must be principled.'[190] That neatly summarises the theme of this essay. It has been argued that the reactions to two significant private law decisions of the House of Lords have failed to display legislative integrity. The legislative enactments represent checkerboard solutions.

Professor Cane alleges that 'Accusations that legislative modifications of common-law rules are arbitrary and unprincipled typically rest on a normative objection to the particular balance the legislature has struck between competing interests.'[191] It is crucial to stress that I do not see my argument as based on a normative objection to the particular balance struck: my objection is that the executive and legislative engagement with the relevant decisions betray a fundamental lack of desire or respect for the coherence of the law. Nor is it an *ad homines* argument against particular legislators: on the contrary, the works of MacCormick and Dworkin provide an explanation of how we can reasonably disagree with a legislative enactment which does not seem to offend against fairness.

For Dworkin, our intuitive disapproval of checkerboard statutes, such as the Compensation Act 2006 and the Damages (Asbestos-Related Conditions) (Scotland) Act 2009, is because they involve the state 'acting in an unprincipled way, even though no single official who voted for or enforces the compromise has done anything which, judging his individual actions by the ordinary standards of personal morality, he ought not to have done.'[192] For MacCormick, our task is to try to make sense of the law, and the difference between the legislator and the judge (or academic) may be one of perspective:

> A statute represents a new input into an already ongoing legal system. So to make sense of the newly-enacted law one has to read it in the light of the existing legal system to see what it has changed and how the new rules enacted can best make sense in the light of the continuing-but-altered legal system. Not surprisingly, a lawyer's or a judge's understanding of the enacted law may well be different from that of politicians who participated in enacting it as law. It will certainly be formed in a different context, based on awareness of the law more than on attention to a particular political programme.[193]

[190] [2002] UKHL 22 [36].
[191] Cane, 'Taking Disagreement Seriously' (n 16) 414.
[192] Dworkin, *Law's Empire* (n 32) 183.
[193] MacCormick, *Institutions* (n 42) 178.

Thus we find that legislative responses to the decisions in *Barker v Corus* and *Rothwell v CIC*, while commanding widespread Parliamentary support and motivated by understandable concerns for victims of exposure to asbestos, have nevertheless introduced incoherence to the law. These incidents fail to display legislative integrity because of a disregard for principle. The incoherence from s 3 of the Compensation Act 2006 resulted from an apparent lack of consideration, let alone understanding, of the nature of the exception recognised in *Fairchild*. While the UK Government's more measured response to *Rothwell* is less alarming, it is hard to reconcile the new approach with the attitude adopted towards *Barker*. Indeed, the Scottish Parliament has already acted to reverse *Rothwell*, relying, as seen above, on the previous example set by s 3 of the Compensation Act.

What is more, it would appear that the politicians are developing principles which they intend to determine when it is appropriate for Parliament to intervene to reverse a particular decision, without any consistent basis. During a debate on pleural plaques, the Minister justified the Labour Government's disinclination to legislate, citing 'the complexities of the problems involved [which] explains why we have taken far longer to come up with a plan for pleural plaques than for mesothelioma, which was a much more straightforward case.'[194] It has been demonstrated that the problems were not straightforward in either *Barker* or *Rothwell*. These purported legislative reversals of two decisions are unhappy interventions, based on an apparent misunderstanding of, or a reluctance to engage with, the complexities of the legal issues involved. Let us return to Blackstone. The danger is that Parliament's attempts to reverse specific private law decisions often result in mischievous and inconsiderate alterations in our law.

---

[194] Bridget Prentice: Hansard HC col 269WH (4 June 2008).

# 6

# (Dis)owning the Convention
# in the Law of Tort

JENNY STEELE*

## I INTRODUCTION

ARDEN LJ HAS described the influence of the Human Rights Act (HRA) on the law of tort as a neglected aspect of its overall impact.[1] In some ways this appears odd, since the transformative effect of Convention rights on certain areas of civil liability has provoked intermittent political controversy,[2] as well as more consistent academic interest. It remains true, however, that there has not been any *general* retrospective assessment of the effect of the HRA on the law of tort.[3] Analysis has tended to focus on one part of the field or another, usually where there has been some exciting development (such as the emergence of privacy as a protected interest), or some puzzling lack of development, without attempting to identify or make sense of the fuller picture.

Equally importantly, given the purpose of the present volume, neither has there been particular cause to focus on the role of the House of Lords specifically. In this chapter, it is on the record of the House of Lords in respect of Convention rights that I focus, asking what the overall pattern of development shows when it is broadened to the whole law of tort, but narrowed to a focus on the House of Lords per se. This, in turn, yields some insights into the approach of the House to the Convention rights. These insights however relate specifically to their use in the context of *civil liability*. In other words the analysis may reveal as much

---

* Thanks are due to colleagues at York Law School for discussion of the ideas at a seminar in October 2009, and to Richard Mullender and TT Arvind for most valuable comments on a draft. I would also like to thank Richard Clayton, James Lee and Gavin Phillipson for their part in the session at which this paper was presented at the 'Judges and Jurists' seminar, London, November 2009.

[1] Arden LJ, 'Human Rights and Civil Wrongs: Tort Law Under the Spotlight' [2010] *Public Law* 140.

[2] Not surprisingly, given the ability of the media to create and sustain controversy, this has been particularly apparent in respect of developments which restrict media freedom.

[3] J Wright, *Tort Law and Human Rights* (Oxford, Hart Publishing, 2001) was published early in the career of the Act. It predicted a failure to give appropriate effect to the rights in the law of tort, but for very different reasons from those identified here (see further n 67 and associated text). The second edition is due for publication in December 2010.

about the attitude of the House to the law of tort, as about its attitude to the new role of Convention rights.

In the 11 years between enactment of the HRA and the end of the Judicial Committee, members of the House disagreed about many aspects of the HRA. In relation to the law of tort, however, disagreements of principle have been allowed to overshadow an underlying consistency in the overall pattern of development. Oddly, given the nature of the Convention,[4] it is in 'horizontal' cases that there has been most change in the law of tort.[5] Attention to these alone might give the false impression that wholesale change has been initiated by the HRA. But in 'vertical' cases meanwhile (claims made against public authorities), the overwhelming pattern has been of non-change, and possibly even restriction, in tort liability in response to the Act. In these cases, the House of Lords most certainly did not pursue the possibility that Arden LJ went on to propose, namely that the HRA might be used in order to 'energise' common law rights in this sphere.[6] Instead, the House (but generally not the lower courts) took steps to insulate domestic tort law from the influence of the rights.

The restrictive role of the House of Lords is clearest in the vertical cases. Even in the horizontal cases, though, the role played by the House of Lords is open to question. Certainly, the Court of Appeal has played a leading role in the development of the law in these cases, both before and after the decision of the House of Lords in *Campbell v MGN*,[7] initiating the most fundamental changes and taking the influence of the rights far further. By contrast in the vertical cases the end result (non-change, or even restriction) has been brought about chiefly through the efforts of the House of Lords, often reversing developments in the Court of Appeal.

In this chapter, I will illustrate the general pattern just sketched, and show how isolated *Campbell v MGN* appears to be when looked at in the context of the whole set of tort decisions of the House of Lords over this period, both vertical and horizontal. I will also suggest some reasons behind this pattern. Two key factors may be argued to underlie the House of Lords' increasing reluctance over time to allow the rights to 'cascade' through the law of tort, or to be 'interwoven'

---

[4] The Convention imposes duties only upon states. However, in some circumstances this includes a duty to ensure that there are domestic legal remedies in place to protect at least certain of the rights (positive duties). The big pre-commencement question arising in respect of the law of tort was whether and to what extent the rights would take any effect in 'horizontal' cases. The jurisprudence of the European Court of Human Rights on positive duties has developed rapidly in the period explored here.

[5] The language of horizontality is not universally liked in this context. In this chapter, I use the expression very simply, to refer to the nature of the claim itself—whether it was against a public authority defendant, or not.

[6] Arden, 'Human Rights and Civil Wrongs' (n 1) 153. Arden LJ draws here on the judgment of Lord Scott in *Ashley v Chief Constable of Sussex* [2008] UKHL 25, [2008] 1 AC 962, which, as she notes, stands alone in that case. The analysis below suggests that if we confine our analysis to the House of Lords, it also stands alone in relation to public authority liability. It may be a better description however of some of the reasoning of the Court of Appeal during the same period.

[7] *Campbell v MGN* [2004] UKHL 22, [2004] 2 AC 457.

into its fabric.[8] The first of these proposed factors was a broad concern with the protection of public authorities from the threat of tort liability, whether through the influence of human rights, or not. The second was a fear of losing control of the substantive content of obligations and liabilities, ceding control of some such matters to the European Court of Human Rights in Strasbourg. While neither 'cascading' nor 'interweaving' conveys an idea of supremacy on the part of Convention rights, both imply intermixing which either has its own momentum, or is in other respects very difficult to unpick. To some degree therefore, both may give rise to a feared loss of control.[9] It will be explained that the addition of the 'mirror principle' (leaving interpretive supremacy with Strasbourg) has deepened the effect of this second factor. The two factors are linked, of course, since ceding control may itself be disliked particularly where, as here, there is a preference for restraint in the expansion of liabilities, and where positive obligations are growing in the Strasbourg jurisprudence. But the second concern may also make itself felt in cases where liability to pay money damages and potential exposure to costly litigation are not the key issues.

It is not suggested that concern with both these factors was shared by all members of the House of Lords, to the same extent. The point is that the pattern presented by the cases is stronger than the variety of views apparently present in the House might lead one to expect. This might point to overlapping reasons for support of certain outcomes; or it might suggest that certain key arguments or concerns became sufficiently dominant to overcome underlying disagreements. In any event, the very existence of such a diversity of views makes it eminently possible that the balance in the Supreme Court will turn out to be different.[10] Indeed, the overall set of operating influences may push in a different direction.

---

[8] These expressions are preferred over 'horizontality' by Stephen Sedley in *Freedom, Law and Justice* (London, Sweet and Maxwell, 1999) ch 2, 'Private Power and Public Power'. I take it that they are more descriptive terms than 'horizontality', in that they begin to describe the *nature* of the impact of the rights, rather than purely (and mechanically) stating the applicability of the rights to a particular type of dispute. 'Cascading' brings to mind the idea that rights once introduced do not remain static but that their influence becomes dynamic: equally, that their progress through different layers of the law is unpredictable, and that this progress has its own momentum. 'Interweaving' implies that the rights become intertwined with domestic legal principles, forming a part of the fabric of domestic law and contributing in subtle ways to its overall pattern. In both cases, there is an element of unpredictability about the impact of the rights and, equally importantly, a difficulty in dividing the impact of the rights very clearly from the indigenous legal principles of which they become part.

[9] This is entirely different from the suggestion that common law judges cannot recognise broad general principles of an overarching nature (Wright, *Tort Law and Human Rights* (n 3)), and suggests instead that the rights would have their greatest impact if absorbed into the details of common law (for a consistent analysis see R Mullender, 'Tort, Human Rights, and Common Law Culture' (2003) 23 *Oxford Journal of Legal Studies* 301, and see also n 67). It is this absorption which has been resisted, for reasons explored here.

[10] At the time of writing, six months after the initiation of the Supreme Court, there have still been no decisions on the law of tort from that Court. This would surely have been most unusual for the House of Lords, and raises the question whether the Supreme Court is planning less intervention into private law than its predecessor.

## II THE GENERAL PICTURE

### A  Change and non-change

Clearly, there are areas of tort law which have been deeply transformed in the wake of the HRA.[11] Equally clearly, there are other areas which have not, despite early indications (and predictions) to the contrary, and moves toward change on the part of the Court of Appeal. Two of the most notable instances of this involved a Court of Appeal led by Lord Phillips, now President of the Supreme Court.

The Court of Appeal decision in *D v East Berkshire* seemed to indicate that radical change in the tort of negligence was certain, at least where public authorities were concerned, since the Court decided there that a policy judgment reached in a recent House of Lords decision could not survive the HRA.[12] The House of Lords did not comment on this, but drew the line against further extension in the form of a duty to suspected parents (Lord Bingham dissenting). Since then, the normal role of precedent has been (in fact rather quickly) strongly reasserted. In *Leeds City Council v Price*,[13] Lord Phillips himself said that to depart from a House of Lords judgment in order to act compatibly with a European Court of Human Rights decision would be 'iconoclasm of a different dimension' from what had been involved in *D v East Berkshire* (implying, one might think, that there had been iconoclasm of some order in *D v East Berkshire* itself).[14] The approach exemplified by the Court of Appeal in *D v East Berkshire* certainly now seems to be a thing of history, and was explained away by Lord Phillips in *Price* as depending specifically on the undermining of the *policy* issues (rather than legal principles?) in *X v Bedfordshire*.[15] More recently, in *Lawrence v Pembrokeshire CC* the Court of Appeal has emphasised that the passage of the HRA does not mean the 'consignment to history' of the conflict of interest point reaffirmed by the House of Lords in *D v East Berkshire*; nor does the new role of art 8 ECHR in domestic law displace the traditional approach to duty questions.[16]

Turning to the law of nuisance, in *Marcic v Thames Water Utilities*[17] the Court of Appeal stated unequivocally that radical reform to the torts of private

---

[11]  The commencement date of the HRA was 2 October 2000, and its application was prospective only. But its influence in judicial decisions became apparent much sooner. *Reynolds v Times Newspapers* [2001] 2 AC 127 was decided before commencement. Legislative intent expressed in the HRA was used to justify a revised role for freedom of expression.

[12]  *D v East Berkshire* [2003] EWCA Civ 1151, [2004] 2 WLR 58 [83].

[13]  *Leeds City Council v Price* [2005] EWCA Civ 289, [2005] 1 WLR 1825.

[14]  ibid [33].

[15]  *X (Minors) v Bedfordshire CC* [1995] 2 AC 633. Since, as we know from the rejection of *Osman v UK* on this point, that policy judgments are an inherent aspect of negligence principles, this is a very fine line to draw.

[16]  *Lawrence v Pembrokeshire CC* [2007] EWCA Civ 446, [2007] 1 WLR 2991 [32]–[33].

[17]  *Marcic v Thames Water Utilities* [2002] EWCA Civ 64, [2002] BLR 174.

nuisance and *Rylands v Fletcher* would (again *of necessity*)[18] flow from the HRA: the House of Lords firmly reasserted orthodoxy, without comment on this.[19]

Though the Court of Appeal has continued to attempt some innovations in the law of tort on the basis of Convention rights and their new status, some areas of tort liability have subsequently become *more* restricted than might have been the case in the absence of the HRA. In *Watkins v Secretary of State for the Home Department*,[20] the House used the existence of a new remedy under the HRA as a reason against the development of the tort of misfeasance in a public office (a damage-based tort) to protect 'constitutional rights' (as the Court of Appeal had proposed). Lord Rodger described previous efforts to extend the common law in this way as 'heroic' (presumably implying a degree of activism), and as no longer necessary.

This section maps out the different areas which make up the general picture, and suggests that in terms of the record of the House of Lords in particular, if we step aside from detailed analysis of the judgments and just look at the outcomes of various types of case, a remarkably consistent pattern can be observed. This consistency can be seen by making an initial division between 'horizontal' and 'vertical' cases, although the horizontal cases then need some closer attention. The stark truth is that outside the well-trodden area of privacy, where the role of the House of Lords was in any event relatively muted, the House never used the HRA as a reason to expand liability in tort.[21] Apart perhaps from *Campbell* (which needs further exploration), the occasion where the House of Lords most clearly took ownership of the Convention rights in respect of the law of tort predated commencement, and resulted in a new defence, rather than new liability.[22]

## B 'Horizontal' cases

There has been significant activity around 'horizontal' cases. In *Campbell v MGN*,[23] the House of Lords continued the transformation in the law of confidence which had earlier been effected by the Court of Appeal in *Douglas v Hello!*,[24] and *A v B Plc*,[25] and endorsed the approach to arts 8 and 10 set out by the Court of Appeal in *Re S*.[26] The principles in *Re S* were further developed by the House itself

---

[18] This kind of thinking—that domestic private law would be *forced* to change to give better effect to the Convention rights—has become extinct as the HRA has bedded down, but is familiar in cases that followed in the wake of *Osman*.

[19] *Marcic v Thames Water Utilities* [2003] UKHL 66, [2004] 2 AC 42.

[20] *Watkins v Secretary of State for the Home Department* [2006] UKHL 17, [2006] 2 AC 395.

[21] Two 'rights-based' decisions which favoured claimants during the period were *Chester v Afshar* [2004] UKHL 41, [2005] 1 AC 134, and *Ashley* (n 6), but these were not based on reasoning from Convention rights (other than in the opinion of Lord Scott in *Ashley*).

[22] *Reynolds v Times Newspapers* (n 11).

[23] *Campbell* (n 7).

[24] *Douglas v Hello!* [2001] QB 967, [2001] 2 WLR 992.

[25] *A v B Plc* [2002] EWCA Civ 337, [2003] QB 195. In neither of these cases did the Court of Appeal grant an injunction, and in *Campbell* the claim was one for damages.

[26] *Re S* [2003] EWCA Civ 963.

on appeal, with reference to *Campbell*.[27] This is significant, as here the House underlined that there was to be no 'presumptive priority' between the rights. Significant though this period of activity certainly was, from a greater distance we can see that in the field of tort and tort-like liabilities, the decision in *Campbell* stands alone, so far as the House of Lords is concerned. It is the only case in which the House of Lords used the Convention rights to extend liability in tort (if it is correctly seen as a case of tort).[28]

In truth, even in *Campbell,* the warmth of the House of Lords' embrace of the rights as an aspect of private law was a little tepid. Although the dissents of Lords Hoffmann and Nicholls indicated disagreement as to the outcome, but not in respect of the applicable legal principles, they remain highly significant in light of the analysis below. Lord Hoffmann, for example, drew attention to the protection for responsible journalism (and for freedom of expression) underlying the earlier decision in *Reynolds*, and emphasised the need to respect this approach in relation to privacy also. This highlights that the use of art 10 to create a public interest defence in *Reynolds* is a very different matter from the use of art 8 to create a new variation of a right of action, in breach of confidence. Certainly, the lower courts have since gone considerably further in expanding liability in this area, and indeed in further intensifying the influence of the Convention rights.[29]

Breach of confidence is not the only area where horizontal liability has been affected by the Convention rights. The law of defamation has also undergone considerable change under the influence of the HRA,[30] and this process has imbued the law of defamation with important hallmarks of Convention jurisprudence such as proportionality and, as Eric Barendt has put it, 'ad hoc' (fact-specific) balancing.[31] And while questions might be asked about the particular role of the House of Lords in privacy cases, in respect of defamation the House of Lords has plainly been the initiator. Even so, it is in the hands of the lower courts that the infiltration of Convention influence has quietly gathered pace in the last year or two, as we will explain in section IV. The effect may be quite different from what the House in *Reynolds* intended.

---

[27] *Re S (A Child)* [2004] UKHL 47, [2005] 1 AC 593, setting out the correct approach to arts 8 and 10 in terms of what was called 'the ultimate balancing test' (Lord Steyn [17] and [23]). This was not a case of civil liability, but concerned the correct approach to reporting restrictions.

[28] Lord Nicholls referred to the action as a 'tort': *Campbell* (n 7) [14] and [15].

[29] The House did not accept a number of subsequent opportunities to hear appeals in respect of privacy, refusing leave. I am grateful to Hugh Tomlinson for making this point in the course of the 'Judges and Jurists' seminar.

[30] The Act was referred to a number of times in *Reynolds*, and it is suggested that its influence was strong—though the full implications of that (given subsequent developments in privacy) were not recognised by the House of Lords. More recent cases in the lower courts make the link between *Reynolds* and the Convention much more apparent (see section IV).

[31] E Barendt, *Freedom of Speech*, 2nd edn (Oxford, Oxford University Press, 2005) 222–26 (contrasting 'ad hoc' balancing with 'definitional balancing' to be found in US law and more traditionally, perhaps, in common law generally). The UK has successfully defended applications to Strasbourg in respect of defamation since *Reynolds*: see *Times Newspapers v UK* [2009] EMLR 14; *Wall Street Journal v UK* (2009) 48 EHRR SE19.

Whilst the House of Lords did, in *Reynolds v Times Newspapers*, instigate a deep though subtle revolution in this area,[32] it did so in order to create a new defence (which was designed to be securely under judicial control), and not in order to extend liability. It made this abundantly clear when it returned to the new defence in *Jameel v Wall Street Journal*,[33] criticising lower courts for their excessive caution in their protection of public interest reporting. Only now is it beginning to be apparent that the *Reynolds* approach could ultimately lead to further and potentially opposite transformation to the contours of defamation, as reputation itself acquires new, and rather different, force as falling within art 8. The House of Lords neither intended, nor anticipated, that this would occur, and it seems doubtful whether it would have welcomed it. The recasting of this action as involving *two* Convention rights, which must therefore be balanced, rather than just one, potentially makes a very significant difference to the likely development of the law,[34] for example making it much harder to justify an entirely different approach to the award of an injunction in privacy rather than defamation cases.

At the very least, developments in the law of defamation do not show the House of Lords taking an enthusiastic lead in extending tort liability in response to the Convention rights, though Convention rights permeated its reasoning. What it wanted perhaps was the *freedom* to use Convention reasoning. As we will see when we turn to our two key threads (in section IV), this freedom seems increasingly elusive in horizontal cases, partly because of the positive obligation to protect the Convention rights of *both* parties to the action.

In privacy too, although the House of Lords refined—outside the area of tort—the 'ultimate balance' between arts 8 and 10, there are indications that the House itself would not have struck the balance in the same way that lower courts have more recently done under the influence of *Von Hannover v Germany*.[35] In respect of privacy, the approach to balancing taken by the House on the facts of *Campbell* was consistent with a stronger leaning towards freedom of press reporting (interpreted primarily as a public interest issue) than is reflected in recent decisions.[36] Even among the majority there were suggestions that protection

---

[32] The wider ripples of *Reynolds* include the creation of a new 'reportage' defence and the recognition of reputation itself as protected within the terms of art 8 ECHR. The House of Lords in *Reynolds* constructed its approach on the foundations of an adventurous decision by the Court of Appeal.

[33] *Jameel v Wall Street Journal* [2006] UKHL 44, [2007] 1 AC 359.

[34] In 'Bringing Rights Home—Time to Start a Family?' (2008) 28 *Legal Studies* 327, 330, Sedley LJ made this very clear: 'we have embarked on a rebalancing of our libel law by dovetailing the Art 8 privacy right more precisely than before with the Art 10 right of free expression, each involving respect for others in equal measure with personal liberty'. By contrast, in light of his comments both in *Campbell* and (more recently) in 'The Universality of Human Rights' (2009) 125 *Law Quarterly Review* 416, it is hard to envisage Lord Hoffmann endorsing a development along these lines.

[35] *Von Hannover v Germany* (2004) 40 EHRR 1.

[36] The two dissentients in *Campbell*—who regarded freedom of expression as outweighing privacy on the facts—have subsequently retired. See now the UKSC decision in *R(L) v Commissioner of Police of the Metropolis* [2009] UKSC 3, [2009] 3 WLR 1056. The Supreme Court by a majority held that the claimant's art 8 rights had to be respected when disclosing information for inclusion

would be confined to intrusive pictures, not extending to mundane pictures taken when a claimant 'pops out to buy a bottle of milk', for example.[37] In *Von Hannover*, however, the European Court of Human Rights held that publication of some unremarkable everyday photographs of the applicant ought to have been restricted by German law. An interpretation of *Von Hannover* resting on intrusion rather than on the nature of the images themselves has been rejected by the UK courts,[38] and the case has had a direct impact on the development of domestic law. This now provides a level of protection for privacy (and a level of intrusion into freedom of press reporting) not envisaged in *Campbell*.[39]

Looking at the general record of the House of Lords in respect of protection of privacy through private law, it is hard to deny that the most decisive move of the House was its refusal to extend protection beyond publication of private information in *Wainwright v Home Office*.[40] This observation is reinforced by noting that after his retirement, Lord Hoffmann reserved particular criticism for the leading source of guidance on the balance to be struck in English breach of confidence cases where privacy is engaged—which is, pertinently, *Von Hannover v Germany*.[41] The statement of one Strasbourg judge, that in his view freedom of expression had received too much priority to date, was subjected to particularly vehement criticism.[42] While on one view this reason for the antagonism could be substantive (the conclusion as to appropriate balance differing from his own conclusions in *Jameel*, *Reynolds*, and (in dissent) *Campbell*), on another view the primary reason is the presumptuousness involved in making decisions about the right balance on behalf of a domestic legal system.

The legacy of *Von Hannover* can be seen clearly reflected in domestic law, as the balance between freedom of expression and privacy has shifted over time. The ground-breaking case of *Douglas v Hello!* did not result in an injunction in the claimants' favour, despite the reorientation effected by the Court of Appeal in that case, because the invasion of privacy was considered too modest to outweigh an inherent right to freedom of expression (no matter how modest the value of

---

in an enhanced criminal records certificate (ECRC). An approach based on the proportionality of protection was adopted by the majority. Lord Scott, disagreeing on the issue of the status of the art 8 rights in these circumstances, argued that the information to be disclosed in such a certificate was inherently likely to include information about the claimant's private life. This dissenting position expressly 'accords priority to the social need to protect the vulnerable' ([44]). The majority's approach is a strong vindication of proportionality between art 8 and pressing social needs, and appears very different from the spirit of the later decisions of the House of Lords.

[37] *Campbell* (n 7) [154] (Baroness Hale).

[38] *McKennitt v Ash* [2006] EWCA Civ 1714, [2008] QB 73.

[39] See in particular *Murray v Express Newspapers* [2008] EWCA Civ 446, [2008] 3 WLR 1360.

[40] *Wainwright v Home Office* [2003] UKHL 53, [2004] 2 AC 406. This (a vertical privacy claim) led to a successful complaint against the UK in Strasbourg on the basis of violation of privacy: *Wainwright v UK* (2007) 44 EHRR 40. Strangely perhaps, this is the sort of development which seemed to concern the House of Lords less once the HRA had bedded in than it had in the days of *Osman*, *Barrett*, and *Phelps*.

[41] Lord Hoffmann, 'The Universality of Human Rights' (n 34).

[42] ibid 429.

the publication). Later, in *Douglas v Hello! (No 3)*,[43] a different Court of Appeal took the view that an injunction should in retrospect have been granted, and that this was clear in the light of intermediate changes—including the decision in *Von Hannover v Germany*.[44] The outcome in the early case of *A v B plc*,[45] where the most lightweight freedom of speech outweighed the privacy interests of the claimant in the circumstances, can be contrasted with more recent decisions such as *CC v AB*,[46] and *Mosley v News Group Newspapers*:[47] sexual encounters, whether adulterous, commercial, or orgiastic give rise to an expectation of privacy, and it will require some specific public interest justification to outweigh this expectation.[48] All of these were decisions of the lower courts, not of the House of Lords. Since the House of Lords did not grasp opportunities to hear appeals from significant privacy cases after *Campbell*,[49] can it be concluded that the House did not think that change in the balance was possible, given the *Von Hannover* decision?

In summary, the House of Lords made one significant contribution to the development of a remedy for one particular form of invasion of privacy. This was not however the first decisive step in the development of the privacy remedy, and it was taken before the full implications of the development became clear. On the debit side where privacy is concerned, the House of Lords headed off the development of other varieties of privacy action in *Wainwright*, leading to a successful application against the UK in Strasbourg,[50] and has not been involved in the subsequent development of the privacy remedy. In defamation meanwhile, the House clearly used Convention rights, and significantly contributed to their interweaving into (or cascade through) this area of domestic law. But it did so in order to create a new defence, clearly conditional on the court's judgment as to responsible reporting, rather than to extend liability. Once again, the fuller implications of this, and particularly the equality this would create through conceptualising defamation cases in terms of arts 8 and 10, were certainly not anticipated at the time, as we will see in section IV.

---

[43] *Douglas v Hello! (No 3)* [2005] EWCA Civ 595, [2006] QB 125.

[44] *Von Hannover* (n 35).

[45] *A v B plc* (n 25).

[46] *CC v AB* [2006] EWHC 3083 (QB), [2007] Fam Law 591.

[47] *Mosley v News Group Newspapers* [2008] EWHC 1777 (QB).

[48] For example, Eady J considered that had the orgies in *Mosley* been genuinely 'Nazi themed', then this might have led to a public interest justification. The question arises of whether newspapers will feel the need to devise increasingly damaging allegations in order to justify their intrusion. As things stand, a claim which is essentially concerned with reputation will be unlikely to result in an injunction restraining publication: defamation rules, and therefore *Bonnard v Perryman* [1891] 2 Ch 269 will apply, and s 12 HRA will have no impact. Meanwhile, claims concerned essentially with private information, rather than reputation, will be addressed under the balanced approach set out in *Campbell* (n 7) and *Re S* (n 27): no presumptive priority to either right. See the discussion of this awkward distinction in *John Terry v Persons Unknown* [2010] EWHC 119 (QB).

[49] See n 29.

[50] *Wainwright v UK* (2007) 44 EHRR 40.

## C  'Vertical' cases

Outside the realm of these typically 'horizontal' actions,[51] the broader picture is one of notable *non-change* in the law of tort in response to the new status of Convention rights, and perhaps even of restriction of potential liability. It is easy to lose sight of this more general trend, given the excitement over 'horizontality'. The weight of expectation that change would follow enactment in these particular areas may also help to explain why the true picture has not always (and then only very slowly) been correctly perceived. It is not only commentators who have been misled. As recently as 2008, in the Court of Appeal decision in *Smith v Chief Constable of Sussex*,[52] Rimer LJ responded to the claimant's argument that the development of common law principles in this area should be affected by the positive obligations under art 2 ECHR by suggesting that 'it is arguable that they should, on the basis that where a common law duty covers the same ground as a Convention right, it should, so far as practicable, develop in harmony with it'.[53] As such, he suggested, the policy reasoning articulated by the House of Lords in *Hill v Chief Constable of West Yorkshire*[54] may need to be revisited: an argument resembling the Court of Appeal decision in *D v East Berkshire*. The approach subsequently taken in the House of Lords was entirely the reverse of this, and effectively took the law back to a position very close to *Hill* itself.[55] In this area, the House of Lords itself has been by far the most active court in securing the status quo, firmly reversing Court of Appeal efforts to extend tort liability on the basis of a 'Convention rights' argument on more than one occasion.

It is true that soon after enactment of HRA, the House of Lords expanded the reach of public authority liability, in *Barrett v Enfield*[56] and *Phelps v Hillingdon*.[57] But these cases in their origins really belong to an earlier, pre-HRA era. They were, in essence, decided in the shadow of *Osman v UK*, during the period before the European Court of Human Rights recanted on its approach to policy issues in English negligence law, in *Z v UK*.[58] They therefore belong to a period of time where the Convention rights had not yet gained their new status in domestic law, and the key influence was interpretation of the right of access to a court under art 6. Further, *Z v UK* itself, combined with continuing bitterness over *Osman*, seems to have led to a much greater confidence in the freedom of domestic courts to restrict the development of negligence on policy grounds.

---

[51] There is no reason why a defamation or breach of confidence action should not be brought against a public authority. But the core examples of such cases are actions against media defendants.

[52] *Smith v Chief Constable of Sussex* [2008] EWCA Civ 39, [2008] HRLR 23.

[53] ibid [45].

[54] *Hill v Chief Constable of West Yorkshire* [1989] AC 53.

[55] *Hertfordshire Police v Van Colle; Smith v Chief Constable of Sussex Police* [2008] UKHL 50, [2008] 3 WLR 593.

[56] *Barrett v Enfield* [2001] 2 AC 550.

[57] *Phelps v Hillingdon* [2001] 2 AC 619.

[58] *Z v UK* (2002) 34 EHRR 3, [2001] 2 FLR 612.

As it progressively shuffled off the immediate influence of *Osman*, the House of Lords shifted its stance, deliberately truncating the development of tort actions against public authorities where Convention rights were concerned, and entering what might be described as a period of reaction. In its final five years, the trend was one of *increasing* restrictiveness. In the area of police liability for example, the House emphasised in *Brooks v Chief of Police of the Metropolis*[59] that the door was open to exceptional claims: the particular case disclosed no duty of the sorts claimed, but even so there was to be no general immunity along the lines of *Hill v Chief Constable of West Yorkshire Police*.[60] Perhaps concerns over art 6 continued to operate. Later, in *Smith v Chief Constable of Sussex*,[61] it was said clearly by a majority of the House that the principles weighing against a duty of care must be applied in a *general* manner in order to protect the police from litigation. Lord Bingham, in dissent, thought the case in hand fell within a limited 'liability principle', fulfilling the possibility left open by *Brooks*; but it seems that door is now closed. *Brooks*, in retrospect, represents a stage on the route between *Phelps* and *Smith*—which is also in effect the route back to *Hill*, so far as tort liability on the part of the police is concerned. An HRA action will in future be possible on facts like *Smith*, its success depending on whether the 'imminent danger' criterion is fulfilled. Article 6 is thus no longer a concern. The new sense of security in domestic negligence law allowed the House to give vent to its inclination to restrict public authority liability.

Explaining the cases of *Phelps* and *Barrett* as we have, the role of the House is much easier to plot in this part of the terrain. The trend over time was one of increasing restrictiveness. *Smith* was one of a sequence of cases where the existence of an alternative remedy under the HRA itself, modelled on the Strasbourg action, was treated as a reason for *not* allowing a tort remedy.[62] Extensions in tort liability made by the Court of Appeal were knocked back where public authority defendants were concerned, whereas equally adventurous Court of Appeal innovations in respect of 'horizontal' cases were not. The completeness of this trend, which is more evident with hindsight than it was as it unfolded, together with the relatively weak intentions of the House in horizontal cases, is illustrated in section V.

### III EXPLAINING THE PICTURE: GENERAL ISSUES

Why has this pattern emerged? Before exploring two key threads of importance to tort law whose conjunction I think will help to explain this picture, it is worth

---

[59] *Brooks v Chief of Police of the Metropolis* [2005] UKHL 24.

[60] *Hill* (n 54).

[61] *Smith* (n 55).

[62] The clearest case perhaps was *Jain v Trent Strategic Health Authority* [2009] UKHL 4, [2009] 2 WLR 248, since here members of the House to one degree or another thought or suspected that the claimant's rights might have been violated. This stands in marked contrast with concern over challenges in Strasbourg which was evident in earlier cases such as *Barrett* (n 56) and *Phelps* (n 57).

observing three broader underlying developments: the House of Lords' approach to the new action under the HRA itself; the House of Lords' general approach to the new status of the Convention rights; and the timing of the crucial cases.

## A  The approach to the HRA action

One of the less heralded features of the HRA was the introduction by ss 7–8 of a new civil action directly against public authorities, with a monetary remedy in suitable cases. Gradually over the career of the HRA, this action came to be conceptualised by the House of Lords as a clearly distinct and more appropriate alternative to an action in tort, with remedies more suited to cases where there has been a breach of Convention rights. This is not because the remedies were more generous, but precisely because there was less emphasis on monetary remedies at all in respect of these actions: the House of Lords has interpreted the provisions as essentially tying the domestic HRA remedy to the Strasbourg remedy; and the quantum awarded in Strasbourg is less than the quantum of tort damages.[63] This alternative does not exist where the defendant is not a public authority (such as the defendants in *Campbell* and *Reynolds*, and the magazine in *Douglas v Hello!*).

This approach to the remedies under s 8 was not predicted either by commentators or by the Law Commission, which after exhaustive review concluded that such damages could for the most part be based on tort awards.[64] It is not clear whether this interpretation is chiefly a cause or an effect of the House's approach to tort claims involving Convention rights during the same period. It seems most likely that they stem from common causes. In any event, the interpretation of the remedies as different and distinct has had a significant, and not always widely noted, impact in restraining the development of tort in response to the HRA.

## B  Nature of the Convention rights

Equally importantly, the House of Lords took a decision at a pivotal moment in the career of the HRA to interpret the Convention rights as essentially 'international law' rights which had been given new status through the Act.[65] Their correct interpretation could only be 'authoritatively expounded' by the Strasbourg court. Very shortly before this, in *Re McKerr*,[66] Lord Hoffmann

---

[63]  See the exploration by J Steele, 'Damages in Tort and Under the Human Rights Act: Remedial or Functional Separation?' (2008) 67 *Cambridge Law Journal* 606. The Strasbourg remedy is available in the absence of an appropriate domestic remedy. It does not logically follow that the domestic remedy should be modelled on the international remedy, but that is what the House of Lords concluded.

[64]  Law Commission, 'Damages Under the Human Rights Act 1998' (Law Com No 266, 2000).

[65]  *R (Ullah) v Special Adjudicator* [2004] UKHL 26, [2004] 2 AC 323: decided in the same crucial year as *Campbell v MGN* (n 7).

[66]  *Re McKerr* [2004] UKHL 12, [2004] 1 WLR 807.

had proposed that the Convention rights set out in the HRA were new domestic law rights, related of course to the international rights whose text they restated but a part of domestic law and, critically, for domestic courts to interpret and develop. This view, if fully accepted, might have amounted to a powerful means of 'owning' the Convention rights,[67] as an integral part of domestic law, and as clearly under the control of domestic courts. Instead, the House in *Ullah* and subsequent cases adopted what is now known as the 'mirror principle' or, even more descriptively, the 'Strasbourg ceiling', ensuring that English courts will go no further than the Strasbourg court in interpretation of the rights.

In respect of tort law, the restrictive effect of this 'disowning' of the rights became increasingly obvious over time. In *Ullah* itself, Lord Bingham said that the protection offered by domestic law to the interests guaranteed by the Convention rights would be 'no more, and certainly no less' than was offered in Strasbourg. By 2007, Lord Brown had turned this around: domestic protection of the rights would be 'no less, and certainly no more' than Strasbourg had to offer.[68]

The mirror principle meant that the Strasbourg court was conceded to have supremacy, in effect, in the definition and development of the rights. This may have fed directly into the increasing resistance to interweaving of these rights through domestic law. If that interweaving had come with greater ownership, would it have been so strongly resisted? Both the mirror principle, and the resistance which follows from it, are creations of the House of Lords.

## C  Timing

The decisive changes in horizontal cases happened at an early stage in the career of the HRA, before its full implications had been realised, and before the House of Lords had settled on its present restrictive approach. The pattern of vertical cases emerged more slowly as the House of Lords left behind *Barrett* and *Phelps*, both decided before commencement and both a legacy of *Osman v UK*. It is suggested that the timing of the crucial cases in each stream, given gradual emergence of the mirror principle and the separation of tort and the HRA action, may have

---

[67] Pertinent here is the valuable exploration by Mullender, 'Tort, Human Rights, and Common Law Culture' (n 9), discussing the interaction between Convention rights and common law principles in terms derived from M Walzer, *Thick and Thin: Arguments at Home and Abroad* (Notre Dame, University of Notre Dame Press, 1994). The analysis in this chapter is consistent with the view expressed by Mullender that the common law does not lack the resources to embrace broad general principles, such as the Convention rights (as proposed by Wright, *Tort Law and Human Rights* (n 3)). Other factors in play are also explored in this chapter.

[68] *R (Al-Skeini) v Defence Secretary* [2007] UKHL 26, [2008] 1 AC 153. Note also Lord Brown's analysis in *Van Colle* (n 55), particularly at [137]: the possibility of a Human Rights Act claim now 'to some extent weakens the value of the '*Hill* principle' insofar as that is intended to safeguard the police from the diversion of resources involved in having to contest civil litigation'; but even so, that is 'no good reason for mirroring the *Osman* principle by the introduction of a common law duty of care in this very limited class of case, still less for weakening the value of the *Hill* principle yet further by creating a wider duty of care.'

been critical in the degree to which the rights 'cascaded' through the different areas.

To suggest that timing is important in this way is not, however, to dismiss the pattern as purely the product of historical accident. It seems pretty clear that developments in respect of privacy and defamation occurred soon after enactment (and in the case of *Reynolds* even before commencement), largely because courts were eager to achieve developments in these areas of law. In other words, the timing of developments is itself explicable in terms of the intentions of the higher courts. As time went on, the deeper implications of changes in breach of confidence and (much more slowly) defamation became more apparent. Foresight of these implications, had that been possible, might have made a decisive difference.

## IV  EXPLAINING THE PICTURE:
### TWO DOMINANT THREADS IN TORT CASES

Against the background of these broader developments, it is time to suggest two dominant threads explaining the House of Lords' adoption of an increasingly restrictive approach to the Convention rights in the area of tort law in particular.

### A  Vertical cases: protecting public authorities from liability

The first thread is the more straightforward, but there is still room for diversity in how we explain it. In its last few years, the House of Lords showed itself— not without a degree of internal division[69]—to be reluctant to extend monetary remedies in tort against public authorities (and to some extent, against any defendant).[70] This provides a reason why the use of the Convention rights might have been restricted in 'vertical' cases, even though this is the primary area in which those rights could be expected to operate.

Underlying this reluctance may be a number of different potential reasons. The influence of some of these can be clearly observed from the expressed policy reasons employed by the House of Lords, and from some extra-judicial comment; others require more speculative interpretation. Certainly, the House was concerned that the expansion of tort liability would be costly and might threaten to interfere with the distribution of scarce public resources; that public

---

[69] Note the discussion by Brice Dickson in his chapter in this volume.

[70] The next section of this chapter provides a brief but complete overview of tort cases before the House of Lords, 2004–09. No tort claimant succeeded before the House in 2009. In 'The COMBAR Lecture 2001: Separation of Powers' [2002] *Judicial Review* 137, Lord Hoffmann expressly recognised that liabilities in general have distributive implications, and that all such liabilities ultimately generate costs for the public (at [24]): 'When . . . the courts create a new head of tort liability, they are creating a new head of public expenditure . . .'. This makes the link between public authority liability, and other tort liability. The same paragraph proceeds to relate this to the impact of *Osman*.

authority defendants were already a tempting target in situations where they were not the primary wrongdoer;[71] and that the very threat of litigation would have considerable nuisance value and might adversely affect public decision-making.[72] All of these considerations were expressed from time to time, and they undoubtedly fed into the general position adopted by the House, that private law monetary remedies are not the appropriate response to claims against public authorities in respect of human rights violations. In all of this, the nature of the *remedy* in tort is crucial. Having interpreted the civil remedy under s8 HRA as modelled on the international remedy in Strasbourg, not on the law of tort, the House of Lords proceeded to treat this as the more appropriate and proportionate response to cases engaging human rights.[73]

These concerns over the impact of liability on public authorities help to explain why Lord Bingham was forced into dissent in respect both of his proposed 'liability principle' in *Smith v Chief Constable of Sussex*,[74] and his proposed exception for cases of gross negligence in *D v East Berkshire*.[75] These approaches would allow for exceptionally strong claims to succeed, and are compatible with Lord Bingham's general argument for incorporation of the Convention, namely that it is needed for those rare cases where things go badly wrong. Such approaches, which had significant academic support,[76] were regarded by other members of the House as providing insufficient certainty in the sense that they would not remove the *threat* of litigation in the way that the 'no duty' conclusion can do. Perhaps also, they would provide too much temptation to lower courts to award remedies. Our study in the next section shows that this trend is not confined to negligence.

There are however other potential factors. Here it is necessary to be more hesitant. But it could be said that these concerns are more than merely practical. One additional factor, linked no doubt to the first, is increased sensitivity to the political impact and popular visibility of the law of tort itself, particularly where monetary remedies (and now litigation costs) are concerned. In other words, the House of Lords has positioned itself as protector of the public interest, and of socially beneficial risk-creating activities more generally, through restraint of

---

[71] *Stovin v Wise* [1996] AC 923 is a clear example of this, outside the area of application of the Convention rights; *Mitchell v Glasgow City Council* [2009] UKHL 11, [2009] 2 WLR 481 provides a more recent example where art 2 was in issue.

[72] This concern was most clearly expressed perhaps in *Hill*.

[73] Extra-judicial statements of regret about advancements in liability (or potential liability) include Lord Hoffmann's comments about education authority liability in the COMBAR lecture (n 70), [19] (calling attention to the distributive implications); and Lord Phillips' comments on the House of Lords' decision not to strike out a misfeasance action against the Bank of England in *Three Rivers DC v Bank of England* [2001] UKHL 16, [2003] 2 AC 1. In Lord Phillips' words, this allowed the continuation of 'the most expensive piece of hopeless litigation the commercial court has ever seen': N Phillips, 'Introductory Tribute: Lord Bingham of Cornhill', in M Andenas and D Fairgrieve (eds), *Tom Bingham and the Transformation of the Law* (Oxford, Oxford University Press, 2009) xlviii.

[74] *Smith* (n 55).

[75] *D v East Berkshire* [2005] UKHL 23, [2005] 2 AC 373.

[76] See for example S Bailey, 'Public Authority Liability in Negligence: the Continued Search for Coherence' (2006) 26 *Legal Studies* 155; discussed by Auld LJ in *Lawrence v Pembrokeshire* (n 14) [49].

liability. Not only are clear and robust general rules required to avoid litigation, but these should be set out in equally clear and robust judicial language, to avoid room for doubt and the temptation to further litigation.[77] Thus a sense of the political profile of tort helps to explain the robust and plain-speaking style of some of the House of Lords' later pronouncements. All of this no doubt reflects an understanding that private law is currently subject to the bright light of publicity to an unprecedented extent. But it also reflects concern over the assertion of human rights in cases involving distributive decision-making. Vertical tort claims engaging Convention rights therefore lie at an intersection of various factors, all of which militate against liability: protection of scarce resources; protection of the integrity of public reasoning; restraint in the judicial role; and protection of the reputation of the law against a perception that there is a compensation or rights culture. All of these are particularly strong in respect of vertical cases, though their reach is demonstrably wider.

Before turning to the second thread, which is most strongly applicable to horizontal cases, we should take from the first a general lesson: the particular remedies offered by private law are fundamental to the perceived problems.

## B  A horizontal thread: control

The relatively half-hearted influence of the House of Lords in horizontal cases is slightly harder to explain. In *Reynolds v Times Newspapers*, as we have seen, the House was perfectly prepared to allow an action between private parties to be deeply influenced by the Convention right to freedom of expression. This, however, was on the basis that the court would thereby achieve a greater level of control over the scope of liability. This element (control) was an unexplored factor in the House of Lords' growing resistance to the 'interweaving' or 'cascade' of Convention rights through domestic law. I suggest it is the gradual dawning of realisation about this factor which explains why the House did not repeat the sorts of changes it had wrought in civil remedies in *Reynolds* and *Campbell*. We can illustrate this by looking more closely at *Reynolds* in the context of the evolution of defamation from pre-HRA to post-HRA development.

In *Reynolds*, the House approached the law of defamation as raising one Convention right, namely art 10 (freedom of expression). By giving the right to freedom of expression a more central role in these cases, the House thereby aimed to take control of the balance between public interest reporting and protection of reputation, because art 10(2) recognises the need for a judgment as to proportionality of protection. This perception of the role of the Convention in defamation actions owes a great deal to the pre-HRA case law, not surprisingly

---

[77] 'Normally . . . the House will decide what the law is according to what it thinks is a fair and sensible conclusion and the reasoning in the speeches will support the result in the usual polemical style which judges find it necessary to adopt in order to persuade their colleagues and the public that no other answer is possible.' Lord Hoffmann, COMBAR lecture (n 70) [8].

given its chronology. During the period before the HRA, the existence of a right to freedom of expression (art 10) which was recognisably applicable to the UK whilst at the same time extraneous to domestic law gave the courts considerable freedom to decide how much use to make of that right.[78]

It is clear from the speeches in *Reynolds* that the House saw the new status of art 10 as a way of strengthening the role of freedom of expression in defamation actions, so that freedom of expression could be claimed to be the starting point (its restriction requiring justification), rather than a residual concern marking the boundaries of legitimate protection of expression:

> The starting point is now the right to freedom of expression, a right based on a constitutional or higher legal order foundation. Exceptions to freedom of expression must be justified as being necessary in a democracy. In other words, freedom of expression is the rule and regulation of speech is the exception requiring justification. The existence and width of any exception can only be justified if it is underpinned by a pressing social need. These are fundamental principles governing the balance between freedom of expression and defamation.[79]

On the other hand, art 10 itself appeared to give considerable latitude for domestic courts to determine whether or not a particular restriction of freedom of expression was (or was not) 'necessary in a democratic society'—and it expressly mentions the balance between freedom of expression, and reputation. This has in effect been preferred over the US-style priority to freedom of expression, which has led to a general privilege for speech concerning public officials (and a wide range of others), lost only on proof of malice.[80] The distinction helps to explain precisely why the *Reynolds* 'privilege' is not a true privilege. Its very application to a particular case depends on the court's verdict on the appropriate balance between interests in all the circumstances. This is entirely in sympathy with the Convention, and is also attractive to the House of Lords in a way that it would not have been attractive to the US Supreme Court at the time of *Sullivan*, for example.[81]

Subsequent development has cast doubt on the implications of this approach, in two ways. First, the 'mirror principle' adopted by the House itself is inclined

---

[78] Consider for example its use by the Court of Appeal in *John v MGN* [1997] QB 586, and by the House of Lords in *Derbyshire v Times Newspapers* [1993] AC 534: the prospect of losing a potential claim in Strasbourg was used as a reason for deploying art 10; but there were plentiful references also to *NYT v Sullivan* 376 US 254, 279-80 (1964).

[79] *Reynolds* (n 11) 208 (Lord Steyn).

[80] For an argument (extra-judicially) that the US approach should not be the preferred route, see S Sedley, 'The First Amendment: A Case for Import Controls?' in I Loveland (ed), *Importing the First Amendment: Freedom of Speech and Expression in Britain, Europe and the USA* (Oxford, Hart Publishing, 1998).

[81] This is a question of *whom* the superior court is trying to control. The House of Lords was asserting control over journalists to some extent, while also wishing to achieve a greater degree of restraint in the law of defamation. The way to achieve this was to place the balance in the hands of the courts. In *Sullivan v NYT*, decided against a background of institutional racism in Alabama, control of the local courts will have been one of the objectives of the Supreme Court's decision to prioritise speech: see further I Loveland, *Political Libels* (Oxford, Hart Publishing, 2000).

to restrict the freedom of domestic courts to determine the appropriate level of protection for the Convention rights, even in a 'horizontal' action. Secondly, the wider implication of the development of the action to protect privacy has cast doubt on any perception that there is just one Convention right at stake in defamation actions (freedom of expression). If reputation is treated as an element of privacy—as the European Court of Human Rights has treated it,[82] and as the Court of Appeal and lower courts have now quite clearly accepted[83]— then something uncomfortably akin to the shadow of *Osman* begins to cross the horizon. The new-found freedom to determine the balance between reputation and freedom of expression, provided that freedom of expression is at least adequately protected, proves short-lived because the balance is now one between two Convention rights. In cases where there is a balance to be struck between different Convention rights, both sides of the balance are susceptible to Strasbourg's interpretive supremacy (a supremacy created not by the HRA, but by the House of Lords itself). This is all the more pertinent because the dominant interpretation of the media defendant's freedom of expression in *Reynolds* is itself an interpretation which gives priority to the interests of the *public* in the availability of information, true or false. The new status of art 10 in *Reynolds* was of a piece with the House of Lords' protectiveness towards the public interest explored in respect of vertical cases, below. The new status of reputation as an aspect of the Convention right to privacy is not.

A feared loss of control may therefore have led to a more recent wariness not of 'horizontality' in the simple sense (application of the rights in claims involving no public authority), but of the very *cascading* or *interweaving* of Convention rights through domestic law which was put into effect in *Douglas v Hello!* and reflected by the House of Lords in *Campbell v MGN* and *Re S*. Quite simply, to allow the interweaving into domestic private law of rights whose interpretive home is elsewhere might be to surrender control over the pattern of liabilities and remedies (and indeed over the behaviour of lower courts). If this seems far-fetched, then we should consider the chain of events in respect of privacy since *Campbell*, outlined above. But we should also remember *Osman v UK*, and the judicial reaction to it.[84]

---

[82]   *Radio France v France* (2004) 40 EHRR 706; *Cumpana and Mazare v Romania* (2005) 41 EHRR 14.

[83]   In *Roberts v Gable* [2007] EWCA Civ 721, [2008] QB 502, the Court of Appeal identified reputation with art 8 as though this was entirely uncontroversial, and discussed the balance struck in *Reynolds* as though it had expressly taken the form of a balance between art 8 and art 10 ([48]–[49]). At first instance, in *Flood v Times Newspapers* [2009] EWHC 2375 (QB), Tugendhat J followed the logic of this and applied the 'ultimate balance' test in *Re S*—a privacy case—to the determination of a case involving the *Reynolds* defence. In *John Terry v Persons Unknown* [2010] EWHC 119 (QB), he addressed the awkward overlap between privacy and defamation that this creates in respect of the injunctive remedy in particular (n 48).

[84]   For judicial objections to *Osman v UK*, see comments of Lord Browne-Wilkinson in *Barrett* (n 56) and Lord Hoffmann's article, 'Human Rights and the House of Lords' (1999) 62 *Modern Law Review* 159. Many of the issues in the latter article continue to resonate through Lord Hoffmann's more recent speeches, particularly 'The Universality of Human Rights' (n 34), and 'The Separation of Powers' (n 70).

The 'control' thread identified here does not indicate mistrust of the substantive rights in the abstract, nor a lack of comfort with proportionality and balancing, provided the determination of the balance is within the reach of domestic courts (the cases of *Reynolds* and *Campbell* both saw the House of Lords engaging in these techniques). The most pertinent problem is not the principle, the rights, or the technique, but the threat of domestic law being controlled or restricted by some other court; and the flexibility of that law being curtailed by the need to balance two rights whose contents are not primarily determined by domestic jurisprudence. A concern along these lines would help to explain the relatively muted response of the House of Lords to liability in horizontal cases and its role in limiting use of the rights in vertical cases. It also potentially explains the clean separation between actions in tort, and under the HRA: this too is an attempt to keep responses to the Convention rights proportionate and confined.

The horizontal cases therefore have turned out to raise once again the *Osman* nightmare, that areas ostensibly quite far removed from the traditional core of human rights—such as the liability of particular parties to pay monetary damages[85]—might come to be determined according to the preferences of another set of judges, taking them outside the control of domestic courts (and especially the House of Lords). The irritation is all the greater to the extent that the domestic courts have advocated caution in their use of civil remedies, in the public interest. The overall concern may be to avoid too great a 'cascade' through domestic law—perhaps because this will turn out to be a cascade of remote influence, lost control, and excessive liability. The clearest statement of this position is to be found in Lord Hoffmann's recent article, 'The Universality of Human Rights':

> As the case law shows, there is virtually no aspect of our legal system, from land law to social security to torts to consumer contracts, which is not arguably touched at some point by human rights. But we have not surrendered our sovereignty over all these matters. We remain an independent nation with its own legal system, evolved over centuries of constitutional struggle and pragmatic change. . . . I . . . argue that detailed decisions about how it could be improved should be made in London, either by our democratic institutions or by judicial bodies which, like the Supreme Court of the United States, are integral with our own society and respected as such.[86]

This is an argument directly against 'cascading' through the law as that idea has been identified here.[87] It is also an argument against the surrender of control. There is no way of knowing to what extent it was a view adopted by other members of the House of Lords. But it is at the very least consistent with the way in which the early expectation of wholesale change became quietly reversed.

---

[85] This links the first reason with the second: it is the extent of *tort liability* which is in question in these cases—and therefore the justification for imposition of damages.

[86] Lord Hoffmann, 'The Universality of Human Rights' (n 34) 430.

[87] See n 8.

## V  THE PATTERN ILLUSTRATED

In order to supply evidence for some of the broader statements above, and in order to compare Convention rights cases with other actions in tort, this section will outline the decisions of the House of Lords in respect of tort law as a whole from the start of 2004 until the final judgments in 2009. This period (somewhat over five years, given that the final judgments were delivered in July) is more manageable than the full eleven years from enactment, but it also allows us to focus on the pattern which emerged after the initial preconceptions about the Act had had time to settle. *Ullah*, which I have described as an important moment in setting the House of Lords' view of the nature of the Convention rights under the HRA, was decided near the start of this period. The period includes *Campbell v MGN* and *Jameel*, but excludes *Phelps* and *Barrett*, which I have suggested are legacies of the pre-HRA relationship between domestic law, and the Convention.

The general pattern which emerges from the exercise is one of restrictiveness in respect of the common law of tort, subject to some notable exceptions. Apart from *Campbell*, those exceptions are not related to Convention rights. Nor are they generally 'vertical' cases. For these purposes, I have categorised the decisions as either 'for the claimant' or 'for the defendant'.[88] Statutory cases of tort-like liability are included, as is breach of confidence, so there is a broad interpretation of tort, but I have excluded any actions under the HRA itself. Claims against public authorities are in bold;[89] claims where Convention rights were strongly implicated are marked with an asterisk.

During the period 2004–09, the following cases relating to the law of tort were decided by the House of Lords in favour of defendants:

1.  ***Adams v Bracknell*** [2004] **UKHL 29.** A relatively restrictive interpretation of s 14 Limitation Act 1980 was adopted, in a negligence claim against a public authority in respect of educational failure (undiagnosed dyslexia). Though this decision was not ostensibly based on Convention rights, it is relevant to our story. It softened the impact (principally to the benefit of public authorities) of the liability established in *Phelps v Hillingdon*, which was itself influenced by the Convention (but not the HRA) as already explained.
2.  *\*Cream Holdings v Banerjee* [2004] UKHL 44. This was a breach of confidence action. Applying s 12 HRA 1998, the balance came down against an interim injunction.

---

[88] For this reason, I have omitted *OB v Aventis Pasteur* [2008] UKHL 34, [2008] 4 All ER 881, an action under the Consumer Protection Act 1987, where proceedings were adjourned in order to secure a clear ruling from the ECJ. Obviously the stark distinction ought to be qualified in some cases, such as *OBG v Allan*, where the claimants were not all defeated on all points. But for other reasons it seems appropriate to keep that claim in the list of restrictive cases. This is a decision *not* to innovate in the law of confidence, since privacy on the part of one claimant did not alter the analysis of the breach of confidence action brought by another.

[89] This is not a category without controversy, so a judgment has to be made in this respect.

3. *Gorringe v Calderdale* [2004] UKHL 15. This was a decisive victory for public authority defendants, firmly closing the door to negligence duties arising out of failures to exercise statutory powers. As such it removed the last vestiges of *Anns v Merton* in domestic law, and protected public authorities to some extent from liability for negligent failure to act.

4. *Moy v Pettmann-Smith* [2005] UKHL 7. On the facts, there was no breach of the advocate's duty of care to a client. Though not a vertical case, this decision bears some comparison with *Adams v Bracknell*. It cushioned the effect of the abolition of advocates' immunity in *Hall v Simons*.[90] The abolition was itself arguably, though not explicitly, influenced by Convention rights. On this interpretation, it formed one of the less obvious parts of the UK courts' response to *Osman v UK*, on the assumption that immunities at common law may violate art 6 ECHR.[91]

5. *\*Brooks v Commissioner of Police for the Metropolis* [2005] UKHL 24. No duty of care was owed to the claimant eye-witness by the police, in respect of their treatment of him. It appeared to be accepted that there might be cases in respect of the investigation and suppression of crime where duties of care would be owed by the police. The full force of the immunity in *Hill v Chief Constable* would no longer apply. Even so, it is from this point that the *Hill* 'immunity' appears to have been resurrected in the guise of a 'principle'.

6. *Gregg v Scott* [2005] UKHL 2. There was no liability in negligence for a lost chance of a cure from cancer, where the claimant's survival had never been a probability. Though an action against an individual GP, this has particularly significant implications for the National Health Service.

7. *\*JD v East Berkshire* [2005] UKHL 23. No duty of care in negligence is owed to parents whose children are wrongly removed from their care, on unfounded suspicion of abuse, no matter how gross the incompetence of the professional making the relevant judgment. The reasoning applied by the Court of Appeal in recognising a duty to the children was not criticised, but the duties did not extend to the parents even in limited circumstances, because of potential conflicts of interest. Lord Bingham dissented.

8. *Re Deep Vein Thrombosis and Air Travel Group* [2005] UKHL 72. Deep vein thrombosis could not be injury 'by accident' attracting strict liability under the Warsaw Convention on Carriage by Air 1929 art 17.

9. *Commissioners of Customs and Excise v Barclays Bank* [2006] UKHL 28. No duty was owed by a bank to guard the Inland Revenue against economic loss by taking reasonable care to comply with a freezing order. This was an unsuccessful claim *by* a public authority claimant.

10. *Barker v Corus* [2006] UKHL 20. This stands out as more restrictive than the general run of industrial disease cases. After the notably pro-claimant

---

[90] *Hall v Simons* [2002] 1 AC 615.
[91] See the discussion of *Hall v Simons* by R English, 'Forensic Immunity post-*Osman*' (2001) 64 *Modern Law Review* 300, and more recently by R Merkin and J Steele, 'Advocates' Immunity: A UK Perspective' (2008) 14 *New Zealand Business Law Quarterly* 45.

decision in *Fairchild v Glenhaven*,[92] the House of Lords held here that liability of employers for materially contributing to the risk of mesothelioma under *Fairchild* was measured according to their contribution to the risk: claimants must therefore pursue all tortfeasors to secure full compensation. This outcome was reversed in respect of mesothelioma claims by s 3 Compensation Act 2006.

11. *\*Jameel v Wall Street Journal* [2006] UKHL 44. The *Reynolds* privilege assisted the defendant newspaper under the circumstances. The defence should not be drawn too narrowly, and should be understood to be a new 'public interest defence'.

12. *Sutradhar v Natural Environment Research Council* [2006] UKHL 33. An organisation researching water quality did not owe a duty of care to the claimants who were consumers of the water, to ensure that it was safe.

13. *\*Watkins v Home Office* [2006] **UKHL 17.** The action for misfeasance in a public office depended on material damage. Contrary to what the Court of Appeal had decided, interference with a 'constitutional right' did not suffice.

14. *OBG v Allan* [2007] UKHL 21. A number of claims were involved in this case, engaging economic torts and conversion. Most ended in failure for the claimants. *OK! Magazine* succeeded however in its breach of confidence action.

15. *Rothwell v Chemical and Insulating Co Ltd* [2007] UKHL 39. Asymptomatic pleural plaques caused by exposure to asbestos were not material injury capable of grounding a claim in negligence. The effect has been reversed in Scotland by legislation. It has not however been reversed for England and Wales, no doubt because of the likely cost to insurers and potentially also public bodies in their guise as employers. The UK Government did not propose legislation on the point, and a private Member's Bill introduced by Mr Andrew Drismore eventually failed to become law before the Parliamentary session came to a close in time for the election in May 2010.[93]

16. *\*Van Colle v Chief Constable of Hertfordshire; Smith v Chief Constable of Sussex* [2008] **UKHL 55.** The claim in *Van Colle* was argued under the HRA, but the claim in *Smith* was argued in negligence. Both failed.[94] Lord Bingham's proposed 'liability principle', which seemed to be consistent with dicta in *Brooks* (above), was rejected by the majority. The policy reasons against police liability in the investigation and suppression of crime required the 'no duty' area to be defined in general terms, or the police would be exposed to excessive liability or the threat of it.

17. *\* Austin v Chief Commissioner of the Metropolis* [2009] **UKHL 5.** This was only weakly a tort case, since it was argued before the House only in terms of

---

[92] *Fairchild v Glenhaven* [2002] UKHL 22, [2003] 1 AC 32.

[93] Damages (Asbestos-related Conditions) Bill (No 2) 2009–10: see the chapter in this collection by James Lee.

[94] It may be that a case like *Smith* would in future stand a better chance of success under the HRA, given that there arguably was foreseeability of imminent danger to life.

art 5 ECHR. For the purposes of appeal to the House, the claimant conceded that if her claim under art 5 failed (which it did), so too would her claim in false imprisonment. This was despite the fact that the Court of Appeal had reasoned very differently in respect of the two actions. Since the House of Lords read into art 5 a condition that it applied only to *arbitrary* deprivations of liberty, it was probably literally true that the tort claim would have been hopeless.

18. *Gray v Thames Trains* [2009] UKHL 33. A claimant convicted of manslaughter and detained in a secure institution could not claim for losses flowing from his own crime (even though this crime was the result of psychological damage caused by the negligence of the defendant). *Ex turpi causa non oritur actio*, even in cases where the crime could not conceivably have come about but for the defendant's tort. The claimant's loss of earnings claim therefore did not extend to the period of detention.

19. *\*Mitchell v Glasgow City Council* [2009] UKHL 11. No duty of care was owed by a local authority to a tenant murdered by another tenant, to warn him of the meeting and the chance of violence that it generated.

20. *Smith v Northamptonshire* [2009] UKHL 27: a ramp at a patient's house which was regularly used by an employee to transfer the patient to an ambulance was not 'work equipment' within the Provision and Use of Work Equipment Regulations 1998. Strict (or absolute) liability under the Regulations therefore did not bite when the ramp collapsed.

21. *\*Trent Strategic Health Authority v Jain* [2009] UKHL 4. There was no liability in negligence for economic loss caused by an unnecessary and unjustified ex parte application to shut down a care home, destroying the claimants' livelihood, for the same sorts of reasons that were used to deny a duty to suspected parents in *D v East Berkshire*: there was a potential conflict of interest and this should not be allowed to affect decision-making for the benefit of the vulnerable residents of the care homes.[95]

22. *Moore Stephens v Stone & Rolls Ltd* [2009] UKHL 39. A claim by a company which was a vehicle of fraud on the part of its sole director was (by a narrow majority) barred as *ex turpi causa*.

The following tort cases were determined in favour of claimants by the House of Lords during the period 2004–09:

1. *Simmons v British Steel* [2004] UKHL 20: this was an industrial injury claim, taking an expansive approach to liability for psychiatric injury.

2. *Chester v Afshar* [2004] UKHL 41. By a majority, negligence liability was established on the part of a surgeon who did not warn of a risk associated with surgery, even though he did not enhance the risk by his failure to warn. The reasoning was based on patient 'autonomy', not Convention rights.

---

[95] It may well be argued that the principles are consistent with *Customs and Excise v Barclays Bank* (item 9 above), where there was a public authority *claimant*: ie, the consistent principle is that no duty of care is owed between parties to litigation. Our exercise though is to explore the pattern, rather than the expressed principles on which the components of that pattern are based.

Like *Gregg v Scott*, this has important implications for the National Health Service—though it is suggested that these are in no way as far-reaching as the introduction of liability for lost chances of recovery would have been. The chief impact is in advice as to risks that must be provided.

3. *\*Campbell v MGN* [2004] UKHL 22: by a majority, the balance came down in favour of a remedy in respect of some elements of a publication, on the basis of the claimant's right to privacy.

4. **Barber v Somerset CC [2004] UKHL 13.** This was a case endorsing liability for work-related stress. The House broadly approved the criteria stated by the Court of Appeal.

5. *Robb v Salamis* [2006] UKHL 56: interpretation of the Provision and Use of Work Equipment Regulations 1998.

6. **Majrowski v Guy's and St Thomas's NHS Trust [2006] UKHL 34.** Vicarious statutory liability of employer under Protection from Harassment Act 1998.

7. *Law Society v Sephton & Co* [2006] UKHL 22. Commencement of limitation period interpreted to claimants' advantage.

8. *Horton v Sadler* [2006] UKHL 38. Limitation periods again. The House adopted a wide interpretation of the discretion to allow a claim outside the statutory limitation period.

9. *Spencer-Franks v Kellogg Brown and Root* [2008] UKHL 46: another decision under the Provision and Use of Work Equipment Regulations 1998.

10. *Total Network v Her Majesty's Revenue and Customs* [2008] UKHL 19: a successful claim *by* a public authority.

11. *Corr v IBC* [2008] UKHL 13. This was a successful claim under the Fatal Accidents Act 1976 in respect of suicide arising from depression caused by industrial injury. The claimant's success was somewhat balanced by observations about contributory negligence in future cases.

12. **A v Hoare [2008] UKHL 6.**[96] This concerned removal of an anomalous distinction between trespass and negligence in respect of the applicable limitation period. The case has very significant implications for public authorities. Having said that, it means actions will generally now be framed in terms of trespass (sexual assault), and defendant authorities and institutions are less likely to be called upon to defend broad-ranging claims of institutional negligence, which was the artificial result of *Stubbings v Webb*[97] (departed from here), in association with *Lister v Hesley Hall*.[98] Convention rights were not in issue because *Stubbings v Webb* had already survived an unsuccessful application to the European Court of Human Rights:[99] even the shorter limitation period held by the House of Lords in that case to be applicable to trespass actions was compliant with the Convention.

---

[96] Although the defendant in the 'lead' claim was an individual, there were also several public authority defendants.
[97] *Stubbings v Webb* [1993] AC 498.
[98] *Lister v Hesley Hall* [2001] UKHL 22, [2002] 1 AC 215.
[99] *Stubbings v UK* (1997) 23 EHRR 213.

13. ***Ashley v Chief Constable of Sussex* [2008] UKHL 25.** A claim against the police in trespass to the person after a fatal shooting could be pursued even though the defendant had admitted liability in negligence. Convention rights were not at the forefront, though they were treated as relevant by Lord Scott in particular. Monetary remedies were also not at the forefront, since liability in full had already been admitted (even in respect of aggravated damages): their Lordships adopted different approaches, according to which the trespass action would either be an alternative route to the same remedy, or a route to a declaration of unlawfulness, rather than a distinct monetary remedy (rather like the 'vindication' of rights by the HRA remedy).

We can observe that there were considerably more unsuccessful tort claims than successful claims before the House of Lords during this period. Of the 13 successful claims, three involved liability under statute rather than at common law,[100] and three more were interpretations of the Limitation Act 1980. Only one successful claim turned on Convention rights, and this was not an action against a public authority: *Campbell v MGN*. Therefore, significant though *Campbell* is, it should not distract from the fact that there was *no* successful claim against a public authority in this period where Convention rights were clearly important to the arguments. By contrast of the 22 unsuccessful claims, nine could be said to have involved significant argument about Convention rights (and others could be said to have important underlying connections to the Convention rights: *Adams v Bracknell*, and *Moy v Pettman-Smith*). All but one of the unsuccessful claims involving Convention rights arguments (the exception being *Cream Holdings*, a breach of confidence action) were actions against public authorities. Leaving aside *Austin* as not primarily a tort claim (though it is pretty clear that such a claim would also have failed), there were no fewer than seven unsuccessful tort claims against public authorities where Convention rights were clearly relevant, and no successful tort claims in the same category. Every tort action against a public authority before the House of Lords where Convention rights were considered important ended in failure for the claimant.[101]

*Campbell* has been closely analysed as one aspect of a move towards 'horizontality'. But seen in the context not of horizontal actions across all courts and concerned with a variety of substantive topics, but in terms of the House of Lords' record in respect of the law of tort, it stands out as the one case during this period where the House of Lords allowed liability to be extended against a defendant on the basis of the new status of Convention rights. Given what we have said about *Phelps* and *Barrett* (really responses to *Osman*, not to the HRA) and *Reynolds* (which was an exercise in restricting liability, rather than intentionally expanding it), *Campbell* is unique as the one case where the House

---

[100] The existence of statutory liability introduces elements of specific Parliamentary intent that there should be a remedy.

[101] It would be interesting to contrast Privy Council decisions during the same period. 'Vindicatory damages' for breach of constitutional rights were developed during this period. Back home, the approach to HRA damages was in the other direction—restraint.

of Lords extended tort liability (if it is tort)[102] against any defendant on the basis of Convention rights arguments. Even in this one area, privacy, it has been argued here that the role of the House was equivocal.

## VI CONCLUSIONS

The final full stop to the Judicial Committee of the House of Lords provides a good moment to reflect that principles of law are developed by particular people at a particular time in a particular context, and to look back at these developments as aspects of history, recent though they are.[103] It is clear that, during the period explored, the House deliberately decided not to take up the challenge of overhauling this branch of the law in response to the new status of the Convention rights.[104] Where the rights are concerned, their cascade through the law of tort was helped along for a time by the House of Lords but developed much more enthusiastically by lower courts. In vertical cases they retained a 'bolted-on' character in which the House of Lords was the prime mover, frustrating the expectations both of the Court of Appeal, and of commentators. I have tried to set out some reasons— some more clearly evidenced than others—why this might be the case.

For the future, it is entirely possible that the move to a Supreme Court, in combination with a partial change in personnel, will come to make a decisive difference to the approach to the Convention rights in this context—assuming, that is, that the HRA is not repealed.[105] Will the Supreme Court feel less impressed by the sense of cohesion or partnership with other public decision-makers? Will it come to feel more friendly to fellow judges in Strasbourg and more able to enter into dialogue about the interpretation of the rights? If so, then perhaps the Supreme Court will be willing to take ownership of the rights, and assume a 'world-leading', rather than a 'little Englander' role.[106]

Leaving aside the potential for repeal, the final question of course is *why* the two concerns I have noted, if I am right about them, should have become so dominant at this particular time and for this particular group of people. The

---

[102] See n 28. However, the equitable nature of the remedy is no mere accident of detail: the existing balance provided the opportunity for a Convention-style balancing process to be accommodated.

[103] The pressure, generally, is to provide an analysis which feeds into the continuing development of principle. This means that commentators have an incentive to seek principled and forward-looking explanations over contingent and historically situated ones.

[104] Lord Hope predicted around the time of commencement that the 'entire legal system' would be subjected to a process of review and reform by the judiciary: see Arden LJ, 'Human Rights and Civil Wrongs' (n 1) 14, citing Lord Hope, *R v DPP, ex p Kebilene* [2000] 2 AC 326, 375.

[105] If it is, then the 'bolted-on' action under the HRA can clearly be unbolted. The effect of rights which have cascaded or been interwoven cannot so easily be removed, even if courts wished to do so.

[106] These are expressions used by Arden LJ, 'Human Rights and Civil Wrongs' (n 1) 156, to describe the position in the event of leaving the Convention altogether: 'The Strasbourg court can bring about remarkable change and the raising of standards throughout Europe, in my experience its influence stretches far beyond the shores of Europe. As things stand, we have the opportunity to influence and contribute to its jurisprudence. If we left the Convention, we would be little Englanders rather than potential world leaders in the field of human rights'.

answers must remain speculative to some extent. A possible reason is overlap in different concerns. One of these may have been a desire to maintain public confidence in the law at a time of rights-scepticism (though that may be too grand a title for resistance to the HRA), by actively and publicly restraining the growth of liabilities. I propose that there is an element of this behind the pattern, though it is not completely compelling, since the House showed no fear of controversy in the introduction and development of the *Reynolds* defence, for example. As already noted however, this was not a development which had primary application against public authorities; nor did it increase liabilities. A second potential explanation is a sense of cohesion with other public decision-makers: on the whole, public decision-makers were perceived by the House as generally acting in the public interest, and this function was thought to require protection against private law claims.[107] A third explanation is that there was an underlying sense that the violations of human rights claimed in these cases were not the most serious or were not at the core of human rights protection. Cases of abuse, neglect, fatal attack, removal of children, and false accusation are, certainly, very serious. Perhaps then the crucial factor is that in many such cases the fault of the public authority was a fault of omission.[108] But in a different context, a majority of the House of Lords during this period also refused legal challenge to the actions of the state in a case of very serious human rights violations—permanent, forcible eviction from the homeland to a life of exile and penury.[109] This encourages the view that cohesion and separation of powers are the stronger factors.

Ultimately perhaps, the most compelling explanations relate to the House of Lords' perception of the distributive implications of common law liabilities during this particular period, even if not all of their Lordships would have expressed their thoughts in quite this way. Quite possibly, concern over the distributive implications was combined with a wish to keep control of these liabilities. In embracing these concerns, the House of Lords did not see itself as usurping a political role, but as safeguarding the political and public interest role of other decision-makers. The nature of the remedies offered by private law caused the House particular concern. While this chapter has also explored a further potential argument, based in the fear that control through the Convention rights might ultimately mean control by the Strasbourg court, not by the UK courts,[110]

---

[107] As mentioned already, Lord Bingham took a different view on two occasions what this should mean for tort liabilities.

[108] Not so, however, in the (unsuccessful) claim by parents whose children are removed on the basis of false suspicion; or in cases of police shooting or detention, for example.

[109] *R (On the Application of Bancoult) v Secretary of State for Foreign and Commonwealth Affairs* [2008] UKHL 61, [2008] 3 WLR 955. This was a majority decision, and not concerned with civil liability, so that the parallel should be treated with caution. It has been proposed however that this decision—which is hard to explain—is best understood as connected with the approach taken to the separation of powers by the majority judges: see TT Arvind, '"Though it Shocks One Very Much": Formalism and pragmatism in the *Zong* and *Bancoult*' (unpublished paper delivered at York Law School, October 2009).

[110] See the analysis of superior courts' greater resistance to the 'supremacy' of EU law in K Alter, *Establishing the Supremacy of European Law* (Oxford, Oxford University Press, 2001).

the existence of a belief in the need to restrain liabilities works to strengthen the foundation of this concern also.

I suggest that this underlying concern with distributive issues, and at least ostensibly with the location of legitimate decision-making as to such decisions,[111] deeply affected the House of Lords' approach to the Convention rights,[112] but also affected its approach to tort liabilities more generally. Where these coincided, there was the recipe for some quite determined and occasionally surprising judicial restraint of liability. The addition of a Convention rights argument may therefore have been an additional reason for confining liabilities, not for developing them, in the minds of the House of Lords. That is the phenomenon illustrated in this chapter.

---

[111] It is notable that in both *Barker v Corus* and *Rothwell,* legislatures (though in the latter case so far only the Scottish Parliament) have thought that restraint of civil liability by the House of Lords went too far: *cf* James Lee's chapter in this collection.

[112] Note *Austin v CPM* [2009] UKHL 5, [2009] 1 AC 564, where the House of Lords treated art 5 as though it was qualified by 'proportionality'.

# 7

# Keeping Their Heads Above Water? European Law in the House of Lords

ANTHONY ARNULL*

. . .[The] flowing tide of Community law is coming in fast. It has not stopped at high-water mark. It has broken the dykes and the banks. It has submerged the surrounding land. So much so that we have to learn to become amphibious if we wish to keep our heads above water.[1]

## I INTRODUCTION

THIS CHAPTER IS concerned with the reception of European law[2] by the House of Lords prior to the abolition of its appellate jurisdiction pursuant to the Constitutional Reform Act 2005. The discussion will focus mainly on two types of case: those referred by the House of Lords to the European Court of Justice (ECJ) for a preliminary ruling and those raising questions of European law which were disposed of by the House of Lords without a reference to the ECJ. Purely domestic cases decided by the House of Lords where the outcome was influenced by its understanding of the position in European law will also be briefly considered. The chapter will conclude with some general reflections on the relationship between the House of Lords and the ECJ and early evidence of the likely stance towards the latter of the former's successor, the Supreme Court of the United Kingdom established under the 2005 Act on 1 October 2009.

* The comments of Martin Borowski, Graham Gee, Martin Trybus and participants at the SLS Annual Seminar in November 2009 are gratefully acknowledged, with the usual disclaimer.
[1] Lord Denning MR in *Shields v E Coomes (Holdings) Ltd* [1979] 1 All ER 456, 462.
[2] ie the law based on the Treaties establishing the European Communities and the European Union. The European Community was replaced and succeeded by the European Union on the entry into force of the Treaty of Lisbon on 1 December 2009, when the EC Treaty was renamed the Treaty on the Functioning of the European Union (TFEU). That Treaty has the same legal status as the Treaty on European Union (TEU). The EAEC remains a distinct legal entity. The ECSC expired in July 2002.

## II THE PRELIMINARY RULINGS PROCEDURE

Under art 267 TFEU (ex-234 EC/177 EEC), national courts may ask the ECJ for guidance on questions of European law they need to decide before giving judgment. Most national courts enjoy a discretion in deciding whether to refer and may if they wish decide questions of European law for themselves. However, national courts 'against whose decisions there is no judicial remedy in national law' are obliged by art 267(3) to refer such questions to the ECJ.

There was never any doubt that the House of Lords was covered by that paragraph. Although in most cases permission to appeal had to be sought, this did not have the effect of transferring the obligation to refer to the court below. Where a question of European law needed to be resolved, the House was therefore subject to the obligation to refer, either when considering whether to grant permission to appeal[3] or at a later stage in the proceedings. As the Court of Appeal put it in *Chiron Corporation v Murex Diagnostics*,[4] the possibility of asking the House for permission to appeal constituted a 'judicial remedy' for the purposes of art 267(3).

The Court of Appeal did not itself refer a question on the interpretation of that paragraph to the ECJ in the *Chiron* case. However, the latter came to a similar conclusion in *Lyckeskog*,[5] a reference by the Court of Appeal for Western Sweden, whose decisions could only be challenged before the Swedish Supreme Court if it declared the appeal admissible.[6] The ECJ held that a court such as the referring court was not subject to the obligation to refer laid down in art 267 (3).

The purpose of that obligation is 'to prevent a body of national case-law that is not in accordance with the rules of Community law from being established in a Member State'.[7] It provides a safeguard against incorrect application of European law by lower national courts. However, notwithstanding the use in art 267(3) of the word 'shall', the obligation it lays down is a qualified one.

In *CILFIT v Ministry of Health*,[8] the ECJ held that final courts are in the same position as other national courts in deciding whether they need to resolve a question of European law before giving judgment. A final court is not therefore

---

[3] Provision for the House of Lords to make a reference before determining whether to grant permission to appeal was made by Practice Directions and Standing Orders Applicable to Civil Appeals (2007-08 edition) direction 34.3, and by Practice Directions and Standing Orders Applicable to Criminal Appeals (2007-08 edition) direction 32.3. This possibility is also envisaged by the Supreme Court Rules 2009: see r 42(2).

[4] *Chiron Corporation v Murex Diagnostics* [1995] All ER (EC) 88.

[5] Case C-99/00 *Lyckeskog* [2002] ECR I-4839. See also Case C-210/06 *Cartesio Oktató és Szolgáltató Bt*, judgment of 16 December 2008 [75]–[79].

[6] *Lyckeskog* (n 5) [18].

[7] See Case C-495/03 *Intermodal Transports* [2005] ECR I-8151 [29]; Case C-393/98 *Gomes Valente* [2001] ECR I-1327 [17].

[8] Case 283/81 *CILFIT v Ministry of Health* [1982] ECR 3415. See also Case 107/76 *Hoffmann-La Roche v Centrafarm* [1977] ECR 957, where the Court held that national courts of last resort are not required to make a reference in interlocutory proceedings as long as the point of Community law at issue can be referred at a later stage in the proceedings.

obliged to ask for a preliminary ruling where the answer to the question raised cannot affect the outcome of the case.[9] Even where a question of European law is relevant, the ECJ went on to hold that a final court is under no obligation to refer if: (a) 'previous decisions of the Court have already dealt with the point of law in question';[10] or (b) the correct application of European law is so obvious as to leave no scope for any reasonable doubt as to the manner in which the question raised is to be resolved (a situation known as '*acte clair*').

Before the national court concludes that the answer to a question of European law is obvious, it must be convinced that the matter would be equally obvious to the courts of the other Member States and to the ECJ. In that regard, it must take account of the characteristic features of European law and the particular difficulties to which its interpretation gives rise. The ECJ emphasised that:

1. the different language versions of a European provision are all equally authentic and may have to be compared;
2. European law uses its own terminology and legal concepts do not necessarily have the same meaning in European law as in the national laws of the Member States;
3. every provision of European law must be placed in its context and interpreted in the light of European law as a whole, having regard to the objectives of European law and its present state of development.

The *CILFIT* criteria therefore allow national courts of last resort to decide questions of European law for themselves in certain limited circumstances.[11] They do not prevent such courts from seeking a preliminary ruling where they consider it appropriate to do so. The ECJ made clear in its judgment[12] that, even where it has dealt with the point at issue previously, the national court remains free to refer the point to it again. Similarly, the ECJ will not entertain a challenge to the admissibility of a reference on the basis that the national court should have treated the point at issue as *acte clair*.[13]

The *acte clair* doctrine is controversial. Advocate General Caportorti[14] advised the ECJ in *CILFIT* that it would undermine the preliminary rulings procedure, but the doctrine was later criticised for depriving national courts of last resort of any real freedom to decide questions of European law for themselves.[15] A minor concession to the latter view was made in *Intermodal Transports*, where the ECJ made it clear that the *acte clair* doctrine did not require national courts of last

---

[9] See also Case C-344/04 *IATA and ELFAA* [2006] ECR I-403 [28].

[10] *CILFIT* (n 8) [14].

[11] The obligation to refer is qualified only in cases concerning the interpretation of European law. It remains unqualified in cases where the validity of a Union act is challenged: see Case C-461/03 *Gaston Schul Douane-Expediteur* [2005] ECR I-10513 [19].

[12] *CILFIT* (n 8) [15].

[13] See Case C-340/99 *TNT Traco* [2001] ECR I-4109 [35]. Cf art 104(3) of the Court's Rules of Procedure.

[14] *CILFIT* (n 8) 3439.

[15] See A Arnull, *The European Union and its Court of Justice*, 2nd edn (Oxford, Oxford University Press, 2006) 122–25.

resort 'to ensure that . . . the matter is equally obvious to bodies of a non-judicial nature such as administrative authorities.'[16] However, there has been no significant retreat from the *CILFIT* criteria since they were laid down in the early 1980s. They did not in any event constrain the House of Lords unduly, as we shall see.

There is no direct remedy available to the parties if a national court of last resort declines to make a reference to the ECJ: no appeal lies to the latter against the former's decision. This does not mean that there are no potential repercussions if such a court fails to refer, but in practice they are limited in scope. If the effect of the national court's decision is to uphold the validity of an administrative measure and a later decision of the ECJ establishes that the measure in question should have been quashed, it may have to be reviewed by its author.[17] Infringement proceedings may in principle be brought against a Member State by the European Commission where the established case law of its courts on a particular issue is inconsistent with European law, particularly where that case law has been confirmed by its supreme court.[18] However, 'the Commission (and it is not alone) rightly considers that it is not really feasible, and even less advisable, in such cases to bring an action for failure to fulfil an obligation. . .'[19]

In *French and Others v Council and Commission,*[20] an unsuccessful attempt was made to force the Commission's hand. The applicants were involved in litigation in the United Kingdom in which they sought a reference on the interpretation of a European directive. They were eventually refused leave to appeal by the House of Lords without a reference having been made. They then made a complaint to the Commission alleging that the United Kingdom courts had failed to fulfil their obligations under art 267. The Commission subsequently informed the applicants that it had secured a change to the rules of procedure of the House of Lords, so that reasons would in future be given when it declined to make a reference for a preliminary ruling.[21] This was a worthwhile reform, but the applicants were not satisfied and brought an action for damages against the respondent institutions. The action was dismissed by the Court of First Instance (now the General Court)[22] as manifestly inadmissible, a decision upheld by the ECJ.[23]

An additional remedy emerged in *Köbler,*[24] where the ECJ held that non-compliance by a top national court with its obligations under art 267(3) might render the competent state liable in damages to litigants who were thereby

---

[16] *Intermodal Transports* (n 7) [39].

[17] See Case C-453/00 *Kühne & Heitz* [2004] ECR I-837.

[18] See Case C-129/00 *Commission v Italy* [2003] ECR I-14637. Infringement proceedings may result in the imposition of financial sanctions on the state concerned: see art 260 TFEU (ex-228 EC).

[19] See AG Tizzano in *Lyckeskog* (n 5) [65].

[20] Case T-319/03 *French and Others v Council and Commission* [2004] ECR II-769.

[21] See Practice Directions and Standing Orders Applicable to Civil Appeals (2007-08 edition) direction 34.2; Practice Directions and Standing Orders Applicable to Criminal Appeals (2007–08 edition) direction 32.2 (both referring to *CILFIT*); Supreme Court Rules 2009 r 42(1).

[22] See art 19 TEU.

[23] Case C-190/04 P, Order of 22 June 2005 (unpublished).

[24] Case C-224/01 *Köbler* [2003] ECR I-10239. See also Case C-173/03 *Traghetti del Mediterraneo* [2006] ECR I-5177.

deprived of their rights under European law. However, such liability arises 'only in the exceptional case where the [national] court has manifestly infringed the applicable law.'[25] This very high threshold had not been met in the circumstances of that case, and successful claims are likely to be rare.[26]

### III REFERENCES TO THE ECJ BY THE HOUSE OF LORDS

Between United Kingdom accession in 1973 and the creation of the Supreme Court, the House of Lords made a total of 40 references to the ECJ.[27] The three largest categories (leaving aside three withdrawn references) were in the fields of social policy (10 references, of which eight concerned equal treatment for men and women), value added tax (eight references) and jurisdiction and the recognition and enforcement of judgments in civil and commercial matters (five references).[28]

It is hard to compare the number of references made by the House of Lords with the corresponding figures for courts of last resort in other Member States. This is because allowance has to be made for such factors as the size of the state concerned; the organisation and culture of its legal system; the jurisdiction and case load of its top court or courts; length of membership; the evolution of the substantive scope of European law; and the volume of economic exchange with other Member States, which has been shown to have a major effect on national reference rates.[29] However, the figures[30] show that, if the House of Lords was not a particularly enthusiastic interlocutor of the ECJ, other top national courts were even less keen to refer. Indeed, some—notably the *Bundesverfassungsgericht* (German Federal Constitutional Court)—have never made a reference.

The House of Lords made its first reference just over six years after United Kingdom accession. The case in question was *R v Henn and Darby*,[31] which was referred in February 1979 and was the first in which the ECJ had been called upon

---

[25] *Köbler* (n 24) [53].

[26] See further B Beutler, 'State Liability for Breaches of Community Law by National Courts: Is the Requirement of a Manifest Infringement of the Applicable Law an Insurmountable Obstacle?' (2009) 46 *Common Market Law Review* 773.

[27] For a complete list, see A Arnull, 'The Law Lords and the European Union: Swimming with the Incoming Tide' (2010) 35 *European Law Review* 57, 86–87. In 2008, the House of Lords disposed of 96 appeals and 207 petitions for leave to appeal: *Judicial and Court Statistics 2008* (Cm 7697, September 2009) tables 1.3 and 1.4, http://www.justice.gov.uk/publications/judicialandcourtstatistics.htm. See further, B Dickson, 'Judicial Activism in the House of Lords 1995–2007' in B Dickson (ed), *Judicial Activism in Common Law Supreme Courts* (Oxford, Oxford University Press, 2007) 366.

[28] For details, see Arnull, (n 27) 61–62.

[29] See J Golub, 'Modelling Judicial Dialogue in the European Community: The Quantitative Basis of Preliminary References to the ECJ', EUI Working Paper RSC No 96/58, 23; A Stone Sweet, *The Judicial Construction of Europe* (Oxford, Oxford University Press, 2004) 55–62 and 98–106; G Tridimas and T Tridimas, 'National Courts and the European Court of Justice: A Public Choice Analysis of the Preliminary Reference Procedure' (2004) 24 *International Review of Law and Economics* 125, 132–33.

[30] See Table 20, Statistics concerning the judicial activity of the Court of Justice (2008), available at http://curia.europa.eu/jcms/upload/docs/application/pdf/2009-03/ra08_en_cj_stat.pdf.

[31] Case 34/79 *R v Henn and Darby* [1979] ECR 3795.

to consider the scope of the exception contained in art 36 EEC (now 36 TFEU) 'on grounds of public morality' from the prohibition between Member States of 'quantitative restrictions and all measures having equivalent effect' laid down in art 30 EEC (now 34 TFEU). One of the questions referred to the ECJ was whether that prohibition applied to a total ban on imports. The Court of Appeal had concluded that it did not,[32] a view described by Advocate General Warner as 'plainly wrong'.[33] The ECJ declared that art 30 covered 'a prohibition on imports inasmuch as this is the most extreme form of restriction' and referred to the use in art 36 of the expression 'prohibitions or restrictions on imports'.[34]

When the ECJ's ruling came to be applied by the House of Lords, Lord Diplock[35] said that the case showed 'the danger of an English court applying English canons of statutory construction to the interpretation of the EEC Treaty or, for that matter, of regulations or directives.'[36] He explained that, in view of the established case law of the ECJ,

> it appeared to me to be so free from any doubt that an absolute prohibition of importation of goods of a particular description from other member states fell within art 30 that I should not have been disposed to regard the instant case as involving any matter of interpretation of that article that was open to question. But the strong inclination expressed by the Court of Appeal to adopt the contrary view shows that there is involved a question of interpretation on which judicial minds can differ. It serves as a timely warning to English judges not to be too ready to hold that because the meaning of the English text (which is one of six of equal authority) seems plain to them no question of interpretation can be involved.[37]

As one would expect, some of the references made by the House of Lords led to important developments in European substantive law. A notable example is *Foster v British Gas plc*,[38] referred by the House of Lords in 1989, which remains the leading authority on the types of body (sometimes called 'emanations' or 'organs' of the state) against which directives may be enforced directly in the national courts. However, some references are more notable for their impact on the domestic law of the referring court than their importance for the development of European law. A good illustration is provided by the famous *Factortame* litigation, which concerned the compatibility with European law of the conditions for the registration of fishing vessels introduced by Part II of the Merchant Shipping Act 1988. That litigation produced three references to the ECJ, including one by the House of Lords, and three important judgments of the House of Lords. The 1988 Act also led to the institution by the European Commission of infringement proceedings against the United Kingdom.

---

[32] See *R v Henn (Maurice Donald)* [1978] 1 WLR 1031.

[33] *Henn* (n 31) 3820.

[34] ibid [12].

[35] With whom Lords Wilberforce, Salmon, Fraser and Scarman agreed.

[36] *R v Henn (Maurice Donald)* [1980] 2 All ER 166, 196.

[37] ibid 197.

[38] Case C-188/89 *Foster v British Gas plc* [1990] ECR I-3313. See also Case C-271/91 *Marshall v Southampton and South-West Hampshire Area Health Authority* [1993] ECR I-4367.

The main steps in the *Factortame* litigation were as follows.

1. The applicants brought proceedings in the Divisional Court challenging the compatibility of the 1988 Act with European law and sought interim relief to protect their position pending final judgment. The Divisional Court[39] made a reference to the ECJ on the substance of the case and suspended the contested provisions of the 1988 Act as regards the applicants.

2. On appeal,[40] the Court of Appeal held that English courts had no power under national law to suspend an Act of Parliament in the absence of a definitive ruling that it was incompatible with European law.

3. On further appeal,[41] the House of Lords upheld the Court of Appeal's decision on the position in national law. Applying the criteria laid down in *CILFIT*, however, it concluded that it was obliged to ask the ECJ whether European law required interim protection to be granted in such circumstances.

4. In the course of the infringement action brought by the European Commission, the President of the ECJ made an order requiring the United Kingdom to suspend the application of certain provisions of the 1988 Act, pending judgment in the main proceedings.[42]

5. In response to the reference by the House of Lords, the ECJ held that 'the full effectiveness of Community law would be . . . impaired if a rule of national law could prevent a court seised of a dispute governed by Community law from granting interim relief . . . [A] court which in those circumstances would grant interim relief, if it were not for a rule of national law, is obliged to set aside that rule.'[43]

6. The House of Lords duly granted the applicants interim relief.[44]

7. In response to the reference by the Divisional Court on the substance of the case, the ECJ in effect held that the 1988 Act was incompatible with European law.[45]

8. The infringement action brought against the United Kingdom was upheld by the ECJ.[46]

9. The Divisional Court made a further reference to the ECJ asking for guidance on whether, and if so in what circumstances, the applicants were entitled to compensation for the losses they claimed to have suffered as a result of the infringements of European law which had now been established.

---

[39] *R v Secretary of State for Transport* [1989] 2 CMLR 353.

[40] ibid.

[41] *Factortame Ltd and Others v Secretary of State for Transport* [1990] 2 AC 85.

[42] Case 246/89 R *Commission v United Kingdom* [1989] ECR 3125. Effect was given to that order by the Merchant Shipping Act 1988 (Amendment) Order 1989 (SI 1989/2006), which entered into force on 2 November 1989.

[43] Case C-213/89 R *v Secretary of State for Transport, ex p Factortame* [1990] ECR I-2433 [21].

[44] *R v Secretary of State, ex p Factortame* [1991] 1 AC 603.

[45] Case C-221/89 R *v Secretary of State for Transport, ex p Factortame* [1991] ECR I-3905.

[46] Case C-246/89 *Commission v United Kingdom* [1991] ECR I-4585.

10. The ECJ gave guidance on the circumstances in which European law required compensation to be paid by Member States who had failed to comply with their Treaty obligations.[47]

11. The House of Lords held that the United Kingdom's breach of its European obligations was sufficiently serious to entitle the respondents to compensation for damage directly caused by that breach.[48]

This saga contributed to the development of European law in at least two respects. From a substantive point of view it elucidated the relationship between, on the one hand, the system of national fishing quotas established by European legislation and, on the other hand, the right of establishment and the principle of non-discrimination on grounds of nationality. The litigation also helped to clarify the scope of the principle of state liability. The issue of interim relief was perhaps more straightforward from a European law perspective, but its domestic implications were profound. In considering whether to refer that issue to the ECJ, Lord Bridge[49] was influenced by the effect he thought European law would produce if the applicants were to succeed. Section 2(4) of the European Communities Act 1972, he declared, had

> precisely the same effect as if a section were incorporated in Part II of the Act of 1988 which in terms enacted that the provisions with respect to registration of British fishing vessels were to be without prejudice to the directly enforceable Community rights of nationals of any member state of the EEC. Thus it is common ground that, in so far as the applicants succeed before the ECJ in obtaining a ruling in support of the Community rights which they claim, those rights will prevail over the restrictions imposed on registration of British fishing vessels by Part II of the Act of 1988.[50]

Sir William Wade[51] argued that to say that the terms of the European Communities Act 'are putatively incorporated in the Act of 1988 is merely another way of saying that the Parliament of 1972 has imposed a restriction upon the Parliament of 1988. This is exactly what the classical doctrine of parliamentary sovereignty will not permit.' Sir John Laws, writing extrajudicially, was more guarded, arguing that Parliament could always repeal the European Communities Act and that there were 'a number of areas where a particular statutory construction is only likely to be accepted by the courts if it is vouchsafed by express provision.'[52] Whatever view is taken on this issue,[53] it remains the case that the House of Lords' apparently unquestioning acceptance of the primacy of European law involved an

---

[47] Joined Cases C-46/93 and C-48/93 *Brasserie du Pêcheur and Factortame* [1996] ECR I-1029.

[48] *R v Secretary of State for Transport, ex p Factortame Ltd and Others* [1999] All ER (D) 1173.

[49] With whom Lords Brandon, Oliver, Goff and Jauncey agreed.

[50] *Factortame* (n 41) 140.

[51] HWR Wade, 'Sovereignty—Revolution or Evolution?' (1996) 112 *Law Quarterly Review* 568, 570.

[52] See J Laws, 'Law and Democracy' [1995] *Public Law* 72, 89. He gave as examples statutes imposing taxes or criminal liability or having retroactive effect.

[53] See further P Craig, 'Sovereignty of the United Kingdom Parliament after *Factortame*' (1991) 11 *Yearbook of European Law* 221; TRS Allan, 'Parliamentary Sovereignty: Law, Politics and Revolution' (1997) 113 *Law Quarterly Review* 443.

interpretation of the European Communities Act that was by no means a foregone conclusion.[54] The result was a significant reinforcement of the status of European law in the United Kingdom. It paved the way for the later ruling of the House of Lords, delivered after the ECJ had pronounced on the question of interim relief, suspending the application of the 1988 Act at a time when its compatibility with Community law had still not been conclusively determined.[55] In its third judgment in the *Factortame* litigation, the House of Lords dealt in a remarkably matter-of-fact way with the principle of state liability, notwithstanding the considerable financial implications for the British Government.

*Factortame* marked a sea-change in the attitude of the English courts to European law. The suspicion and defensiveness evident in earlier case law[56] gave way to an awareness of how European law might strengthen the capacity of the courts in general, and the House of Lords in particular, to uphold the rule of law and protect individual rights. This necessarily entailed some reduction in the deference traditionally accorded to the wishes of Parliament.

The magnitude of the shift was underlined in *R v Secretary of State for Employment, ex p Equal Opportunities Commission*.[57] In that case, the applicants challenged the compatibility with European law of provisions of the Employment Protection (Consolidation) Act 1978 granting protection against unfair dismissal and redundancy on the basis that they discriminated against part-time workers, the majority of whom were women. They sought judicial review of a letter written to them by the Secretary of State claiming that the contested provisions were justified and refusing to reconsider them. Lord Keith[58] observed: 'The question is whether judicial review is available for the purpose of securing a declaration that certain United Kingdom primary legislation is incompatible with European Community law.'[59] The *Factortame* case was, he said, 'a precedent in favour of the EOC's recourse to judicial review for the purpose of challenging as incompatible with European Community law the relevant provisions of the Act of 1978.'[60] The EOC was simply seeking 'to obtain a ruling which reflects the primacy of European Community law enshrined in section 2 of the [European Communities] Act of 1972' and to establish whether the relevant provisions of the 1978 Act were compatible with European law.'[61] He went on to conclude—without making a

---

[54] *cf* the remarks of Lord Diplock in *Garland v British Rail Engineering Ltd* [1983] 2 AC 751, 771, and Lord Denning in *Macarthys v Smith* [1979] 3 CMLR 44, 47. See TRS Allan, 'Parliamentary Sovereignty: Lord Denning's Dexterous Revolution' (1983) 3 *Oxford Journal of Legal Studies* 22.

[55] See E Wicks, *The Evolution of a Constitution: Eight Key Moments in British Constitutional History* (Oxford, Hart Publishing, 2006) 156.

[56] See, eg, the famous decision of the Court of Appeal in *HP Bulmer Ltd and Another v J Bollinger SA and Others* [1974] Ch. 401.

[57] *R v Secretary of State for Employment, ex p Equal Opportunities Commission* [1995] 1 AC 1. The Equal Opportunities Commission (EOC) was replaced in 2007 by the Equality and Human Rights Commission, established under the Equality Act 2006.

[58] With whom Lords Lowry, Browne-Wilkinson and Slynn agreed; Lord Jauncey dissented.

[59] ibid, 26.

[60] ibid, 27.

[61] Ibid.

reference to the ECJ—that those provisions were not objectively justified and granted the declarations sought.

## IV  THE EFFECT OF EUROPEAN LAW IN PURELY DOMESTIC CASES

The impact of *Factortame* was not confined to cases concerned with European law. It had a direct impact on the outcome of the purely domestic case of *M v Home Office*,[62] which raised the question whether a finding of contempt of court could be made against a minister of the Crown. The alleged contempt arose from the failure of the Home Secretary to comply with an injunction requiring an asylum-seeker to be brought back to the United Kingdom. The case had no factor linking it with European law. However, Lord Woolf [63] referred to *Factortame* and pointed out that 'the unhappy situation now exists that while a citizen is entitled to obtain injunctive relief (including interim relief) against the Crown or an officer of the Crown to protect his interests under Community law he cannot do so in respect of his other interests which may be just as important.'[64] He concluded that the relevant legislation offered no support for the view, endorsed by the House of Lords in *Factortame* before the issue was referred to the ECJ, 'that in respect of ministers and other officers of the Crown alone the remedy of an injunction, including an interim injunction, is not available.'[65] There was in Lord Woolf's view nothing to prevent a court from making a finding of contempt against a government minister.

*M v Home Office* is far from being the only example of a purely domestic case decided by the House of Lords in which the outcome was affected by European law. Two further examples confirmed the Law Lords' growing awareness of the potential of European law to reinforce the rule of law and individual rights. One was *Woolwich Building Society v IRC*,[66] which involved a claim for the recovery of tax paid pursuant to regulations which had been found to be ultra vires. Lord Goff referred to a decision of the ECJ making it clear that national rules 'making it virtually impossible or excessively difficult to secure the repayment of charges levied contrary to Community law'[67] would be unlawful. He observed: '. . .it would be strange if the right of the citizen to recover overpaid charges were to be more restricted under domestic law than it is under European law.' He therefore concluded 'that money paid by a citizen to a public authority in the form of taxes or other levies paid pursuant to an ultra vires demand by the authority is prima facie recoverable by the citizen as of right.'[68] The other example is *National*

---

[62]  *M v Home Office* [1994] 1 AC 377.

[63]  With whom Lords Keith, Templeman, Griffiths and Browne-Wilkinson agreed.

[64]  *M v Home Office* (n 62) 407.

[65]  *M v Home Office* (n 62) 422.

[66]  *Woolwich Building Society v IRC* [1993] AC 70.

[67]  See Case 199/82 *San Giorgio* [1983] ECR 3595 [14].

[68]  *Woolwich* (n 66) 177.

*Westminster Bank plc v Spectrum Plus Ltd,*[69] where Lords Nicholls and Hope referred to the practice of the ECJ[70] in concluding that the House of Lords might exceptionally deliver a ruling with prospective effect only (although they did not think it should do so in the instant case).

## V DECLINING TO MAKE A REFERENCE TO THE ECJ

We turn now to cases where the House of Lords decided a question of European law without making a reference to the ECJ. When a national court of last resort persuades itself, perhaps on the basis of the *CILFIT* criteria, that a reference is not required, the result may be the development in the state concerned of a line of case law which is inconsistent with European law.[71] The effect of such cases may in due course be corrected, but they all involve a potential denial of justice to the parties in the instant case and in later cases where the decision reached there is applied.

Some cases where the House of Lords decided a point of European law without making a reference to the ECJ are uncontroversial.[72] In others, there is room for argument about whether or not a reference should have been made.[73] But in some instances the failure of the House of Lords to seek the guidance of the ECJ is open to serious criticism. One of several examples is *Freight Transport Association Ltd and Others v London Boroughs Transport Committee.*[74] That case involved a requirement introduced by the appellant committee that heavy goods vehicles using residential streets in Greater London at night should be fitted with an air-brake noise suppressor. The requirement was challenged by the respondent, who represented the transport and distribution industries, as contrary to two directives adopted by the Council under art 100 EEC (now 115 TFEU), one to do with brakes, the other to do with sound levels.

The brake directive was concerned with the approximation of the laws of the Member States relating to the braking devices of certain categories of motor vehicles and of their trailers.[75] It prevented Member States from prohibiting the use of a vehicle on grounds relating to its brakes where they satisfied the requirements set out in annexes to the directive. The Court of Appeal held that the requirement laid down by the appellant committee was incompatible with

---

[69] *National Westminster Bank plc v Spectrum Plus Ltd* [2005] AC 680.

[70] See eg, Case C-209/03 *Bidar* [2005] ECR I-2119.

[71] *Intermodal Transports* (n 7).

[72] See eg, *R v Chief Constable of Sussex, ex p International Trader's Ferry Ltd* [1999] 2 AC 418.

[73] See eg, *White v White and the Motor Insurers' Bureau* [2001] 2 CMLR 1; *Crehan v Inntrepreneur Pub Co* [2007] 1 AC 333.

[74] *Freight Transport Association Ltd and Others v London Boroughs Transport Committee* [1991] 3 All ER 915. See also *Duke v GEC Reliance Ltd* [1988] AC 618; *Finnegan v Clowney Youth Training Programme* [1990] 2 AC 407; *Re Sandhu*, The Times, 10 May 1985; *Three Rivers DC v Bank of England (No 3)* [2003] 2 AC 1. For discussion of these cases, see Arnull, (n 27) 69–79.

[75] Dir 71/320, OJ 1971 L 202/37.

the directive, but Lord Templeman[76] said the directive 'has got nothing to do with sound levels and is not concerned with traffic regulation . . . [it] harmonises the technical requirements of brake devices used in vehicles throughout the Community and ensures that the brake systems of all vehicles are efficient and safe.'[77] Conversely, the disputed requirement 'does not prohibit the use of a vehicle on grounds relating to its braking devices.' It regulated traffic and protected the environment by providing that certain roads remained banned to certain vehicles 'whose brake sound levels create a nuisance unnecessarily.'[78]

The sound level directive was concerned with the approximation of the laws of the Member States relating to the permissible sound level and the exhaust system of motor vehicles.[79] It prevented Member States from prohibiting the use of a vehicle on grounds relating to the permissible sound level and exhaust system where the sound level and exhaust system satisfied the requirements set out in an annex to the directive. The Court of Appeal again thought that the requirement laid down by the appellant committee was incompatible with the directive, but Lord Templeman declared that '[t]he sound level directive does not deal with the sound of compressed air brakes and is not concerned with traffic regulation.'[80]

In Lord Templeman's view, the fact that a vehicle complied with the technical requirements contained in Council directives based on art 100 'and is therefore entitled to be used in every member state throughout the Community' did not mean that it was 'thereby entitled to be driven on every road, on every day, at every hour throughout the Community.' He was impressed with the level of disturbance caused by unsuppressed brakes and the relatively low cost of fitting noise suppressors.[81] He therefore upheld the validity of the disputed requirement and rejected the respondents' suggestion that the case should be referred to the ECJ for a preliminary ruling: 'No plausible grounds have been advanced for a reference to the European Court.'[82]

It seems self-evident that, as a court of last resort, the House of Lords was at the very least obliged to refer questions to the ECJ on the meaning and effect of the two directives.[83] Lord Templeman did not refer to *CILFIT* in his speech, but it could not plausibly have been argued that a conclusion that seemed to fly in the face of their wording was *acte clair*.

---

[76] Whose speech was endorsed by Lords Keith, Roskill, Oliver and Goff.
[77] *Freight Transport Association* (n 74) 922.
[78] ibid.
[79] Council Directive 70/157, [1970] OJ L42/16.
[80] *Freight Transport Association* (n 74) 923.
[81] See, in particular, *Freight Transport Association* (n 74) 920.
[82] ibid 928.
[83] For a detailed analysis of issues on which the Court's guidance should have been sought, see S Weatherill, 'Regulating the Internal Market: Result Orientation in the House of Lords' (1992) 17 *European Law Review* 299.

VI AN ASSESSMENT

## A The Record of the House of Lords

The House of Lords was undoubtedly aware of the capacity of European law to reinforce its role as guardian of the rule of law and fundamental constitutional principles. It would also have known that, if it did not come to an accommodation with the ECJ and European law, it might find itself outflanked by lower national courts entering into direct dialogue with Luxembourg. Be that as it may, the House of Lords was never an enthusiastic interlocutor of the ECJ. It might have helped if some Law Lords had served on the ECJ, but only one with direct experience was ever appointed.[84] Another barrier may have been the form of the ECJ's judgments. Although this has evolved over the years, it remains reminiscent of that of the top French courts, the Conseil d'Etat and the Cour de Cassation.[85] Judgments of the ECJ are collegiate and there are no separate or dissenting opinions. Although they contain a description of the factual background and the arguments of the parties and give reasons for the decision—and nowadays seek to situate it within the evolving mosaic of the ECJ's case law—the analysis often appears superficial by the standards of common law judgments and may have contributed to a certain loss of respect on the part of the House of Lords.[86] It certainly seems to have inhibited the development of a dialogue[87] as healthy as that which it came to enjoy with the European Court of Human Rights in Strasbourg.[88]

---

[84] Lord Slynn, an Advocate General at the ECJ from 1981 to 1988 and a Judge from 1988 to 1992, served as a Law Lord from 1992 to 2002.

[85] See M Lasser, *Judicial Deliberations* (Oxford, Oxford University Press, 2004); Arnull, *The European Union and its Court of Justice* (n 15) ch 17.

[86] In some cases, the House of Lords found it necessary to ask the Court for further guidance in cases which had been the subject of references earlier in the same proceedings: see eg, Case C-309/06 *Marks & Spencer* [2008] ECR I-2283; Case C-358/08 *Aventis Pasteur SA v OB*, judgment of 2 December 2009.

[87] See further Lord Mance, 'The Common Law and Europe: Difference of Style or Substance and Do They Matter?', University of Birmingham, Holdsworth Club Presidential Address, 24 November 2006, available at www.law.bham.ac.uk/documents/holdsworth-address2007.pdf. Perhaps the only area in which a fundamental difference of approach emerged between the House of Lords and the ECJ was private international law: see J Harris, 'Understanding the English Response to the Europeanisation of Private International Law' [2008] *Journal of Private International Law* 347; Mance, ibid 19–22. See also the chapter by Professor Briggs in this collection. Compare also *West Tankers Inc v RAS Riunione Adriatica di Sicurta SpA ('The Front Comor')* [2007] UKHL 4 with Case C-185/07 *Allianz (formerly Riunione Adriatica di Sicurtà)*, judgment of 10 February 2009. A judgment in an equal treatment case that attracted particularly forceful criticism for its alleged failure to engage properly with the issues was Case C-167/97 *R v Secretary of State for Employment, ex p Seymour-Smith and Perez* [1999] ECR I-623. See C Barnard and B Hepple, 'Indirect discrimination: interpreting *Seymour-Smith*' (1999) 58 *Cambridge Law Journal* 399.

[88] See A Le Sueur, 'A Report on Six Seminars About the UK Supreme Court', Legal Studies Research Paper No 1/2008, Queen Mary University of London (available at http://ssrn.com/abstract=1324749) 47–52; D Anderson, 'The Law Lords and the European Courts' in A Le Sueur (ed), *Building the UK's New Supreme Court: National and Comparative Perspectives* (Oxford, Oxford University Press, 2004) 214–15.

The House of Lords' subtle approach to European law may therefore be described as one of guarded enthusiasm. It never displayed the euroscepticism that has become so prevalent in politics and the media in the United Kingdom. It made just enough references to avoid being seen as obstructive of the wishes of Parliament as expressed in the European Communities Act 1972. It applied the rulings of the ECJ faithfully and sometimes seemed to welcome the opportunity given to it by European law to extend new principles to domestic cases lacking any European element. However, impatience with the delay involved in references[89] and diminishing confidence in the capacity of the ECJ to deal convincingly with its concerns led the House of Lords on several occasions to deal with questions of European law itself. Not only did this sometimes result in decisions which were difficult to reconcile with its Treaty obligations as a court of last resort, but it may ultimately have proved counterproductive because it reduced the opportunities for the House of Lords to educate the ECJ in the principles underlying the English legal system, and the concerns of English courts. It also meant that the House of Lords was unable to exert any significant influence on the development of European law.[90]

The national court which has proved most effective at shifting the direction of European law has adopted a markedly different approach. Despite never yet having made a reference, the *Bundesverfassungsgericht* has succeeded in focusing the attention of the ECJ on such issues as the protection of fundamental rights and the limits of the Union's powers.[91] Its success has been due less to persuasion (although the judgments concerned were fully and closely reasoned) than to its status as the Constitutional Court of the most powerful Member State and the implied threat that it might itself review the validity of European acts if the institutions of the EU were allowed to act in a way which was inconsistent with its own conception of fundamental rights and the limits of the powers conferred on them. Its case law to that effect has influenced the approach of the supreme courts of other Member States, such as Denmark, Poland and the Czech Republic. Working within the confines of the European Communities Act 1972, the House of Lords was never likely to exercise a similar degree of influence on the development of European law.

---

[89]   Though *cf* the remarks of Lord Walker in proposing a further reference in *Marks and Spencer plc v Customs and Excise Commissioners* [2005] STC 1254, 1270.

[90]   Though F Jacobs and D Anderson, 'European Influences', in L Blom-Cooper, B Dickson and G Drewry (eds), *The Judicial House of Lords 1876–2009* (Oxford, Oxford University Press, 2009) 497 note the valuable contribution made by Law Lords to the work of Sub-Committee E (Law and Institutions) of the influential European Union Committee of the House of Lords. The creation of the Supreme Court deprived the Committee of the expertise of the United Kingdom's most senior judges and the judges themselves of the benefits of membership.

[91]   See eg, *Internationale Handelsgesellschaft mbH v Einfuhr- und Vorratsstelle für Getreide und Futtermittel* ('Solange I') [1974] 2 CMLR 540; *Wünsche* ('Solange II') [1987] 3 CMLR 225; *Brunner v European Union Treaty* [1994] 1 CMLR 57; judgment of 30 June 2009 on the German act approving the Treaty of Lisbon.

## B  Prospects for the Supreme Court

Is the Supreme Court likely to behave differently? Its decision in *Office of Fair Trading v Abbey National plc and Others*[92] suggests that, for the time being at least, it will maintain the arm's-length relationship with the ECJ established by the House of Lords. The issue in *Abbey National* was the extent to which the OFT could challenge the fairness of certain charges imposed by the respondent banks on their customers pursuant to standard terms agreed between them. Customers incurred the contested charges when they allowed an account to go overdrawn without having obtained permission from their bank beforehand. Charges of this kind helped the banks to avoid imposing charges on customers who kept their accounts in credit. Thousands of claims had been brought in the county courts by individual litigants affected by the contested charges. Nearly all those claims had been stayed pending the outcome of the proceedings between the OFT and the banks.

The case turned on the effect of reg 6(2) of the Unfair Terms in Consumer Contracts Regulations 1999,[93] which provided:

> In so far as it is in plain intelligible language, the assessment of fairness of a term shall not relate –
>
> (a)  to the definition of the main subject matter of the contract, or
> (b)  to the adequacy of the price or remuneration, as against the goods or services supplied in exchange.

The 1999 Regulations were introduced to give effect to Directive 93/13 on unfair terms in consumer contracts.[94] The provision of that directive which corresponded to reg 6(2), art 4(2), was in similar terms and the two provisions were treated as having the same effect.

The crucial provision was reg 6(2)(b). As Lord Phillips explained,[95] the question was whether, for the purposes of that provision, the contested charges constituted the price or remuneration, as against the services supplied in exchange. Both the High Court and the Court of Appeal had concluded that reg 6(2)(b) did not have the effect of limiting the assessment of fairness that the OFT was entitled to carry out. The Supreme Court disagreed. Lord Walker (with whom Lords Phillips, Mance and Neuberger and Lady Hale agreed) said:[96]

> I would declare that the bank charges levied on personal current account customers in respect of unauthorised overdrafts . . . constitute part of the price or remuneration for the banking services provided and, in so far as the terms giving rise to the charges are in plain intelligible language, no assessment under the Unfair Terms in Consumer Contracts Regulations 1999 of the fairness of those terms may relate to their adequacy as against the services supplied.

---

[92]  *Office of Fair Trading v Abbey National plc and Others* [2009] UKSC 6.
[93]  SI 1999/2083.
[94]  [1993] OJ L95/29.
[95]  *Office of Fair Trading* (n 92) [57].
[96]  ibid [51].

Even though the ECJ had yet to rule on the scope of the underlying provision of Directive 93/13, the Supreme Court declined to make a reference for a preliminary ruling. The question whether the Court was obliged to make a reference was discussed by Lords Walker, Phillips, Mance and Neuberger. Lord Walker acknowledged that reg 6(2) 'does indeed follow closely the English text of Article 4(2) of the Directive',[97] which he proceeded to set out. He went on: 'The Court has had available the texts of Article 4(2) in French, German and some other languages, but they cast little light on the interpretation of the English text.' While there may be room for argument about whether, in a Union of 27 Member States, the *CILFIT* case requires all the language versions to be considered,[98] there is little evidence in the judgment of the Supreme Court of a serious attempt to compare any of the language versions. Lord Mance seemed sceptical whether looking at other language versions would provide any help: 'In the present case, we are concerned with a relatively simple sentence, using simple and basic concepts, and the scope for different readings of different language texts seems very limited.'[99]

Any such comparison as might have been made does not appear to have started from the correct premise. As the ECJ made clear in *CILFIT*, all the language versions of European legislation are equally authentic. The object of comparing the language versions of a provision is therefore to find a meaning which is consistent with all (or nearly all) of those versions and if possible with the purpose and context of the provision, bearing in mind the need to ensure its uniform application throughout the Member States. That object is unlikely to be met if those making the comparison ask whether other language versions cast any light on the meaning of the text in their own language. This is certainly not how the ECJ would conduct the comparative analysis, yet the national court is supposed to satisfy itself that the answer to the question of interpretation that has arisen would be equally obvious to the ECJ before concluding that it leaves no scope for any reasonable doubt.

Towards the end of his judgment, Lord Walker devoted three further paragraphs[100] to the question whether a reference should be made. They are worth setting out here in full:

> This court, as the national court of last resort, is under an obligation to make a reference to the Court of Justice under art 234 of the Treaty if a decision on the correct interpretation of the Directive is necessary to enable the court to give judgment, and the point is not *acte clair*. Neither side showed any enthusiasm for a reference, because of the further delay that would be occasioned in a very large number of claims at present stayed. The court is entitled to take the likely delay into account, although not as an overriding consideration, in deciding whether to make a reference.

---

[97]   ibid [5].

[98]   See AG Jacobs in Case C-338/95 *Wiener v Hauptzollamt Emmerich* [1997] ECR I-6495, 6517; AG Tesauro in *Lyckeskog* (n 5) 4869.

[99]   *Office of Fair Trading* (n 92) [115].

[100]   ibid [48]–[50].

If (as I understand to be the case) the court is unanimous that the appeal should be allowed, then in my opinion we should treat the point as *acte clair*, and decide against making a reference. It may seem paradoxical for a court of last resort to conclude that a point is clear when it is differing from the carefully-considered judgments of the very experienced judges who have ruled on it in lower courts. But sometimes a court of last resort does conclude, without any disrespect, that the lower courts were clearly wrong, and in my respectful opinion this is such a case.

Even if some or all of the court feel that the point is not *acte clair*, I would still propose that we ought not to incur the delay involved in a reference under art 234, since a decision on the correct construction of art 4(2) of the Directive is not essential for the determination of this appeal. The correct construction of art 4(2) is a question of Community law, but the application of the Article, properly construed, to the facts is a question for national law. Even if the Court of Appeal was not clearly wrong on the issue of construction, it was in my respectful opinion clearly wrong in applying its construction to the facts. In other circumstances it might be regarded as rather unprincipled to take that means of avoiding an important issue of Community law, but in the special circumstances of this case I would regard it as the lesser of two evils. There is a strong public interest in resolving the matter without further delay.

This passage calls for several comments.

The parties' lack of enthusiasm for a reference to the ECJ appears to be the reason why no reference was seriously considered by the courts below.[101] However, neither the wishes of the parties nor the delay a reference would cause are relevant to the scope of the obligation imposed by the Treaty on national courts of last resort. One may in any event question whether the proceedings were urgent for any reason other than commercial and judicial convenience. The Court gave no reason for believing that the further delay a reference would entail would cause hardship to any of the individuals whose claims had been stayed pending the outcome of the proceedings. Certainly they were not urgent in the same sense as proceedings involving persons in custody[102] or the interests of children. If, however, the Supreme Court had felt there was a pressing need for a swift decision, it could have asked the ECJ to apply the accelerated procedure provided for in art 104a of its Rules of Procedure. In 2008, references handled under that procedure were dealt with by the ECJ in an average of four and a half months. This is less than the period which elapsed between the hearing of the case before the House of Lords in June 2009 and the judgment of the Supreme Court the following November.

Lord Walker could be understood as suggesting, in the second paragraph of the passage quoted above, that a point which is not *acte clair* may be treated as if it were where the Supreme Court is unanimous about how it should be resolved. This was presumably not his intention, because the result would effectively be to abrogate the obligation to refer imposed by the Treaty on national courts of last resort. In any event, Lord Walker clearly felt uncomfortable about describing

---

[101] *Abbey National Plc & Ors v The Office of Fair Trading* [2009] EWCA Civ 116, [2009] 1 All ER (Comm) 1097, 1100 (Sir Anthony Clarke MR).

[102] See art 267(4) TFEU.

as *acte clair* an issue which had been decided differently in the courts below in judgments whose quality was praised by the Supreme Court. The fact that the top court disagrees—even that it ultimately has no hesitation in disagreeing—with lower courts cannot suffice to establish that a point is *acte clair*. On the contrary, a top court mindful of its duties under the Treaty would see this as evidence that 'there is involved a question of interpretation on which judicial minds can differ', as Lord Diplock put it in *R v Henn and Darby*,[103] and as militating in favour of a reference.

Lord Walker did not seem to have much confidence in the additional reason he put forward for not making a reference, namely that the correct interpretation of art 4(2) of the Directive was not after all essential. His lack of confidence may be readily understood. The judgment of the Court of Appeal contained a lengthy section[104] on the principles to be applied in interpreting directives. The Supreme Court heard 'submissions about the background to the Directive, its *travaux préparatoires*, and academic commentaries on it',[105] some of which it referred to in its judgment. The outcome of the case was determined essentially by the meaning attributed by the Court to the term 'price or remuneration' in reg 6(2). That term (although intriguingly the word 'or' is replaced by 'and') is used in art 4(2) of Directive 93/13. To maintain that the case did not require its correct interpretation to be established is therefore unpersuasive. Lord Walker seemed to admit a sliver of doubt as to whether the Court of Appeal might have been right on the issue of construction, even though he thought it had been 'clearly wrong in applying its construction to the facts.' But what if the correct interpretation did not correspond precisely to that preferred by either the Supreme Court or the Court of Appeal (whose reasoning differed from that of Andrew Smith J)? What confidence could one then have about the application of the contested provision to the facts? As for the public interest, this was ill served by a judgment based on what may turn out to be an incorrect view of the law, especially in view of the number of claims liable to be affected.

Lord Phillips said that he did 'not find the resolution of the narrow issue before the court to be *acte clair*', but agreed with Lord Walker that 'it would not be appropriate' to make a reference for a preliminary ruling.[106] Lord Mance took essentially the same position as Lord Walker, but expressed greater confidence that the decisive issue could properly be regarded as *acte clair*. He observed:

> Bearing in mind the general Community aim of legal certainty, the likelihood of the Court of Justice (or any other Member State's court) accepting the Court of Appeal's approach to the interpretation of article 4(2) seems to me to be remote indeed. I would regard the position as *acte clair* and not as requiring a reference.[107]

---

[103]  *R v Henn and Darby* [1980] 2 All ER 166, 197. See above text to n 31.
[104]  See [2009] EWCA Civ 116, [2009] 1 All ER (Comm) 1097, 1124.
[105]  *Office of Fair Trading* (n 92) [6].
[106]  ibid [91].
[107]  ibid [115].

Lord Neuberger considered it possible that the ECJ would interpret art 4(2) in the way preferred by the Court of Appeal: '[I]f the resolution of that issue were essential to the determination of this appeal, I would, very reluctantly, have concluded that a reference was required.'[108] However, for the reasons given by Lords Walker and Mance, he did not think the issue needed to be resolved for the purpose of the appeal. Lady Hale did not express a view of her own on whether or not a reference should be made. So of the five Justices sitting in the case, two thought the correct interpretation of the Directive was not *acte clair*, one thought it was and one thought it should be treated as if it were. Four thought that no reference needed to be made because the essential question was not the meaning of the Directive but its application to the facts, which was a matter for national law. One of the Justices who took that view admitted that it might be regarded as 'rather unprincipled'.

## VII CONCLUSION

The *Abbey National* case sits squarely alongside the decisions of the House of Lords mentioned above where it failed to comply with its obligation to refer relevant questions of European law to the ECJ. The issue is no longer whether the *CILFIT* criteria should be relaxed, but how their abuse can be prevented. In the United Kingdom, it seems clear that there has been a profound loss of confidence in the ECJ among senior members of the judiciary. This would be consistent with the growing truculence of other national supreme courts. The standard bearer remains the *Bundesverfassungsgericht*, whose judgment on the Treaty of Lisbon[109] seems to increase the possibility of direct conflict with the ECJ.[110]

The consequences of any such trend for the European Union would be serious. The preliminary rulings procedure, once described by the ECJ as 'the veritable cornerstone of the operation of the internal market',[111] acquired its central role through the success of the ECJ in the 1960s and 1970s in winning the confidence of the national courts. According to Joseph Weiler,[112] part of the reason for the ECJ's success was the eminence of its members and the persuasive force of its judgments. In a more democratic and sceptical age, the eminence of the ECJ's members is no longer assumed and its reluctance to engage directly with the concerns of national courts risks undermining its authority.

How can the contagion be arrested? A reform of the procedure for appointing members of the ECJ, which took effect on the entry into force of the Treaty

[108] ibid [120].

[109] Judgment of 30 June 2009 (n 91).

[110] See D Thym, 'In the Name of Sovereign Statehood: A Critical Introduction to the Lisbon Judgment of the German Constitutional Court' (2009) 46 *Common Market Law Review* 1795, 1807–08.

[111] See the Court's report on the application of the TEU in 'The Proceedings of the Court of Justice and Court of First Instance of the European Communities', 22-26 May 1995 (No 15/95) [11].

[112] See J Weiler, *The Constitution of Europe* (Cambridge, Cambridge University Press, 1999) 32–33.

of Lisbon and which requires a special panel to be consulted by the Member States on the suitability of candidates,[113] may help. It is true that the final decision remains with national governments acting collectively.[114] Nonetheless, a welcome trace of disquiet among Member States about the effect of the new procedure was evident in the haste with which the Spanish Advocate General, Mr Dámaso Ruiz-Jarabo Colomer, who died in office on 12 November 2009, was replaced.[115] The ECJ itself must do more to identify and respond to the problems confronting national courts in applying European law and to make the process of ratiocination underlying its judgments more visible to its national interlocutors. The national courts for their part must learn to accept the role attributed to them by the Treaties in a multi-level polity based on a variety of legal traditions and cultures.

---

[113] See art 255 TFEU.

[114] See art 253 TFEU.

[115] His successor, AG Pedro Cruz Villalón, was appointed by the Member States on 30 November 2009, the day before the Treaty of Lisbon entered into force. See ECJ Press Release No 109/09, 14 December 2009.

# 8

# The Development of Principle by a Final Court of Appeal in Matters of Private International (Common) Law

### ADRIAN BRIGGS

## I INTRODUCTION

A S IT WAS presented at the conference in November 2009, this paper had two modest aims, and one rather morose conclusion. The first aim was to look at the effect of foreign judgments in private international common law, and to consider whether some of the later decisions of the House of Lords and Privy Council may point the way to a new and different understanding of which judgments the common law rules of private international law ought to direct us to recognise, and why. The second aim was to use these to demonstrate that an important function, maybe the most important function, of the House of Lords lay in the elucidation of principles of common law, to explain why answers are as they are, and to fit them into a broader, rational, pattern which is derived from the underlying philosophy of the common law. For if it be accepted that judgments are written not only for the litigants themselves—judgments in the sense of orders are for the parties, but judgments in the sense of reasons are for those interested in the law—then judgments are the more persuasive if they are derived from the common law and rooted in common sense than if they are rested upon some special or idiosyncratic principle of private international law. This may involve accepting that the subject-matter of the enquiry is private more than it is international law. The morose conclusion was that as English private international law moves into its twilight zone, to be replaced by the statutes and habits of thought of a new European private international law, it means that the Supreme Court of the United Kingdom—the birth of which was half of the reason for this conference—will be (i) less likely to deal with private international common law, and (ii) more likely to be asked to apply, but not to interpret, the new European material in which our private international law is now increasingly written. There will be an inevitable alteration in technique associated with that.

At the point in our history when the court was better placed than ever before to take hold of private international law and understand it, the opportunity for it to do so is as diminished as it has ever been.

## II  THE COMMON LAW OF FOREIGN JUDGMENTS

It is necessary to start with foreign judgments. The point of departure is that the English (which includes Australian, but excludes Canadian) common law recognises foreign judgments on the basis of there being a particular connection between the foreign court and the party to be bound.[1] As to that party, it is usual to speak of the defendant, but only because we are generally more commonly concerned with judgments against a defendant; the principle works in like manner for the plaintiff when we are dealing with the effect in England of judgments against the plaintiff. The principle is that the defendant assumed an obligation to abide by and obey the judgment, and that this is what is binding on and enforceable against him. Whether by his submitting to the jurisdiction of the foreign court before or after service of the writ on him, or by his being present within the jurisdiction where the writ was served on him, the obligation by which he is bound results from his own, individual, decision to act in a particular way. Two things follow. The first is that if he is not present, and does not submit, no such obligation arises; and the second is that the fact that the court in which proceedings were brought had some other sensible connection, or some other reason to adjudicate the dispute, is irrelevant.

However, when the law is written in terms of obligations, the immediate question is what gives rise, or what else may give rise, to that obligation. There are several ways to define an obligation, or to define the steps which give rise to an obligation, including the obligation to obey a judgment. The common law of contract enforces promises, but then has to decide which promises to enforce; the common law of constructive trusts enforces agreements but then has to decide which agreements should create property rights; the common law of proprietary estoppel enforces expectations but then worries both about which expectations and about what enforcement should mean. And the common law of foreign judgments enforces obligations and may now be starting to worry about which obligations, or which facts might be seen to create that obligation.

It is this question which is considered here. More particularly, the question is whether there is another useable, useful, legal principle, which may be deployed to provide an explanation for certain recent decisions in private international law cases which, at first sight, do not otherwise seem to have convincing explanations. That principle might be formulated along the lines of saying that you 'lent yourself' to a particular event or outcome, that you 'chose to put yourself' in

---

[1] See generally Dicey, Morris and Collins, *The Conflict of Laws*, 14th edn (London, Sweet & Maxwell, 2006) ch 14.

a position where someone else could affect your legal rights without further reference to you, and that as a result, the ordinary rules of private international law are irrelevant. The hand and brain of Lord Hoffmann have been at work here. If there is such a principle, we will need to identify the intellectual basis for it: that sounds grander than is prudent, but we need to make claims.

In private international law, English law places a lot of weight on the notions of agreement and consent as justifications for doctrine.[2] Their importance is that they provide the intellectual and rhetorical underpinning for the individual and detailed rules which develop on the surface of the law. So, for example, in recent days they have provided the framework for analysis of whether agreements on jurisdiction and on choice of law are really capable of being understood as giving rise to private law rights and obligations, enforceable by demand and discretion as other contract terms are. More particularly they allow one to ask whether a claim for damages may be advanced where a claimant is able to say that his counterparty has acted in defiance of or inconsistently with, or has breached, an agreement on jurisdiction or governing law. The questions are answered, or at least they are asked, in terms of what the parties agreed to, and which among the items upon which they agreed is it possible to for them to hold each other. An active and energetic debate has now grown up.[3] In the common law of private international law, the private has begun to eclipse the international. The responses will not be derived from the analysis of authority and detail, but by an examination of a more fundamental principle: are these contracts or agreements? Is this subject matter as to which one may contract and make agreements? Is there an intelligible distinction between a contract and a procedural contract? And so forth.[4] The analysis is, or ought to be, in terms of what is going on at a deeper level than may meet the eye.

Much may be derived from the law on agreements. But there are still some legal effects in the common law of private international law which cannot be explained by these principles, yet for which the common law, including private international law, needs a principled explanation. This issue has arisen in particular and recent connection with the private international law of cross-border insolvency, but not only there. It may be seen that, working alongside these basic principles, there is another: that one who lent himself to it in advance has only himself to blame

---

[2] See generally Briggs, *Agreements on Jurisdiction and Choice of Law* (Oxford, Oxford University Press, 2008).

[3] In addition to the work mentioned in the previous footnote, see also K Takahashi, 'Damages for Breach of a Choice-of-Court Agreement' (2008) 10 *Yearbook of Private International Law* 57.

[4] Though this paper is concerned with the common law, it is sensible to note that, according to some legal traditions in continental Europe, the idea that one may make an agreement to give up a right of access to a court or judge is regarded with suspicion. Whereas it may be acceptable to hold merchants to such agreements, and maybe to an obligation to pay damages if it is departed from, it does not follow that this should hold for an ordinary person. It is only a small step from the particular law on insurance, consumer, and employment contracts, where jurisdiction and arbitration agreements are strictly controlled in their effect, to a general rule that individuals may not be bound to an agreement on jurisdiction, at least with the same degree of stringency as is applied to a merchant or commercial party.

when the consequences of that are drawn out and given effect. The argument here is that what the House of Lords and Privy Council have done is to develop, if not quite to complete the articulation of, a rational and structural principle of common law private international law; and that this was precisely what they were meant to do.

In its detail, the reasoning will look as though it is a close cousin of the principle in *Penn v Lord Baltimore.*[5] That case was one in which two landowners had made an agreement to settle the boundary line between their two properties by arbitration: not just average landowners, though, for the lands in question were the two American proto-states of Pennsylvania and Maryland. It followed from this subject matter that they had made an agreement to settle colonial boundaries, which was something which the King, and only the King, had legal power to do. As the subject matter of the agreement was therefore outside the jurisdiction of the courts, it was argued that the agreement could not be enforced, that the court might not do indirectly something which it could not do directly. But the Chancellor took the view that the ordinary courts were bound and entitled to enforce the private agreement which the parties had made, that *their* differences should be settled by arbitration. The court had no power to determine the state boundaries, but it did have power to enforce the agreement which the parties had made, or the equities which flowed from the agreement which the parties had made. It will be necessary to return to this. It may mean that though a foreign judgment has no effect in England, as the act of a foreign sovereign cannot have any effect in England, the manner in which the parties deal with each other may mean that they assume, take to themselves, an obligation which each owes to the other, analogous to a contract; and that this is the obligation which the court can enforce. The enforcing of foreign judgments is, in this respect, *Penn v Baltimore* all over again.

It is important to keep sight of the fundamental importance of this principle, and not to underestimate the width of its influence. In *Penn v Baltimore*, the court accepted that it had no jurisdiction to examine and to rule on the drawing of colonial boundaries, but it was entitled to enforce an agreement which the parties had made. Indeed, in the case of title to foreign land, an English court has no jurisdiction to determine title,[6] but it has jurisdiction to enforce, and will enforce, an agreement made between parties who are tussling over foreign land. In the case of foreign judgments, a court will not enforce in England a foreign sovereign act,[7] so they will not enforce a foreign judgment as such; but they will enforce the obligations arising from the agreement or quasi-agreement which the parties have made in relation to the foreign court. In the case of stays of English proceedings, a court will not consider that parties may oust or otherwise limit the jurisdiction of an English court by private agreement, for the jurisdiction of courts is a matter for Parliament to define; but it will enforce an agreement

---

[5] *Penn v Lord Baltimore* (1750) 1 Ves Sen 444.
[6] *British South Africa Co v Companhia de Moçambique* [1893] AC 602.
[7] Dicey, Morris and Collins, *The Conflict of Laws* (n 1) Rule 3.

which the parties have made in respect of that jurisdiction.[8] An English court will not adjudicate, and may have no jurisdiction to adjudicate on whether a foreign court has jurisdiction according to the law of that foreign court; but it will enforce an agreement which the parties have made in respect of that jurisdiction.[9]

## III  RECENT DECISIONS AND THE SEARCH FOR A PRINCIPLE

To make the points which it is hoped to demonstrate, one may look to five decided cases which set the scene. They are most conveniently taken in chronological order.

The first case is this: suppose that one has made a contract, expressed to be governed by English law, with a foreign company, and that the foreign company was then dissolved; or that one has made a contract, expressed to be governed by English law, with a foreign bank which was dissolved and amalgamated with another bank. The dissolution may mean the rights generated by the contract are no longer precisely the same as they were, even though there has been no alteration to English law as the law applicable to the contract. Several old Russian cases,[10] and a couple of newer Greek cases,[11] suggest that a foreign legislature can alter the contractual rights which were created by virtue of an English contract. Can it be correct that these rights may still be altered by the act of a foreign legislator?

The second case is as follows. Suppose that a contract had been made with the Chittagong branch of a Cayman Island bank, BCCIO, which was a part of the BCCI banking group, as counter-party. Suppose that the bank had failed to perform its side of the contract, and has become insolvent, leaving the claim unmet, and that the contract was expressed to be governed by the law of Bangladesh. Suppose that the Bank of Bangladesh, acting under powers granted by Bangladeshi law, makes a scheme for the reconstruction of all the business activities of BCCIO in Bangladesh, and this law purports to extinguish all contractual rights against BCCIO. If it is asserted, in the Cayman insolvency of BCCIO, that the contract should be admitted by the liquidators, the claim will be rejected as unfounded in law, on the ground that Bangladeshi law destroyed the basis on which the claim was rested, with the result that there is nothing to prove, and nothing to admit.[12]

The third case may be put this way. Suppose that you are a shareholder in a Manx company which is in financial trouble and against which proceedings have been brought before a court in the United States. Suppose that the company submits, as defendant, to those proceedings before the US court. Suppose that an order is made by the US court, which demands or requests the confiscation by the Manx authorities of your shareholding in the defendant Manx company,

---

[8] *Donohue v Armco Inc* [2001] UKHL 64, [2002] 1 Lloyd's Rep 425.
[9] ibid.
[10] Such as *Re Russian Bank for Foreign Trade* [1933] Ch 745.
[11] Such as *Adams v National Bank of Greece and Athens SA* [1961] AC 255.
[12] *Wight v Eckhardt Marine GmbH* [2003] UKPC 37, [2004] 1 AC 147 (PC, Cayman Is).

and the issue of new shares to a committee of creditors of the company. It may be objected that to accede to this request or demand would amount to the Manx court enforcing a foreign confiscatory decree against you and your property, in circumstances where you neither participated in the foreign proceedings, nor otherwise submitted to the jurisdiction of the foreign court; and in circumstances in which the property is not within the territorial jurisdiction of the American court. However, the Manx courts may be required to give effect to the demand or request of the American court, regardless of whether the shareholder played any part in the foreign proceedings.[13]

For a fourth case, suppose that you have dealt with or invested in an Australian multinational company, which has gone into insolvent liquidation in Australia, and which fact precipitated an ancillary liquidation in England. Suppose that the Australian administrators make an application to have funds located in England remitted from England, where you and your class of creditor would have had a claim against them for the partial satisfaction of debts, to Australia, where you would not have such a claim. You point out that the Insolvency Act 1986 gives you a right to claim against assets within the jurisdiction of the court, and that your rights under this legislation should not be set aside on the application of the liquidators or at the request of a foreign court. But the English courts will hold that the assets may be and should be remitted to Australia, for disposal in the Australian administration, and that this may even be done on the basis of a general judicial discretion.[14]

The fifth and final case is this. Suppose that you submitted to the jurisdiction of an English court in a substantial commercial claim, and after judgment was entered against you, you found yourself subject to a variety of further measures, by way of enforcement and execution, which you did not expect and did not agree to. It may be, for example, that a receiver was appointed by way of equitable execution to try to collect money owed to you by your trade debtors;[15] that you were restrained by injunction from taking steps overseas to question or undermine the conclusions of the English judgment, even to prevent you from contending that it should not be recognised by a foreign court.[16] And not only that: persons holding senior office in your corporate structure, resident in Greece and never having been to England in their professional lives, may find themselves on the receiving end of a judicial command that they make themselves available to give evidence about the whereabouts of your assets.[17] You object to all of these,

---

[13]    *Cambridge Gas Transport Corp v Committee of Unsecured Creditors of Navigator Holdings plc* [2006] UKPC 26, [2007] 1 AC 508 (PC; Isle of Man).

[14]    *Re HIH Casualty & General Insurance Ltd, McGrath v Riddell* [2008] UKHL 21, [2008] 1 WLR 852.

[15]    *Masri v Consolidated Contractors International (UK) Ltd (No 2: appointment of receiver)* [2008] EWCA Civ 313, [2009] QB 450.

[16]    *Masri v Consolidated Contractors International (UK) Ltd (No 3: anti-suit injunction)* [2008] EWCA Civ 621, [2009] QB 503.

[17]    *Masri v Consolidated Contractors International (UK) Ltd (No 4: order for examination of officers)* [2008] EWCA Civ 876, [2009] 2 WLR 699; rev'd [2009] UKHL 43, [2010] 1 AC 90.

and the court says that you do not have any sustainable defence, but the corporate servants or office-holders, not resident in England, do have a defence.

However, if you were to approach these cases as though they raised orthodox questions of private international law, the results might not have come out as the decisions actually did. For example, in the first case, the rights in question were contained in a contract governed by English law. If a Greek judgment purporting to declare that those rights were unenforceable would not have been binding on you, and if a rule of Greek law purporting to annul your contractual rights would have been disregarded as irrelevant to the functioning of an English contract, a piece of Greek legislation altering the legal identity of the party to whom you are contractually indebted, or who is indebted to you, might be thought to have no more of an effect. After all, if it were given effect, what would be to stop the Greek legislator transferring by legislation all debt liabilities owed to foreign creditors from a bank with assets to a bank of straw? Contrast this with the second case. There, if the case is thought of as one about the governmental confiscation of rights, the rights against the Cayman bank were located in the Caymans, for that was where the debtor resided. If that is so, the law of Bangladesh cannot reach out and confiscate property outside the territorial jurisdiction of Bangladesh. The case is accurately and properly seen as amounting to the legislative confiscation of property, where the principle is that the *lex situs*, and only the *lex situs*, applies. If the decree of a Bangladeshi court would not have been binding on you, a piece of subordinate Bangladeshi legislation should have no more effect.

In the third case, an order from an American court made against a defendant shareholder is only binding on, and liable to be enforced against him personally, if he submitted to the jurisdiction of the American court or was present within its jurisdiction when the proceedings were begun. If neither of these conditions is met, it cannot be argued that the judgment and decree of the American court should be considered as binding on him, and all the more so if it purports to confiscate his assets in the Isle of Man for, as said above, where the confiscation of property is concerned, the *lex situs* applies to the exclusion of all other laws.[17A]

In the fourth case, English insolvency law, which is mostly statutory, allows a person with a claim against an insolvent debtor to make a claim against the assets of the insolvent in England subject to the set-off of mutual debts.[18] If the assets are remitted overseas, that statutory right will, in effect, have been abrogated, as may other English priority rules, with the result that a discretion to send the money overseas is inconsistent with that legislative statement of rights found in the insolvency legislation.

In the fifth case, you may have submitted to the adjudicatory jurisdiction of the English court, but that, as a matter of its construction, was as far as your submission went. It did not entail the further conclusion that you would be subject to its powers so far as these relate to enforcement of judgments outside England

---

[17A] Though as to this, see also *Rubin v Eurofinance SA* [2010] EWCA Civ 895 (on which, see Briggs [2010] LMCLQ 532).

[18] Insolvency Rules 1986 (SI 1986/1925) r 4.90.

and after the event; but if it is true that your submission to the jurisdiction carried with it a submission to the post-judgment enforcement jurisdiction, on the basis that you cannot pick and choose which aspects of the jurisdiction to submit to, any more than you can choose which parts of a claim form you will submit to, your directors and office-holders are carried along on the tide.

## IV  WHAT PRINCIPLE MIGHT HAVE SUGGESTED

In all of the cases mentioned, the answers reached in the cases are, if to varying degrees, not wholly consistent with the underlying theory of English private international law. The reason appears to be that, in all these cases, the person to be affected has entered, voluntarily, into a relationship with another as a consequence of which he allowed—permitted, authorised, empowered—that other to affect his legal rights without further reference to him. It is important to say that the courts did not rest their conclusion plainly on this principle, but the judgments do not betray much doubt about the result to be reached, which tends to suggest that there was something beneath the surface which drove the detailed legal reasoning to the conclusion arrived at. Take the first case, for example. If one makes a contract with a natural person, one accepts, for it cannot be otherwise, that the counterparty may naturally die. But if you make a contract with an artificial person, with an entity which is only a person in the artificial sense that it was created under and because of a law, it seems inescapable that one must also accept that the counterparty may be made to die artificially. The person who makes a contract with a Greek bank must accept that the bank may be killed off by the Greek legislator, and that if this comes to pass, there is nothing more to be done about it. It follows that the Greek debtor may be dissolved and the liabilities vested in an entity with no assets: if one makes a contract with a Greek artificial person, this is the chance one elects to take. If this signposts the way to bad practice by the Greek legislator, that can hardly be said to be surprising, or unprincipled. It might be rather too bold to assert that it was agreed that the Greek state might behave in that way: but it seems quite correct that it was the obvious risk that was taken, or to which the complainant laid himself open, and that this is why there is no general ground for complaint when this event comes to pass.

One may now proceed to the second case, which represents the other side of the coin. The person who makes a contract governed by the law of Bangladesh, especially if the choice of Bangladeshi law to govern it is express, makes a bargain with his contractual counterparty which means, in part, that if the law of Bangladesh changes before the contract is performed, so also may his rights be changed. Either he makes an agreement that Bangladeshi law applies to regulate his rights and to govern his disputes, or he makes an agreement that the law of Bangladesh may alter his right, for good or for ill; and that if this happens, he will simply abide by the consequences, for even if this is not what he agreed to, it is what he laid himself open to. We can find all the answers we need from an examination of what was agreed to and accepted, and there is no need to look to rules of private international law to find a better answer. Of course, the reasoning may have to be different if there is no express choice of law, but a decision not to make and express a choice of law is itself a decision to accept the default option which will be provided by the court before which the dispute arises, and in the end the result and the reasoning may be almost exactly the same. The whole of the answer can be found from the fact that this is what was actually agreed to, or from the fact that in making the agreement, the contracting parties laid themselves open to this particular consequence, and cannot properly complain about it now.

The third case, when it was decided, looked really rather shocking, especially in a world in which the European Convention on Human Rights gives certain guarantees about the right to be heard and as to the security of property. However, if you subscribe for shares in a corporation, it seems inevitable that you accept that the corporation may do something which damages your interest in your capacity as shareholder. As the advertisement has it: the value of your investment may go down as well as up. The company in which you invest may make unwise or improvident commercial decisions: in modern times, those who subscribed for shares in banks may be able to bear vivid witness to this truth. It may issue new share capital and so dilute your stake; it may get involved in foolhardy litigation; and it may submit to the jurisdiction of a foreign court. If it does any or all of these, you will find that you have already agreed to accept and abide by the outcome of the proceedings before the foreign court, for as the corporation chose to submit, it carried your interest, as shareholder, with it. One does not need to look beyond the agreement arising from the shareholding: it is all you need to know, and there is no need to look to rules of private international law to find a better answer. When you subscribed for the shares, you laid yourself open to this. No rule of private international law is required to give any further answers.

The fourth case also looked puzzling, for if there is a statutory right to claim against English assets, in accordance with English priority rules, when insolvency strikes, it may come as a surprise when that is set at naught by a judicial discretion. However, if you make a contract with an Australian corporation, you realise that the corporation may be killed off by Australian legal process, as the Greek legislator did with the Greek bank. And that which may be done quickly may also be done more slowly: the bank may also be killed in stages, as the process of insolvent liquidation did also. The effects and consequences of that legal death may therefore be considered to be part of the bargain which you have struck, and that means that you get the same right to claim in the deceased estate as Australian law gives you; and there should be no need to look to rules of private international law to find a better answer. It may not be what you agreed to, but it was what you laid yourself open to when you made the agreement which you did make, and that is all you need to know. Or, to put it another way, when you place yourself into a creditor–debtor relationship with an Australian company, you can hardly complain if the insolvency and liquidation is carried on according to Aussie rules.

But when it comes to the fifth case, we begin to see the limits and the lessons of this. If a company has submitted to the adjudicatory jurisdiction of a court, it has probably exposed itself to the post-judgment enforcement process as well. That deals with the defendant who happens to be a corporation. But the position of the corporate officers is really rather different. On the one hand, they chose to hold office in a company which submitted to the jurisdiction of the English court. The Court of Appeal would have allowed them to be summoned, acting as though they accepted that the officers had put themselves in the frame by agreeing to serve the corporation, but certainly driven (some might say carried away) by the perception that the more that could be done to make its judgments effective, the better. The House of Lords took a rather different view: perhaps sensing that officers were more in the nature of employees, and it was a significant error of principle to suppose that they had so identified themselves with the corporation that their legal fate should be tied to and made dependent on that of the company they served. It is probably correct to say that initial reactions to the judgment of the House of Lords were negative, for it makes it more difficult to enforce an English judgment; it removes a remedy which would have made it harder for judgment-evaders to get away with their evasions. On the other hand, it has to be said that although a master may be responsible for things done by his servant, it does rather stand the world on its head for the servant to have the responsibility of answering for his master.

There is a really fundamental choice to be made, but one which is really only obscured if one focuses, as the judgments in the House of Lords appear to do, on the history of CPR Part 71 and the presumption of legislative territoriality. Indeed, one reason why the judgment of the House of Lords may not have been received with applause may have been the way it did not quite square up the principle beneath the surface of the question before it. If one were to accept that officers are analogous to the shareholders, and are an integral part of the organisation, one might deduce that they have placed their fate in the hands of the corporation, and have agreed to accept the outcome of proceedings which may be contrary to their own private interests, as this is the effect of agreeing to hold office in a company. It would therefore be appropriate to draw the conclusions which follow from that agreement to become embedded in the company, and to hold that there is nothing inappropriate in exercising a jurisdiction to summon them for interrogation. So far as their liability to be summoned to give evidence is concerned, that liability should be seen to follow from the agreement which they have made with the company, and there is nothing else which needs to be said. However if one does not see that analogy as persuasive, there is no real basis for saying that the officers brought this particular consequence upon themselves and now have to live with it. On reflection, the House of Lords probably made an accurate assessment of what corporate officers should be taken to have exposed themselves to; and from that perspective, and even though this is not quite how they put it, they got it right.

## V THE BROAD RESPONSIBILITY OF THE FINAL COURT OF APPEAL

None of these conclusions may be particularly profound, though as each case had to get as far as the Privy Council or the House of Lords for its answer, it is fair to say that the issues may have appeared to be more difficult at the time than they do now. The institutional point is surely, however, this: that a central function of a final court of appeal is to deliver judgments which are as technically well-founded as they also reflect the fundamental values of the common law from which they stem. In other words, they should deliver judgments which make good legal sense just as much as they make good law.

There are plenty of other examples in the field of private international law which make this point. The best recent example can be found in the law on arbitration and jurisdiction agreements. In *Fiona Trust & Holding Corp v Privalov*[19] it was held that an arbitration agreement in a charterparty contract which was, as it was pleaded, not binding on the shipowner whose agent had been bribed to conclude it, was still binding on the shipowner and meant he had to proceed by way of arbitration. Lord Hoffmann attributed this conclusion to a principle of severability of the dispute-resolution agreement from the rest of the contract, but there is probably a better answer which he knew very well. That is that if the parties had not entered into this contract, the shipowner would have entered into another charter, for that was its business, and as that charterparty would have contained an arbitration agreement, as the Shelltime 4 standard form does, the agreement to arbitrate was not caused by the bribery. In this there are unmistakeable echoes of Lord Hoffmann's analysis of cause and consequence in *South Australia Asset Management Corp v York Montague Ltd.*[20] It was argued in that case that losses, resulting from buying or investing in property on a falling market, had all been caused by the wrongful inducement to buy; but a more thoughtful analysis allowed the court to conclude that although the property investment company had been induced to invest as it had by the negligent valuation provided by the solicitor, it could not recover those losses which resulted from its exposure to the general fall in the value of property. This was because if it had not made that investment, it would have made another, for that was the business it was in, and that was why the loss from the fall in property values was not caused by the surveyor. If one looks at *Fiona Trust* through that lens, it is obvious that the shipowner may not be heard to say that his agent had no authority to bind him to the charterparty, or to any part of it, including the arbitration agreement. For had the shipowner not entered into this charterparty it would have entered into another, as this was its business, and it would have still agreed to arbitrate its disputes. A good judicial answer is one which comes to the right conclusion; a convincing judicial answer is one which appeals to

---

[19] *Fiona Trust & Holding Corp v Privalov* [2007] UKHL 40, [2007] Bus LR 1719.
[20] *South Australia Asset Management Corp v York Montague Ltd* [1996] UKHL 10, [1997] AC 191.

deeper reason. An explanation which is able to rest on the principle that a person is bound by the consequences of what he agreed to, or by the consequences of something which he lent himself to, is a good answer. It reaches parts which the rules of private international law, just sometimes, cannot otherwise reach. In common law systems, in particular, that is what final courts of appeal are there to do, and in these recent cases, the House of Lords and the Privy Council may have been doing it.

## VI  OTHER CASES WHICH MIGHT BE RECONSIDERED BY A FINAL COURT OF APPEAL

If there is a principle at work in the law of foreign judgments, along the lines best described by the proposition that if the defendant lent himself to it, he is bound to accept the consequences which flow from it naturally or in the ordinary course of things, there will be a number of other cases in which it may be appropriate to ask whether the judgment of a foreign court ought to be recognised, and recognised for this reason. They might include the following five cases.

First, it should be considered whether the fact that a person did business within the territorial jurisdiction of a foreign court, which court has now given judgment against him for damages in a claim arising out of the business which he did there, might be reason enough to recognise the judgment of that court. The traditional answer of the common law is that the judgment will not be recognised in England unless the defendant was present when the proceedings were begun, or submitted to the jurisdiction of the court when served with the writ. The fact that, because of what he did there, he could and should have anticipated being sued there is not currently of significance. The fact that he did business there is not, apparently, significant.

However, if a person has done business within the territorial jurisdiction of the foreign court, and now a court in that jurisdiction has, at the behest of the claimant, given judgment against him, ordering him to pay damages, it may be argued that someone who has chosen to engage in the commercial sphere of that country, who has purposefully availed himself of the jurisdiction in question, he has laid himself open to having his legal rights affected by the acts of the other, that he realised or should have realised that he could be affected by the acts of another, perhaps rather more so than the person who was merely present.

So *is* it persuasive to say that because you have taken advantage of the laws of a country by doing business there, you have laid yourself open to the recognition of judgments against you? One might say yes: that you take the rough with the smooth, the bitter with the sweet, and so forth. And if you have taken advantage of the market in which to do business, you may be taken, surely to goodness, to have laid yourself open to its exercise of jurisdiction: at least in relation to the claims which arise out of the business which you did there. But at the moment,

English law, as set out in *Adams v Cape plc*[21] denies this proposition, preferring to say that whether you are bound by the judgment has only ever been answered by looking at the defendant's response to the court when served with its writ. There is no agreement with the claimant to accept that he may do something to alter your legal position, and in the absence of that agreement, the fact that you may have foreseen that this is something which the claimant might do is not enough to give rise to an obligation. However, to put it in those terms may be to present a false antithesis. If the question is whether you lent yourself to being sued there, an answer, which is neither wholly yes nor wholly no, suggests itself: that you lent yourself to the extent that you did business there, and that principle should define the limits within which the judgment should be enforced.

Secondly, consider whether a judgment in respect of a tort which is given by the courts for the place of the tort ought to be recognised in England. The traditional answer is that the judgment will not be recognised unless the defendant was present when the proceedings were begun, or submitted to the jurisdiction of the court when served with the writ. The fact that he could and should have anticipated being sued there is not currently of significance.

However, it does not follow that the principle under consideration yields the same answer in this case. True, if one were to accept that the justification for the application of the *lex loci delicti commissi* to answer questions of choice of law may be justified, as indeed it is, on the ground that this is what a reasonable man would have expected to be applied, it might be taken to follow that the judgment of a court at that place should also be regarded as conclusive, on the ground that this is what the defendant, by participating in the business or social environment of the foreign court, had left or lent himself to: that he should have realised that this was a predictable consequence of his decision to act and breach his duty in a particular place. On the other hand, it is plausible that the prior connection with the place where the tort was committed will sometimes be weaker than the prior connection with the place where business was done. The question which this raises may be whether it is sufficient to say that the defendant realised or should have realised (foresaw or should have foreseen) that there might be litigation in the place where the tort occurred, with the result that his realisation or foresight is the basis for his being obliged by the judgment. Again, at the moment, English common law says no. It could perfectly rationally say yes. Perhaps one can see that a rational legal principle could explain why you should be bound by the judgment of a foreign court within the territorial jurisdiction of which you chose to act or interact, by holding that you lent yourself to being sued in that place. Perhaps one can also see that to hold that you have lent yourself to this is not so obvious: it may be a *Masri*[22] case, all over again.

Thirdly, suppose that you were one of a huge number of victims of a tort committed by a company, which was made the defendant in proceedings certified

[21] *Adams v Cape plc* [1990] Ch 433.
[22] *Masri* (n 17).

as a class action in the United States. Suppose then that you were notified of the proceedings, and of your membership of the class, and were invited to opt in or out, but simply threw the notice away and did not otherwise respond. Suppose then that judgment or settlement in the proceedings is entered and that, as a matter of American law, you are now bound by the judgment or settlement and precluded from bringing proceedings of your own; and that you then bring proceedings of your own in England. The plain answer is that the American judgment and order, and its effects, will not be recognised unless you yourself submitted to the jurisdiction of the American court or were present there when the proceedings were begun. The fact that you had a fair opportunity to opt out of the class, and chose not to do so, will be of no significance, even if true. The fact that you were told what the consequences would be is irrelevant.

But if you had a claim in tort against a company which submitted, as defendant, to class action proceedings in the courts of the United States, it might be argued that if you have entered into a relationship with another, and that other has accepted the jurisdiction of the foreign court, you are then bound by what that other has done. English law says no: you have not entered into a voluntary relationship with another which allows that other to affect your legal position by what that other does, and the question whether you are bound by the judgment which purports to tie your hands can only be answered by looking at *your* response, not at your opponent's response, to the court when served with its writ. Quite right, too. It is one thing to say that you lent yourself to becoming bound because you took shares in, or made a contract with, the person who was then able to adversely affect your legal position. But if the opposite conclusion follows in the case where you were a servant or officer of the company, the proposition that you can be bound simply because you were the victim of the company as tortfeasor is irrational, adding insult to injury.

So, for example, it will not be possible to say that you knew or should have known, when you bought the product or subscribed for the shares in a European market, for example, that you should have realised that a judge in the United States might make an order which debarred you from bringing a claim of your own. Although there may be social reasons to support class action litigation, and the settlement of such consumer claims against large corporations, it does not seem possible to identify a rational[23] principle which allows it to be said that the risk of such litigation, and class action settlement preclusion, was one to which you laid yourself open. It is thought that that there is nothing which the common law can do, and if reform is called for, it has to take legislative form.

Fourthly, suppose you left property within the jurisdiction of a foreign court, which proceeded to allow an attachment of the property as the basis for the exercise of jurisdiction,[24] and the judgment is now sought to be enforced

---

[23] Though irrational ones, presented by authors who seemed to think they were rational, are not unknown. There is no need to draw attention to them here.

[24] For example, art 23 ZPO (Germany), or the arrest of a sea-going vessel against which or the owner or operator of which there is a claim.

against you in England. The traditional answer is that the judgment will not be recognised unless the defendant was present when the proceedings were begun, or submitted to the jurisdiction of the court when served with the writ. The fact that property was left and found within the jurisdiction of the foreign court is of no significance.

But if you did leave property within the jurisdiction of a court, the answer ought to be that by leaving the assets within the grasp of the court, you have only yourself to blame when jurisdiction is taken and exercised, but that if the principle is that you lent yourself to being sued in that country, you only did so up to the limit of the assets which were within the jurisdiction of the foreign court. It would also follow that enforcement of the judgment overseas, to try and recover more than that is not justifiable. You have not made an agreement with the other party which would allow a court to say that you had made an agreement to accept and be bound by the judgment obtained by the claimant. The extent to which you laid yourself open to litigation before the foreign court is the extent to which you left assets within its territorial jurisdiction.

Fifthly—and at this point we are looking at whether it would be better to refuse to recognise a judgment which the law currently would recognise—suppose you were present when the proceedings were instituted, but that you had arrived only shortly before, and left soon after, the proceedings were begun. You are taken to be bound by the judgment against you. The fact that there was no other basis for finding a connection between you and the court is of no significance. The recognition of judgments on the basis of presence appears to be justifiable. It may be justified, as the common law seems to do, on the basis of a feudal relationship between sovereign and those present within his or her jurisdiction; but it may also be that you can be said to have laid yourself open to the jurisdiction. One should prefer the second explanation. If this is right, it makes perfect sense, but it also means that a number of other decisions and recognitions become comprehensible.

One might ask whether the answers in some or all of these cases could be different. If the justification for the results of the cases mentioned earlier is that by engaging with a foreign entity you exposed yourself to certain risks of which you cannot later complain, and if you chose a foreign law to govern your contract you exposed yourself to certain risks of which you cannot later complain, should it not follow that if you acted or carried on business in a particular country, you exposed yourself to certain risks of which you cannot later complain; and that one of the risks in question—rationally foreseeable and reasonably predictable— is that what you did there might result in litigation there? One might think so. In none of these five cases can it be said that you have made any kind of agreement with the other party to abide by the outcome of litigation. In some at least of these cases, you may not be surprised by the fact that litigation ensues in a particular court, or that it is governed by a particular law. But in none of them does it seem possible to say that you have made some form of agreement by which you can be said to be liable to be held by your counterparty. One may come very close in the tort cases, at least where the tort arises out of a prior relationship. One may come close in the 'purposeful availment' cases, if it said that if you chose to interact with another and do business in a particular country, that you accepted that he may go to the courts of that country and, by doing so, he may affect your legal position. The proposition that you brought it upon yourself, and that this is so even in the absence of an agreement to bring the legal consequences upon yourself, is plausible. It seems that it may have more than just abstract attraction.

It may be objected that it would be hard to see the difference between these cases and any other case in which it may be said that you should have been able to see that your counterparty would sue you in his own courts. That does not seem good enough: there is no agreement or acceptance that this will be done and will be accepted without further reference to you. Those who take a different view may well say that this is sufficient: that in these circumstances you knew or ought to have known that this might happen, and that you are bound by it if that is so. But there may be not so much a gap as a gulf between the two positions: 'you realised that it may happen' and 'you agreed to put yourself at the mercy of another' are two very different ideas.

If however the line is to be drawn where the English common law seems to have drawn it, there must be a principle at work here, and it seems to be this: that a person may be bound, in the sense of being conclusively adversely affected, by a decision of a foreign court *where it is fair to say that he has lent himself to the possibility of being affected by the decision of the foreign court.* It explains why the person who subscribes for shares in a company may be adversely affected by decisions taken by the company, including by the decision to appear in foreign proceedings. It explains why the person who lends to or otherwise invests in a foreign company may be adversely affected by a decision to liquidate that company with such legal consequences as are provided for by the law of the place of incorporation and disincorporation. It explains why the person who makes a contract with a particular bank may find that his counterparty has been changed to another when the laws under which the bank was incorporated dissolve it or amalgamate it with another. In all of these, it is possible, or is not fanciful, to find an agreement to accept certain legal consequences, and for the court to give effect to that agreement, almost despite what the rules of private international law might otherwise have said. It also explains what we should be asking, in any event, when asked to accept that if the company in which you hold office has accepted the jurisdiction of an English court, you as office-holder are adversely affected by that.

If we are going to resist this extension to the law of foreign judgments, this is where the link to the principle in *Penn v Lord Baltimore* comes in. For when we try to move from 'you agreed, or are to be treated as though you agreed' to accept that it is just the same if 'you put yourself in a position where it is reasonable to say that you lent yourself to it', then we may have crossed a line which is, at the moment, just too well established to cross. If ever there was an issue for the reflection of a Supreme Court, this is it.

VII  THE CHANGING ROLE OF THE SUPREME COURT:
A MOROSE CONCLUSION

There were two reasons for looking at this collection of common law authority. It was intended to allow those who find their interest confined to private international law, to ask whether there was an explanation which was perhaps invisible but evidently influential in the recent jurisprudence of the House of Lords and Privy Council. It seemed arguable that there was, and that this unspoken explanation may be why in some instances the result of the cases seems more convincing than the published legal reasoning actually does. The proposition that a legal result follows because the person against whom it is asserted 'lent himself to it' is inherently and broadly attractive. It underpins the liability of an accomplice or a joint entrepreneur; it seems probable that a sizeable mass of the law of tort rests on the same broad and generous foundation. But it is the fact that judgments in as arcane a corner of the common law as private international law sometimes seem to as well, that they may also be seen to have their roots in a deep, common, and broader truth, which is a happy surprise.

It is also part of the task of the final court of appeal in a common law system to look out for this and, where possible, to develop it. One would suppose that this remained a central task for the new Supreme Court: to identify the principle or principles which prevent the jurisprudence generated by the legal system amounting to nothing more that a wilderness of single instances. The court will still be the judicial apex of the common law, after all. The irony is that, at least as far as private international law is concerned, we are on the threshold of a world in which there is less, and will soon be even less, recourse to the common law to regulate the domain of private international law. The source material with and from which the court must find the answer will now be, increasingly, all legislative. And this legislative material was not made to develop and refine, or to alter but still live alongside, the common law. It was and is instead made to replace it with a common European law. If, then, there are any truly fundamental principles which hold this new material together and give it intellectual coherence and practical sense, they will need to be found in a very different place. This is going to require a distinctly different approach.

Many will regret that it will not be the Supreme Court which has the opportunity and the task of producing the answer. This is because, in any case in which a serious question of statutory interpretation arises, the Supreme Court will be increasingly obliged to make a reference to the European Court for a preliminary ruling, rather than answer the question for itself. The laws on jurisdiction and foreign judgments in civil and commercial matters,[25] on choice of law for contracts,[26] torts and unjust enrichment,[27] on jurisdiction, foreign judgments

---

[25]  Council Regulation (EC) 44/2001; Brussels I.
[26]  Council Regulation (EC) 593/2008; Rome I.
[27]  Council Regulation (EC) 864/2007; Rome II.

and choice of law in insolvency,[28] divorce and dissolution of marriage,[29] financial support,[30] and wills and succession,[31] are now primarily contained in European legislation. The encroachments on the private international law of companies and of insurance are a little less easy to summarise, but they are making relentless progress. According to the 'Draft Stockholm Programme'[32] there is still more to come. Our private international law is to be a European private international law, not an English private international law, and still less a common law private international law.

To be sure, there will be a run-off period during which the common law principles of choice of law will continue to apply: torts committed before August 2007 (and defamation); contracts made before December 2009 (except that those made after 1991 were subject to the Rome Convention in any event); insolvencies of entities whose centre of main interest is not in a Member State; such marginal and scattered cases concerning civil jurisdiction which fall outside the current scope of the Brussels I Regulation; recognition of divorces from non-Member States, and so on. But they are a motley collection, and their future is precarious, as one can clearly see.

For as art 81(2)(c) of the Lisbon Treaty is now in force, there will be no part of the conflict of laws over which the European Union does have legislative authority:

**Article 81**
**(ex Article 65 TEC)**

1. The Union shall develop judicial cooperation in civil matters having cross-border implications, based on the principle of mutual recognition of judgments and of decisions in extrajudicial cases. Such cooperation may include the adoption of measures for the approximation of the laws and regulations of the Member States.
2. For the purposes of paragraph 1, the European Parliament and the Council, acting in accordance with the ordinary legislative procedure, shall adopt measures, particularly when necessary for the proper functioning of the internal market, aimed at ensuring:

   (a) the mutual recognition and enforcement between Member States of judgments and of decisions in extrajudicial cases;
   (b) the cross-border service of judicial and extrajudicial documents;
   (c) the compatibility of the rules applicable in the Member States concerning conflict of laws and of jurisdiction;
   (d) cooperation in the taking of evidence;
   (e) effective access to justice;
   (f) the elimination of obstacles to the proper functioning of civil proceedings, if necessary by promoting the compatibility of the rules on civil procedure applicable in the Member States;

---

[28] Council Regulation (EC) 1346/2000 (non-geographic).
[29] Council Regulation (EC) 2201/2003; Brussels II*bis*.
[30] Council Regulation (EC) 2201/2003; Council Regulation (EC) 4/2009.
[31] Proposal by Commission of 14 October 2009; Brussels IV.
[32] www.se2009.eu/polopoly_fs/1.19577!menu/standard/file/Draft_Stockholm_Programme_16_October_2009.pdf.

    (g)  the development of alternative methods of dispute settlement;

    (h)  support for the training of the judiciary and judicial staff.

3.  Notwithstanding paragraph 2, measures concerning family law with cross-border implications shall be established by the Council, acting in accordance with a special legislative procedure. The Council shall act unanimously after consulting the European Parliament.

There is nothing which is obviously excluded from this formulation of legislative power: its extension to the field of civil procedure is particularly unwelcome. The materials we currently have, and the materials we are about to receive, are clearly and deliberately alien to the common law. They are not designed to blend into a common law structure; and it would be quite wrong to interpret them as though they were. For a Supreme Court which has been created with unparalleled strength in private international law, dealing with this material would present a worthy challenge. But for the law to be located in these various legislative instruments will in fact remove from the Supreme Court one of the functions which it would have been brilliantly well placed to discharge, even if (as is suggested here) it would not be relying on its accumulated skill as a common law tribunal to do the work required. The Supreme Court will instead be limited, in this area, to checking the application—in a non-interpretive sense—of legislative rules whose meaning is not open to serious question. Look at art 267 of the Treaty of Lisbon:

### Article 267
### (ex Article 234 TEC)

The Court of Justice of the European Union shall have jurisdiction to give preliminary rulings concerning:

    (a)  the interpretation of the Treaties;

    (b)  the validity and interpretation of acts of the institutions, bodies, offices or agencies of the Union;

Where such a question is raised before any court or tribunal of a Member State, that court or tribunal may, if it considers that a decision on the question is necessary to enable it to give judgment, request the Court to give a ruling thereon.

    Where any such question is raised in a case pending before a court or tribunal of a Member State against whose decisions there is no judicial remedy under national law, that court or tribunal shall bring the matter before the Court. . .

This will make two changes to existing law in this area. First, any court or tribunal will be entitled to make a reference to the European Court 'on the interpretation of acts of the institutions . . . if it considers that a decision on the question is necessary to enable it to give judgment'. That widens the power to refer which is, under the former version of the Treaty, confined to courts from which there is no appeal.

Secondly, when the court is one from which there is no appeal, art 267 ties the hands of the court. If the text is taken at face value, the duty to bring the matter before the European Court is not confined to cases in which the court (from which no appeal lies) considers that a decision is necessary to enable it to give judgment.

It appears to arise in any case in which a question of the interpretation of the acts of the institutions is raised. If that is right (and even if it is not) it will remove any significant opportunity for the Supreme Court to apply its powers of reason and analysis to these new statutory rules.

For example, a really interesting question such as arose before the Dutch courts and which was referred to the European Court in *ICF v Balkenende Oosthuizen*[33] will not be the kind of thing for the Supreme Court to decide for itself. The tricky and much-litigated relationship between what are currently arts 4(2) and 4(5) of the Rome Convention, and which will soon be reborn as arts 4(1) and 4(4) of the Rome I Regulation, Regulation (EC) 593/2008, was something on which Lord Mance and Lord Collins, in particular, might have been expected to produce an analysis which was as legally literate as it was appropriate to the needs of commercial practice. But unless the meaning of the legislative rules is so clear as not to require any clarification, it will not be for the Supreme Court, but for the European Court to supply the thinking. It would be indelicate to go any further into why that is a matter for deep and real regret, but the impact of the European Court on matters of private and commercial law has not been greeted with stormy and prolonged applause. The principal function for a Supreme Court, over a very large area of modern private international law, will be taken away from it and placed in unsafe hands.

The bitter irony is, therefore, that at the point when the law is more uncertain than it has ever been—all this new legislation is bound to throw up endless problems of interpretation, as it drives deeper and deeper into private law—and when the final court of appeal in the United Kingdom is as brimming with expertise as it has ever been, there will be practically nothing for it to do. If this is what progress looks like, it is perhaps unsurprising that some of us are still struggling to recognise it for what it is said to be.

---

[33] Case C-133/08 *ICF v Balkenende Oosthuizen*, [2010] All ER (EC) 1, [2010] 1 All ER (Comm) 613.

# 9

# *The Law of Unjust Enrichment in the House of Lords: Judging the Judges*

## GRAHAM VIRGO

**T**HE UNJUST ENRICHMENT principle was created by the House of Lords on 6 June 1991 in *Lipkin Gorman v Karpnale Ltd*.[1] Before then there was evidence of the existence of a concept of unjust enrichment in the case law, and the phrase was sometimes used by the judiciary, but it was not clear that it formed a coherent part of English law which could be used to underpin a claim for restitution. Any doubt about its existence was resolved by *Lipkin Gorman*.

In 2009, unjust enrichment celebrated its 18th birthday and came of age. As it moves into adulthood, it is an appropriate time to consider its legitimacy and how it has been nurtured by the judiciary since its birth. In a collection of essays reflecting on the role of the House of Lords it is especially significant to examine the role of that court in recognising and developing this principle. Arguably, the unjust enrichment principle is the greatest testament to the creativity of the House of Lords in the late twentieth and early twenty-first centuries.

This paper analyses the development of the unjust enrichment principle by the House of Lords. Rather than simply seeking to trace a chronological progress, it will consider key themes in the development of the law and will identify judicial traits and trends of general significance to our understanding of it. It will reveal a close partnership between judge and jurist in legal creativity and rationalisation, but it will also reveal a tension, often hidden beneath the surface, but one that it is vital to acknowledge as regards the different contributions of the judge and the jurist to legal analysis.

## I LOCATING THE LAW OF RESTITUTION ON THE PRIVATE LAW MAP

The unjust enrichment principle has often been equated with the law of restitution. So Goff and Jones in the preface to the first edition of their *Law of Restitution*[2] said:

---

[1] *Lipkin Gorman v Karpnale Ltd* [1991] AC 546.
[2] R Goff and G Jones, *The Law of Restitution* (London, Sweet and Maxwell, 1966).

the law of Restitution is the law relating to all claims, quasi-contractual or otherwise, which are founded on the principle of unjust enrichment.[3]

The reality, however, is that the law of restitution is simply that body of law which is concerned with the award of a generic group of remedies that are assessed with reference to the defendant's gain, by either giving back (literal restitution) or giving up (disgorgement) to the claimant what the defendant has obtained. Three distinct principles underpin the award of these gain-based remedies: unjust enrichment of the defendant at the expense of the claimant; the vindication of legal or equitable property rights; and the commission of a wrong, whether tort, breach of contract or an equitable wrong.[4] The House of Lords has had a vital role in developing the law of restitution in all three areas, but especially as regards unjust enrichment. That is what this paper will focus on. The recent role of the House of Lords as regards the law of restitution for wrongs has been more limited, save for the recognition that gain-based remedies are exceptionally available for breach of contract,[5] but that has had only a very limited impact on the nature of the remedies awarded for breach of contract.

## II THE CONCEPTION OF THE UNJUST ENRICHMENT PRINCIPLE

The seeds of unjust enrichment can be traced back to the old forms of action, especially the action of *indebitatus assumpsit* which was developed in the seventeenth century.[6] The conception of what would eventually become the modern principle of unjust enrichment can be identified in the judgment of Lord Mansfield in *Moses v Macferlan*,[7] who recognised that the action for money had and received, one of these forms of action, lay:

for money paid by mistake; or upon a consideration which happens to fail; or for money got through imposition, (express or implied) or extortion; or oppression; or an undue advantage taken of the plaintiff's situation, contrary to laws made for the protection of persons under those circumstances.

This list proved highly significant to the subsequent rationalisation of the law by jurists, notably William Evans in 1801.[8]

But it took 230 years for the unjust enrichment principle to be recognised explicitly by the House of Lords. Two reasons can be identified for this. First,

[3] ibid v. See also main text, 5. This became the opening sentence of the text in the second edition (1978) and in subsequent editions.
[4] See G Virgo, *The Principles of the Law of Restitution*, 2nd edn (Oxford, Oxford University Press, 2006) 3–18.
[5] *Attorney-General v Blake* [2001] 1 AC 268.
[6] See J Baker, 'The History of Quasi-Contract in English Law' in W Cornish, R Nolan, J O'Sullivan and G Virgo (eds), *Restitution: Past, Present and Future* (Oxford, Hart Publishing, 1998); and D Ibbetson, *A Historical Introduction to the Law of Obligations*, Part IV (Oxford, Oxford University Press, 1999).
[7] *Moses v Macferlan* (1760) 2 Burr 1005, 1012.
[8] W Evans, 'An Essay on the Action for Money Had and Received' [1998] *Restitution Law Review* 1.

the development of the law occurred within four forms of action, namely money had and received to the defendant's use, money paid to the defendant, *quantum valebat* to recover the reasonable value of goods and *quantum meruit* to recover the reasonable value of services. This artificial division of claims prevented their unification in a single unjust enrichment principle. The artificiality of the distinction became even more marked following the abolition of the forms of action by the Common Law Procedure Act 1852. But the language of the forms of action continued to be used, and still appears to rule us from beyond their grave.[9]

The second reason for the late recognition of unjust enrichment was the implied contract theory. The old forms of action originally required the claimant to prove that the defendant owed money to the claimant and had promised to repay this money. Over time this promise to pay was implied and became fictional.[10] Eventually the artificiality of this implied contract was recognised by Lord Atkin in *United Australia Ltd v Barclays Bank Ltd*:[11]

> These fantastic resemblances of contracts invented in order to meet requirements of the law as to forms of action which have now disappeared should not in these days be allowed to affect actual rights. When these ghosts of the past stand in the path of justice clanking their medieval chains the proper course for the judge is to pass through them undeterred.

The rejection of the implied contract theory[12] opened the way for the recognition of a unified unjust enrichment principle. In fact, the first recognition of unjust enrichment in the House of Lords occurred two years later in the judgment of Lord Wright in *Fibrosa Spolka Akcyjna v Fairbairn Lawson Combe Barbour Ltd*:[13]

> It is clear that any civilised system of law is bound to provide remedies for cases of what has been called unjust enrichment or unjust benefit, that is to prevent a man from retaining the money of or some benefit derived from another which it is against conscience that he should keep. Such remedies in English law are generically different from remedies in contract or tort, and are now recognised to fall within a third category of the common law which has been called quasi-contract or restitution.

---

[9] See text to n 60 ff.

[10] It was explicitly recognised by the House of Lords in *Sinclair v Brougham* [1914] AC 398, 452 (Lord Sumner).

[11] *United Australia Ltd v Barclays Bank Ltd* [1941] AC 1, 29. The theory was 'unequivocally and finally' rejected by the House of Lords in *Westdeutsche Landesbank Girozentrale v Islington LBC* [1996] AC 669, 710 (Lord Browne-Wilkinson), 718 (Lord Slynn), 720 (Lord Woolf), 738 (Lord Lloyd). See also *Kleinwort Benson Ltd v Glasgow CC* [1999] 1 AC 153.

[12] But the implied contract still makes an appearance. So in *Guinness plc v Saunders* [1990] 2 AC 663, 689, Lord Templeman accepted it as providing the basis of quantum meruit claims.

[13] *Fibrosa Spolka Akcyjna v Fairbairn Lawson Combe Barbour Ltd* [1943] AC 32, 61. See also *Brook's Wharf and Bull Wharf Ltd v Goodman Bros* [1937] 1 KB 534, 545, where, as the Master of the Rolls, he referred to an obligation arising by operation of the law where the defendant was 'unjustly benefited at the cost of the plaintiffs'. On Lord Wright's general contribution as a judge see N Duxbury, 'Lord Wright and Innovative Traditionalism' (2009) 59 University of Toronto Law Journal 265.

Lord Wright had clearly been influenced in his recognition of unjust enrichment by the work of Seavey and Scott in the United States who had used the principle as the foundation of the American Law Institute's *Restatement of the Law of Restitution, Quasi-Contracts and Constructive Trusts*, promulgated in May 1936.[14] In November 1937 he delivered a lecture to the Cambridge University Law Society[15] on *Sinclair v Brougham*,[16] which he explained as giving relief:

> to prevent unjust enrichment, or to achieve restitution, if we accept the useful term which has been employed in the recently published American Restatement of the Law of Restitution. The word itself is only an echo of the language which will be found in English judgments . . . It is therefore important not merely to recognise the existence of this separate head in the law (in which word I include law and equity) but to enumerate to classify and to distinguish.[17]

Although the course seemed to be set for the assimilation of the unjust enrichment principle into English law by the House of Lords,[18] this did not occur. In *Reading v Attorney-General*[19] Lord Normand stated that the 'exact status of the law of unjust enrichment is not yet assured.' Further, Lord Diplock in *Orakpo v Manson Investments*[20] stated that:

> there is no general doctrine of unjust enrichment recognised in English law. What it does is to provide specific remedies in particular cases of what might be classified as unjust enrichment in a legal system that is based on the civil law.

This rejection of a 'doctrine' of unjust enrichment by the House of Lords is mirrored by the recent attitude of the High Court of Australia to unjust enrichment. Although the High Court has recognised a principle of unjust enrichment in Australia,[21] more recently it has expressed scepticism about its relevance,[22] most significantly in *Bofinger v Kingsway Group Ltd*,[23] where the

---

[14] American Law Institute, 1937. On the history of the Restatement and the recognition of the unjust enrichment principle in the United States see A Kull, 'James Barr Ames and the Early Modern History of Unjust Enrichment' (2005) 25 *Oxford Journal of Legal Studies* 297.

[15] '*Sinclair v Brougham*' (1938) 6 *Cambridge Law Journal* 305.

[16] *Sinclair* (n 10).

[17] '*Sinclair v Brougham*' (n 15) 306. See also Lord Wright, '*United Australia Ltd v Barclays Bank Ltd*' (1941) 57 *Law Quarterly Review* 184 and A Denning, 'The Recovery of Money' (1949) 65 *Law Quarterly Review* 37, 48. It is ironic that Lord Wright used *Sinclair v Brougham* as the peg on which to hang his extra-judicial analysis since that case was overruled by *Westdeutsche Landesbank Girozentrale v Islington LBC* [1996] AC 669, one of the leading decisions of the House of Lords on the modern unjust enrichment principle, and anyway principally concerned restitutionary proprietary claims.

[18] Although it was also recognised by Lord Pearce in *Attorney-General v Nissan* [1970] AC 179, 228.

[19] *Reading v Attorney-General* [1951] AC 507, 513–14.

[20] *Orakpo v Manson Investments* [1978] AC 95, 104. Other sceptics included Lord Radcliffe in *Bossevain v Weil* [1950] AC 327, 341, Lord Simonds in *Ministry of Health v Simpson* [1951] AC 251, 275 and Lord Templeman in *Guinness Plc v Saunders* [1990] 2 AC 663, 689, although the latter changed his tune soon afterwards in *Lipkin Gorman* (n 1).

[21] *David Securities Pty Ltd v Commonwealth Bank of Australia* (1992) 175 CLR 353.

[22] See, eg, *Roxborough v Rothmans of Pall Mall Australia Ltd* (2002) 185 ALR 335, 355, where Gummow J preferred to describe the action for money had and received as being founded on a principle of unconscientious receipt rather than unjust enrichment.

[23] [2009] HCA 44, (2009) 260 ALR 71.

Court rejected the notion that unjust enrichment was a 'definitive legal principle according to its own terms' and confirmed that it was 'just a concept'.[24] Other Australian courts were bound accordingly. Although the significance of the distinction between a principle and a concept might be regarded as unclear, the sense appears to be that, in Australia at least, unjust enrichment as a concept has descriptive but not explanatory force. In other words, the claimant cannot obtain restitution by pleading unjust enrichment, but a claim to restitution which can be established in some other way, such as by subrogation, constructive trust or *quantum meruit*, can be described after the event as involving the reversal of an unjust enrichment.

## III THE BIRTH OF UNJUST ENRICHMENT

It is not much of an exaggeration to say that the modern unjust enrichment principle was created by Lord Goff and it was strongly influenced by his own writings as a jurist and his subsequent judgments. The seminal *Law of Restitution*, written with Gareth Jones, was published in 1966 and showed that the recognition of the unjust enrichment principle by the courts would be a natural legal development. When Robert Goff became a judge he used the unjust enrichment principle to explain the operation of the Law Reform (Frustrated Contracts) Act 1943.[25] On elevation to the House of Lords he had an opportunity to recognise formally the unjust enrichment principle in *Lipkin Gorman (a firm) v Karpnale*,[26] where he said that:

> A claim to recover money at common law is made as a matter of right; and even though the underlying principle of recovery is the principle of unjust enrichment, nevertheless, where recovery is denied, it is denied on the basis of legal principle.

Although this decision of the House of Lords is of profound significance to the recognition and subsequent development of the unjust enrichment principle, careful analysis of the facts and the reasoning indicates that it was an inappropriate vehicle for its recognition and should not be considered to have been a case about unjust enrichment at all.

---

[24] Referring to the language of Deane J in *Pavey and Matthews Pty Ltd v Paul* (1987) 162 CLR 221, 256–57.

[25] *BP Exploration Co (Libya) Ltd) v Hunt (No 2)* [1979] 1 WLR 783, 799. See also *Barclays Bank v WJ Simms (Southern) Ltd* [1980] QB 677, 697 (restitution of mistaken payment, where the language of unjust enrichment was not used but restitution was); *British Steel Corporation v Cleveland Bridge and Engineering Co Ltd* [1984] 1 All ER 504, 511 (anticipated contract) and in the Court of Appeal in *Whittaker v Campbell* [1984] QB 318, 327 (rescission preventing unjust enrichment).

[26] *Lipkin Gorman* (n 1), 578. This had been prefigured in *R v Tower Hamlets LBC, ex p Chetnik Developments Ltd* [1988] AC 858, 882.

## A  The decision in *Lipkin Gorman*

The case concerned Cass, one of the partners of the claimant firm of solicitors, who had authority to draw on the firm's client bank account on his signature alone. Cass was a compulsive gambler and stole over £300,000 from the account, which he used to fund his gambling habit at the defendant casino. On discovering what had happened, the firm sought to recover the stolen money from the club. The House of Lords held that the claim against the club for money had and received should succeed because the club had been unjustly enriched, although the liability to make restitution was reduced to the extent that the club had changed its position in paying out when Cass had occasionally won on a bet.

Four distinct strands can be identified in the reasoning of their Lordships, with substantial judgments being handed down by Lords Templeman and Goff, with whom the other Law Lords agreed.[27] First, the claim for money had and received was recognised as involving a claim for restitution such that the defendant was required to give up its gain of the stolen money, but without it having to suffer a net loss.[28] Lord Goff specifically recognised that the case turned on the application of the principles of the law of restitution.[29]

Secondly, the unjust enrichment principle was recognised as underpinning the claim for money had and received, with specific reference to the judgment of Lord Wright in *Fibrosa*.[30] But surprisingly little was said about the elements of this principle, other than that the defendant's enrichment must have been obtained at the claimant's expense. Lord Goff did, however, emphasise that the principle did not enable the court to reject a claim simply because it was considered to be unfair or unjust.

Thirdly, it was recognised that no valuable consideration had been provided by the club in respect of the gambling transactions, since these were void. Consequently, the club had no defence based on the validity of these transactions.[31]

Fourthly, the defence of change of position was recognised. It was in this context that most of the analysis about the unjust enrichment principle occurred. Lord Goff analysed the older authorities, relating to agents and bills of exchange, which he considered to have partially recognised the defence. He also had regard to authorities in the US, Canada, New Zealand and certain Australian states which had recognised the defence. He concluded that change of position should be recognised as a general defence in England. Very little was said about what was needed to establish the defence, other than that it was available where it would be inequitable to require the defendant to make restitution and that it was not available where the defendant had acted in bad faith, such as where the defendant was aware of the restitutionary claim or was a wrongdoer. Further,

---

[27] Lords Bridge, Griffiths and Ackner.

[28] *Lipkin Gorman* (n 1) 563 (Lord Templeman).

[29] ibid 572.

[30] [1943] AC 32, 61.

[31] See further the analysis of the presence of basis principle, see section IVD(iii), below.

the mere fact that the defendant had spent money was not sufficient to establish the defence.[32] Beyond this, Lords Bridge and Goff considered that the defence should be allowed to develop on a case by case basis. The defence did apply on the facts so that, of the £300,000 which had been received by the club, it was liable to pay just over half of this back to the firm, since it had changed its position to the extent that it had paid gambling winnings to Cass.

## B  The significance of *Lipkin Gorman*

In addition to the recognition of the unjust enrichment principle, the most significant aspect of *Lipkin Gorman* was the recognition of the change of position defence, which has been vital to the subsequent development of the law of unjust enrichment by the House of Lords. For it is only because such a defence has been recognised that it was possible to expand the unjust enrichment principle itself, as Lord Goff acknowledged would be the case.[33] For the essence of that principle is that the defendant is liable without proof of any wrongdoing or bad faith; liability is strict. This would make the award of restitutionary remedies difficult to justify if, for example, the claimant has made a mistake, for why should the defendant be required to make restitution when the claimant was to blame? But the award of a restitutionary remedy in such circumstances is much easier to justify when innocent changes in the defendant's position can be taken into account. If the defendant's position has not changed then it is much more clearly appropriate that the defendant should make restitution to the claimant, to return the parties to their original position. With the defence firmly in place, despite its ambit being left unclear, the courts could confidently expand the grounds of restitution which are available.[34]

Despite this significant contribution to the development of unjust enrichment, *Lipkin Gorman* is not in fact what it appears to be. The supreme irony is that what has been considered to be the leading case on the principle is not about unjust enrichment at all. If the case is analysed as involving a claim founded on unjust enrichment it is clear that it is difficult to identify what made the enrichment unjust. Neither Lord Templeman nor Lord Goff broke down the principle into its component parts and consequently neither judge identified a recognised reason why the enrichment was unjust. It is true that Lord Templeman did cite *Hudson v Robinson*[35] where, in the context of a claim to recover money which had been paid for goods which were not delivered, Lord Ellenborough CJ recognised that 'the absence of any consideration entitles the plaintiffs to maintain this action

---

[32] Rejecting the contrary suggestion of Lord Simonds in *Ministry of Health v Simpson* [1951] AC 251, 276.

[33] *Lipkin Gorman v Karpnale* [1991] 2 AC 548, 581.

[34] Especially the abolition of the bar on the recovery for mistake of law: *Kleinwort Benson Ltd v Lincoln CC* [1999] 2 AC 349, 371–72 (Lord Goff). See text to n 140, below.

[35] *Hudson v Robinson* (1816) 4 M and S 475, 478.

[for money had and received]'. Absence of consideration has been recognised as a ground of restitution in its own right as regards payments made in respect of void contracts,[36] and it could certainly have been relevant in *Hudson* where the contract of sale was void because the partner who had made the contract with the claimant had acted fraudulently. But the facts of *Lipkin Gorman* were different, because Cass did have authority to draw the money from the client account; this was a valid transaction. An alternative 'ground' of restitution appears to have been suggested by Lord Goff, who said it would be unconscionable for a third party to retain stolen money.[37] But this notion of unconscionability is so vague that it cannot constitute a principled ground of restitution. No recognisable ground of restitution can be identified on the facts of *Lipkin Gorman*.

A further reason why unjust enrichment cannot be established is because the club's enrichment was not obtained directly at the expense of the firm but was obtained at the expense of Cass, who had paid the money to the club.[38] Unjust enrichment requires there to be a direct causative connection between the defendant's receipt and the claimant's loss,[39] and this could not be shown.

In fact the reason why Lords Templeman and Goff considered that the claimant should make restitution was because the money which had been stolen from the client account continued to belong to the firm of solicitors. So Lord Templeman recognised that:

> in a claim for money had and received by a thief, the plaintiff victim must show that money belonging to him was paid by the thief to the defendant and that the defendant was unjustly enriched and remained unjustly enriched.[40]

The claim should properly be analysed as being based on the vindication of the firm's property rights in the money and was in fact analysed in this way by Lords Templeman and Goff. Lord Templeman's analysis was rather unsophisticated. He asserted that the claim depended on the defendant's retention of the money, although this appeared to reflect a confusion about the role of the defence of change of position. In fact Lord Goff emphasised that the claim for money had and received did not depend on the club's retention of any money; it was a personal claim which turned on whether the club had received money in which the firm had a continuing proprietary interest at the time of the defendant's receipt. But Lord Goff acknowledged that the firm needed to establish a basis on which it was entitled to the money and it could do so by showing that the money was its legal property. Particular reliance was placed on the decision of Lord Mansfield in *Clarke v Shee and Johnson*[41] where the claimant recovered money which had

---

[36] See section IVD(ii), below.

[37] *Lipkin Gorman* (n 1) 572.

[38] ibid.

[39] *Banque Financière de la Cité v Parc (Battersea) Ltd* [1999] 1 AC 221, 237 (Lord Clyde); see section IVC(ii) below. See further G Virgo, 'Causation and Unjust Enrichment' in S Degeling and J Edelman (eds), *Unjust Enrichment in Commercial Law* (Sydney, Law Book Co, 2008).

[40] *Lipkin Gorman* (n 1), 559–60.

[41] *Clarke v Shee and Johnson* (1774) 1 Cowp 197.

been stolen by his servant, who had used it to buy lottery tickets. The claimant successfully sued the defendants who ran the lottery. Crucially, Lord Mansfield specifically recognised that the claimant sued 'for his identified property'.[42] The significance of this to Lord Goff was that the claim was:

> founded simply on the fact that, as Lord Mansfield said, the third party cannot in conscience retain the money—or, as we say nowadays, for the third party to retain the money would result in his unjust enrichment at the expense of the owner of the money.[43]

Now it is true that Lord Goff used the unjust enrichment principle to justify restitution in that case, but he did not need to do so, because the claim turned on the vindication of a property right. That is why in *Lipkin Gorman* itself, rather than searching for a recognised reason why the enrichment was unjust, Lord Goff focused instead on showing that the defendant had received money which belonged to the firm at common law. He held that the firm did not have any proprietary rights in the money which was credited to the client bank account because Cass had authority to draw money from the account. However, he concluded that, since the bank owed the money to the firm, it owned a chose in action at law which it could trace into the cash drawn from the bank account by the solicitor and into the money received by the club. But this does not satisfactorily deal with the fact that the money drawn by Cass belonged to him because he had authority to draw on the account. True, his act of drawing the money constituted theft, because he had interfered with another's property rights dishonestly, but this did not render the withdrawal unauthorised. Lord Goff's analysis was half-hearted and he seemed almost too ready to reach the desired result of allowing restitution but without providing convincing reasons, especially as to how it was possible to identify a continuing proprietary interest in money which clearly belonged to the thief.[44]

There was a further difficulty in establishing a proprietary claim, since the money drawn from the client account might have been mixed with Cass's own money when he gambled at the club, so that it would have lost its identity. This is because tracing at law is defeated by mixing in a fund.[45] But counsel for the defendant had conceded that title to the money would not have been lost had it been mixed. This is a very odd concession. Had it not been made, it is possible that the claim for restitution would have failed or, perhaps more likely, the House of Lords would have taken the opportunity to remove the distinction between tracing at law and in equity, and concluded that it was possible to trace at law even through a mixture.

---

[42] ibid 200–01. See also *Black v S Freedman and Co* (1910) 12 CLR 105 (albeit a case involving a trust) and *Banque Belge pour l'Etranger v Hambrouck* [1921] 1 KB 321.

[43] *Lipkin Gorman* (n 1) 572.

[44] That a thief can be guilty of a crime whilst still obtaining property rights has been explicitly recognised by the House of Lords: *R v Hinks* [2001] AC 241.

[45] *Trustee of the Property of FC Jones v Jones* [1997] Ch 159, 168 (Millett LJ).

There was an alternative proprietary claim available to the firm, but this had not been pursued. Although the effect of Cass having authority to draw money meant that legal title to the money passed to him, his reason for doing so was such that he would have been acting in breach of fiduciary duty,[46] so the money would be held on constructive trust for the firm, which would have been able to trace it in equity to the defendant. This would have been a lot easier to establish, since tracing in equity is not defeated by money becoming mixed. But counsel for the firm did not make such a claim, presumably because the personal claim would have been for what is now known as unconscionable receipt, which would have required proof of fault on the part of the defendant at the time of receipt and would have been difficult to establish on the facts.[47]

The reasoning of the House of Lords could have been much clearer without the distraction of unjust enrichment. If instead the focus had been on the vindication of property rights at law it would have been clear that the firm had to show that it had title to the money paid to the defendant. It could not have shown this, and so the claim should have failed.

## C  Lessons as to judicial methodology

Analysing *Lipkin Gorman* as a case which did not actually turn on unjust enrichment provides some valuable insights into the methodology of the House of Lords. First, there is a sense that the Law Lords had been waiting for an opportunity to recognise formally the unjust enrichment principle in English law and considered that *Lipkin Gorman* gave them such an opportunity, especially because of the apparent significance of change of position

Secondly, the result was clearly influenced by the way it was argued. It is unfortunate, for example, that counsel for the defendant had conceded that it was possible to trace into the money received by the defendant despite mixing and that counsel for the claimant had not pursued a claim in equity, which would have enabled the House of Lords to clarify whether fault is required for such a claim.

Finally, the relevance of the unjust enrichment principle was asserted, rather than analysed logically and rigorously. There is a real danger that this could have transformed the principle into a concept which enables judges to reach a fair result, but without the benefit of predictability or rationality.[48] Thankfully, many

---

[46] As Lord Goff acknowledged: *Lipkin Gorman* (n 1) 572.

[47] But a strict liability claim in equity would have been available to recover any money which was still identifiable. Note also L Smith, 'Simplifying Claims to Traceable Proceeds' (2009) 125 *Law Quarterly Review* 338, who argues that common law actions for money had and received in respect of the proceeds of an unauthorised disposition can be analysed as a common law claim for money held on trust. This might mean that the solicitor held the money on trust for the firm, which would explain how the firm could trace to the property received by the club, but it would still depend on the solicitor's withdrawal of the money being unauthorised.

[48] See section II above.

of the judges in the House of Lords have subsequently avoided the temptation to interpret this principle in this way, and the necessary rigour of analysis has been applied.[49] But *Lipkin Gorman* itself was something of a damp squib as regards its rigorous analysis of the unjust enrichment principle. For unjust enrichment was used by Lord Templeman and even Lord Goff as an ex post justification for restitution.

## IV  THE FORMATIVE YEARS

Since 1991 the House of Lords has considered issues relating to the unjust enrichment principle in 10 leading cases.[50] Issues relating to unjust enrichment have been considered in other cases, but those issues have been less significant to the reasoning and the result.[51] Analysis of the 10 leading decisions show how the components of unjust enrichment have been clarified, but different judges have adopted different styles and methods of analysis.

## A  Unjust enrichment as a cause of action

Although the decision of the House of Lords in *Lipkin Gorman* can be considered to be seminal, and although Lord Goff did emphasise that unjust enrichment involved a right to restitution and the denial of restitution was made by reference to principle,[52] no details were given as to how this principle could be established. It was not until 1998 that the principled nature of unjust enrichment was acknowledged. In *Banque Financière de la Cité v Parc (Battersea) Ltd*[53] Lord Steyn talked of 'established principles of unjust enrichment' and acknowledged that unjust enrichment ranks next to contract and tort within the law of obligations and was an independent source of rights and obligations.[54] Lord Steyn adopted the distinction drawn by Birks in *An Introduction to the Law of Restitution*[55]

---

[49] Although, in 1992, Lord Browne-Wilkinson in *Woolwich Equitable Building Society v IRC* [1993] AC 70, 197 described unjust enrichment as a concept and not a general rule of law.

[50] *Woolwich Equitable Building Society v IRC* (n 49); *Westdeutsche Landesbank Girozentrale v Islington LBC* [1996] AC 669; *Stocznia Gdanska SA v Latvian Shipping Co* [1998] 1 WLR 574; *Kleinwort Benson Ltd v Glasgow CC* (n 11); *Banque Financière de la Cité* (n 39); *Kleinwort Benson Ltd v Lincoln CC* (n 34); *Foskett v McKeown* [2001] 1 AC 102; *Deutsche Morgan Grenfell Group plc v IRC* [2006] UKHL 49, [2007] 1 AC 558; *Sempra Metals Ltd v IRC* [2007] UKHL 34, [2008] 1 AC 561; and *Yeoman's Row Management Ltd v Cobbe* [2008] UKHL 55, [2008] 1 WLR 1752.

[51] See, eg, *Pan Ocean Shipping Co Ltd v Creditcorp Ltd, The Trident Beauty* [1994] 1 WLR 161 (primacy of contract over unjust enrichment); *Dubai Aluminium Co Ltd v Salaam* [2003] 2 AC 366 (contribution); *Marks and Spencer plc v Her Majesty's Commissioners of Customs and Excise* [2009] UKHL 8, [2009] 1 All ER 939 (passing on defence as regards claims for recovery of VAT).

[52] *Lipkin Gorman* (n 1) 578.

[53] *Banque Financière de la Cité* (n 39).

[54] ibid 227. This positioning of unjust enrichment within the law of obligations had already been recognised by Lord Wright in *Fibrosa* (n 13) 61, see section II above.

[55] P Birks, *An Introduction to the Law of Restitution* (Oxford, Oxford University Press, 1985).

between unjust enrichment by wrongdoing and by subtraction. In fact Birks had the previous month rejected this distinction at a conference[56] where he argued that gain-based remedies for wrongdoing had nothing to do with the law of unjust enrichment, since the underlying cause of action was the wrong rather than unjust enrichment.[57] This analysis appears now to have been accepted in *Attorney-General v Blake*[58] where the House of Lords accepted that gain-based remedies were available for breach of contract but without making reference to unjust enrichment to explain why these remedies were available.

The real significance of *Banque Financière de la Cité* is that unjust enrichment was clearly recognised as a distinct cause of action[59] with its own key elements which need to be established. These elements were recognised by Lord Steyn[60] as follows:

1.   that the defendant had been benefited or enriched;
2.   this was received at the expense of the claimant;
3.   the enrichment was unjust; and
4.   there was no available defence.

With the clear recognition of a new cause of action, albeit one that was developed from the old forms of action, it might be thought that the legacy of the forms of action and the implied contract theory could be consigned to a footnote of legal history. Unfortunately that is not the case and the old forms of action do appear to rule us still from their graves. It was the last pronouncement of the House of Lords on the law of unjust enrichment in *Yeoman's Row Management Ltd v Cobbe*[61] which unfortunately confirms this continued and confusing legacy. Although that case was primarily concerned with an unsuccessful claim founded on proprietary estoppel, a claim in restitution succeeded. What makes the case so significant, and unsettling, is that three distinct causes of action were recognised for which gain-based remedies were considered to be available, when in fact each cause of action was a different way of describing the same thing.

In *Yeoman's Row* the claimant had entered into an oral agreement in principle with the defendant to buy the defendant's land. No written contract was made. The claimant successfully made an application for planning permission to develop

---

[56] Marking the retirement of Gareth Jones from the Downing Professorship in the University of Cambridge.

[57] 'Misnomer' in W Cornish, R Nolan, J O'Sullivan and G Virgo (eds), *Restitution: Past, Present and Future* (Oxford, Hart Publishing, 1998).

[58] *Blake* (n 5).

[59] The latest view as to the function of unjust enrichment is that a number of different causes of action exist within the unjust enrichment principle, each with their own requirements, such as the cause of action for unlawfully demanded tax and that for the recovery of money paid under a mistake of law: *FJ Chalke Ltd v The Commissioners for Her Majesty's Revenue and Customs* [2009] EWHC 952 (Ch) [127] (Henderson J); affirmed on appeal, [2010] EWCA Civ 313. See also *Deutsche Morgan Grenfell* (n 50) [17] (Lord Hoffmann).

[60] *Banque Financière de la Cité* (n 39) 227. At 234, Lord Hoffmann added that a further question was whether there were any reasons of policy for denying a remedy.

[61] *Yeoman's Row* (n 50).

the land. Negotiations broke down and the claimant sought a restitutionary remedy from the defendant. This claim succeeded on the basis that the defendant had obtained the benefit of the planning permission.[62] Lord Scott, with whom the other judges agreed,[63] recognised that there were three causes of action available to the claimant:

1. unjust enrichment—on the basis that the defendant had obtained a benefit at the expense of the claimant;
2. *quantum meruit*—on the basis that the defendant's benefit consisted of the claimant's services in obtaining planning permission;
3. failure of consideration—on the basis that the claimant had expected to obtain the land in respect of which the planning permission had been obtained and this was not forthcoming.

That the claimant could obtain a personal restitutionary remedy in these circumstances was not controversial; that the claimant had three distinct ways to obtain this is. The only claim available was one in unjust enrichment, for which the only appropriate remedy would have been *quantum meruit* (the reasonable value of the services provided) and for which the unjust element would be satisfied by showing that there had been a total failure of consideration. In identifying three distinct claims Lord Scott was simply describing one claim, but from three different perspectives: the underlying cause of action, the remedy and the ground of restitution.

The most worrying aspect of Lord Scott's analysis was the proposition that *quantum meruit* was a cause of action in its own right. But that cause of action was abolished in 1852. Even if the cause of action could still be considered to exist in its own right, what are the elements of the claim which need to be established? Lord Scott gave no indication of this, and it is difficult to see what would be required, other than that the defendant had benefited from the receipt of the services provided by the claimant, and there was a reason why the defendant should be required to pay for this service. But that is what unjust enrichment establishes. There is a growing body of law on the identification and valuation of enrichment, which has been contributed to by the decision in *Yeoman's Row*, and reliance on a recognised ground of restitution shows why a remedy should be awarded. Nothing can be gained by simply asserting a claim in *quantum meruit*.

It is, perhaps, rather too easy for a commentator to criticise the House of Lords for adopting three different methods to reach the same result, especially when one of them is analysed properly. But judges in the appellate courts have a responsibility for accuracy of analysis and, crucially, to avoid unnecessary complexity. Probably the tripartite analysis was a consequence of the way the case was argued before the court, and Lord Scott was simply trying to reflect the

---

[62] As to the identification and valuation of this enrichment, see section IVB below.
[63] Lords Hoffmann, Walker, Brown and Mance.

nature of the argument in his judgment. But that will not do. If the underlying cause of action is not understood by counsel, then the judge needs to explain clearly why they have got it wrong. Judges, especially in appellate courts, do not just decide the case before them; they clarify and rationalise the law for the benefit of those who do not or cannot go to court.

## B  Enrichment

The notion of whether a defendant has been enriched lies at the heart of the unjust enrichment principle. It is, however, the part of the unjust enrichment formula which has not been subject to much judicial analysis in the House of Lords, largely because most of the restitutionary claims which have reached that court have involved claims for money which is incontrovertibly beneficial, being the measure of enrichment, and so uncontroversial. Nevertheless, recently some of the most difficult and technical unjust enrichment issues have involved enrichment questions.

### (i)  Use value of money

The judgment of most of the judges in *Sempra Metals Ltd v IRC*[64] constitutes a master-class in principled analysis of a difficult enrichment question, which has put the law on a much more secure foundation as to the definition and proof of an enrichment. The case arose from a decision of the European Court of Justice[65] which had ruled that the denial of group income tax relief to companies with a non-resident parent was unlawful since it was discriminatory under EC law. Consequently, certain taxpayers had paid corporation tax prematurely without the benefit of the relief which would have enabled them to defer payment. Claims for restitution were pursued. The House of Lords had held that a claim in unjust enrichment grounded on mistake of law was available,[66] but the issue for the House of Lords in *Sempra Metals* concerned the identification and valuation of the enrichment. What is crucial to this case was that the claim did not concern the restitution of money paid, since the tax which was paid was ultimately due to the Revenue. Rather, the claim related to the Revenue's use of the money until the time when the money would otherwise have been paid had the taxpayer been allowed to elect to delay payment.

The House of Lords recognised that the defendant's use of money could constitute an enrichment. This was a significant development, and one that surprisingly has had little impact in subsequent cases. For the effect of the decision is that if, for example, A pays money to B by mistake, A will have two claims in

---

[64] *Sempra Metals* (n 50).
[65] C-410/98 *Metallgesellschaft Ltd v IRC; Hoechst v IRC* [2001] Ch 620.
[66] *Deutsche Morgan Grenfell* (n 50).

unjust enrichment, because B will have been enriched in two ways: by receipt of the money and by its use until judgment.[67]

The analysis of both the majority and the minority as to whether the use value of money could constitute an enrichment and, if it did, how that use could be valued, is of more general significance in showing how the Law Lords have sought to clarify and develop the law with reference to clearly defined principles, although in fact the identification of these principles could have been even clearer.

It was first necessary to determine whether the Revenue had been enriched by the premature payment of the tax money. The majority[68] assumed that the Revenue had been negatively enriched by the receipt of the tax, in that it had the opportunity to use the money paid by the claimant rather than to borrow an equivalent amount from elsewhere. The minority[69] considered this to be a wholly conceptual benefit and wanted the claimant to bear the burden of proving that the defendant had actually relied on the receipt of the money. The approach of the majority is preferable, since it is appropriate to assume that the recipient of money has relied on it in some way, and the defendant is in the best position to show there was no reliance on the receipt, for example because it was put in a box under a bed or credited to a non-interest bearing current account. Consequently, the majority presumed that the Revenue had been enriched, since if the Government had not been paid the tax money prematurely, it would have borrowed an equivalent amount from another source.

It was accepted by the parties that the appropriate method for valuing the defendant's use of this money was by reference to interest. The objective value of this enrichment was considered to be the reasonable cost of borrowing an equivalent amount of money, which was to be assessed by reference to compound interest, this being the conventional interest for ordinary commercial borrowings. However, the majority also recognised that the Revenue could subjectively devalue this enrichment since it could establish that the Government would have been able to borrow at a lower rate of interest. The value of the enrichment of the use of the money was consequently assessed with reference to this rate of interest. The approach of the majority in focusing on objective benefits and subjective devaluation is consistent with key principles underpinning the law on enrichment.

*(ii) Services*

Another controversial issue relating to the identification of an enrichment involves the claimant performing a service for the defendant which has the effect of increasing the value of the defendant's property. Should the defendant be considered to be enriched by the value of the service or the increase in the

---

[67] After judgment, interest can be awarded on the amounts due. Following the decision in *Sempra Metals* this is likely to be assessed as compound interest.

[68] Lords Hope, Nicholls and Walker.

[69] Lords Scott and Mance.

property's value? This issue arose in *Yeoman's Row Management Ltd v Cobbe*[70] since the claimant's work in obtaining planning permission had increased the value of the defendant's land. Lord Scott concluded that the relevant enrichment was the service and not the end product. He drew an analogy with a locked cabinet which is believed to contain valuables but the key is missing. If the claimant locksmith makes a key which enables the defendant to obtain the valuables inside, the defendant will only be enriched by the cost of the key and not by the value of the valuables, because everything which is inside the cabinet is already owned by the defendant. So, in *Yeoman's Row*, Lord Scott concluded that the planning permission did not 'create the developmental potential of the property; it unlocked it.'[71] This is a significant decision to the law on enrichment since it shows that the defendant can only be considered to be enriched to the extent that the claimant has caused the defendant to be benefited.

## C  At the expense of the claimant

### (i)  Direct benefit

The second element of the unjust enrichment formula is that the enrichment was received at the expense of the claimant. At its most basic this involves proof that the enrichment which was received by the defendant was received directly from the claimant. This was recognised by the House of Lords in *Banque Financière de la Cité v Parc (Battersea) Ltd.*[72] The claimant had entered into a refinancing transaction involving the payment of a sum of money to the chief financial officer of a holding company, which was transmitted to a subsidiary of that company to discharge a debt which the subsidiary owed. It was conceded that the discharge of this debt enriched the defendant, another subsidiary of the holding company which was also owed money by the first subsidiary, because the discharge of the first debt meant that the defendant's debt was more likely to be repaid. One of the questions for the House of Lords was whether this enrichment could be considered to have been at the claimant's expense, even though the claimant had paid money to the chief financial officer rather than to the first subsidiary directly. The court was prepared to consider the realities of the case and the role of the financial officer was ignored, so that the benefit obtained by the defendant, namely the reduction of the other subsidiary's liabilities, was considered to have been obtained directly at the claimant's expense.

### (ii)  Correspondence of loss and gain

Another issue is embodied within the 'at the expense of the claimant' test, namely whether the enrichment which was received by the defendant must correspond

---

[70]  *Yeoman's Row* (n 50).
[71]  ibid [41].
[72]  *Banque Financière de la Cité* (n 39).

with the loss suffered by the claimant. On one view[73] it is not necessary to show an exact correspondence between gain and loss, because the function of the requirement that the benefit was obtained at the claimant's expense is simply to show that there is a causal link between the claimant's loss of an enrichment and the defendant's gain. Other commentators[74] have emphasised that the claimant should only be able to obtain restitution to the extent that the defendant's gain corresponds with the claimant's loss. This is because the unjust enrichment principle is considered by many jurists to be founded on a principle of corrective justice, and it is only appropriate to correct the injustice of the defendant's unjust enrichment to the extent that the claimant has suffered loss, since the function of the law of unjust enrichment is not the giving up of enrichment but the reversal of transactions.[75] So, for example, if the claimant has provided services worth £500 to repair the defendant's car, which consequently increases the value of that car by £1,000, if correspondence between gain and loss is required the claimant is only able to obtain restitution of £500.

The existence of such a correspondence principle was rejected by some members of the House of Lords in *Sempra Metals Ltd v IRC*.[76] Lord Hope expressly rejected any requirement that the defendant's gain must correspond with the claimant's loss. He recognised that the defendant in that case had to give back the whole of the benefit it had received from the claimant without regard to the extent of the claimant's loss and that the process was 'one of subtraction, not compensation.'[77]

This focus on the defendant's gain rather than the claimant's loss is reflected also in recent controversy about whether the fact that the claimant has passed on its loss to a third party should operate as a defence to the restitutionary claim. So, for example, if A pays money to B by mistake and then passes this loss on to C by, for example, increasing its prices, should the fact that A has no longer suffered a loss bar the restitutionary claim against B? The Court of Appeal had rejected the defence of passing on,[78] but the House of Lords had the opportunity to consider the defence in the specific context of restitution of overpaid VAT. Section 80(3) of the Value Added Tax Act 1994[79] recognises a defence of unjust enrichment which applies where the consequence of recovering overpaid VAT will be to unjustly enrich the claimant. Marks and Spencer had sought restitution of overpaid VAT

---

[73] See P Birks, *Unjust Enrichment*, 2nd edn (Oxford, Oxford University Press, 2005) 78–86. See also M Rush, *Passing On* (Oxford, Hart Publishing, 2006) 172.

[74] See L Smith, 'Restitution: The Heart of Corrective Justice' (2001) 79 *Texas Law Review* 2115; M McInnes, 'Interceptive Subtraction, Unjust Enrichment and Wrongs—A Reply to Professor Birks' (2003) *Cambridge Law Journal* 697, 708; R Grantham and C Rickett, 'Disgorgement for Unjust Enrichment?' (2003) *Cambridge Law Journal* 159. See also Lord Wright '*Sinclair v Brougham*' (1938) 6 *Cambridge Law Journal* 305, 306.

[75] C Mitchell, 'The New Birksian Approach to Unjust Enrichment' [2004] *Restitution Law Review* 260, 267.

[76] *Sempra Metals* (n 50).

[77] ibid [31].

[78] *Kleinwort Benson Ltd v Birmingham CC* [1996] 4 All ER 733.

[79] As amended by the Finance Act 1997 s 46.

which had been incorrectly charged on teacakes it sold. Its restitutionary claim was met with the defence of unjust enrichment on the ground that it had passed on its loss to its customers. The House of Lords[80] determined that the validity of this defence should be referred to the European Court of Justice, but Lord Walker did state that the passing on defence was recognised in English law as a possible defence to any restitutionary claim.[81] He relied on a decision of the High Court of Australia[82] in support of that conclusion, even though that decision had expressly rejected the defence in Australia.[83] The European Court of Justice[84] stated that the English court had to consider the validity of the unjust enrichment defence in the light of European Community principles of equal treatment and fiscal neutrality. In the light of that decision the House of Lords has now rejected the defence in the VAT context as being discriminatory.[85]

Consequently it appears that the passing on defence does not exist in England in any form. This is right as a matter of principle, simply because the loss suffered by the claimant after the defendant has been enriched is not causatively linked to the defendant's enrichment. It arises from a distinct transaction, a *novus actus interveniens*, between the claimant and a third party and is not directly linked to the defendant's receipt of the enrichment.

### (iii)  Recovery of indirect benefits

This treatment of the 'at the claimant's expense' requirement as embodying a causation principle can be used to explain one of the other difficult issues which the House of Lords had to face in *Sempra Metals v IRC*,[86] concerning whether the claimant could recover compound interest from the defendant in respect of its use of the claimant's money and, if so, whether the claimant could recover other benefits from the defendant arising from the use of the money. In particular, if the money paid by mistake to the defendant has been used to buy a winning lottery ticket, can the claimant recover the lottery jackpot? It is undoubtedly the case that where the claimant brings a claim founded on the vindication of property rights it is possible to recover all the proceeds of the enrichment. In *Sempra Metals*, Lord Walker accepted that indirect benefits could also be recovered in a claim for unjust enrichment:

> income benefits are more accurately characterised as an integral part of the overall benefit obtained by a defendant who is unjustly enriched. Full restitution requires the whole benefit to be recouped by the enriched party. . .[87]

---

[80]  *Marks and Spencer plc v Commissioners of Customs and Excise* [2005] UKHL 53, [2005] CMLR 3.
[81]  ibid [25].
[82]  *Roxborough v Rothmans of Pall Mall Australia Ltd* (2002) 76 ALJR 203.
[83]  The defence has also been rejected in Canada: *Kingstreet Investments Ltd v New Brunswick* [2007] 1 SCR 3.
[84]  Case 309/06 *Marks and Spencer plc v Commissioners of Customs and Excise* [2008] ECR I-2283.
[85]  *Marks and Spencer plc v Her Majesty's Commissioners of Customs and Excise* [2009] UKHL 8, [2009] 1 All ER 939.
[86]  *Sempra Metals* (n 50).
[87]  ibid [178].

The better view, however, is that benefits which are obtained following the receipt of the enrichment as a result of a distinct transaction are not received at the expense of the claimant and so cannot be recovered. Claims for the use of the money paid to the defendant are different because this is an enrichment which is received directly at the claimant's expense, since the defendant has the use of money which should have been paid to the claimant immediately the liability arose.

## D  The grounds of restitution

The traditional analysis of the law of unjust enrichment is that, once it has been established that the defendant has been enriched at the expense of the claimant, the defendant is only liable to make restitution if the receipt of the enrichment can be considered to be unjust. This is not simply an opportunity for judges to exercise their discretion to determine what justice requires. Rather, specific grounds of restitution have been recognised within which the claim must fall. The recognition of these so-called 'unjust factors' provides what has been described as 'a principled ground for granting a restitutionary remedy'.[88]

### (i)  Interpretation of grounds of restitution

The House of Lords has clarified the meaning of a number of long recognised grounds of restitution. So, for example, a number of the cases have concerned mistake. The House of Lords has made clear that it is sufficient that the claimant has made a mistake, either of law[89] or fact, which caused the claimant to transfer a benefit to the defendant,[90] and has examined what state of mind of the claimant might negate a claim.[91] Similarly, the ground of total failure of consideration has been clarified, initially by Lord Wright in *Fibrosa Spolka Ackyjna v Fairbairn Lawson Combe Barbour Ltd*[92] who recognised that, where payment is made subject to a condition which fails, the right to retain the money must fail because the claimant did not intend to enrich the defendant in those circumstances. Subsequently, the House of Lords has confirmed the requirement that the consideration must fail totally[93] and that the test of total failure is not whether the claimant has received any benefit from the defendant but whether the defendant has performed any part of their contractual duties.[94]

---

[88]  *Banque Financière de la Cité* (n 39) 227 (Lord Steyn).
[89]  See *Kleinwort Benson Ltd. v Lincoln City Council* (n 34).
[90]  *Banque Financière de la Cité* (n 39), *Kleinwort Benson Ltd v Lincoln CC* (n 34), *Deutsche Morgan Grenfell* (n 50).
[91]  *Deutsche Morgan Grenfell*, ibid.
[92]  *Fibrosa Spolka Akcyjna* (n 13) 64–65.
[93]  *Stocznia Gdanska* (n 50) 588 (Lord Goff).
[94]  ibid.

The House of Lords has also recognised the limits to unjust enrichment claims, including that the existence of a contractual regime between the parties means that, as a general rule, the law of restitution is excluded.[95] This is a significant restriction on the law of unjust enrichment to ensure that it is kept within reasonable bounds and does not undermine the law of contract.

### (ii) Development of the grounds

Although a number of grounds of restitution have been recognised for many years, there is nothing to prevent the courts from developing those grounds or even recognising new ones. This power of judicial creativity was recognised in dramatic terms by Lord Goff in *Westdeutsche Landesbank Girozentrale v Islington LBC:*[96]

> An action of restitution appears to me to provide an almost classic case in which the jurisdiction should be available to enable the courts to do full justice . . . The seed is there, but the growth has hitherto been confined within a small area. That growth should now be permitted to spread naturally elsewhere within this newly recognised branch of the law. No genetic engineering is required, only that the warm sun of judicial creativity should exercise its benign influence rather than remain hidden behind the dark clouds of legal history.[97]

There are many examples of this judicial creativity in operation since *Lipkin Gorman*. So, for example, in *Kleinwort Benson Ltd v Lincoln City Council*[98] the House of Lords unanimously rejected the common law bar on mistakes of law operating as a ground of restitution, with Lord Goff particularly acknowledging the work of scholars as providing 'the prime cause for the rejection' of the bar.[99] Although the Law Commission had recommended legislation to abolish to bar,[100] the House of Lords considered that judicial abolition was appropriate because the issue was before the court and it took a 'robust view of judicial development of the law'.[101]

The application of the law of unjust enrichment to the facts of *Kleinwort Benson* was, however, more controversial. The claim in that case related to payments made in respect of an interest rate swap contract which was subsequently declared to be void. A majority[102] recognised that, where the claimant relies on a judicial decision as requiring money to be paid and that decision is subsequently

---

[95] *Pan Ocean Shipping Co Ltd v Creditcorp Ltd, The Trident Beauty* [1994] 1 WLR 161, 164 (Lord Goff).

[96] *Westdeutsche* (n 17) 697.

[97] In the context of recognising that compound interest could be awarded in respect of common law claims. This was finally recognised in *Sempra Metals* (n 50).

[98] *Kleinwort Benson Ltd v Lincoln City Council* (n 34).

[99] ibid 372–73.

[100] Law Commission, 'Restitution: Mistakes of Law and Ultra Vires Public Authority Receipts and Payments' (Law Com No 227, 1994).

[101] *Kleinwort Benson v Lincoln CC* (n 34) 372 (Lord Goff).

[102] Lords Goff, Hoffmann and Hope.

overruled, this was sufficient to establish a mistake of law. This is because the effect of the declaratory theory of judicial law-making is that the change in law operates retrospectively so that the claimant can be considered to have been mistaken since the money was not due when it was paid. A mistake of law could similarly be identified where the law is subsequently clarified by the courts, since the effect of this clarification was considered to falsify the claimant's assumption that the money was due. A minority[103] concluded that a mistake of law could not be created by means of the declaratory theory.

Ultimately, whether the view of the minority is preferred turns on how we wish to use the declaratory theory of judicial law-making. If we wish to apply that theory literally it is possible to construct a mistake of law artificially, because the declaratory theory means that when the claimant transferred a benefit to the defendant the claimant's belief as to the validity of the payment was incorrect. Alternatively, since we know that judges do not just declare the law but actually change it, and because the ground of mistake is concerned with the claimant's thought process at the time of the payment,[104] the declaratory theory is a fiction which should not be used to construct a mistake.[105] In reality, if the claimant was liable to pay the defendant at the time of payment and it is only subsequently that the law changed, the claimant should not be considered to have made a mistake as to the existing law but made a misprediction as to what might happen in the future.[106] The approach of the minority is preferable. Indeed Lord Hoffmann in *Deutsche Morgan Grenfell plc v IRC*[107] effectively recognised the artificiality of constructing a mistake by virtue of the declaratory theory of law-making by describing it as a 'deemed mistake' and justified it by reference to practical considerations of fairness. Nonetheless this mistake was effective to ground a restitutionary claim in that decision arising from the premature payment of tax.

There are other examples of the creativity of the House of Lords in developing grounds of restitution. One of the most significant arises from the decision in *Woolwich Equitable Building Society v IRC*.[108] The claimant building society in that case had been assessed by the Inland Revenue to pay tax by reference to regulations which were subsequently declared to be *ultra vires*. It followed that the claimant had paid more than £57 million than was actually due. The Revenue repaid this money but refused to pay interest, amounting to £6.73 million, from the date it had received the money until the regulations had been declared void. It was held by a majority[109] that the Revenue was liable to pay this interest because it had been liable to repay the overpaid tax at common law from the moment of receipt, by virtue of the unjust enrichment principle. The ground of restitution was not mistake, since the building society believed that it was not liable to pay

---

[103] Lords Browne-Wilkinson and Lloyd.
[104] See in particular Lord Hoffmann: *Kleinwort Benson v Lincoln CC* (n 34) 398.
[105] P Birks, 'Mistakes of Law' (2000) 53 *Current Legal Problems* 205.
[106] *Kleinwort Benson v Lincoln CC* (n 34) 360 (Lord Browne-Wilkinson), 394 (Lord Lloyd).
[107] *Deutsche Morgan Grenfell* [2006] UKHL 49, [2007] AC 558 [23].
[108] *Woolwich* (n 50).
[109] Lords Goff, Browne-Wilkinson and Slynn. Lords Keith and Jauncey dissented.

the tax but had paid anyway for fear of adverse publicity. The House of Lords recognised a new ground of restitution, namely that the Revenue had received an *ultra vires* payment and, for constitutional reasons,[110] public authorities were not entitled to receive or retain such payments. This principle was specifically recognised by Lord Goff as follows:

> [Money] paid by a citizen to a public authority in the form of taxes or other levies paid pursuant to an *ultra vires* demand by the authority is *prima facie* recoverable by the citizen as of right.[111]

The analysis of their Lordships which enabled them to recognise this new ground is significant. The ground of *ultra vires* receipt was built on the old principle of extortion by colour of office (*colore officii*) which applied where a public officer demanded money to which he was not entitled for the performance of his public duty.[112] But, whereas that ground was founded on notions of compulsion, this does not provide the rationale for the recognition of *ultra vires* receipt. This was instead identified as being an independent ground of restitution which was recognised simply because of fundamental constitutional principles, arising from the Bill of Rights 1677, that no public authority can retain money which it had no authority to receive.[113] In recognising this new ground of restitution the House of Lords was explicitly influenced by the work of commentators which had argued for such a ground.[114] The attitude of the minority in this case is in marked contrast to that of the majority. Lords Keith and Jauncey dissented, on the ground that previous authorities, which were laboriously analysed, recognised that restitution would only be available against a public authority when the claimant had paid as a result of some improper pressure. Lord Keith specifically refused to recognise a new ground of restitution in this case because it would amount to 'a very far reaching exercise of judicial legislation.'[115] This harks back to the conservative approach to the recognition and development of the unjust enrichment principle before *Lipkin Gorman*. The minority's focus on previous cases is a vital component of decision-making in the House of Lords, but it was their failure to extract a more fundamental principle of general application which was especially disappointing. The majority were aware that limits would need to be placed on restitutionary claims against public authorities, since defences such as change of position might not be sufficient or might need to be interpreted in a

---

[110] The constitutional significance of this principle has caused the Supreme Court of Canada to conclude that restitution on this ground has nothing to do with the unjust enrichment principle: *Kingstreet Investments Ltd v Province of New Brunswick* (2007) SCC 1.

[111] *Woolwich* (n 50), 177. See also 196 (Lord Browne-Wilkinson) and 201 (Lord Slynn).

[112] See *Mason v New South Wales* (1959) 102 CLR 108, 140.

[113] *Woolwich* (n 50) 172 (Lord Goff).

[114] ibid 163 and 168 (Lord Goff). Notably W Cornish, 'Colour of Office: Restitutionary Redress against Public Authority' [1987] JMCL 41 and P Birks, 'Restitution from the Executive: A Tercentenary Footnote to the Bill of Rights' in P Finn (ed), *Essays on Restitution* (Sydney, Law Book Company, 1990). The work of the Law Commission was also relevant: Law Commission, 'Restitution of Payments Made Under a Mistake of Law' (Law Com No 120, 1991).

[115] *Woolwich* (n 50) 161.

different way, but preferred to leave this open for future development. That the House of Lords did not explicitly deal with this in *Woolwich* certainly illustrates the limitations of so-called 'judicial legislation'.

But there have been limits to the creativity of the House of Lords in developing the grounds of restitution, often in the face of the demands of commentators, including sometimes judges in the House of Lords themselves. This is especially illustrated by the much more conservative development of the ground of failure of consideration. This ground was recognised by Lord Mansfield in *Moses v Macferlan*,[116] but the requirement that the consideration must fail totally before restitution can be obtained has proved to be controversial. So, for example, if the claimant pays £1,000 for 1,000 pineapples and receives 100 of them, it will not be possible for the claimant to recover £900, because the consideration will not have failed totally.[117] The need for consideration to fail totally has been side-stepped by the House of Lords in the context of void contracts. So in *Westdeutsche Landesbank Girozentrale v Islington LBC*[118] the House of Lords was concerned with a restitutionary claim arising from a void contract. The issue before the court was primarily concerned with a claim for interest, which turned on whether the claimant had an equitable claim, but Lords Goff and Browne-Wilkinson did examine a claim for money had and received grounded on failure of consideration.[119] The problem with establishing failure of consideration on the facts was that the claimant, who had paid money to the defendant bank pursuant to the void contract, had also received payments from the defendant; so the consideration for the claimant's payments would not have failed totally. The trial judge and the Court of Appeal had concluded that the restitutionary claim succeeded because of a new ground of absence, rather than failure, of consideration, since as a matter of law the defendant could never provide any consideration for the payments received because they were invalid. Although Lord Goff did not express a concluded view, he did express doubts about the validity of absence of consideration as a ground of restitution and said that he would have preferred that the ground of restitution was failure of consideration.[120] Earlier in his judgment, however, he had noted that:[121]

> There has long been a desire among restitution lawyers to escape from the unfortunate effects of the so-called rule that money is only recoverable at common law on the ground of failure of consideration where the failure is total, by reformulating the rule upon a more principled basis; and signs that this will in due course be done are appearing in judgments throughout the common law world.

---

[116] (1760) 2 Burr 1005, 1012. See section II above.

[117] The claimant could sue for compensatory damages for breach of contract and this would provide a satisfactory remedy, save where the contract is a losing one, which might in itself be considered to be an adequate reason to confine the claimant to a compensatory remedy.

[118] *Westdeutsche* (n 17).

[119] A claim founded on mistake of law was not considered because of the then existence of the mistake of law bar, as discussed earlier in this section.

[120] *Westdeutsche* (n 17) 683.

[121] ibid 682.

In the light of this dictum, and his preference for failure of consideration rather than absence of consideration reasoning, it would be reasonable to conclude that he was assuming that restitution should have been awarded on the ground of partial failure of consideration. Lord Browne-Wilkinson did appear to recognise the validity of absence of consideration as a ground of restitution, although he too used the language of total failure of consideration, but he was willing to discount the claimant's receipt of benefits since those benefits could not have been validly received as a matter of law. That is the essence of absence of consideration as a ground which is distinct from that of total failure of consideration.

Although Lord Goff's analysis of failure of consideration in *Westdeutsche* was obiter, his reference to reformulation of the rule to make it more principled suggests that, if given the opportunity to do so, he would have been willing to replace the total failure with a partial failure requirement. The perfect opportunity to do so arose in *Stocznia Gdanska SA v Latvian Shipping Co*,[122] involving a claim for restitution arising from a contract to build and sell ships. Lord Goff recognised that the rule requiring failure of consideration to be total had:

> been subject to considerable criticism in the past; but it has to be said that in a comparatively recent Report (Law Com. No. 121(1983) concerned with Pecuniary Restitution on Breach of Contract) the Law Commission has declined to recommend a change in the rule, though it was there considering recovery by the innocent party rather than by the party in breach. I for my part am unpersuaded by matters such as these to exercise the power under the *Practice Statement (Judicial Precedent)* . . .[123]

His Lordship consequently, with other members of the House of Lords,[124] confirmed the total failure requirement. This meant that restitution was not available on the facts since the relevant contract was for the design and sale of vessels and, since the shipbuilder had started to design and build the ships, it had performed part of the contractual duties for which payment was due.[125] This conservative approach to the interpretation of the law is at odds with the wide jurisdiction for judicial development which he identified in *Westdeutsche*. Maybe this change of heart was due to the commercial context of the case, and the consequent need for certainty in the law, although this is not apparent on the face of the judgment.[126]

It is clear from the decisions of the House of Lords over the last 18 years that their Lordships are willing to develop the law on an incremental basis, but radical reform which may have unintended implications will be resisted, as in *Stocznia*. A similar approach to development of the criminal law by the House of Lords

---

[122] *Stocznia Gdanska* (n 50).

[123] ibid 590.

[124] Lords Lloyd, Hoffmann, Hope and Hutton.

[125] This is consistent with the decision of the House of Lords in *Hyundai Heavy Industries Co Ltd v Papadopulos* [1980] 1 WLR 1129.

[126] In fact counsel for both parties had accepted that the key issue to be resolved was whether the failure of consideration could be considered to be total: *Stocznia Gdanska* (n 50) 588 (Lord Goff).

was identified in *C (a Minor) v DPP*[127] where the House of Lords recognised, for example, that fundamental legal doctrines should not be lightly set aside and that judges should not make a change in the law unless they can achieve finality and certainty. Clearly the rejection of the mistake of law bar was considered to achieve finality whereas, arguably, abolition of the total failure requirement would not. What is particularly significant is that on a number of occasions the House of Lords has reformed the requirements for establishing unjust enrichment but has purposely left defences to be developed as required.[128] This would be unacceptable for Parliamentary legislation and should equally be regarded as unacceptable for 'judicial legislation', precisely because it does not achieve finality.

### (iii) Absence of basis

The House of Lords has approached the question of whether the defendant's enrichment can be considered to be unjust with reference to identifiable grounds of restitution.[129] Birks in *Unjust Enrichment*[130] developed a new approach to the principle which focused on there being no explanatory basis for the defendant's receipt of an enrichment, rather than whether the case fell within one of the recognised grounds of restitution.[131] He argued that there would be a basis for receipt if, for example, the enrichment was transferred to discharge a contractual or other obligation or was a gift.[132] This analysis of the unjust enquiry was clearly influenced by civilian legal systems, but it had been specifically rejected by Lord Goff in *Woolwich Equitable Building Society v IRC*.[133] Nevertheless, Birks's influence on the development of the law of unjust enrichment was such that some members of the House of Lords were willing to contemplate the move to an absence of basis approach. The most significant judicial analysis of the absence of basis principle can be found in the judgment of Lord Walker in *Deutsche Morgan Grenfell v IRC*, where he said that:[134]

> The recognition of 'no basis' as a single unifying principle would preserve. . .the purity of the principle on which unjust enrichment is founded, without in any way removing (as this case illustrates) the need for careful analysis of the content of particular 'unjust factors' such as mistake.

He acknowledged the persuasiveness of Birks's approach and recognised that it might be appropriate to consider its reception into English law. Lord Hoffmann

---

[127] [1996] AC 1. A useful response, perhaps, to Lord Goff's concern expressed in *Woolwich Equitable Building Society v IRC* [1993] AC 70, 173 as to where the boundary between legitimate development of the law by judges and Parliament should be drawn.
[128] See especially *Lipkin Gorman* (n 1) and *Woolwich* (n 50).
[129] *Banque Financière de la Cité* (n 39) 227 (Lord Steyn); *Kleinwort Benson Ltd v Lincoln CC* (n 34) 408 (Lord Hope).
[130] P Birks, *Unjust Enrichment* 2nd edn (Oxford, Clarendon Press, 2005).
[131] ibid chs 5 and 6.
[132] ibid 104.
[133] *Woolwich* (n 50) 172.
[134] *Deutsche Morgan Grenfell* (n 50) [158].

also acknowledged the relevance of absence of basis analysis.[135] Subsequently, in *Sempra Metals Ltd v IRC*[136] Lord Hope referred to 'no legal ground' as the ground of restitution, although he had earlier accepted that the ground was mistake of law.[137]

The debate as to whether the unjust enquiry should be resolved with reference to identified grounds of restitution or by simply showing that there was no basis for a transfer provides a perfect example of the interplay between the academic commentator and the judge. But it also illustrates the disadvantages. Birks's thesis has the attractions of simplicity and practicability and even, according to Lord Walker, of 'purity', undoubtedly traits which are attractive to the appellate judge and especially ones steeped in the commercial and chancery law tradition. But recognition of an absence of basis principle should be rejected for a number of reasons. It is supported neither by authority nor principle. It would actually result in greater analytical complexity because focusing on absence of basis alone cannot be sufficient to justify restitution. Where there is a potential basis for a transfer the grounds of restitution still need to be examined to determine whether the basis was valid.[138] Even as regards cases involving void contracts, Birks acknowledged[139] that it would be necessary to consider whether the claimant was mistaken when paying money to the defendant, since this would indicate that the claimant had not willingly taken the risk that the money was not due. Absence of basis reasoning could also result in too much restitution being awarded. The generally restrictive approach of the common law to unjust enrichment claims means that the defendant's receipt of the benefit is secure, save in the exceptional cases where the claimant establishes that the defendant's enrichment is unjust. This principle of security of receipt is important to the unjust enrichment principle, especially in the commercial field where parties generally need to be certain that benefits have been effectively transferred and will not be upset too readily. A move to an absence of basis approach could destabilise commercial transactions. Consequently, the absence of basis theory should be rejected, since it is not supported by authority, principle nor policy. Indeed, in *Deutsche Morgan Grenfell* itself, where the House of Lords had the opportunity formally to adopt that theory, the traditional approach to grounds of restitution was specifically recognised as regards the identification of a mistake of law.

Nevertheless, there is much in Birks's theory which makes sense in that, if there is a basis for the defendant's receipt of an enrichment, restitution should be denied. It is consequently preferable to recognise that if there is a legally effective basis for the transfer of a benefit to the defendant, such as by virtue of a contract, a statutory liability or a gift, a restitutionary remedy should not be available. Indeed, this was specifically recognised by Lord Hope in *Kleinwort Benson v*

---

[135]   ibid [28].
[136]   *Sempra Metals* (n 50) [25].
[137]   Lord Mance left the point open: ibid [192].
[138]   As Lord Walker himself noted in the dictum above.
[139]   Birks, *Unjust Enrichment* (n 130) 132.

*Lincoln CC.*[140] So, for example, where the claimant has transferred a benefit to the defendant pursuant to a valid statutory obligation, such as a valid tax demand, restitution will not lie because there is a legal basis for the defendant's receipt.[141] The identification of a valid statutory base for tax payments proved to be a matter of particular controversy in *Deutsche Morgan Grenfell v IRC*[142] where the majority allowed a claim for restitution of tax paid prematurely where the claimant had not been able to claim group income relief which would have delayed its liability to pay. Lord Scott dissented on the ground that, since the relief had not been claimed, the claimant was actually liable to pay tax to the Revenue so that the payment was lawfully due. In determining whether Lord Scott was correct, it is vital to remember that this was not a claim for recovery of the tax paid because, as was subsequently recognised in *Sempra Metals Ltd v IRC*,[143] this sum was eventually set off against the corporation tax which was lawfully due. The taxpayer's claim related simply to the early payment of tax in circumstances where the claimant would have wished to delay payment by means of the group income election.[144] If the focus is placed on the entitlement of the Revenue to receive the money when it did, rather than on the language of whether the tax was actually due to the Revenue, it is much easier to understand why the Revenue was required to make restitution. For, during the period when the Revenue had the unlawful use of this money, there was no valid legal basis for its receipt. However, from the time when the tax would have been paid had the claimant elected to defer payment, the Revenue's receipt became lawful and so, at that point, there was a basis for this payment and so the money paid could not be recovered. Presence of basis reasoning can be used to justify the decision of the House of Lords. This is another example where greater attention being given to underlying principles would have assisted the judges in their decision-making.

## E  Unjust enrichment and the law of property

There is one final example of how the House of Lords has sought to clarify the unjust enrichment principle, namely by clarifying the boundary between unjust enrichment and restitutionary proprietary claims. The decision in *Lipkin Gorman v Karpnale Ltd*[145] appeared to recognise that a personal claim to recover money in which the claimant had retained legal title could be explained by reference to the unjust enrichment principle. That this was incorrect has now been recognised by the House of Lords in *Foskett v McKeown*,[146] which provides an excellent illustration of how the analysis of the unjust enrichment principle has become

---

[140]  *Kleinwort Benson v Lincoln CC* (n 34) 408.
[141]  *Deutsche Morgan Grenfell* (n 50) [89] (Lord Scott).
[142]  ibid.
[143]  *Sempra Metals* (n 50).
[144]  *Deutsche Morgan Grenfell* (n 50) [5] (Lord Hoffmann).
[145]  *Lipkin Gorman* (n 1).
[146]  *Foskett* (n 50).

more sophisticated with greater attention being paid to underlying principles of the law of obligations and the law of property.

In *Foskett*, the claimants claimed an equitable proprietary interest in the payment from a life insurance policy, which had been taken out by the claimants' trustee on his own life. The trustee had stolen £20,000 from the trust, which was used to pay two of the five annual premiums for the policy. The trustee committed suicide and his children received a lump sum payment of £1 million. The claimants sued for £400,000 of this, on the basis that they had contributed two-fifths of the premiums, and succeeded in the House of Lords. The real significance of this case is that it was held that the claim did not depend on establishing unjust enrichment. As Lord Millett said:[147]

> The transmission of a claimant's property rights from one asset to its traceable proceeds is part of our law of property, not of the law of unjust enrichment. There is no 'unjust factor' to justify restitution (unless 'want of title' be one, which makes the point). The claimant succeeds if at all by virtue of his own title, not to reverse unjust enrichment.

In other words, it was not necessary to show that the defendant had received money at the claimant's expense and that the case fell within one of the recognised grounds of restitution.[148] It was sufficient that the defendant had received property in which the claimant had an equitable proprietary interest, even though this interest was in different money from that which had been stolen from the claimant. The approach of the House of Lords was rigorously principled. As Lord Browne-Wilkinson said:[149]

> The crucial factor in this case is to appreciate that the [claimants] are claiming a proprietary interest in the policy moneys and that such proprietary interest is not dependent on any discretion vested in the court. Nor is the purchaser's claim based on unjust enrichment. It is based on the assertion by the purchasers of their equitable proprietary interest in identified property.

This decision has proved controversial, especially as to whether it is possible to assert proprietary rights in substitute property without resorting to the unjust enrichment principle to do so.[150] But the real significance of the case is that the House of Lords considered unjust enrichment as a law in its own right. The judges concluded that the elements of that formula could not be and need not be established. This is probably the high-point of rigorous analysis of unjust enrichment. It was 10 years' old; it was growing up.

The rigour of the House of Lords' approach in *Foskett* is reflected in Lord Browne-Wilkinson's assertion that the case involved 'hard-nosed property rights' and not discretion.[151] But even Lord Browne-Wilkinson had previously

---

[147]    ibid 127.

[148]    In the same way that it should not have been necessary to show this in *Lipkin Gorman* (n 1) either. See section IIIB above.

[149]    *Foskett* (n 50) 108.

[150]    See P Birks 'Property, Unjust Enrichment and Tracing' [2001] *Current Legal Problems* 231.

[151]    *Foskett* (n 50) 109.

been willing to recognise the significance of judicial discretion in fashioning property rights. In *Westdeutsche Landesbank Girozentrale v Islington LBC*[152] he was ready to acknowledge the existence of a remedial constructive trust, which he described as 'a judicial remedy giving rise to an enforceable obligation: the extent to which it operates retrospectively to the prejudice of third parties lies in the discretion of the court.' Significantly, in *Thorner v Major*[153] Lord Scott endorsed the recognition of the remedial constructive trust, which he considered should be applicable instead of proprietary estoppel in a case where a representation has been made by the owner of property that the claimant would obtain a future rather than an immediate benefit, such as inheritance of property.

Although this flirting with discretion clearly arises in the context of proprietary rather than unjust enrichment claims, the consequent uncertainty and unpredictability is unacceptable, and it clashes with the general tenor of the principled approach of the House of Lords to the development of unjust enrichment. Even there, justice and conscience are referred to, but as a justification for a result rather than as a principle to be applied to secure a particular result.[154]

## V JUDGING THE JUDGES

The history of the recognition and development of the unjust enrichment principle is of general significance to the legal community. It reveals a tale of a principle emerging uncertainly into the world from confusion and then developing with growing confidence. But in addition it reveals a symbiotic relationship between the judge and the jurist working together for a common goal.[155] The relationship may not always be for the benefit of the principle. The recent flirting with the absence of basis principle is rather like a teenager being tempted with a drug from behind the bike-sheds 'to make things easier to understand'. But, for the most part, the judges and the jurists learn from each other and, of course, the judges themselves have increasingly participated in academic debates outside the court, at conferences and by publishing articles.[156]

There is one particular lesson for academics to learn from these cases, namely that there are times when a radical or principled solution might be considered to be desirable but the judges do not consider it to be open to them because of the way the case was pleaded or argued. So counsels' concession as to tracing in

---

[152] *Westdeutsche* (n 17) 714.

[153] *Thorner v Major* [2009] UKHL 18, [2009] 1 WLR 776 [20].

[154] See, eg, *Woolwich* (n 50) 172 (Lord Goff) and 199 (Lord Browne-Wilkinson) and *Banque Financière de la Cité* (n 39) 237 (Lord Clyde). Even in *Moses v Macferlan* (1760) 2 Burr 1005, 1012 Lord Mansfield spoke of the 'ties of natural justice and equity'.

[155] See especially *Kleinwort Benson Ltd v Lincoln CC* (n 34) 372 (Lord Goff).

[156] See in particular the influential papers of Lord Nicholls, 'Knowing Receipt: The Need for a New Landmark' in W Cornish, D Nolan, J O'Sullivan and G Virgo (eds), *Restitution: Past, Present and Future* (Oxford, Hart Publishing, 1998) 23 and Lord Millett in S Degeling and J Edelman (eds), *Equity in Commercial Law* (Sydney, Thomson Reuters, 2005).

*Lipkin Gorman* and the total failure requirement in *Stocznia* need to be borne in mind when analysing those decisions. Similarly, Lord Scott's acceptance of three distinct causes of action in *Yeoman's Row v Cobbe*, which were actually different ways of describing the same thing, may have been simply a replication of the way counsel had pleaded his case. But should the errors of counsel be allowed to determine the result and the analysis in this way? Surely the judges in the House of Lords and now the Supreme Court should comment on and reject artificial pleadings and inappropriate concessions, at least as regards the identification and development of principles for the future, if not for the case before the court. Further, jurists need to be aware that the court is limited by the chance of the right case coming on appeal at the right time, but, when it does, the court should remember the comment of Lord Goff in *Woolwich*: 'this opportunity will never come again. If we do not take it now it will be gone forever.'[157]

As the unjust enrichment principle has matured the judiciary's development of it has been more confident. The treatment of unjust enrichment in *Lipkin Gorman* itself is frankly disappointing, with very little exposition or analysis but just assertion, and a reluctance to say anything of real significance about the nature of the change of position defence. It was probably two years later in *Woolwich* that the potential of this newly emerged principle became apparent in enabling restitution to operate in a public law context.[158] In *Westdeutsche*, Lord Goff's judgment indicated that the courts could be even more radical in developing the law, but there was subsequently a lull, exemplified by *Stocznia*, where a more conservative and restrictive attitude was adopted.[159] Thereafter, with the abolition of the mistake of law bar in *Kleinwort Benson*, and the recognition of the distinction between unjust enrichment and property claims in *Foskett v McKeown*, the approach of the courts has been much more forthright and clear-sighted. This has continued through the decisions in *Deutsche Morgan Grenfell*, *Sempra Metals* and *Yeoman's Row*, where the elements of the unjust enrichment formula have been elaborated. But these more recent cases have been characterised by unnecessary complexity of reasoning and analysis. Giving greater attention to the underlying principles would certainly have assisted the judges in their decision-making. This, perhaps, is where jurists have an especially useful role since they can step back from the particular case and look at the wider picture; they can show how the pieces of the jigsaw should fit together.

---

[157] *Woolwich* (n 50) 176.

[158] Even in that case, a conservative approach to the development of the law can be discerned, with Lord Keith dissenting as regards the recognition of a new ground of restitution relating to public authorities and confirming that the mistake of law bar was 'too deeply embedded in English jurisprudence to be uprooted judicially': *Woolwich* (n 50) 154. But this is what happened to it just six years later.

[159] See also *Kleinwort Benson Ltd v Glasgow* CC (n 11), although that case was concerned with the specific interpretation and application of the Brussels Convention on Jurisdiction and the Enforcement of Judgments in Civil and Commercial Matters 1968 as regards the jurisdiction of the English court to hear a claim founded on unjust enrichment.

Analysis of the 10 leading decisions of the House of Lords involving unjust enrichment reveals the judges engaging rigorously with the authorities, old and new, engaging with comparative material, and increasingly being influenced by the doctrinal and taxonomical work of commentators. But what is surprising, at least so far, is the almost complete absence of reference to the more theoretical and jurisprudential approaches to analysis. So, for example, the relevance of corrective justice to explain why the unjust enrichment principle needs to be recognised is never acknowledged. It means that the House of Lords has side-stepped the big questions about the law of unjust enrichment which are common topics of discussion in the law schools. So, for example, the judges have not examined how a claim in unjust enrichment can be justified where the defendant is enriched without fault. It is assumed that, if a claimant has paid money to the defendant by mistake, the defendant should be required to make restitution, subject to the defence of change of position, but the judges do not explain why this should be so. Further, why should a defendant who has breached a contract be liable to make restitution to the claimant if there has been a total failure of consideration, rather than being limited to compensating the claimant for loss suffered? Too often the judges have applied and developed the unjust enrichment principle and said that the result was just, but without explaining why that is so. What is especially noteworthy is that in eight[160] of the 10 leading cases, a restitutionary remedy was awarded. It has been left to the jurists to seek to justify these results.

## VI  THE LAW OF UNJUST ENRICHMENT

The creation and nurturing of the unjust enrichment principle is one of the most significant legal developments of the late twentieth and early twenty-first century. It is a testament to the work of Lord Goff, but Lords Wright, Steyn, Hope and Millett have made particularly significant contributions to its growth. Over the years the approaches of the judges have been ever more rigorous, adopting an ever more sophisticated analysis. That analysis more recently can be criticised as being unnecessarily complicated, and there has been a tendency to ignore the need to identify underlying principle clearly and to engage with the larger more theoretical questions. That is what the Supreme Court should be expected to do. Lord Hope's analysis of the principle in *Deutsche Morgan Grenfell v IRC*[161] needs to be remembered, namely that the purity and simplicity of the principle should not be disturbed unless there are clear reasons of policy or principle for doing so.

In tracing the development of the principle it is noteworthy that in its early years the judges, notably Lord Goff, spoke of the law of restitution rather than

---

[160] Restitutionary relief would not have been available in *Stocznia Gdanska* (n 50) and the interpretation of the Brussels Convention in *Kleinwort Benson Ltd v Glasgow CC* (n 11) meant that England did not have jurisdiction over the unjust enrichment claim.

[161] *Deutsche Morgan Grenfell* (n 50) [41].

a law of unjust enrichment.[162] Unjust enrichment used to be thought of as a concept,[163] then it became recognised as a principle, now, as it comes of age, we should recognise that we have, at last, a law of unjust enrichment.[164]

---

[162] See, for example, *Woolwich* (n 50) 163; *Pan Ocean Shipping Co Ltd v Creditcorp Ltd, The Trident Beauty* [1994] 1 WLR 161, 164 and *Westdeutsche* (n 17) 697, where he spoke of an action of restitution. See also Lord Hutton in *Kleinwort Benson Ltd v Glasgow City Council* (n 11) 186.

[163] See *Woolwich* (n 50) 197 (Lord Browne-Wilkinson).

[164] As Lord Hope described it in *Sempra Metals* (n 50) [8].

# 10

# Use of Scholarship by the House of Lords in Tort Cases

KEITH STANTON*

## I INTRODUCTION

I N RECENT YEARS, I have written a number of pieces[1] concerning judicial methodology in the context of the tort of negligence. The theme behind these pieces is that much can be learned by studying in detail the methodology used by members of the judiciary when constructing their judgments.[2] This essay seeks to develop this project by looking at how academic work and other forms of scholarship have been used by members of the House of Lords in deciding tort[3] cases in the period from 1990 to 2009.

The starting point is the words of Professor Peter Birks in his FA Mann lecture in 1997:

> We know already in our hearts . . . that the self-image of the common law as judge-made is incomplete. It is judge-and-jurist-made. The common law is to be found in its library, and the law library is nowadays not written only by its judges but also by its jurists. The juristic function is to analyse, criticise, sift, and synthesise, and thus to play back to the judges the meaning and direction of their own daily work, now conducted under ever increasing pressure. Everyone who writes even so much as a case-note in a journal joins in that law-making function.[4]

* I would like to thank the participants in the seminar who responded to this paper and the members of my primary unit at Bristol for their comments on an early version of this work.

[1] In particular: K Stanton, 'Incremental approaches to the duty of care' in N Mullany (ed), *Torts in the 90's* (Sydney, LBC Information Services, 1997); K Stanton, 'Professional negligence: duty of care methodology in the twenty first century' (2006) 22 *Journal of Professional Negligence* 134 and K Stanton, 'Decision-making in the tort of negligence in the House of Lords' (2007) 15 *Tort Law Review* 93.

[2] It is probably inevitable that this work has unsettled many views that I have held about the tort of negligence for many years. The task of considering how a judge has constructed a judgment proves to be radically different from that of distilling a summary of the outcome from a number of judgments.

[3] This essay covers a wider subject matter than the earlier pieces in extending beyond the tort of negligence.

[4] Published as P Birks, 'The academic and the practitioner' (1998) 18 *Legal Studies* 397, 399.

I do not seek to disagree with the assertion that the work of jurists is today a recognised source of law. But, it has to be remembered that Birks made this assertion as part of a paper which was addressing the role of academic law in the training of lawyers: he was not attempting to conduct a full survey of the use made of academic writing by the judiciary. This paper takes a different approach by looking in detail at what juristic writing is being cited in tort cases and at the kind of use which is being made of it. From that perspective, I am not sure that I see the picture in the same way that Birks did. Times have moved on. Birks clearly appreciated that he was writing at a time when approaches were changing. My view is we can now see that a very significant change took place a couple of years earlier, but that the picture in 2010 is a complex one.

One can see things changing by looking at the leading cases on negligently inflicted psychiatric damage. When the House of Lords laid down the framework for the modern law in 1991 in *Alcock v Chief Constable of the South Yorkshire Police*[5] it made no reference to juristic writings at all. When it returned to the issue in the 1995 case of *Page v Smith*,[6] Lord Lloyd referred to a passage in *Clerk & Lindsell on Torts*[7] and some periodical literature of considerable vintage.[8] Four years later, in *White v Chief Constable of South Yorkshire*[9] the picture is totally changed, with modern academic criticism of the law being engaged with in considerable detail (although not adopted). This is a good example of the change in methodology which occurred in the period in which Birks was writing. However, it would be wrong to read too much into this example: the overall picture is a complex one which defies easy classification.[10]

## II METHODOLOGY

This essay, in line with the larger project of which it forms a part, concentrates on decisions of the judicial House of Lords.[11] The particular subject is tort[12] cases decided in the years 1990 to 2009. This concentration brings the pragmatic advantage of keeping the work within bounds. However, the fact that the House of Lords has led the development of tort in the period in question and has

---

[5] *Alcock v Chief Constable of the South Yorkshire Police* [1992] 1 AC 310.

[6] *Page v Smith* [1996] AC 155.

[7] RWM Dias (ed) *Clerk & Lindsell on Torts*, 16th edn (London, Sweet and Maxwell, 1989) 587–88.

[8] RWM Dias, 'Negligence—Remoteness—The *Polemis* Rule' [1961] *Cambridge Law Journal* 23 and JA Jolowicz 'The Wagon Mound—A Further Comment' [1961] *Cambridge Law Journal* 30; AL Goodhart, 'Emotional Shock and the Unimaginative Taxicab Driver' (1953) 69 *Law Quarterly Review* 347 and 'The Shock Cases and Area of Risk' (1953) 16 *Modern Law Review* 14.

[9] *White v Chief Constable of South Yorkshire* [1999] 2 AC 455.

[10] A Paterson, *The Law Lords* (London, Macmillan, 1982) ch 2, found evidence that the Lords were becoming more receptive to academic writing in the 1960s.

[11] I have not included tort cases decided by the Judicial Committee of the Privy Council.

[12] I have made no attempt to consider whether the results obtained by considering tort cases hold good for other areas of law. On criminal law, see N Duxbury, *Judges and Jurists* (Oxford, Hart Publishing, 2001) 108–12.

achieved very significant advances,[13] means that its work would dominate even if the research had extended to cases in lower courts. In the context of the Society of Legal Scholars centenary, there was an attraction in taking the research back to 1909. However, the work which has been done on the pre-1990 period has indicated that there is little data of significance to be extracted from such cases: the methodology used in that era would, at the most, make passing use of leading textbooks which set out the applicable rules of law.[14]

In spite of the limitations placed on the research, it still covers an extensive range of issues, and the policies associated with those issues. In terms of torts, negligence appears, in relation to a variety of subjects, alongside nuisance, the rules in *Rylands v Fletcher* and *Wilkinson v Downton*, battery, harassment, false imprisonment, breach of statutory duty, claims under the Warsaw Convention, defamation and breach of confidence, misfeasance in public office, malicious prosecution, conversion, interference with trade and conspiracy. When one moves away from nominate torts we can also see issues of causation, assessment of damages, vicarious and joint liability, limitation of actions and, of course, the arrival of the European Convention on Human Rights as a fundamental element of English law. The policies at issue include both the scope of public authority liability to compensate individuals, theoretical issues concerning causation and ethical issues surrounding medical practice.

In terms of methodology, I have followed the practice of others who have undertaken work of this kind.[15] The subject matter is thus individual speeches in cases, rather than the cases as a whole, and, as the subject is the construction of speeches, no distinction is drawn between majority and dissenting speeches. To the extent that any quantitative results are drawn, speeches in which a judge simply concurs with others who make reference to juristic writings are not counted. Similarly, I have not counted those references in speeches which are to another speech which includes references to literature.[16]

Unlike some other works which have considered the use of academic writing by courts,[17] I have not conducted a simple counting exercise. Although, I have collected numerical data on the number of citations,[18] I have attempted to make a qualitative assessment by classifying the nature of the use in order to identify

[13] For further comments on this see: R Stevens, 'Torts' in L Blom-Cooper, B Dickson and G Drewry (eds), *The Judicial House of Lords 1876–2009* (Oxford, Oxford University Press, 2009).

[14] This is not to say that academic views did not have unacknowledged influence on decisions of the House of Lords in that period. See Duxbury, *Judges and Jurists* (n 12) 84–98.

[15] See for example, V Black and N Richter, 'Did she mention my name: Citation of Academic Authority by the Supreme Court of Canada, 1985–1990' (1993) 16 *Dalhousie Law Journal* 377.

[16] See for example: Lord Bingham in his speech in *Chief Constable of the Hertfordshire Police v Van Colle* [2008] UKHL 50, [2008] 3 WLR 593 [51], citing a passage of Lord Steyn's speech in *Brooks v Commissioner of Police for the Metropolis* [2005] UKHL 24, [2005] 1 WLR 1495, which refers to standard practitioner works; Lord Phillips in *Stone & Rolls Ltd (in liquidation) v Moore Stephens* [2009] UKHL 39, [2009] 1 AC 1391 [7], citing a portion of McLachlin J's judgment in *Hall v Hebert* (1993) 101 DLR (4th) 129, which cites E Weinrib, 'Illegality as a Tort Defence' (1976) 26 *University of Toronto Law Journal* 28.

[17] See for example, Black and Richter, above, 'Did she mention my name' (n 15).

[18] A summary of this data is included in the Appendix.

the ways in which legal scholarship is used in the structure and logic of speeches. There are several reasons for regarding a simple count of the number of citations of a work as of limited value. First, the fact of citation depends on decisions made by counsel and judges as to how relevant the writing (or, in some cases, a limited portion of it) is to the particular case before the courts: it is not an assessment of the intrinsic merit of the piece.[19] Second, a count of citations is almost certain to favour general works, such as textbooks, which cover a number of subjects. Third, detailed consideration of this subject shows that use of juristic writing is very uneven within both cases and speeches: a counting exercise has the capacity to mislead unless placed in context.[20] Finally, this piece seeks to assess the variety of ways in which a piece of writing can be used: a simple reference to a textbook as authority for an uncontentious rule of law is different in kind from an engagement by a judge with, for example, the arguments for a change in the law which are contained in a law review article.[21]

On occasions, the definition of tort has called for a judgment to be made as to whether to include a case or to exclude some elements of the speeches because of the subject matter. The public international law elements of a case such as *Kuwait Airways Corpn v Iraqi Airways Co (Nos 4 and 5)*[22] provide an obvious example of work which merits exclusion.[23]

Practically, it is often impossible to distinguish writings by practitioners from those by academics. Not only would one need a full biography of the author of every piece of writing one encounters; one would also need to devise a classification for those individuals who move between the two camps (or who have roles which

---

[19] A good example of this is provided by Lord Walker's use of C Witting's case note ((2002) 118 LQR 214) on the decision of the High Court of Australia in *Perre v Apand Pty Ltd* (1999) 198 CLR 180 in his speech in *Customs & Excise Commissioners v Barclays Bank* [2006] UKHL 28, [2007] 1 AC 181. Witting's note considers the current status in the High Court of the three-fold test for the duty of care. Lord Walker does not address the substance of Witting's piece, but uses it as a way of avoiding having to list the modern Australian authorities. For a further example, see below (n 53).

[20] For example, in 1996 the House decided five tort cases. Juristic writing was cited in the speeches delivered in four of them. There were only six substantive speeches delivered in these cases (one of which was a dissent) and we obviously have no way of telling the extent to which the 19 decisions to agree with another judge's speech were influenced by juristic writings. In total there were 28 references to juristic writing in four of the speeches delivered in that year. Further research reveals that all but four of those references were made in two speeches. Numerically, Lord Nicholls made reference to 16 pieces of literature in his dissenting speech in *Stovin v Wise* [1996] AC 923 and Lord Steyn to eight in *Smith New Court Securities Ltd v Citibank NA* [1997] AC 254. A qualitative assessment shows Lord Steyn's use to be of greater significance than Lord Nicholls's. In the latter case, a mass of literature is referenced in a single paragraph as support for the proposition that the law on the liability in negligence of public authorities is unsettled. It is difficult to see why Lord Nicholls felt the need to support this proposition in this way.

[21] Lord Goff made 10 references to juristic writings in his speech in *Cambridge Water Co v Eastern Counties Leather plc* [1994] 2 AC 264. Three of those were to textbook statements concerning the right to extract percolating water from land. Lord Goff's adoption of the arguments made in F Newark, 'The Boundaries of Nuisance' (1949) 65 *Law Quarterly Review* 480 was of much greater importance in serving to change the conceptual basis of the tort of private nuisance and the rule in *Rylands v Fletcher*.

[22] *Kuwait Airways Corpn v Iraqi Airways Co (Nos 4 and 5)* [2002] UKHL 19, [2002] 2 AC 883.

[23] As the thrust of the research is to provide a qualitative assessment of the work of the House in the area and not a statistical analysis, these definitional problems are not a major consideration.

straddle both). This paper therefore attempts to identify all legal literature, other than case law and statutes, which is referred to in speeches and makes no attempt to classify such literature according to the professional status of the writer. The adoption of a broad approach to the subject matter permits a consideration of the relative weight attached by the judiciary to different forms of literature. As a result of these decisions, the word 'juristic'[24] will be used in preference to 'academic' writing.[25] One of the advantages of this is that it allows consideration to be given to whether judges give particular weight to extra-judicial writing and lecturing by other judges.

I have included data on the use made by members of the House of Lords of publications by the Law Commission and other law reform bodies. There are several reasons for doing this (albeit that I have not integrated this data into that on journals and books etc). The first is that academic lawyers feed their views into the work of the Law Commission and like bodies in a number of ways. If an academic wishes to have an impact on the development of the law this is a legitimate way of making views known (although one which is unlikely to lead to a great deal of attribution, even when the individual is appointed by the Commission as consultant on a project). Second, it is worth considering whether, and to what extent, judges regard views on law reform emanating from official law reform bodies as more authoritative than academic views making similar arguments. Finally, this approach reveals that empirical research conducted by academics into relevant issues does, on occasion, get fed into the thinking of the judiciary via the work of the Commission.[26]

## III PROBLEMS

The problem of identifying a causal link between scholarship and the judgments of courts must be addressed.[27] The process under consideration relates to the transmission and evolution of bodies of knowledge and thought. The influences of a piece of writing can be felt in a variety of ways and the origins of an idea can become lost as it is developed by others over time.

Judges, like all lawyers, base their work on knowledge and skills acquired from a wide variety of sources over many years. A judge's thinking and approach

---

[24] In general, I have avoided using the word 'scholarship', because its use may raise the issue of whether a piece of purely descriptive writing qualifies for inclusion as a piece of scholarship. The balance in the use of descriptive and more critical literature is one of the issues I wish to explore.

[25] 'Academic' will be used when it is clear that writing emanating from an academic institution is being referred to.

[26] The classic example of this is the use made by the House in *Wells v Wells* [1999] AC 345 of the research conducted by H Genn into the use made of awards of damages by successful claimants. This research was published by the Law Commission as Report No 225. There are other examples of the Commission's review of medical research on post traumatic stress disorder being used as an authoritative statement of the accepted position when claims for damages for negligently inflicted psychiatric damage are under discussion.

[27] For a more detailed discussion of this issue see Duxbury, *Judges and Jurists* (n 12).

to an issue will inevitably have been moulded by books and articles read when they trained and over the course of a career in the law, even before counsel commences arguing a case based on their own training, experience and thinking. The members of the modern judiciary and the counsel who argue before them learned their skills in law schools at a time when periodicals, textbooks and monographs had become part of the basic materials used by law students. Some of the individuals involved have had careers as academic lawyers. Juristic writing is readily available nowadays in both paper and electronic form to those developing arguments on behalf of their clients and to the judges. It therefore contributes to the body of knowledge within the legal community as well as to the judicial process. There are occasions on which one can identify the influence of a particular piece of writing within a judgment. However, such cases are rarities. All lawyers build their own understanding on foundations laid by others and it is commonly an impossible task to identify this kind of influence.

When we turn to consider the use of juristic writing in particular cases it is necessary to accept that the structure of judgments is heavily influenced by the arguments and the materials put before the judges by counsel.[28] There is also no convention, equivalent to those which operate in the academic world, requiring a judge to attribute views drawn from another person's work. As a result, attributing the source of an idea is a matter of judicial taste. The task facing counsel of convincing a judge to accept an argument is designed to ensure that the judge owns the idea. If a student cuts and pastes a portion of a law journal article into an essay without proper attribution the conduct counts as plagiarism; if counsel find that a judge accepts arguments and cuts and pastes them into a judgment it is a job well done. The source of the ideas (whether acknowledged or not) doesn't matter in a process in which the outcome of a piece of litigation is the primary consideration.

When juristic writing is used in the construction of a speech it will commonly be only one component in a complex reasoning process. For example, a section of Lord Goff's speech in *Hunter v Canary Wharf Ltd*[29] deals with the standing requirement in an action in private nuisance. The starting point of his reasoning on that point is Professor Newark's classic article on the boundaries of nuisance[30] which argued that the essence of a private nuisance is that it is a tort protecting the enjoyment of rights in land. This reliance on academic literature is supported by reference to a number of House of Lords cases[31] and then to Fleming's textbook

---

[28] Paterson, *The Law Lords* (n 10).

[29] *Hunter v Canary Wharf Ltd* [1997] AC 655. I have chosen this speech both because it is one of the main examples of the use of Newark's article as the basis of developments in nuisance and because Lord Goff was notably open to basing his speeches on a wide variety of sources. In the earlier part of his speech (dealing with the possibility that conduct interfering with television reception could constitute a nuisance) he had traced authority back to the sixteenth century and also referred to decisions in Canada, New Zealand and Germany.

[30] F Newark, 'The Boundaries of Nuisance' (1949) 65 *Law Quarterly Review* 480.

[31] *Sedleigh-Denfield v O'Callaghan* [1940] AC 880, 902–03 (Lord Wright); *Read v J Lyons & Co Ltd* [1947] AC 156, 183 (Lord Simonds); *Tate & Lyle Food and Distribution Ltd v Greater London Council* [1983] 2 AC 509, 536–37. Note that the first two pre-dated Newark's article. It is not referred to in the *Tate & Lyle* decision.

on Torts.[32] The following section of the speech comprises a standard application of caselaw to the problem in hand leading to the conclusion that the decision of the Court of Appeal in *Khorasandjian v Bush*[33] was inconsistent with the classic authority of *Malone v Laskey*.[34] Lord Goff then considers whether the House should reject the established principle. At this point he identifies a 'developing school of thought' to the effect that personal injury claims should be handled by the tort of negligence and excluded from nuisance. Schools of thought can, of course, exist as easily within the judiciary as in academia, however this one is attributed to Newark and to a much more recent academic article.[35] The passage which follows this is, on its face, an assertion of Lord Goff's own views on the boundaries of nuisance. No authority is cited for his Lordship's rejection of the Court of Appeal's 'substantial link' test: he seems merely to be working out in his own mind the consequences of the new test and finding them unacceptable. The creativity here is simply found in Lord Goff's reasoning that the proposed test will not work. He then concludes his speech by making some general comments about his use of academic material. He says that he cites those materials which he has found helpful but that on this topic he has found much of the material arguing for a wider test to be a matter of assertion and not based on analysis of the issues. He is clear that the latter approach is more helpful.

The fact that literature is being used to support arguments made by counsel and conclusions expressed by judges can produce a tendency to use the work of authors perceived to be of eminence, and well established books of recognised authority. However, this tendency may be counteracted by the fact that a particular piece of work is directly relevant to the point in issue. In the latter case, the chances of an author being cited in court will be dependent both on the quality of the work and on accidents of litigation making it highly relevant to the particular case. The wide range of sources cited in the cases surveyed suggests that information technology is enabling counsel to find material of this kind which would have gone unnoticed in earlier years. While some eminent authors and venerable textbooks appear time and again, there is also significant use being made of the work of a wide range of little known authors publishing in periodicals which would not be available in many law libraries.

Of course, personal preference plays a significant part in the way in which materials are built into a speech. In this context it pays to remember the words of Lord Goff in *Hunter v Canary Wharf Ltd*:

> I would not wish it to be thought that I myself have not consulted the relevant academic writings. I have, of course, done so as is my usual practice; and it is my practice to refer to those which I have found to be of assistance, but not to refer, critically or otherwise, to those which are not.[36]

---

[32] J Fleming, *The Law of Torts*, 8th edn (Sydney, LBC Information Services, 1992) 416.

[33] *Khorasandjian v Bush* [1993] QB 727.

[34] *Malone v Laskey* [1907] 2 KB 141.

[35] C Gearty, 'The Place of Private Nuisance in a Modern Law of Torts' [1989] *Cambridge Law Journal* 214.

[36] *Hunter v Canary Wharf* (n 29) 694.

Lord Mustill adopted a different approach in his speech in *White v Jones:*[37]

> ... the judgment of Steyn L.J. remarked on the sparseness of reference to academic writings in the argument before the Court of Appeal. No such complaint could be made of the proceedings in this House. There can be few branches of contemporary law on which the commentators have had so much to say. Citation has been copious, and of great value. If I refer to none of the writings it is only because, as with the reported cases, the volume is too large to permit accurate and economical exposition; and the selection of some in preference to others would be invidious.

All of these considerations emphasise the point that any survey of this area needs to be careful not to jump to conclusions based on simple numerical data. On one hand, while it seems reasonable to accept that scholarly writing is playing a significant role if a judge cites it, there are a variety of forms of use and a failure to cite can be attributable to a number of possible explanations. The task of tracking the influence of ideas through a number of people's thinking is commonly an impossible one.[38]

## IV  WHAT DO WRITERS DO?

Writing about law, whether in books or articles, takes a variety of forms. There are no firm barriers between the different forms: an author's work will commonly progress from one to another. Even highly theoretical writing on law may include elements of descriptive writing. For example, the history of the development of the topic may be given, as may facts which serve as background to criticism of the law.

The traditional role of the textbook author is seen as synthesising a body of case law into workable rules of law.[39] This role is predominantly one of description, although it is liable to become creative as theories as to the correct approach emerge and critical when cases which do not fit the rules are discounted. The problem commonly faced by textbook writers is one of space: fitting a description of a body of law into the confines of a book (whether aimed at students or practitioners) is liable to place severe constraints on the amount of critical or constructive work that the book can contain.

---

[37] *White v Jones* [1995] 2 AC 207, 292.

[38] At times, judges have used academic sources without specifying what they were. For example, Lord Hoffmann in *Hunter v Canary Wharf* (n 29) 704-5 stated that: 'This reasoning, which is echoed in some academic writing and the Canadian case of *Motherwell v Motherwell*, 73 DLR (3d) 62 which the Court of Appeal followed, is based upon a fundamental mistake about the remedy which the tort of nuisance provides' and Lord Millett in *Rees v Darlington Memorial Hospital NHS Trust* [2003] UKHL 52, [2004] 1 AC 309, 343 said that: 'Experience has not shown there to be unforeseen difficulties in application (of the *McFarlane* decision); nor has it shown that the decision is productive of injustice. It has not been universally welcomed by academic writers; nor has it been universally condemned.'

[39] See Birks, 'The academic and the practitioner' (n 4) 401: 'It was the common law's faith in the new armour of reason that brought forth the university jurist. There was a pressing need to make sense of the mass of material. Books had to be written, lawyers had to be helped to understand the medium in which they had their being.'

However, modern legal scholarship, particularly when published in journals or collections of essays, commonly moves beyond the descriptive work found in textbooks and emphasises evaluation and criticism of the law and proposals as to how it should be developed. A piece of academic writing of this nature will commonly consist of a description of the law or of its operation, an analysis of the problem that this law creates, and some form of thesis as to how the law should be developed. The variety of methodologies used in modern legal scholarship and which serve as the basis for writers to produce evaluative and critical work of this kind can be seen as a distinctive and important feature of the discipline of which law schools should be proud.

It is important to evaluate changes in judicial methodology against the background of changes in writing on law. The emergence of a research culture in English law schools through the 1960s and 1970s[40] and the impact of demand for originality set by successive Research Assessment Exercises has undoubtedly taken the attention of legal academics away from the writing of textbooks, towards more critical work.[41] This process has been aided by the explosion in the number of specialist law journals published and the appearance of a greater number of volumes of essays based on conference papers. Information technology nowadays gives counsel easy access to such materials when they are preparing cases.

## VI  USES OF JURISTIC WRITING IN THE HOUSE OF LORDS

All of the different forms of juristic writing can be seen in the speeches in the modern House of Lords.

### A  Providing factual or historical background

Members of the House of Lords are only provided with limited support and research facilities and they are therefore heavily reliant on the work of others to supply the factual basis to underpin their decisions. At times, the facts relate to the commercial world in which the problem arises.[42] It is also possible to find examples of data on medical science, particularly psychiatric damage, and suicide rates being used. Interestingly, there is a tendency to take such data

---

[40] See, in particular, G Wilson, 'English Legal Scholarship' (1987) 50 *Modern Law Review* 818.

[41] It is worth noting that when Peter Birks (Birks, 'The academic and the practitioner' (n 4)), in 1997, identified a number of scholars whose writings had had a major impact on the law, he pointed to a generation of senior scholars whose reputation was heavily dependent on writing major textbooks: often ones aimed at the practitioner market. I do not believe that there is a new generation of academic scholars taking on this work.

[42] There are a number of references in *Marc Rich & Co AG v Bishop Rock Marine Co Ltd* [1996] AC 211 to writings detailing the work of classification societies.

from secondary sources, such as Law Commission papers, rather than from the original sources.[43]

The most notable use of factual data is to be found in the reliance in *Wells v Wells*[44] on research conducted for the Law Commission[45] on the uses to which awards of damages are put. This data played a central role in the assumptions made by the House as to the investment returns likely to be derived from the award and thus on the discount rate to be assumed when calculating the damages to be awarded.

The House commonly makes reference to writings which explain the history which produced a rule of law. Many of these references are to the reports of the Law Commission or other law reform bodies on which legislation was based. If the proposed legislation was enacted and is under consideration in the case in question this is the process of interpretation based on the materials which produced it.

More infrequently, members of the House delve into historical writings in order to provide the context in which to interpret a case. Thus in *Watkins v Secretary of State for the Home Department*,[46] Lord Rodger insisted that the case of *Ashby v White*[47] had to be understood in its historical context. He said:

> That is to put the dispute in purely legal terms, but there was much more to it. It was really a set-piece battle in a war between the two Houses of Parliament and between the Whigs and the Tories, with Ashby, a poor cobbler, being backed by the most prominent Whig and the constables by the Tory lord of the manor. See E Cruickshanks, 'The case of the men of Aylesbury, 1701–4' in C Jones (ed), *Party and Management in Parliament, 1660–1784* (1984) 87.

Similarly, there are a number of references in *Transco plc v Stockport MBC*[48] to Simpson's article 'Legal Liability for Bursting Reservoirs: The Historical Context of *Rylands v Fletcher*'.[49] Lord Hoffmann said:

> Although the judgment of Blackburn J is constructed in the traditional common law style of deducing principle from precedent, without reference to questions of social policy, Professor Brian Simpson has demonstrated in his article '*Legal Liability for Bursting Reservoirs: The Historical Context of Rylands v Fletcher*' (1984) 13 J Leg Stud 209 that the background to the case was public anxiety about the safety of reservoirs, caused in particular by the bursting of the Bradfield Reservoir near Sheffield on 12 March 1864, with the loss of about 250 lives. The judicial response was to impose strict liability upon the proprietors of reservoirs. But, since the common

---

[43]  See below text to n 109 ff.

[44]  *Wells v Wells* (n 26).

[45]  Law Commission, 'Personal Injury Compensation: How Much is Enough?' (Law Com No 225, 1994).

[46]  *Watkins v Secretary of State for the Home Department* [2006] UKHL 17, [2006] 2 AC 395 [51].

[47]  *Ashby v White* (1703) 1 Sm LC (13th ed, 1929) 253.

[48]  *Transco plc v Stockport Metropolitan Borough Council* [2003] UKHL 61, [2004] 2 AC 1.

[49]  AWB Simpson, 'Legal Liability for Bursting Reservoirs: The Historical Context of *Rylands v Fletcher*' (1984) 13 *Journal of Legal Studies* 209.

law deals in principles rather than ad hoc solutions, the rule had to be more widely formulated.[50]

## B Summarising/collecting a list of cases

At times, juristic writing is used simply as a method of removing the need to cite authorities: in this way cases are introduced into a judgement by a reference which treats the writing as a substitute for a law report. This usage may do no more than marginally shorten the judgment. However, it may also use the writing of an expert to introduce specialised material which has not found its way into a series of law reports.[51] A comparative law element may also be introduced into a speech in this way. So, for example, Lord Walker in *Customs & Excise Commissioners v Barclays Bank plc*[52] stated that:

> It would be an unnecessary distraction to go into the more recent jurisprudence in the High Court of Australia, noted by Christian Witting, 'The Three-Stage Test Abandoned in Australia—or Not?' (2002) 118 LQR 214.[53]

Judicial referencing of non-common law sources is commonly achieved in this way. A good example which shows a contrast in approach to common law and civil law sources occurs in Lord Scott's speech in *Re Deep Vein Thrombosis and Air Travel Group Litigation:*[54]

> There have been attempts by claimants in several signatory states to establish article 17 liability for DVT brought about, or said to be brought about, by air travel. I have already referred to *Scherer v Pan American World Airways Inc* 387 NYS 2d 580 in which a DVT article 17 claim was rejected by the Supreme Court of New York. In October 2001 a similar claim was rejected by the Frankfurt am Main Regional Court: see *Shawcross & Beaumont, Air Law*, looseleaf ed, vol I, VII, para 702.

This usage cannot be regarded as using juristic writing as a source of law: the source is the case which the writing is reporting.

---

[50] *Transco* (n 48) [28]. See also Lord Bingham ([3]) who includes the factual data that Simpson had inspected the site before writing the article and had found that Rylands' reservoir was still in use, with a capacity of over 4 million gallons.

[51] See for example, Lord Cooke's use of *Carter-Ruck on Libel and Slander*, 5th edn (London, Butterworths, 1997) 145, fn 4, in his speech in *McCartan Turkington Breen v Times Newspapers Ltd* [2000] UKHL 57, [2001] 2 AC 277, 301 to direct the reader to a group of unreported cases.

[52] *Barclays* (n 19) [71].

[53] Describing these cases was clearly not the reason that the author wrote this piece. Lord Nicholls, in his speech in *Campbell v MGN Ltd* [2004] 2 AC 457, 466 similarly uses the first three pages of G Phillipson's article 'Transforming Breach of Confidence? Towards a Common Law Right of Privacy under the Human Rights Act' (2003) 66 *Modern Law Review* 726, 726–28 as a summary of recent cases. The substance of the article is to be found in the 30 pages which follow this section. See also Lord Slynn's speech in *McFarlane v Tayside Health Board* [2000] 2 AC 59 (n 121), and Lord Bingham in *Rees* (n 38) [5], referring to a stream of American authority by citing an article which lists those cases. The cases are not referred to by name.

[54] *Re Deep Vein Thrombosis and Air Travel Group Litigation* [2005] UKHL 72, [2006] 1 AC 495.

## C  Stating the law

At other times, juristic writing is used in a very different form: it appears as authority for a rule (at times on its own: at other times alongside cases and other sources of law). Standard practitioner reference works, such as *Halsbury's Law of England*, have long been used in this way. An example can be found in the following passage of Lord Cooke's speech in *Reynolds v Times Newspapers Ltd*:[55]

> The established common law rule, for which *Adam v Ward* [1917] AC 309 is the leading authority, is that disputed questions of fact relevant to an issue of qualified privilege are for the jury, but otherwise it is for the judge to determine whether the privilege applies: see *Gatley on Libel and Slander*, 9th ed (1998), p 862, para 3415.

Similarly, Lord Bridge in his speech in *Charleston v News Group Newspapers Ltd*[56] uses another standard work on defamation, without the support of any case, as authority for a basic proposition of law:

> The first formidable obstacle which Mr. Craig's argument encounters is a long and unbroken line of authority the effect of which is accurately summarised in *Duncan & Neill on Defamation*, 2nd ed. (1983), p. 13, para. 4.11 as follows:
>
>> 'In order to determine the natural and ordinary meaning of the words of which the plaintiff complains it is necessary to take into account the context in which the words were used and the mode of publication. Thus a plaintiff cannot select an isolated passage in an article and complain of that alone if other parts of the article throw a different light on that passage.'

This use of descriptive legal scholarship published in textbooks remains very common and was not a new development in the 1990s.

On rare occasions, a rule produced by an author and accepted as a correct statement of the law is identified with the author. The classic example of this is the 'Salmond' test defining the notion of the 'course of employment' in the context of vicarious liability. This was treated for many years as stating the law correctly, until challenged and replaced in *Lister v Hesley Hall*.[57]

A variant of this approach sees juristic writing placed on a par with more traditional sources of law such as cases. Thus, in an important section of his speech in *Hunter v Canary Wharf Ltd*, Lord Goff supports a proposition of law (which is itself derived from previously approved juristic writing) both by dicta found in previous decisions of the House and by a textbook statement:

> There are many authoritative statements which bear out this thesis of Professor Newark. I refer in particular to *Sedleigh-Denfield v O'Callaghan* [1940] AC 880, 902-903, per Lord Wright; *Read v J. Lyons & Co. Ltd.* [1947] AC 156, 183, per Lord Simonds; *Tate & Lyle Food and Distribution Ltd. v Greater London Council* [1983]

---

[55] *Reynolds v Times Newspapers Ltd* [2001] 2 AC 127.
[56] *Charleston v News Group Newspapers Ltd* [1995] 2 AC 65, 70.
[57] *Lister v Hesley Hall* [2001] UKHL 22, [2002] 1 AC 215.

2 AC 509, 536–537, per Lord Templeman; Fleming, *The Law of Torts*, 8th ed. (1992), p. 416.[58]

Lord Steyn does the same in his speech in *Three Rivers DC and Others v Governor and Company of The Bank of England (No 3)*:

> The tort of misfeasance in public office is an exception to 'the general rule that, if conduct is presumptively unlawful, a good motive will not exonerate the defendant, and that, if conduct is lawful apart from motive, a bad motive will not make him liable': *Winfield & Jolowicz on Tort*, 15th ed (1998), p 55; *Bradford Corpn v Pickles* [1895] AC 587; *Allen v Flood* [1898] AC 1.[59]

An even more emphatic use of academic writing can be seen in Lord Goff's use of *Fleming on the Law of Torts* in his speech in *Cambridge Water Co v Eastern Counties Leather plc*:

> It is widely accepted that this conclusion [on the role of foreseeability in nuisance], although not essential to the decision of the particular case, has nevertheless settled the law to the effect that foreseeability of harm is indeed a prerequisite of the recovery of damages in private nuisance, as in the case of public nuisance. I refer in particular to the opinion expressed by Professor Fleming in *Fleming on the Law of Torts* 8th ed. (1992), pp. 443–444.[60]

In short, although doubts may have survived the judicial decision, they have been settled by the textbook.

There is no indication in these statements that the textbook is any less authoritative than the House of Lords cases which are also being cited to support the proposition. Indeed, the fact that the references are made without comment is an indication of the extent to which no one would question the fact that such writings are an accepted source of law.

## D   Providing food for judicial reasoning

On other occasions judges engage with writing which argues that a particular result should be adopted as opposed to stating an established rule of law. For example, an author may argue that words should bear a particular meaning. A good example of this can be found in the use made by the House of Lords in *Morris v KLM Royal Dutch Airlines*[61] of writings considering whether the meaning of the words '*lésion corporelle*' in the Warsaw Convention of 1929 could extend to psychiatric damage.

*OBG Ltd v Allan*[62] shows a significant degree of reliance being placed on juristic writing on a number of topics posed by the case. In that case there are examples of a member of the House setting out the two sides of the academic debate and then

---

[58] *Hunter v Canary Wharf* (n 29) 688.
[59] *Three Rivers DC and Others v Governor and Company of The Bank of England (No 3)* [2001] UKHL 16, [2003] 2 AC 1, 190.
[60] *Cambridge Water* (n 21) 301.
[61] *Morris v KLM Royal Dutch Airlines* [2002] UKHL 7, [2002] 2 AC 628.
[62] *OBG Ltd v Allan* [2007] UKHL 21, [2008] 1 AC 1.

adopting one of them. For example, Lord Hoffmann, on the question of defining 'unlawful means' in the context of the economic torts, says:

> Sales and Stilitz, *'Intentional Infliction of Harm by Unlawful Means'* (1999) 115 LQR 411-437, take a very wide view of what can count as unlawful means, arguing that any action which involves a civil wrong against another person or breach of a criminal statute ('any act that the defendant is not at liberty to commit') should be sufficient. In their opinion, a requirement of a specific intention to 'target' the claimant should keep the tort within reasonable bounds. Tony Weir in the Clarendon Law Lectures *'Economic Torts'* is of much the same opinion. But other writers consider that it would be arbitrary and illogical to make liability depend upon whether the defendant has done something which is wrongful for reasons which have nothing to do with the damage inflicted on the claimant: see Roderick Bagshaw's review of Weir in (1998) 18 Oxford JLS 729-739 at p. 732. I agree.[63]

Much the same occurs in *Chester v Afshar*,[64] in which Lords Steyn and Hope place considerable weight on academic discussion of the causation problem which was before the House. Indeed, approval by academics of the decision in the case at lower levels seems to have been regarded as relevant.[65] In these cases, the juristic literature is setting the framework in which a decision on the future shape of the law is being made.

On occasions, the House directly engages with academic arguments that the law should be changed. Commonly, this occurs when a writer has criticised a case or the reasoning in one and argued that a subsequent court should overrule that case or declare the reasoning to be fallacious. It seems reasonable to assume that many examples of such criticism are presented to courts by counsel who are using the academic work to add weight to attempts to get the court to accept their arguments. Viewed in this way a judicial decision to accept or reject academic work should be regarded more as a response to counsel than as an academic discourse on how the law should be developed.

A good example of this can be found in *Williams v Natural Life Health Foods Ltd.*[66] The history of the duty of care since the decision of the House of Lords in 1963 in *Hedley Byrne & Co Ltd v Heller & Partners Ltd*[67] has contained a strand centring on the notion of 'assumption of responsibility'.[68] The utility of this concept has been hotly debated and it has moved in and out of fashion. In *Williams*, academic criticism of the concept as resting on a fiction in the majority of cases in which no express assumption of responsibility has occurred[69] was

---

[63] ibid [59].

[64] *Chester v Afshar* [2004] UKHL 41, [2005] 1 AC 134.

[65] Lord Bingham in his dissenting speech said: 'I am of course impressed by the weight and distinction of the academic opinion supporting the decisions of the judge and the Court of Appeal in this case': *Chester* (n 64) [9].

[66] *Williams v Natural Life Health Foods Ltd* [1998] 1 WLR 830.

[67] *Hedley Byrne & Co Ltd v Heller & Partners Ltd* [1964] AC 465.

[68] At times 'voluntary assumption of responsibility'.

[69] K Barker, 'Unreliable assumptions in the modern law of negligence' (1993) 109 *Law Quarterly Review* 461; B Hepple, 'The Search for Coherence' (1997) 50 *Current Legal Problems* 67, 88; P Cane, *Tort Law and Economic Interests*, 2nd edn (Oxford, Clarendon Press, 1996) 177 and 200.

rejected as overstated by Lord Steyn in the leading speech. In terms of tracking the influence of ideas, it is interesting to note that, when the House subsequently moved away from Lord Steyn's views in *Customs & Excise Commissioners v Barclays Bank plc*,[70] the rejected critical material was not cited.[71]

There are other important examples of such usage. In *Hunter v Canary Wharf Ltd*[72] considerable attention is paid to academic arguments in favour of expanding standing in the tort of private nuisance beyond persons with title to the affected property. In *White v Chief Constable of South Yorkshire*[73] Lord Goff's speech engages with writings criticising the distinctions drawn by the House in its previous decision in *Page v Smith*.[74] In both of these cases the courts engage with the arguments but reject them.

The most important example of a topic on which juristic writing successfully drove a change in the law is found in the House of Lords adopting the framework of the law of private nuisance and the rule in *Rylands v Fletcher* propounded by Newark in his article 'The Boundaries of Nuisance'.[75] The decisions in *Cambridge Water Co v Eastern Counties Leather plc*,[76] *Hunter v Canary Wharf Ltd*[77] and *Transco plc v Stockport MBC*[78] have settled a host of long standing difficulties which have beset these torts. It is possible to trace the current position: that private nuisance is a tort directed to protecting the amenity of land; that compensation for personal injury is not recoverable under either private nuisance or the rule in *Rylands v Fletcher* and that *Rylands v Fletcher* is to be regarded as a species of private nuisance which is not subject to a requirement of continuity of interference directly back to Newark's thinking being adopted by Lord Goff in his speech in *Cambridge Water*.

## VII IMPACT ON THE DEVELOPMENT OF TORT

There can be no doubt that critical and constructive scholarship has had a significant impact on the development of particular parts of the law of tort by the House of Lords in the period surveyed. However, the picture is not uniform. There are significant examples of academic views being aired and then rejected

---

[70] *Barclays* (n 19).

[71] It appears in none of the speeches and does not appear to have been cited by counsel. Note that a case note by Mitchell and Mitchell, (2005) 121 *Law Quarterly Review* 194, discussing the reasoning of the Court of Appeal in fairly critical terms, was cited by Lord Bingham, *Barclays* (n 19) [4] and [7]. What we have here is criticism of an approach being made by a number of authors over the years, but only the most recent criticism being cited in the case. The influence of the older literature is almost certainly being felt at the later date, but is impossible to quantify as it expresses a view that has come to be widely held.

[72] *Hunter v Canary Wharf* (n 29).

[73] *White v Chief Constable* (n 9).

[74] *Page* (n 6).

[75] F Newark, 'The Boundaries of Nuisance' (1949) 65 *Law Quarterly Review* 480.

[76] *Cambridge Water* (n 21).

[77] *Hunter v Canary Wharf* (n 29).

[78] *Transco* (n 48).

and some areas of law have been developed with scarcely any assistance from jurists.

It is possible to see a major impact in a number of areas. The modern tort of private nuisance and the rule in *Rylands v Fletcher* are, as we have seen, based on the model set out by Newark in a *Law Quarterly Review* article in 1949.[79] The House also made significant use of juristic writing when developing causation in *Fairchild v Glenhaven Funeral Services Ltd,*[80] *Chester v Afshar,*[81] *Gregg v Scott*[82] and *Barker v Corus UK Ltd.*[83] A lesser, but still important degree of impact can be seen in litigation concerning medical issues, in particular: the 'wrongful life' claims in *McFarlane v Tayside Health Board*[84] and *Rees v Darlington Memorial Hospital NHS Trust*[85] and the patient's 'right to know' issue in *Chester v Afshar.*[86] A different example of importance to the development of tort is the fact that the calculation of multipliers after *Wells v Wells*[87] is justified both by empirical research conducted by an academic on behalf of the Law Commission into the use made of awards of damages and by arguments made by one of the leading authors[88] on damages writing in both textbooks and case notes. Finally, although the effect of juristic writing in *OBG Ltd v Allan*[89] was less dramatic, the writings used in the case on the meaning of 'unlawful means' in the economic torts and on the role of conversion in relation to choses in action clearly assisted members of the House in the construction of their speeches.

Elsewhere the picture is less clear-cut. The history of the concept of assumption of responsibility as a touchstone for the imposition of a duty of care in areas of negligence is a good example of the problem of tracking the evolution of ideas. The utility of the concept, which first saw the light of day in *Hedley Byrne & Co Ltd v Heller & Partners Ltd,*[90] has been championed by those who see it as expressing the view that, in the area of pure economic loss,[91] duties of care should only be recognised in the case of a relationship which approximates to a contractual one. To its critics, assumption of responsibility is one of the meaningless concepts used in the area. It is effective as a conclusion to be attached to a result, but wholly ineffective as a tool to be used to achieve the result. Express assumptions of responsibility are rare and to accept that an assumption can be

---

[79] Newark, 'The Boundaries of Nuisance' (n 75).
[80] *Fairchild v Glenhaven Funeral Services Ltd* [2003] 1 AC 32.
[81] *Chester* (n 64).
[82] *Gregg v Scott* [2005] UKHL 2, [2005] 2 AC 176.
[83] *Barker v Corus UK Ltd* [2006] UKHL 20, [2006] 2 AC 572.
[84] *McFarlane* (n 53).
[85] *Rees* (n 38).
[86] *Chester* (n 64).
[87] *Wells v Wells* (n 26).
[88] Various writings of David Kemp QC are cited eight times in the speeches of Lords Lloyd and Steyn.
[89] *OBG Ltd v Allan* (n 62).
[90] *Hedley Byrne* (n 67).
[91] And, possibly, other cases such as public authority liability.

implied is to accept that other factors in the relationship impose the duty of care and leave assumption of responsibility as a redundant fiction.

Support for assumption of responsibility has varied. It is probably correct to say that today the critics have the upper hand, as their thinking was largely adopted in the speeches in *Customs & Excise Commissioners v Barclays Bank plc*.[92] However, the body of critical thinking has built up over the years. Some of the academic criticisms[93] were rejected by Lord Steyn in *Williams v Natural Life Health Foods Ltd*.[94] However, a different article was cited in the *Barclays Bank* case which went a long way to rejecting Lord Steyn's approach.[95] It would be true to say that the body of opinion which opposes 'assumption of responsibility' extends far beyond the items cited in these speeches. Furthermore, this thinking has been strengthened significantly by the fact that some members of the House of Lords have also expressed their doubts.[96] It would also be naive to think that those who have supported the use of assumption of responsibility have not thereby sharpened the thinking of the critics. In short, the current result can be traced to a body of thinking which has been built up over nearly 50 years. Contributions to the debate have been made by judges and jurists. The evolution of ideas is too complex and muddled a process to permit the drawing of a simple causal chain from a result to a piece of thinking.

We can also see significant examples of the views propounded in juristic writing being discussed and rejected. The examples given previously on the issue of standing in the tort of private nuisance in *Hunter v Canary Wharf Ltd*[97] and the criticism of the attack on the reasoning in *Page v Smith*[98] are the most notable.[99] Reasoned calls for a radical redrawing of liability for negligently inflicted psychiatric damage[100] have fallen on stony ground.

The areas which appear to have been least influenced by juristic writing are: misfeasance in public office, tort claims for breaches of health and safety regulations, occupiers' liability and liability under the Animals Act 1971. A possible explanation for this is that these are areas which have attracted little academic attention which could aid decision making. An alternative is that, with the exception of misfeasance, the cases on these topics are exercises in statutory interpretation. One can speculate that the judiciary feels well within its comfort zone and to have no need to call on outside assistance when deciding cases of this kind.

---

[92]  *Barclays* (n 19).

[93]  Detailed at n 69.

[94]  *Williams v Natural Life Health Foods Ltd* (n 66).

[95]  Mitchell and Mitchell (n 71).

[96]  I have detailed the varying judicial contributions to this debate elsewhere: Stanton, 'Incremental approaches to the duty of care' (n 1).

[97]  *Hunter v Canary Wharf* (n 29).

[98]  *Page* (n 6).

[99]  See section I above.

[100]  J Stapleton, 'In Restraint of Tort' in P Birks (ed), *The Frontiers of Liability* Vol 2 (Oxford, Oxford University Press, 1996) (arguing for abolition of this head of recovery) and N Mullany and P Handford, *Tort Liability for Psychiatric Damage* (Sydney, Law Book Company, 1993) (arguing for use of a reasonable foreseeability test).

Finally, there is one significant change to the law which appears to owe nothing to juristic writing. In *Rees v Darlington Memorial Hospital NHS Trust*[101] the House of Lords created a conventional fixed award of damages of £15,000 to apply in a case of a negligently conducted sterilisation which results in an unwanted pregnancy. The conclusion was clearly founded on an obiter suggestion made by Lord Millett in the earlier decision of *McFarlane v Tayside Health Board*.[102] There seems to have been no academic or other discussion which led up to the creation of the award. It is simply a suggestion made by a member of the House which is adopted in a later case. It is a pure judicial creation of law without any prior discussion or consultation.

## VIII  JUDICIAL METHODOLOGY

My main conclusion is that, although there are notable occasions where juristic writing has played a major role in the construction of a speech by a member of the House of Lords, there are many cases in which it has played a minor part, or no visible role[103] at all. It is clear that the last 20 years has seen the House become more willing to admit that a wide range of influences feed into its decision making: but, this has occurred in the context of a judicial methodology which is basically unchanged. The process remains one of analysing and reasoning about the application of a fixed body of materials (cases and statutes) to a particular scenario. Speeches remain the product of a dialogue between judges and counsel on the specific issues raised by the case.[104] Although a wider range of influences are openly being referred to, it would be incorrect to argue that the substance of the process has changed. However, judges have their individual approaches and undoubtedly tailor them to the issue in hand and the way that issue has been presented to the court by counsel. Some are more inclined than others to venture into academic debates on what the law should be.

---

[101]  *Rees* (n 38).

[102]  *McFarlane* (n 53). According to Lord Steyn ([2004] 1 AC 309 [43]), the possibility of such an award was not raised in *Rees* until the case reached the House of Lords.

[103]  There are no references to juristic writings in the following tort cases decided by the House of Lords since 2000: *Darker v Chief Constable of the West Midlands Police* [2001] 1 AC 435; *W 1-6 v Essex County Council* [2001] 2 AC 592; *Goodes v East Sussex County Council* [2000] 1 WLR 1356; *Marcic v Thames Water Utilities Ltd* [2003] UKHL 66, [2004] 2 AC 42; *Barber v Somerset County Council* [2004] UKHL 13, [2004] 1 WLR 1089; *Fytche v Wincanton Logistics plc* [2004] UKHL 31, [2004] ICR 975; *Sutradhar (FC) v Natural Environment Research Council* [2006] UKHL 33, [2006] 4 All ER 490; *Austin v Commissioner of Police of the Metropolis* [2009] UKHL 5, [2009] 1 AC 564; *Trent Strategic Health Authority v Jain* [2009] UKHL 4, [2009] 2 WLR 248.

[104]  See Lord Steyn's approach to the judicial role in *Three Rivers DC v Governor and Company of The Bank of England (No 3)* (n 59): 'Your Lordships are however not asked to prepare an essay on the tort of misfeasance in public office but to state the ingredients of the tort so far as it may be material to the concrete disposal of the issues arising on the pleadings in this case.' The outcome of that case would be central to the scope of the compensation remedies available to individuals against public authorities. See also Alan Paterson's essay, 'Does Advocacy matter in the Lords?' in this volume.

There is a risk of generalising too readily from high-profile examples. For example, it is correct to say that the decision of the House in *Fairchild v Glenhaven Funeral Services Ltd*[105] is a very important example of the use of literature to access comparative law materials as an aid to decision making. A survey of the speeches shows that Lord Bingham made 13 references to juristic writing as he explored the approach of other jurisdictions to the problem of causation raised by the case and that Lord Rodger made a further six (five of which were references to comparative material, including some to Roman law). But, on the other hand, Lord Hoffmann made only two references in his speech in the case, to fairly general statements on causation principles made in Hart and Honoré's *Causation in the Law*, and Lords Nicholls and Hutton made no reference at all to juristic writings. Furthermore, if we place *Fairchild* in the broader context of the four tort cases decided by the House in 2002, the approaches of Lords Bingham and Rodger begin to look exceptional. Nine of the 15 speeches in the other three cases[106] make no reference at all to juristic writings and the majority of those which do are cases of using writing as authority for a basic rule of law. The only speeches in those cases which are worth noting are those of Lords Hope and Steyn in *Morris v KLM Royal Dutch Airlines*,[107] who use writings for the specialised purpose of obtaining information about foreign law when interpreting wording within the Warsaw Convention which controls the scope of liability of airlines for injuries suffered by passengers. It is accepted that judicial reasoning in such an area must attempt to ensure that international conventions receive identical interpretation in different jurisdictions. The standard text books on civil aviation are an obvious source of information on decisions reached elsewhere. However, their use in such a specialist context cannot be taken as evidence that members of the House of Lords are now generally inclined to consult comparative law materials as a matter of course. Although *Fairchild* is not the only case in which comparative law writings have been used by the House, it cannot be taken as setting a standard approach.[108]

A considerable number of speeches make some, but not a very great, use of juristic writing. In such cases there is often no more than a passing reference to a textbook as authority for a proposition of law. Examples of this usage would not have been regarded as exceptional in the 1970s and are certainly not a matter for comment in 2010. Writing is being used as a brick which contributes to the construction of the speech. This is not insignificant although it contributes only marginally to the final result. Semi-authoritative commentary on the law

---

[105] *Fairchild* (n 80).
[106] *Grobbelaar v News Group Newspapers Ltd* [2002] UKHL 40, [2002] 4 All ER 732; *Kuwait Airways Corpn v Iraqi Airways Co (Nos 4 and 5)* (n 22) (the public international law parts of the speeches have been excluded from consideration); and *Morris v KLM* (n 61).
[107] *Morris v KLM* (n 61).
[108] Indeed, it would overstate the position to argue that reference to comparative law writings has become a standard approach for a particular member of the House. Lord Bingham in his speech in *Grobbelaar* makes a single reference to juristic writing as authority defining the inherent jurisdiction of the court.

and proposals for reform such as Law Commission papers are also commonly referred to. For example, *White v Chief Constable of South Yorkshire*[109] was a case in which substantial reference was made to juristic writing, but references to Law Commission materials in the speeches actually total more than 50 per cent of the references made to books and articles. When the House was called on, in *Mirvahedy v Henley*,[110] to interpret the troublesome subpara 2(2)(b) of the Animals Act 1971, North's classic monograph on the subject[111] was not cited by the members of the House, who instead paid attention to the recommendations of the Law Commission on which Parliament had based the 1971 Act.[112]

What is new from 1993 onwards is the willingness of certain members of the House to openly engage (if not always agree) with arguments as to what the law should (or should not) be propounded in academic literature. Use of juristic writing is no longer confined to simple statements of the law derived from an analysis of cases. There is clear evidence that members of the House of Lords are, on occasions, looking for assistance from the academic world. As Lord Cooke of Thorndon said in *Hunter v Canary Wharf Ltd*:

> I have collected the foregoing references . . . to suggest respectfully that on this hitherto unsettled issue the general trend of leading scholarly opinion need not be condemned as erroneous.[113]

He goes further and continues, in support of his decision to dissent from the majority view:

> The reason why I prefer the alternative advocated with unwonted vigour of expression by the doyen of living tort writers is that it gives better effect to widespread conceptions concerning the home and family.

Thus, influences which have led a writer to adopt a particular view are being fed into the judicial process.

The modern judicial function requires an appreciation of a wider range of considerations than was previously the case. The arrival of human rights as a component of English law is an obvious example.[114] The complexity of the issues facing the modern judiciary means that there are topics in relation to which members of the House seek to validate their views by reference to the work of jurists. For example, causation[115] is an area which is of concern to philosophers

---

[109] *White v Chief Constable* (n 9).

[110] *Mirvahedy v Henley* [2003] UKHL 16; [2003] 2 AC 491.

[111] P North, *The Modern Law of Animals* (London, Butterworths, 1972).

[112] North's work appears to have been heavily cited by counsel in argument. Note that Lord Walker does make a passing reference to the book in his speech, but only in the sense of noting that Lloyd LJ had used it in his judgment in the Court of Appeal to access some cases decided under the pre-1971 law.

[113] *Hunter v Canary Wharf* (n 29) 717.

[114] Eady J in *Mosley v News Group Newspapers Ltd* [2008] EWHC 1777 (QB) [130] speaks of 'the task which judges are now required to carry out in the context of the rights-based environment' as 'a question of taking account of conflicting public interest considerations and evaluating them according to increasingly well recognised criteria'. See too Jenny Steele's chapter in this volume.

[115] Medical ethics provides another example.

and which has been directly at issue in a number of tort cases. A doctrine of case-based precedent is possibly not the best tool with which to build jurisprudential or ethical considerations into judgments. It is therefore not particularly surprising to find that Hart and Honoré's *Causation in the Law*[116] has been cited in six cases[117] decided in the House between 1996 and 2009. A judgment which did not consider the leading theoretical writing on the topic would be open to criticism and conversely one which adopts the views of leading authors gains authority. Lord Rodger has said that modern judgments have become more academic because judges appreciate that their work may be subject to academic scrutiny.[118] This process may have been assisted since 1999 by the employment of judicial assistants in the House.[119] Furthermore, it seems likely that counsel's contribution to the dialogue which occurs in the House has become more academic as the balance has shifted towards a greater reliance on written, as opposed to oral, submissions.[120] Such processes have a tendency to be self-perpetuating: if the House of Lords is increasingly prepared to consider juristic writing, there is every reason for counsel to use it if they feel that it will strengthen a case. Inevitably, the changes reflect the changing nature of the judiciary. The fact that modern House of Lords is more open to considering and using a wider range of sources than its predecessors should not be a surprise, given that the membership of the House contains individuals who are experienced authors and lecturers, former Law Commissioners and university staff.

As domestic systems of law are increasingly seen as part of a globalised society, the role of the academic comparativist continues to grow in importance. Some members of the House have shown a real desire to go beyond the formal boundaries of precedent in order to make use of material from other countries. Comparative law is, of course, a preserve of academics, as few practitioners can have the time to study or the resources to access other systems in any detail. There are clear examples of members of the House wishing to learn from the experience of other systems before reaching a decision[121] and it is not surprising that academic

---

[116] HLA Hart and T Honoré, *Causation in the Law,* 2nd edn (Oxford, Oxford University Press, 1985).

[117] *Smith New Court Securities Ltd v Citibank NA* [1997] AC 254; *Banque Bruxelles Lambert SA v Eagle Star Insurance Co Ltd* [1997] AC 191; *Reeves v Comr of Police of the Metropolis* [2000] 1 AC 360; *Fairchild* (n 80); *Chester* (n 64); *Mitchell v Glasgow City Council* [2009] UKHL 11, [2009] 1 AC 874.

[118] 'Judges, anticipating scrutiny of that kind, may produce a judgment which shows, on its face, that the judge too has read the literature and has got the academic tee-shirt': Lord Rodger, 'The Form and Language of Judicial Opinions' (2002) 118 *Law Quarterly Review* 226, 237.

[119] Although the level of influence the judicial assistants have in the construction of speeches is certainly far less than that of judges' clerks in America.

[120] A Paterson 'Does Advocacy Matter in the Lords?' in this volume.

[121] See, eg: Lords Bingham and Rodger in *Fairchild* (n 80); Lord Goff in *White v Jones* (n 37) and Lord Bingham in *D v East Berkshire Community Health NHS Trust* [2005] UKHL 23, [2005] 2 AC 373. In *McFarlane* (n 53), Lord Slynn, having devoted sections of his speech to American and Commonwealth authorities (which are listed in detail) dealt with French, German and Dutch cases by reference to W van Gerven and J Lever (eds), *Cases, Materials and Texts on National, Supranational and International Tort Law* (Oxford, Hart Publishing, 1998). See also Lord Steyn's speech where German (but not French) law is introduced by means of a textbook reference.

writings on overseas systems have been used to access relevant material. There are no signs that the influence of other common law jurisdictions is waning. There is no apparent reason why different courts have chosen in particular cases to concentrate on European jurisdictions or on Commonwealth[122] or US law. What can be said is that use of comparative materials is clearly seen to be a valuable technique by the current members of the House and that, particularly in relation to European jurisdictions, juristic writing is commonly used as the means of accessing such law.

There are few examples of empirical/socio-legal research into the working of the tort system being used. On the rare occasions that this kind of research appears in speeches it tends to be on matters outside of tort which are relevant to the case in hand. It is also notable that judges tend to access such data from secondary sources rather than using the original. As has already been noted, the best example is the use made by Lords Lloyd and Steyn in *Wells v Wells*[123] of research conducted for the Law Commission[124] by Professor Hazel Genn on the use made of awards of damages. This research was used to counter an argument that multipliers should be calculated on the assumption that awards will be invested in equities. Other notable examples are: Lord Browne-Wilkinson in *Page v Smith*[125] and Lord Goff in *White v Chief Constable of South Yorkshire*[126] citing the Law Commission's summary of medical evidence on the prevalence of post-traumatic stress disorder;[127] Lord Scott's references in *Corr v IBC Vehicles Ltd*[128] to statistics concerning the risk of suicide in cases of severe depression;[129] Lord Hoffmann using data on prison suicides in *Reeves v Comr of Police of the Metropolis*[130] which was published in an unofficial report[131] and Lord Brown in *Chief Constable of the Hertfordshire Police v Van Colle*[132] using Home Office figures and a press item as the source of data on criminal offences. I suspect that the lack of reference to empirical studies on the working of the tort system is probably a reflection of the paucity of modern work of this kind, rather than evidence that the House would be unwilling to consider such work. The

---

[122] A good example of positive engagement with academic writings on Commonwealth law can be seen in *Chester* (n 64). The commentaries on the High Court of Australia decision in *Chappel v Hart* (1998) 72 ALJR 1344 were accorded considerable respect.

[123] *Wells v Wells* (n 26).

[124] Law Commission, 'Personal Injury Compensation: How Much is Enough?' (n 45).

[125] *Page v Smith* (n 6).

[126] *White v Chief Constable* (n 9).

[127] Law Commission, 'Liability for Psychiatric Illness' (Consultation Paper No 137, 1995) [3.11]–[3.13]. Lord Goff also cites Mullany and Handford's *Tort Liability for Psychiatric Damage* (n 100) on this.

[128] *Corr v IBC Vehicles Ltd* [2008] UKHL 13, [2008] 1 AC 884 [28].

[129] There is no attribution given for this data. However, the submissions of counsel make it clear that this medical data was introduced into the case by an expert witness.

[130] *Reeves v Comr of Police of the Metropolis* (n 117).

[131] *Suicides at Leeds Prison: An enquiry into the deaths of five teenagers during 1988/89* by H Grindrod and G Black (London, Howard League for Penal Reform, 1989). This was an independent report, concerning the suicide rate among prisoners on remand, produced by the Howard League following rejection of its calls for a public inquiry.

[132] *Van Colle* (n 16).

preference for secondary material almost certainly reflects how much easier it is to access data in that form rather than the original research. Judicial use of such material depends, as always, on the accidents of litigation. For example, there exists a sizeable body of academic work founded on empirical evidence which argues against the notion that the United Kingdom is in the grip of a 'compensation culture.'[133] The decision of the House in *Tomlinson v Congleton BC*[134] is commonly regarded as the Lords' attack on the 'compensation culture'. However, the speeches in the House show little interest in engaging with the wider issue. In fact, they go little further than saying that the injured claimant was fully aware of the risks involved in the activity he chose and that other useful activities might be impeded, or made impossible, if a duty to stop people taking risks was recognised. The academic attack on the 'compensation culture', which was largely aimed at the assumptions behind the enactment of section 1 of the Compensation Act 2006 came too late to feature in *Tomlinson*.

Judicial taste can be seen to play a significant part in the construction of speeches. For example, Lord Hope is keen to ensure that Scottish materials are brought into the discussions. Lords Goff and Bingham have championed the use of comparative law[135] and Lord Rodger has given the House the benefits of his knowledge of Roman Law. The fact that different judges make distinctive contributions to the decisions in the House of Lords is obviously relevant to the debate on whether the Supreme Court should decide cases by the use of single speeches. If the evolution of legal doctrine is a fragmented process to which many contribute, there is a strong argument for seeing the multiplicity of influences which produce a result.

The sources from which juristic writing are drawn are varied: textbooks, articles and the humble case note all feature. Long-established textbooks and journals continue to be favoured and the views of some authors are accorded particular respect. Lectures and articles written by members of the judiciary are also favoured. But, there is also an increasing citation of articles drawn from specialist (and, at times, obscure) law journals. This almost certainly reflects advances in legal information systems which make specialised material instantly available to counsel. If material is useful, it tends to be used. This survey also shows that the attempts which are at times made by authors and editors of law journals to publish a comment on a decision of the Court of Appeal in time to have it considered by the House of Lords can succeed in getting members of the House to consider an academic viewpoint.[136]

---

[133]  R Lewis, A Morris and K Oliphant, 'Tort personal injury claims statistics: Is there a compensation culture in the United Kingdom?' (2006) 14 *Torts Law Journal* 158; A Morris, 'Spiralling or Stabilising? The Compensation Culture and Our Propensity to Claim Damages for Personal Injury' (2007) 70 *Modern Law Review* 349.

[134]  *Tomlinson v Congleton BC* [2003] UKHL 47, [2004] 1 AC 46.

[135]  Lords Goff and Bingham have both been President of the British Institute of International and Comparative Law.

[136]  See *Spring v Guardian Assurance plc* [1995] 2 AC 296; *Marc Rich* (n 42); *Wells v Wells* (n 26); *Morris v KLM* (n 61); *Chester* (n 64); *D v East Berkshire Community Health NHS Trust* (n 121); and *Barclays* (n 19).

## IX  CONCLUSIONS

It is commonly argued that the advantage that academics have over practitioners is that, without the immediate pressure of dealing with clients' cases, they can take a considered, objective and more long-term view of the way in which the law is evolving. It is also easier for an academic to evaluate an issue in its theoretical, ethical or social context. On the other hand, juristic writing will rarely, if ever, have been subject to the levels of consultation, discussion and review utilised by the Law Commission when it is making proposals for law reform. Lord Goff has argued for recognition of the different roles of the judge and jurist, emphasising, in particular, the extent to which the thinking of judges is dominated by the facts of the case before them.[137]

In the early twenty-first century it is impossible to contend that judicial decisions should be immune from comment and criticism. Their correctness should be a subject of public debate. Academic lawyers have the capacity to conduct such a debate by engaging with the issues raised at a level of technicality which the media cannot usually achieve.

The overall picture which emerges from this survey is of a senior judiciary which is prepared to be open about the materials it uses to feed into its decisions, including the fact that it is considering and, at times, placing reliance on juristic writings. For academic jurists this holds out the possibility that their work may, albeit on rare occasions, have an impact on the development of the law, even though a precise assessment of the level of that impact is likely to be impossible.

## APPENDIX

### Data

This research has surveyed 104 cases decided by the House of Lords in the period between 1990 and 2009.

The bare statistical data drawn from this survey is as follows.

### Judges

Statistically, the judge who made the greatest number of references to juristic writings per speech in the period surveyed was Lord Cooke (22 references in five speeches, an average of 4.40 references per case). However, given the larger number of cases in which they sat, Lord Bingham (56 references in 18 speeches,

---

[137]   R Goff, 'The search for principle' (1983) 69 *Proceedings of the British Academy* 169, 183.

averaging 3.11), Lord Goff (68 references in 22 speeches, averaging 3.09) and Lord Steyn (101 references in 37 speeches, averaging 2.73) should be regarded as at the forefront of the developing practice. Most of those who made no use of juristic writings were sitting in the early part of the period surveyed.

## Textbooks

A significant number of textbooks are cited. For these purposes, I am excluding any books that received fewer that six references.

*Clerk and Lindsell on Torts* 22; Salmond (including Salmond and Heuston) *on Torts* 21; Fleming, *Law of Torts* 19; Hart and Honoré, *Causation in the Law* 10; van Gerven, Lever and Larouche, *Cases, Materials and Text on National, Supranational and International Tort Law* 9; Markesinis and Deakin, *Tort Law* 8; Carty, *An Analysis of the Economic Torts* 7; Kemp and Kemp, *The Quantum of Damages* 7; Prosser and Keeton *on Torts* 7; Winfield and Jolowicz *on Tort* 7; Atiyah, *Vicarious Liability in the law of Torts* 6; McGregor *on Damages* 6; *Halsbury's Laws of England* 6; Mullany and Handford, *Liability for Psychiatric Damage* 6.

## Journals

References to periodical literature are heavily biased towards three well-established general journals. The *Law Quarterly Review* is, by some way, the most frequently cited. It was cited on 58 occasions. The *Cambridge Law Journal* was a considerable way behind, with 20 citations and the *Modern Law Review* achieved 17.

Nothing else achieved more than five (*Current Legal Problems, Journal of the Law Society of Scotland* and the *Tort Law Review*). The *Journal of Law and Medicine, Lloyds Maritime and Commercial Law Quarterly* and the *Oxford Journal of Legal Studies* achieved four. References at this level are commonly explicable on the basis of a single article having a particular relevance in a case. For example, the *Journal of Legal Studies* and the *Torts Law Journal* both score three, but in both cases it is the same article being referred to on a number of occasions in one case. Also scoring three are the *Harvard Law Review, Medical Law Review, Professional Negligence*, the *Scots Law Times* and the *Yale Law Journal*. The *Edinburgh Law Review*, the *International and Comparative Law Quarterly, Public Law* and the *Advocate* score two.

The breadth of the material being fed into the decision-making process is shown by the journals which receive a single reference. They are: *Australian Bar Review, Brigham Young University Law Review, California Law Review, Canadian Bar Review, Canadian Journal of Law and Jurisprudence, Columbia Law Journal, Fordham Law Review, Journal of Applied Philosophy, Journal of*

*Legal History, Juridical Review, Michigan Law Review, Monash Law Review, New Law Journal, Otago Law Review, Singapore Journal of Legal Studies, Tel Aviv University Studies in Law, Texas Law Review, The Times* (newspaper), and the *University of Western Australia Law Review*.

I should say that the omission of *Legal Studies*, the journal published on behalf of the Society of Legal Scholars since 1981, from this list is not a mistake. It is undoubtedly true that *Legal Studies* is, as the Society's website states, 'recognised as one of the foremost academic law journals in the UK.' However, nothing published in it was referred to in any of the cases surveyed.

## Authors

The most referenced authors (ignoring fewer than 10 references) were:

Fleming 23, Salmond (including Salmond and Heuston) 23, Weir 20, Markesinis 17, Stapleton 16, Honoré 14, Mullany 14, Prosser 13, Cane (including two to editing of Atiyah's *Accidents, Compensation and the Law*) 12, Kemp 10.

In spite of what has been said about the historical significance of Newark's work on the shape of the modern law of nuisance, it is only referenced on eight occasions.

## Other data

There are 60 references to Law Commission publications in these cases. There are a small number of additional references to the work of other law reform bodies.

I can trace at least 23 references in these cases to extra judicial writings/lectures by members of the judiciary (some are to judges working in commonwealth jurisdictions).

# 11

# *Judges and Academics:*
# *Features of a Partnership*

## ALEXANDRA BRAUN*

We have all secretly known for years that the ultimate source of judicial truth is to be found in the *Law Quarterly Review*; all that is needed is to incorporate this obvious fact into our jurisprudence.[1]

## I INTRODUCTION

IN HIS 1997 FA Mann Lecture, 'The Academic and the Practitioner', which inspired the seminar at the origin of this book, the late Professor Birks spoke of the 'rise of juristic literature to a law-making partnership with the judgments of the courts'. According to the author, 'the juristic function is increasingly shared by academics. There is a partnership, apparent in the law library and hence in the reading which every practitioner does in preparation for a case, between the judgments of the higher courts and the books and journals which emanate, preponderantly from the universities'.[2] Only a few years earlier Lord Goff had reached a similar conclusion in his Maccabaean Lecture in Jurisprudence.[3]

But what is the nature of this partnership and what are its characteristics? A partnership usually involves sharing duties, obligations, profits and losses. It entails being party to something, or taking part in doing something. In the case of judges and academics it means being a sharer or partaker in the development of the law. Do English judges and academics conceive of law-making as a joint enterprise? Can their relationship be described as a partnership between equals, or is one of them stronger or even dominant? Do they co-operate, or

* I would like to thank Alberto Maria Benedetti, Martin Flohr, Mark Freedland, Mauro Grondona, Nils Jansen, James Lee, Ruth Sefton-Green and Stefan Vogenauer for their advice and comments on an earlier version of this paper.

[1] Lord Gardiner, 'Law Reform and the Teachers of Law' (1966–1967) 9 *Journal of the Society of Public Teachers of Law* (NS) 190, 190.

[2] P Birks, 'The Academic and the Practitioner' (1998) 18 *Legal Studies* 397, 400 and 413.

[3] Lord Goff, 'The Search for Principle' in W Swadling and G Jones (eds), *The Search for Principle. Essays in Honour of Lord Goff of Chieveley* (Oxford, Oxford University Press, 1999) 329.

rather compete? Is there mutual respect and understanding? And how does their relationship differ from the relationship judges and academics have in other legal systems, such as, for instance, France, Germany or Italy?

These are the questions I shall address in this paper which will examine the nature of the partnership between the two branches of the legal profession from a comparative perspective. The paper will primarily focus on England and touch only briefly upon foreign experiences, in an attempt to highlight the main characteristics of the partnership between academics and judges in this country, and to identify possible trends. In doing so, I shall not concentrate on any particular area of the law, but instead outline how these two legal actors behave towards one another more generally.

## II  THE NATURE OF THE PARTNERSHIP

### A  A Partnership that evolves mostly between individuals

One feature that stands out when looking at the way judges and academics relate to one another in England is that, contrary to other European legal systems, the partnership evolves between individuals.[4] First of all, unless a composite judgment or a single full judgment has been delivered, in England judges speak as individuals.[5] In other words, judges do not in principle hand down anonymous, formal and collective judgments. Hence, each single opinion reveals different attitudes towards scholarly production. This is quite different in France, Italy or Germany, where courts adhere to a system of collegiality and therefore speak unanimously.

At the same time, English academics too do not feel, act or talk like a group or body, such as the French, the German and the Italian legal scholars who define themselves as 'la doctrine' in France,[6] 'die Rechtslehre'[7] in Germany and 'la dottrina' in Italy. This does not mean that in these countries legal scholars all engage in the same type of work, nor that the group is completely homogenous, but rather that they view and present themselves as a body. By contrast, English academics do not conceive of themselves as a collective entity. This is not altogether surprising, given that in England the study and teaching of law only became a university academic discipline in the second half of the nineteenth century and the community of legal scholars was for a long time small

---

[4] A Braun, 'Professors and Judges in Italy: It Takes Two to Tango' (2006) 26 *Oxford Journal of Legal Studies* 665, 680.
[5] The Criminal Division of the Court of Appeal is required by statute to give a single judgment: Criminal Justice Act 1981 s 59.
[6] P Jestaz and C Jamin, *La doctrine* (Paris, Dalloz, 2004); idem, 'The Entity of French Doctrine: Some Thoughts on the Community of French Legal Writers' (1998) 18 *Legal Studies* 415.
[7] Alongside these terms, other terms such as 'Lehre', 'Schrifttum' and 'Rechtswissenschaft' are employed. See S Vogenauer, 'An Empire of Light? II: Learning and Lawmaking in Germany Today' (2006) 26 *Oxford Journal of Legal Studies* 627, 631.

in number.[8] Correspondingly, neither the legislature nor the courts have ever perceived legal academics as a collective entity. However, that legal academics in England do not feel like an *ensemble* might also be ascribed to the fact that their background and education as well as their nationality is quite heterogeneous.[9] Moreover, in England, in order to become professors, academics do not have to go through a contest or a formal procedure that confers on them the permission to teach, nor do they have to pass a national examination to that effect. A PhD or DPhil is in principle sufficient as professional qualification. Contrary to England, in Germany it is necessary for legal academics to have attained the *Habilitation*, while in France academics have to pass the *agrégation* and in Italy the *concorso pubblico*. Such contests may enhance the level of cohesion among academics and contribute to the fact that they are perceived as a group from the outside.[10]

It is therefore probably not a coincidence that the English language does not know of an equivalent expression to the French term *doctrine*, the German *Rechtslehre* or the Italian *dottrina*, which refer to the collective entity of the academic jurists and of their opinions.[11] In order to describe the activity or the scientific production of legal academics in England, we use expressions such as: 'legal writings', 'academic literature', 'academic writings' or sometimes even 'legal scholarship' (although this expression is more commonly found in the US), while references to legal academics are made by using terms such as 'legal writers', 'university jurists', 'academic writers', 'legal authors', 'commentators', 'jurists' or, in some cases, 'legal scholars'.

The upshot of the fact that English legal academics do not act as a community is that the 'authority' of an author or his work is based principally upon his own reputation and the strength of his arguments, and not upon the power or weight of the group of academics that shares his view. In other words, his opinion is persuasive because it is the author's view and not because he is part of the academic profession that is considered a source of law, albeit only an informal one.[12] This does not, of course, imply that in France, Germany or Italy, the opinion of a legal writer is authoritative only because he is part of the *doctrine majoritaire*, the *herrschende Meinung* or the *dottrina dominante*.

---

[8] Moreover, in England legal academics usually do not employ assistants or PhD students who work for them on a regular basis. As a consequence, compared to the US or continental legal systems such as Germany, Italy or France, schools of thought are less commonly developed in the UK.

[9] Further, according to W Twining in 'The Role of Academics in the Legal System' in P Cane and M Tushnet (eds), *The Oxford Handbook of Legal Studies* (Oxford, Oxford University Press, 2003) 920, the full-time university scholar-teacher of law constitutes only a small minority of people involved in teaching in England.

[10] See Jestaz and Jamin, 'The Entity of French Doctrine' (n 6) 429–30. John Bell suggests that the *agrégation* serves to confirm the status of the academics as a recognised authority: J Bell, *French Legal Cultures* (London, Edinburgh and Dublin, Butterworths, 2001) 93.

[11] For a more detailed analysis see A Braun, *Giudici e Accademia nell'esperienza inglese. Storia di un dialogo* (Bologna, Mulino, 2006) 457–61.

[12] S Vogenauer, 'Sources of Law and Legal Method in Comparative Law' in M Reimann and R Zimmermann (eds), *The Oxford Handbook of Comparative Law* (Oxford, Oxford University Press, 2006) 869.

In recent years, however, one can notice that English judges occasionally refer to the 'weight of academic opinion', the 'weight of academic authority', the 'weighty academic authority' or 'the majority of academic opinion'.[13] Moreover, more frequently than in the past, they make general references to the 'academic discussion', or 'academic comments', 'academic criticism', 'academic debate' or 'academic literature'[14]—a trend that may be ascribed to the increasing amount of legal literature. Nevertheless, in principle English judges still cite mostly individual authors rather than referring to the body of legal scholarship. Thus, unlike in other countries, where the relationship is a relationship mostly between two collective entities, the courts on the one side and the body of academics on the other, in England the communication takes place mostly between single judges and individual academics.

In England, judges and academics meet and talk to each other in several ways. Among the main channels through which this communication occurs are, undoubtedly, legal education and legal literature. Those generations of practitioners and judges who have acquired their knowledge of law at university—either taking a first degree or during the second vocational stage offered by some universities—have entered into contact with the methodology and the modes of thinking of legal scholars already at an early stage. They will have been exposed to the academic approach to law that will shape their minds and legal reasoning for the future. Not only will they have been taught by academics, they will also have studied using their textbooks and reading their academic work. In fact, books as well as articles and case notes represent another important means through which legal scholars can communicate their views to students, academics, practitioners and judges alike. The same is true for judges some of whom, as will be seen later, publish not infrequently.[15]

Legal literature and education aside, there are institutional channels through which in England academics and judges can make their views heard and enter into contact with each other. One such channel is constituted by the Law Commission, which not only represents an important platform for communication between the academic world and the legislature, but also provides a forum where academics meet up with practitioners and judges.[16] Another important setting, where academics can meet with practitioners and future judges, is law firms or barristers' chambers. A number of academics are indeed qualified members of the legal profession.[17] Some of them are associated with or work on an occasional

---

[13] See, for instance, *R (on the application of Al-Jedda) v Secretary of State for Defence* [2007] UKHL 58, [2008] 1 AC 332 [115] (Lord Rodger); *Cantrell v Wycombe DC* [2008] EWCA Civ 866 [8] (Lewison J); *I MacWilliam Co Inc v Mediterranean Shipping Co SA (The Rafaela S)* [2005] UKHL 11, [2005] 2 AC 423 [3] (Lord Bingham).

[14] See section IIB below. See also Braun, *Giudici e Accademia* (n 11) 349. Thus bench and bar are aware of the complexity of the academic debate and not only of the writings of single authors.

[15] Below, text to n 89.

[16] In this sense, P Birks, 'The Academic and the Practitioner' (n 2) 400; J Bell, *Judiciaries within Europe. A Comparative Review* (Cambridge, CUP, 2006) 328.

[17] In Italy, many academics work as practising lawyers. This has partly to do with the fact that academic salaries are not very substantial. However, because the prestige and social status of

basis as a 'door tenant' for a leading set of chambers. Essex Court Chambers, for instance, counts 18 academics among its members. Matrix Chambers, 20 Essex Street, Brick Court Chambers and Fountain Court also have academics collaborating with them. Notably, the chambers and the academic members openly declare their connection on their respective web pages.

Other occasions where academics and judges can meet are represented by university lectures and seminars given by judges, as well as conferences attended by both legal scholars and members of the bench and bar.[18] Also, senior members of the Court of Appeal and the Supreme Court often participate in moot courts organised by universities. Moreover, some legal academics are involved in the continuing education and training of judges organised by the Judicial Studies Board.[19]

However, since the relationship takes place between individuals, the communication often passes also through more informal channels.[20] Personal friendships between members of the bench and legal academics are not rare, and represent an important way of influencing each other's work. Further contacts arise when academics act as advocates in a case. There are many other examples of platforms for the exchange between judges and academics, through meetings at events held by university law societies, such as the Oxford Law Club or the Presidential Address of the University of Birmingham's Holdsworth Club. All in all, therefore, in England occasions for judges and academics to meet do exist.

At the same time, some of the channels that academics and judges use in other European legal systems are not frequently explored in England. Professorial opinions are sought, but probably not as formally or as frequently as in France or Italy. In those legal systems, being a professor qualifies the individual to give legal opinions, whereas in England if an academic wants to have some practice activity he must become professionally qualified.[21] Moreover, unlike in the US, professors

professors is regarded as higher than that of a practitioner (or even a judge), practitioners are also keen on acting as part-time teachers at a university. There has, therefore, always been a strong link between academia and the practising profession, though not so much with the judiciary. In France too, many legal academics practise law. According to John Bell, this is partly due to the need to supplement their low pay. The downside of that is that the quantity and quality of doctrinal legal writing has reduced, because much of the writing is for the use of practitioners. See Bell, *Judiciaries within Europe* (n 16) 84. In Germany, professors may practise if they register as a *Rechtsanwalt*, and many do so, especially those working in the field of criminal law.

[18] One is more likely to meet a member of the Court of Appeal or the Supreme Court at a conference in Oxford, than a member of the *Corte di Cassazione* at a conference in Rome. To a certain extent, this seems to be true also for France, though academics do invite members of the higher courts to their events. German judges do attend conferences, but it seems that they would not usually take part in core academic conferences. They rather attend those that focus on topics relevant to legal practice, where they may also give a paper.

[19] Among the legal scholars involved are Andrew Ashworth, Andrew Burrows, John Cartwright and Edwin Peel.

[20] This is the case also in other legal systems. As for France, see Y Gaudemet, *Les méthodes du juge administratif* (Paris, Librairie générale de droit et de jurisprudence, 1972) 158.

[21] In this sense, Bell, *Judiciaries within Europe* (n 16) 37 and 327. Furthermore, unlike in England, in France some academics act directly as advisers to the *Conseil d'État*. See Bell, *French Legal Cultures* (n 10) 225.

in England do not regularly become judges. However, an increasing number of judges have previously had an academic career, such as, for instance, Beatson J and Cranston J, Buxton LJ and Elias LJ, Lord Collins, Lord Goff, Baroness Hale, Lord Hoffmann, Sir Robert Megarry, Lord Rodger and Lord Wright. In Italy academics are elected to the *Corte Costituzionale*, but may not become members of the *Corte di Cassazione*, while in France, academics can be elected to the *Cour de Cassation*[22] where they serve either as temporary or as permanent members— or, and that is more frequently the case, to the *Conseil Constitutionnel*.[23] As for Germany, several of the members of the *Bundesverfassungsgericht* are professors, while the judges at the *Bundesgerichtshof* or the *Bundesverwaltungsgericht* are pure career judges. Moreover, in Germany a number of professors hold part-time posts in a senate of one of the regional *Oberlandesgerichte* or *Oberverwaltungsgerichte*.[24]

## B  A partnership that is transparent

Given that in England we are talking about a relationship between individuals, it is somewhat difficult to speak of it in general terms. Also, relationships are dynamic and complex, and change over time. Nevertheless, for the purpose of this paper, some general reflections can be made about the attitude academics have towards senior judges, and vice versa. Most of what is said concerns not the English judiciary as a whole, but foremost members of the Court of Appeal and the Supreme Court.

One significant feature of the relationship is that, compared to what can be observed in other legal systems, such as Italy and France, in England the relationship between judges and academics is on the whole transparent. This is so for several reasons. First, the relationship is transparent because the communication is not anonymous. As mentioned earlier, it does not take place between the court and the body of academics, but between single judges and individual academics. Second, the relationship is transparent in the sense that, due to the abandonment of the convention against the citation of living authors as authorities in court, judges are more inclined to openly acknowledging the contribution academics make to the law-making process.[25] In other words, academic scholarship is more explicitly borrowed from today than in the past.

---

[22] Such as A Ponsard, Y Chartier and J-L Aubert.

[23] Bell, *Judiciaries within Europe* (n 16) 87–88 who cites Luchaire, Vedel, Bainter and Robert as examples. Those elected to the *Conseil d'État* are not usually academics, though they may teach at university, participate in conferences and publish legal literature. See, for instance, Bernard Stirn, Roger Errera, Guy Canivet and Guy Braibant. See J Bell, S Boyron and S Whittaker, *Principles of French Law*, 2nd edn (Oxford, Oxford University Press, 2008) 25.

[24] For more details see Vogenauer, 'Learning and Lawmaking' (n 7) 637.

[25] For an analysis of how things were in the past and how they have changed, see A Braun, 'Burying the Living? The Citation of Legal Writings in English Courts' (2010) 58 *American Journal of Comparative Law* 27.

Third, despite the fact that a certain amount of communication passes through personal and informal channels, English judges and academics talk to each other quite overtly and have rendered much of their interaction public. This is particularly evident if one looks at the changes the style and the content of references to academic material have undergone in the course of the past 40 years or so.

In England, some form of communication between certain judges and certain academics has always existed. In particular, legal academics of the late nineteenth century were close to the bench and Bar, and judges referred quite frequently to the works of Frederick Pollock and Albert Venn Dicey. However, the citations were not as complex and comprehensive as today, and the dialogue not made as explicit. Indeed, nowadays, judges openly mention in their judgments which academic literature they have consulted and what material they have read. Occasionally they reproach counsel for not having brought academic literature to their attention,[26] or even draw counsel's attention to academic material.[27] It is almost as if judges felt the need to show how well informed and learned they are.[28] Moreover, judges also praise academic work or acknowledge the assistance they have gained from scholarly writings.[29] They further recognise the contribution academics have made and are making to the development of the common law.[30]

---

[26] For reproaches of counsel, see *White v Blackmore* [1972] 2 QB 651 (CA) 666 (Lord Denning MR); *Rowling v Takaro Properties* [1988] AC 473 (PC) 500 (Lord Keith); *White v Jones* [1993] 3 WLR 730 (CA) 750–51 (Steyn LJ).

[27] See *Apple Corps Ltd v Apple Computer Inc* [2004] EWHC 768 (Ch) [36] (Mann J); *Gregory v Portsmouth City Council* [1997] EWCA Civ 2645 (Schiemann LJ): 'Little or none [persuasive material] was produced at the Bar. The material which I cite is the result of reading after we reserved judgment and has therefore not been exposed to the discipline of being the subject of submissions at the Bar'. In *Istil Group Inc & Anor v Zahoor & Ors* [2003] EWHC 165 [67] Lawrence Collins J declared: 'I was not referred either at the hearing or subsequently to the academic literature on the use of equitable remedies in this context, and the difficult issue of the relationship between legal professional privilege and the law relating to confidentiality. . .'. See also *State Bank of India v Sood* [1997] Ch 276 (CA) 285 (Peter Gibson LJ). For a more recent case see *Transfield Shipping Inc v Mercator Shipping Inc* [2008] UKHL 48, [2009] 1 AC 61 [79] where Lord Walker said: 'My Lords, I had reached this point in drafting my opinion when my noble and learned friend Lord Hoffmann drew to my attention the articles by Adam Kramer, Professor Tettenborn, and Professor Robertson, not cited in argument, that are mentioned in Para 11 of Lord Hoffmann's opinion. These scholars develop ideas about *Hadley v Baxendale* which, although differently formulated, share some common ground . . . I have found all these materials very helpful'. See further *AB v Ministry of Defence* [2009] EWHC 1225 (QB) [235] (Foskett J).

[28] 'These days judges read academic articles as part of their ordinary judicial activity': *Re OT Computers (in administration)* [2004] EWCA Civ 653 [43] (Longmore LJ).

[29] See Braun, 'Professors and Judges' (n 4) 668.

[30] See, eg, *Re (A) (Children) (Conjoined Twins: Surgical Separation)* [2001] Fam 147, 232, where Brooke LJ stated: 'The work of academic writers and of the Law Commission has, however, led to one significant development in the common law. This lies in the newly identified defence of duress of circumstances'. See also the words employed by Lord Mustill in the conclusions in the case *Pan Atlantic Ins'ce Ltd v Pine Top Ltd* [1995] 1 AC 501 (HL) 551: 'In conclusion I wish to acknowledge the painstaking research which founded the arguments addressed on appeal, and in particular the deployment of modern academic and other writings. Throughout its long history the law of marine insurance has owed as much to commentators as to the courts, and although the views of these writers are not fully reflected here, I have taken them carefully into account'. *Jones v Commerzbank AG* [2003] EWCA Civ 1663, [2003] All ER (D) 303 [31] (Mummery LJ): 'Since Lord Goff first formulated

That aside, English judges do increasingly deal with academic ideas in an open manner and sometimes respond to criticisms or challenges coming from the academic branch of the profession. They do so not only in the context of extra-judicial writings,[31] but also through their judgments. One recent example of such an open interaction is the debate that emerged in the aftermath of the 2008 House of Lords decision in *Yeoman's Row v Cobbe*. Mr Ben McFarlane and Professor Andrew Robertson wrote a case note entitled 'The Death of Proprietary Estoppel (*Yeoman's Row v Cobbe*)' for the *Lloyd's Maritime and Commercial Law Quarterly*.[32] As the title reveals, the authors argued that in light of the decision in *Cobbe*, proprietary estoppel was dead. Not long afterwards, in March 2009, the House of Lords decided the case of *Thorner v Major* in which Lord Walker cited the case note with disapproval. His Lordship said:

> I should say at once that the respondents to the appeal did not contend that this House's decision in *Cobbe v Yeoman's Row Management Ltd* [2008] UKHL 55; [2008] 1 WLR 1752 ('*Cobbe*') has severely curtailed, or even virtually extinguished, the doctrine of proprietary estoppel (a rather apocalyptic view that has been suggested by some commentators: see for instance Ben McFarlane and Professor Andrew Robertson, 'Death of Proprietary Estoppel' [2008] LMCLQ 449 and Sir Terence Etherton's extrajudicial observations to the Chancery Bar Association 2009 Conference, paras 27ff.).[33]

Here Lord Walker took the opportunity to express his personal opinion and to criticise the legal writer's comments about a previous decision in which he himself was involved. To this the authors of the case note answered in another case note published in the *Law Quarterly Review*, entitled 'Apocalypse Averted: Proprietary Estoppel in the House of Lords', in which they recognise that proprietary estoppel still exists.[34]

Another good example that involves Lord Walker once again, is his response in the House of Lords decision in *R (Pro-Life Alliance) v BBC* to the criticism Mr Richard Edwards had expressed in an article published in the *Modern Law Review*. Mr Edwards had accused judges of being too deferential and not sufficiently firm in their approach to the principle of proportionality expressed in the Human Rights Act.[35] Lord Walker replied in the following manner:

his great principles there have been other cases and a considerable body of academic writing, this being an area in which legal scholars have been very active and influential in recent years . . .'. *X v Y* [2004] EWCA Civ 662 [44] (Mummery LJ): 'In the year 2000 a wide range of views was published in the Law Quarterly Review. Sir William Wade (whose writings have been of immense influence in the development of English Law over the last 40 years and whose death a few weeks ago was a great loss to legal scholarship) argued that the HRA [Human Rights Act] has horizontal effects between individuals: vol 116 LQR at 217.'

[31] For a good example, see Lord Cooke (former President of the New Zealand CA) in 'The Law Lords: an Endangered Heritage' (2003) 119 *Law Quarterly Review* 49. For more examples of publications by judges see section IIC(ii) below.

[32] [2008] *Lloyd's Maritime and Commercial Law Quarterly* 449–60.

[33] *Thorner v Major* [2009] UKHL 18 [31].

[34] (2009) 125 *Law Quarterly Review* 535.

[35] R Edwards, 'Judicial Deference under the Human Rights Act' (2002) 65 *Modern Law Review* 859.

I add a footnote in relation to the article by Mr Edwards, 'Judicial deference under the Human Rights Act' (2002) 65 MLR 859. . . . The article is critical of the British judiciary for being over-deferential and insufficiently principled in its approach to proportionality under the Human Rights Act. As to deference, I would respectfully agree with Lord Hoffmann that (simply as a matter of the English language) it may not be the best word to use, if only because it is liable to be misunderstood.

However the elements which Mr Edwards puts forward, at pp 873–880, as his basis for a principled approach . . . appear to me by no means dissimilar from the principles which do emerge from *R (Daly) v Secretary of State for the Home Department* [2001] 2 AC 532 and other recent decisions of your Lordships' House. The *Wednesbury* test (*Associated Provincial Picture Houses Ltd v Wednesbury Corpn* [1948] 1 KB 223), for all its defects, had the advantage of simplicity, and it might be thought unsatisfactory that it must now be replaced (when human rights are in play) by a much more complex and contextually sensitive approach. But the scope and reach of the 1998 Act is so extensive that there is no alternative. It might be a mistake, at this stage in the bedding-down of the 1998 Act, for your Lordships' House to go too far in attempting any comprehensive statement of principle. But it is clear that any simple 'one size fits all' formulation of the test would be impossible. For these reasons I would allow this appeal.[36]

Also noticeable is what Lord Walker had to say in the House of Lords' decision in *Deutsche Morgan Grenfell Group plc v Commissioners of the Inland Revenue*:[37]

My Lords, the House is being invited (much more pressingly, it must be said, by scholars than by counsel for the parties) to make a choice at a very high level of abstraction. Most scholars would take the view (though Professor Birks himself would not, I suspect, have agreed, since he regarded taxonomy as very important) that the choice is one which will rarely make much if any practical difference to the outcome of any particular case before the court. For several reasons I doubt whether this is the right time for your Lordships to decide whether to rebase the whole law of unjust enrichment on a highly abstract principle which (although familiar to civilians and to Scottish lawyers, and discussed in the speech of my noble and learned friend Lord Hope of Craighead in *Kleinwort Benson* [1999] 2 AC 349, pp 408–409) would represent a distinct departure from established doctrine:

It is of the nature of the common law to develop slowly, and attempts at dramatic simplification may turn out to have been premature and indeed mistaken.[38]

Equally interesting, for the transparency of the dialogue between academics and judges in England, is the House of Lords' decision in *R v Wang*, in which the Appellate Committee declared that:

In contending for the limited exceptions specified in para 2 above, Mr Perry was able to rely on the powerful support of Lord Justice Auld (*Review of the Criminal Courts of England and Wales*: Report, 2001, paras 99–108, pp 173–176), and on a formidable

---

[36]  *R (Pro-Life Alliance) v BBC* [2003] UKHL 23, [2004] 1 AC 185 [142]–[145].

[37]  *Deutsche Morgan Grenfell Group plc v Commissioners of the Inland Revenue* [2006] UKHL 49, [2007] 1 AC 558 where at [97] and [151]–[158] an analysis of academic material is undertaken.

[38]  See in particular ibid [151]–[156]. As for the impact of academic legal writing on the development of the law of the law of restitution, see Graham Virgo's paper in this volume.

body of academic literature including Professor Glanville Williams, *The Proof of Guilt*, 3rd ed, (1963), pp 261–262, Professor Griew [1972] Crim LR 204 and [1989] Crim LR 768 and Professor McConville [1973] Crim LR 164. He drew attention to the question posed by Professor Glanville Williams (*op. cit.*, p 262): 'If we really wish juries to give untrue verdicts, why do we require them to be sworn?'

...

The answer to Professor Glanville Williams' question is of course that we wish juries to give true and not untrue verdicts, and that is why we require them to be sworn. It is obviously true, as Professor Glanville Williams went on to point out, that in some countries a jury system has proved to be inoperable. But in England and Wales it has been possible to assume, in the light of experience and with a large measure of confidence, that jurors will almost invariably approach their important task with a degree of conscientiousness commensurate with what is at stake and a ready willingness to do their best to follow the trial judge's directions. If there were to be a significant problem, no doubt the role of the jury would call for legislative scrutiny. As it is, however, the acquittals of such high profile defendants as *Ponting*, *Randle* and *Pottle* have been quite as much welcomed as resented by the public, which over many centuries has adhered tenaciously to its historic choice that decisions on the guilt of defendants charged with serious crime should rest with a jury of lay people, randomly selected, and not with professional judges. That the last word should rest with the jury remains, as Sir Patrick Devlin, writing in 1956, said (Hamlyn Lectures, pp 160, 162) 'an insurance that the criminal law will conform to the ordinary man's idea of what is fair and just. If it does not, the jury will not be a party to its enforcement . . .. The executive knows that in dealing with the liberty of the subject it must not do anything which would seriously disturb the conscience of the average member of Parliament or of the average juryman. I know of no other real checks that exist today upon the power of the executive'.[39]

Here the judges openly addressed the issues Professor Glanville Williams had raised in his book. Another interesting example is the Court of Appeal decision in *R v Ireland* in which Swinton Thomas LJ (giving judgment for the court) concluded the opinion by observing that:

Academic writers have indicated that judges should not stretch the ambit of specific crimes beyond their proper limits in order to punish behaviour which members of the public would consider ought to be punished (see, for example, Glanville Williams *Criminal Law, The General Part* (2nd edn, 1961) p 176). We are very mindful of that admonition, but, in this case, and in the case in which Tucker J has just given judgment, *R v Johnson* [1996] Crim LR 828 we are satisfied that the conduct complained of falls squarely within the recognised definition of the offence. For those reasons this appeal against conviction is dismissed.[40]

These examples and many others show that a dialogue is going on between the two branches of the legal profession—or at least some of their members—that they listen to each other and that both parties are not afraid of rendering their

---

[39] *R v Wang* [2005] UKHL 9 [15]–[16].
[40] *R v Ireland* [1997] QB 114 (CA) 122–23.

discussions open and public.[41] The interaction is not the same in every area of the law, and not each judge is equally open. But there is a clear trend towards a greater transparency, across the different branches of the law, of the partnership which the late Professor Birks was referring to. In fact, if we look at the Court of Appeal or, indeed, the Supreme Court, a good number of judges do quite frequently refer to academic material. Among the current members of the Supreme Court appearing to stand out are Lord Clarke, Lord Mance and Lord Walker, while among the members of the Court of Appeal who often cite academic material are Arden LJ and Mummery LJ.[42]

The same transparency cannot be said to exist in France and Italy. This is mostly explained by the fact that in France and in Italy, courts cannot or do not cite academic authors in their judgments and therefore do not openly discuss their work. In France the concise style of judgments of higher courts leaves no room for citations, whilst in Italy the citation of legal writings is expressly forbidden and only general references to the 'body of literature' or the 'body of authors' are admissible.[43] Thus, even though both in France and Italy the two legal actors do communicate with each other, the communication is not made as public and transparent as it is in England.[44]

In Germany, the *Bundesgerichtshof* commonly refers to academic literature and openly deals with the author's view. However, even though the court motivates its opinions with regard to academic criticisms, and possibly also changes its position, citations seem to usually consist of short references—often in brackets—to the relevant author or work.[45] Thus, the communication is transparent, but the style of the judgment different. Although there are exceptions, lengthy analysis of the academic debate or replies to criticism, as one can find them in English judgments, appear to be rather infrequent.[46] Indeed, in recent years English judges have started dedicating entire paragraphs or sections of the judgments to the examination of academic legal writings, which they have at times entitled

---

[41] Equally fascinating is the Court of Appeal decision in *Cowan v Cowan* [2002] Fam 97 (CA) [38]–[42] where Thorpe LJ entitled 'The academic appraisal' that part of his opinion in which he examined the writings of those authors whom he defines as 'the three leading academic commentators' in the field of family law. The authors, whose works he reproduces and comments upon and ultimately approves of, are John Eekelaar, Stephen Cretney and Rebecca Bailey-Harris. See also *Office of Fair Trading v Abbey National Plc* [2009] EWCA Civ 116, [2009] 2 WLR 1286 [70]–[80] (Sir Anthony Clarke).

[42] In the past, references to academic literature were often made by Lord Bingham, Lord Edmund-Davies, Lord Goff, Lord Keith, Mantell LJ, Lord Mustill and Lord Steyn.

[43] See Braun, 'Professors and Judges' (n 4).

[44] For an example of such communication in Italy see ibid, 657–78. As for France see Bell, Boyron and Whittaker, *Principles* (n 23) 34–35. In France, the influence of academics on the judiciary seems to be particularly strong in the field of private law.

[45] Quite often references are made to commentaries. Similar is the style of references to academic literature in the judgments of the *Bundesverfassungsgericht* and the *Bundesverwaltungsgericht*.

[46] That is, for instance, the case when the *Bundesgerichtshof* changes a long-standing position on the basis of criticism expressed in legal literature or when the court deals with a new point of law.

'academic literature',[47] 'academic writing[s]',[48] 'academic writers',[49] 'writings of authors',[50] 'the textbooks',[51] or 'academic authority'.[52]

Be that as it may, as is well known, in England, the communication and relationship has not always been that transparent, it being a development mostly of the last 30 or 40 years. In fact, until quite recently, judges were more reluctant to cite academic work and to engage in an open dialogue. The reasons why judges have become more transparent about their relationship with the academic world are probably several, and cannot be fully explored here. However, among the possible explanations seems to be the fact that judges feel they should outline the sources of their reasoning; that they have changed the way they perceive themselves, no longer as officers of the state but rather as 'highly skilled specialists at the peak of their profession';[53] that, unlike in the past, a good share of the judges have had a university legal education; that the convention against the citation of living authors in court has lost its force; that judges are more open to extra-judicial arguments and that skeleton arguments are submitted to the court and that judges are aided by judicial assistants.[54]

It is, however, not only the judges who openly engage with the work of academics. English academics too do not deny the authority or relevance of case law, nor do they downplay their interest in it. They make no secret of the fact that the major focus of their own scholarly work is often represented by case law and that they have an interest in influencing its development. Although this seems probably quite obvious to an English observer, the situation is different elsewhere in Europe. This has not only to do with the fact that in continental legal systems case law is not a binding source of law, but is also attributable to a power struggle between the different legal actors. In France, for instance, academics were for a long time reluctant to recognise case law as a source of law.[55] In Italy, though academics consider case law an important source of law, the use they make of it is different from the UK.[56] A significant amount of legal literature, be it textbooks or monographs, gives indeed little space to the analysis of case

---

[47] See *A v National Blood Authority* [2001] 3 All ER 289 (QB) 322 (Burton J).

[48] *Quantum Corporation Inc v Plane Trucking Ltd* [2002] EWCA Civ 350 [63]–[65] (Mance LJ); *Office of Fair Trading v Abbey National Plc* [2009] EWCA Civ 116, [2009] 2 WLR 1286 [70]–[80] (Sir Anthony Clarke).

[49] *Re A (Children) (Conjoined Twins: Surgical Separation)* [2001] Fam 147, 229 (Brooke LJ).

[50] For 'writings of authors' see *R v Bow Street Metropolitan Stipendiary Magistrate and others ex pe Pinochet Ugarte* [2000] AC 147 (HL) 283 (Lord Phillips).

[51] See *Re Supply of Ready Mixed Concrete* [1992] QB 213, 237 (Lord Donaldson MR).

[52] See *Item Software (UK) Ltd v Fassihi* [2004] EWCA Civ 1244 [112] (Holman J).

[53] S Hedley, 'Words, Words, Words: Making Sense of Legal Judgments, 1875–1940' in Chantal Stebbings (ed), *Law Reporting in Britain: Proceedings of the Eleventh British Legal History Conference* (London-Rio Grande, Hambledon, 1995) 182.

[54] As to the effects of the abandonment of the convention, see Braun, 'Burying the Living?' (n 25).

[55] See M de S-O-l'E Lasser, *Judicial Deliberations. A Comparative Analysis of Judicial Transparency and Legitimacy* (Oxford University Press, Oxford, 2004) 46 and 172–73, and K Lemmens, 'But Pasteur was French: Comments on Mitchel Lasser's 'The European Pasteurization of French Law'' in N Huls, M Adams and J Bomhoff (eds), *The Legitimacy of Highest Courts' Rulings. Judicial Deliberations and Beyond* (The Hague, T-M-C Asser Press, 2009) 145, 153.

[56] M Lupoi, 'L'interesse per la giurisprudenza: è tutto oro?' (1999) *Contratto e Impresa* 234.

law.[57] Thus, one gets the feeling that in France and Italy quite often academics and judges compete rather than co-operate. In Germany, however, it would seem that a 'state of equilibrium has been reached which is generally regarded as satisfactory'.[58] In other words, law-making is seen as a joint enterprise to which academics, judges and the legislature contribute. German academics have thus lost the predominant position they held for a long time.

## C A partnership to which both sides contribute

So far, we have said that in England the partnership between judges and academics takes place between individuals who are quite open about their relationship. In other words, both legal actors communicate overtly with each other without feeling the need to pretend that they are not or to downplay the relevance of the other. However, not only is the relationship transparent, but both parties initiate and sustain the dialogue. The attempts of English legal academics to make their voice heard, to find their professional legitimacy and to gain recognition from the practising branch of the profession, have thus encountered an interest on the side of the judiciary to establish a dialogue.[59] The monologue academics have for a long time conducted has hence slowly transformed into a dialogue that, over the past decades, has involved a greater number of judges. Needless to say, not all senior judges take part in this dialogue. Some seem to be very keen on interacting and on rendering the dialogue public, while others are more reluctant to engage in a debate with the academic community. On the whole, however, it can be said that both sides contribute to the partnership.

### i Academics seek a dialogue with the judiciary

That academics are keen on establishing a relationship with the judiciary and on influencing the decision-making process is quite evident from the fact that English academics write not only for students or their fellow academics, but also, to a large extent, for practitioners and judges. Their audience is composed of students and colleagues, as well as members of the bench and bar and civil servants. This is true not only for reference books such as *Chitty on Contract* or *Bowstead on Agency*,[60] but also for articles, and even more so, for case notes which are read

[57] Most of the textbooks, treatises and manuals written for students do not contain references to case law. See, for instance, F Galgano, *Diritto privato* (Padua, Cedam, 2000) and A Torrente and P Schlesinger, *Manuale di diritto privato* (Milan, Giuffrè, 2007).

[58] Vogenauer 'Learning and Lawmaking' (n 7) 653.

[59] For a more detailed analysis of this process, see Braun, *Giudici e Accademia* (n 11) 120–28. See also D Sugarman, 'Legal theory, the common law mind and the making of the textbook tradition' in W Twining (ed), *Legal Theory and Common Law* (Oxford, Blackwell, 1986) 26, 29 ff; W Twining, *Blackstone's Tower. The English Law School* (London, Stevens & Sons/Sweet & Maxwell, 1994).

[60] Many academics contribute to or edit reference works such as *Chitty on Contract*, *Benjamin's Sale of Goods*, *Underhill and Hayton: Law Relating to Trustees*, *Clerk and Lindsell on Torts*, *Megarry and Wade, The Law of Real Property* and *Lewin on Trusts*.

by practitioners and judges alike. Moreover, several legal journals edited by academics, or to which academics contribute to, aim at the professional market. This is true, for instance, for the *Law Quarterly Review*, *Lloyd's Maritime and Commercial Law Quarterly*, *The Conveyancer and Property Lawyer* and the *Criminal Law Review*.[61]

Because English academics, especially in certain areas, intend to address the practising branch of the profession, they take into account the interests and needs of that branch and thus tackle questions that are of practical relevance. This is quite different from the American experience where, already in the early 1990s, Judge Harry T Edwards, a former academic, complained about the growing disjunction between legal education and the legal profession in the US.[62] Edwards accused American academics of not producing a type of scholarship which judges, legislatures and practitioners could use in their daily work. He felt that American scholarship was too theoretical and too interdisciplinary. Although in England there has been a significant increase in scholarly production for the academic market, on the whole legal academics are still engaged in publishing a type of legal literature that can ultimately have an impact on the development of the law. They are very much aware of the needs of the legal practice and, at the same time, also interested in having a direct bearing on the decision-making process.[63] Hence, despite a more theoretical and interdisciplinary kind of legal literature being increasingly available in England, it is still less common than elsewhere, and the 'Law &' movements have overall gained less ground in England than they have in the US.

As far as Germany is concerned, some legal academics only write for the academic market, while others publish both for their colleagues and the practising profession. Next to monographs and law journals that are read foremost by

---

[61] The *Civil Justice Quarterly*, the *Industrial Law Journal* and *Trust Law International* are other examples.

[62] HT Edwards, 'The Growing Disjunction between Legal Education and the Legal Profession' (1992–93) 91 *Michigan Law Review* 34; HT Edwards, 'The Growing Disjunction between Legal Education and the Legal Profession: A Postscript' (1993) 91 *Michigan Law Review* 2191. See also the criticism expressed by RA Posner in 'Present Situation in Legal Scholarship' (1980–81) 90 *Yale Law Journal* 1113 and 'The Decline of Law as an Autonomous Discipline: 1962–87' (1987) 100 *Harvard Law Review* 761.

[63] This seems to be visible in the use of certain case-notes that strategically address questions decided by the High Court or the Court of Appeal before they proceed to the next level of jurisdiction. Neil Duxbury demonstrated how Pollock and Goodhart influenced the judiciary through their case notes: N Duxbury, 'When We Were Young: Notes in the Law Quarterly Review, 1885–1925' (2000) 116 *Law Quarterly Review* 474, 491 ff; N Duxbury *Jurists and Judges. An Essay on Influence* (Oxford, Hart Publishing, 2001) 84 ff; N Duxbury *Frederick Pollock* (Oxford, Oxford University Press, 2004) 316–22. For a recent example of such an influence, see the case notes produced in the aftermath of the decision of the Court of Appeal in *Jones v Commerzbank AG* [2003] EWCA Civ 1663, [2003] All ER (D) 303, such as A Burrows, 'Clouding the Issues on Change of Position' (2004) 63 *Cambridge Law Journal* 276 and P Birks, 'Change of Position: the Two Central Questions' (2004) 120 *Law Quarterly Review* 373. See further *Test Claimants In the Franked Investment Group Litigation v Commissioners of the Inland Revenue & Anor (Rev 1)* [2010] EWCA Civ 103 (23 February 2010) [192], where Professor Elise Bant's case note, published in the LMCLQ, is cited.

academics,[64] there is a certain amount of literature aimed at the legal profession. Numerous commentaries of the various German codes target both academics and practitioners, some almost exclusively the latter.[65] Also many law journals, to which academics contribute, are widely read by practising lawyers.[66] In Italy, too, academics seem to publish not only for fellow academics and students, but also for practitioners. Although monographs and academic articles will be read mostly by their colleagues, Italian legal academics also produce literature that is consulted by the legal profession. For instance, Italian academics not only publish in areas of law of direct interest to the practitioner, they also produce series of manuals and books specifically written for a practitioner audience. Also, since many academics practise law, one could say that they inevitably write for practitioners too. The same could be said for France, where many professors practise law. More than in Italy, however, where case notes are often reminiscent of theoretical treatises, rather than commentaries on the case in question,[67] in France case notes appear to be a valuable source for legal practitioners. Besides containing critical comments, the *notes d'arrêt* serve the function of explaining the otherwise cryptic decisions of higher courts.[68] Case notes aside, another type of literature frequently consulted by French legal practitioners are encyclopaedias written by academics and practitioners, as well as textbooks and treatises. Be that as it may, even in France there is a good amount of literature, such as monographs and articles in certain law reviews, mainly by academics.[69]

Aside from addressing questions of practical relevance, English academics also focus more on case law than on legislation. Despite the significant growth of legislation during the past decades, the major emphasis in academic writing is still placed on cases and less attention is given to the interpretative task of legislative material.[70] Both in England and in the US, very little is in fact written in the form of commentaries on statute law.[71] This is of course different in those legal systems that have codified their law and where legislation plays a prominent role. In Germany, France and Italy, much of the legal literature is centred on

---

[64] Such as, for instance, the *Archiv für die civilistische Praxis* and the *Zeitschrift der Savigny-Stiftung für Rechtsgeschichte*.

[65] Though this does not seem to be the case for all branches of the law: see Vogenauer, 'Learning and Lawmaking' (n 7) 650–51.

[66] Such as the *Neue Juristische Wochenschrift, Der Betrieb*, the *Zeitschrift für das gesamte Familienrecht*, the *Zeitschrift für Wirtschafts- und Bankenrecht* and *Zeitschrift für Wirtschaftsrecht*.

[67] Braun, 'Professors and Judges' (n 4) 679.

[68] As for their importance and impact on the development of the law see Lasser, *Judicial Deliberations* (n 55) and Duxbury, *Jurists and Judges* (n 63) 48 ff.

[69] For a critical analysis of French law reviews in the field of private law see G Wiederkehr, 'La culture des revues françaises de droit privé' in A-J Arnaud (ed), *La Culture des revues juridiques françaises* (Milan, Giuffré, 1988) 9.

[70] With the exception, perhaps, of areas such as human rights, company law and administrative law. Certain law journals, however, include statutory commentaries such as, for instance, the *Modern Law Review* or the *International and Comparative Law Quarterly*.

[71] An exception seems to be represented by company law. See B Hannigan and D Prentice, *The Companies Act 2006. A Commentary* (London, LexisNexis Butterworths, 2007); P Davies (ed) *Gower and Davies: Principles of Modern Company Law,* 8th edn (London, Sweet & Maxwell, 2008).

legislation, although case law is considered an important informal 'source of law'.[72]

Moreover, though perhaps less frequently than in the past, occasionally English academics also dedicate their books to judges,[73] or ask judges to write a foreword for their book.[74] Finally, some English academics publish books in honour of judges.[75] Occasionally this seems to happen also in France[76] and Germany,[77] though usually not in Italy.

That English academics seek to establish a relationship with the judiciary is also shown by the fact that they do appreciate their work being cited in a judgment, especially if given by the Court of Appeal or indeed the Supreme Court.[78] It would appear that the citation by a court was recognised as an 'indicator of esteem' in the last Research Assessment Exercise (RAE).[79] French, German and Italian academics too are probably keen on their work being acknowledged in a judgment. However, in France and Italy judgments do not contain references to academic material. It is only by looking at the *rapport* and the conclusions of the *avocat general*, or the conclusions of the *commissaire du gouvernement* that we know what material the French judiciary was influenced by. As for Italy, courts usually only refer to the 'dottrina dominante', the 'dottrina prevalente' or the

---

[72] It has to be said that only recently the French doctrine has recognised case law as a source of law. See n 55 above.

[73] Sir Frederick Pollock, for instance, dedicated the first edition of his *Principles of Contract* to Lord Lindley and the book *The Law of Torts* to the memory of Sir James Shaw Willes and to Oliver Wendell Holmes. Sir WS Holdsworth dedicated *A History of English Law* to the Right Honourable Frederick Edwin Smith, Earl of Birkenhead.

[74] *Sources and Literature of English Law* by WS Holdsworth has a foreword written by Lord Justice Atkin. For recent examples, see Lord Hoffmann's foreword to the book *Torts and Rights* by Robert Stevens, Lord Rodger's foreword to Eric Descheemaeker's *The Division of Wrongs* and Lord Phillips' foreword to Basil Markesinis' *Comparative Law in the Courtroom and Classroom*.

[75] JL Jowell and JPWB McAuslan (eds), *Lord Denning: The Judge and the Law* (London, Sweet & Maxwell, 1984); M Bos and I Brownlie (eds), *Liber Amicorum for The Rt Hon Lord Wilberforce, PC, CMG, OBE, QC* (Oxford, Clarendon Press, 1987); P Rishworth (ed), *The Struggle for Simplicity in Law: Essays for Lord Cooke of Thorndon* (Wellington, Butterworths, 1997); D O'Keefe and A Bavasso (eds) *Liber Amicorum for Lord Slynn of Hadley: Volume I: Judicial Review in European Union Law* (The Hague, Kluwer Law International, 2000); M Andenas (ed), *Liber Amicorum in Honour of Lord Slynn of Hadley: Volume II: Judicial Review in International Perspective* (The Hague, Kluwer Law International, 2000); W Swadling and G Jones (eds), *The Search for Principle. Essays in Honour of Lord Goff of Chievely* (Oxford, Oxford University Press, 1999); M Andenas and D Fairgrieve (eds), *Tom Bingham and the Transformation of the Law. A Liber Amicorum* (Oxford, Oxford University Press, 2009). See also the volume entitled *Lord Woolf: The Pursuit of Justice* edited by Christopher Campbell-Holt (Oxford, Oxford University Press, 2008).

[76] For example, *La Cour de cassation, l'Université et le Droit. Mélanges en l'honneur de André Ponsard* (Paris, Litec—Editions du Juris Classeur, 2003); *La justice entre deux millénaires. Mélanges offerts à Pierre Dray* (Paris, Dalloz, 2000); *Propos sur les obligations et quelques autres thèmes fondamentaux du droit. Mélanges offerts à Jean-Luc Aubert* (Paris, Dalloz, 2005).

[77] In this sense Vogenauer, 'Learning and Lawmaking' (n 7) 661.

[78] This is pointed out by Duxbury, *Jurists and Judges* (n 63) 61. The most prominent example is perhaps the book written by Sir Basil Markesinis which is entirely dedicated to the citation of legal authors: B Markesinis, *Comparative Law in the Courtroom and Classroom: The Story of the Last Thirty-Five Years* (Oxford, Hart Publishing, 2003).

[79] See Twining, 'The Role of Academics' (n 9) at 928.

'dottrina minoritaria'. Be that as it may, those within the academic and practising circles usually know whom the court was actually referring to.

Not only do English academics write for practitioners and judges, and are keen on having an impact, they also enjoy having a close relation with the bench. For instance, they invite judges to their conferences either as speakers or as chairpersons. The same seems to happen with increasing frequency in Italy, France and Germany, with academics inviting senior judges to their events.[80] Be that as it may, what is perhaps striking in the eyes of a continental lawyer is the fact that, since its foundation, the Society of Public Teachers of Law, as the Society of Legal Scholars was known before 2002, has worked at maintaining a close relationship with bench and bar.[81] Italian[82] or French societies that unite academics do not seem to keep such a close connection to the judiciary.[83] The same seems to be true for Germany. At the meetings of the *Zivilrechtslehrervereinigung*, for instance, you will hardly encounter someone who has not successfully defended his or her *Habilitation*.

## ii Judges seek a dialogue with academics

That judges too are interested in entering into a dialogue with academics is partly revealed by the increasing number of citations of academic literature in their judgments over the course of the past three or four decades. Such references have not only augmented in frequency, but also changed in language, style and content.[84] They illustrate that judges not only resort to academic literature as a work of reference, but as a source of legal reasoning and argument. In other words, and as already seen before, judges increasingly listen to comments and criticisms by academic writers and engage with their views. The citations we find in modern judgments do not appear to be merely window-dressing, and are not, I believe, simply expression of the politeness of the judiciary.[85] Rather, they seem to convey the judge's awareness that academics have interesting things to say and that they can provide great assistance. They also indicate that judges have an interest in confronting themselves with academic opinions.

---

[80] Given that in Italy and in France many academics practice law, one wonders whether this is another incentive for them to maintain a good relationship with the judiciary.

[81] Edward Jenks, who is considered to be the chief Founder of the Society, was also Principal and Director of Legal Studies of the Law Society. Since the very beginning, there was thus a strong link between the SLS and the practising branch. See AD Bowers, 'The Founding of the Society' (1959–60) 5 *Journal of the Society of Public Teachers of Law (New Series)* 1; F Cownie and R Cocks, '*A Great and Noble Occupation!' The History of the Society of Legal Scholars* (Oxford, Hart Publishing, 2009). The same seems to be true for the Association of Law Teachers.

[82] That is, for instance, the case of the *Associazione dei civilisti italiani*.

[83] However, the *Société de Législation Comparée* includes practising lawyers, academics and judges.

[84] For a detailed analysis of the changes in language, style and content see Braun, *Giudici e Accademia* (n 11) 314–51.

[85] In this sense Lord Rodger, 'Mrs Donoghue and Alfenus Varus' (1988) 41 *Current Legal Problems* 1, 16. According to his Lordship, judges are just being 'nice' to academics.

Citations aside, judges participate in the doctrinal debate, through the writing of articles or book reviews in academic journals. To tell the truth, English judges have always engaged in legal writing.[86] In fact, up until the end of the nineteenth century, most of the legal literature was produced by bench and bar. At that time, however, the literature was written primarily for practitioners and judges. Nowadays, judges write in academic journals not only to be read by other judges or practitioners, but also in order to participate in the academic debate.[87]

Among the former members of the House of Lords and the forever and current members of the Supreme Court whose names most frequently appear in law journals are Lord Bingham, Lord Collins, Lord Goff, Baroness Hale, Lord Hoffmann, Lord Hope, Lord Mance, Lord Millett, Lord Nicholls, Lord Rodger, Lord Steyn and Lord Woolf. Among the members of the Court of Appeal who publish legal literature, the names of Arden LJ, Buxton LJ, Etherton LJ, Jacob LJ and Sedley LJ stand out. Some judges write while holding office, others once they have retired. Quite frequently their articles are based on a lecture given at a university or at some other institution, or a paper presented at a conference.[88]

Those academic law journals which more regularly feature contributions by judges, are the *Law Quarterly Review*[89] (with the highest number of judicial contributions), the *Cambridge Law Journal* and *Public Law*. Interestingly, the articles published by judges in academic law journals not only concern topics that are at the heart of the academic debate, but are quite often similar in content and style to those produced by academics. They contain a good number of footnotes and references to cases as well as academic material. It would thus seem that when writing, certain judges emulate the academic style. According to some commentators, this is also visible in the judgments of higher courts, which are not only getting longer and longer, but occasionally also contain footnotes[90] and sometimes even resemble mini-treatises.[91] In Italy too, some judges seem to write

---

[86] Among the judges who wrote books in the 19th century were: Charles Abbott (Lord Tenterden) author of *Law Relating to Merchant Ships and Seaman* (1801); Sir TE Scrutton was author of several important works, among which *Contract of Affreightment as Expressed in Charterparties and Bills of Lading* (1886), *Law of Copyright* (1883) and *Merchant Shipping Act* (1894). EB Sugden (Lord St Leonards) produced *Law of Vendors and Purchasers* (1805) and *Treatise on Powers* (1808); Sir PB Maxwell was the author of *The Interpretation of Statutes* (1875) and Sir Mackenzie Dalzell Chalmers wrote several texts among which the *Bills of Exchange Act*. For a later example see Robert Megarry.

[87] For an example see the recent article by Lord Neuberger, 'The stuffing of Minerva's owl? Taxonomy and taxidermy in equity' (2009) 68 *Cambridge Law Journal* 537.

[88] For instance, the Sir David Williams Lectures, often delivered by distinguished judges, are published in the *Cambridge Law Journal*. For the Blackstone Lectures, see below n 101.

[89] One needs, however, to remember that judges have always published in the *LQR*. Sir Frederick Pollock was proud of the fact that among the contributors to the *LQR* were distinguished judges, such as Sir James Stephens, Lord Bowen, Lord Lindley, Lord Wright, Lord Justice Frey, Lord Justice Kennedy, Lord Justice Scrutton, Lord Macmillan, FE Smith and Lord Nicholls of Birkenhead. See F Pollock, 'Our Jubilee' (1935) 51 *Law Quarterly Review* 5, 8.

[90] R Munday, 'Judicial Footnotes: A Footnote (with Footnotes)' (2006) 170 *Justice of the Peace* 864–70; 'Fish with Feathers: English Judgments with Footnotes' (2006) 170 *Justice of the Peace* 444–48. According to Munday, judges mimic the footnotes of the academic text.

[91] In this sense Lord Rodger, 'The Form and Language of Judicial Opinions' (2002) 118 *Law Quarterly Review* 226; AWB Simpson, 'The Survival of the Common Law System' in *Then and*

their judgments as if they were academics. This is clearly not the case in France, where the style of judgments of the higher courts leaves little room for that.

English judges, however, do not solely write articles. Occasionally they write books[92] or case notes[93] and, more frequently, they also publish reviews of books written by academics. This is particularly true for the *Law Quarterly Review* which features numerous reviews produced by members of the bench,[94] a phenomenon that is rather exceptional in Italy, France and Germany.

The fact that English judges write in academic journals can probably be explained in several ways. Partly, it may be due to the editor of the respective journal, who may be keen on publishing contributions by the judiciary; and partly it may be attributed to the fact that it is not uncommon for practitioners to publish.[95] In other words, some judges might have published even before rising to the bench. However, it is suggested that this phenomenon is also to be ascribed to an increasing level of interest judges have in participating in the academic debate. After all, in the context of an article, judges have a greater freedom in expressing themselves and in addressing those points that parties have not brought to discussion. Through the publication of legal writings, judges have thus the opportunity to contribute to the development of the law outside the courtroom.

That judges write in legal journals is quite common also in Germany, but their papers are mostly aimed at practitioners.[96] Articles aside, German judges also

*Now 1799–1974. Commemorating 175 years of Law Bookselling and Publishing* (London, Sweet & Mawell, 1974) 64: 'All that can be observed at present is a slight tendency to imitation in the judicial opinion, which appears to be rivalling the learned article in its self-conscious erudition'.

[92] Lord Rodger, for instance, has recently published *The Courts, the Church and the Constitution*, while Lord Collins is the general editor of *Dicey and Morris on Conflicts of Laws* as well as the author of several other books on conflict of laws and European law. The same is true for Baroness Hale, who has published a number of books in the area of family law. The late Lord Bingham had recently published a book entitled *The Rule of Law* (London, Allen Lane, 2010) and a selection of his essays and speeches: *The Business of Judging* (Oxford, Oxford University Press, 2000).

[93] See Arden LJ in (2004) 120 *Law Quarterly Review* 7 and Lord Mance in the same volume at page 357. Buxton LJ, now retired, published a case note on '*R (on the application of Purdy) v DPP*: complicity in suicide abroad' in (2010) 126 *Law Quarterly Review* 1.

[94] For instance, the last issue of 2004 of the *Law Quarterly Review* contains a book review by Lord Woolf of Barnes of Andrew Ashworth's *Human Rights, Serious Crime and Criminal Procedure*, while the book *Comparative Law in the Courtroom and Classroom: the Story of the Last Thirty-Five years*, by Basil Markesinis, is reviewed by Beatson J. Lord Steyn is the author of the review of the book *Themes in Comparative Law in Honour of Bernard Rudden* written by P Birks and A Pretto. In 2005 Lord Bingham wrote a book review of *Owen Dixon* published by Philip Ayres, while Dyson LJ wrote a review of *English Public Law* edited by David Feldman. Also, Lord Millett produced a review of *Lives of the Judges: Jessel, Cairns, Bowen and Bramwell* by Edmund Heward and Silber J a review of *Excusing Crime* by Jeremy Horder. In the 2007 volume of the *LQR* Lord Millett wrote a review of *Landmark Cases in the Law of Restitution* by Charles Mitchell and Paul Mitchell. There are many more examples in the *LQR*.

[95] It is not uncommon for distinguished members of the bar to publish in academic journals. See, for instance, Richard Clayton QC, who publishes in the area of human rights; Phil Shiner who writes in the areas of human rights and international law, or Michael Beloff QC who has published in different areas of the law. Other examples are Lord Pannick QC and Geoffrey Robertson QC.

[96] German judges contribute, for instance, to law journals such as the *Betriebs-Berater*, the *Neue Zeitschrift für Arbeitsrecht*, the *Neue Juristische Wochenschrift* and the *Zeitschrift für das gesamte Familienrecht*.

contribute to commentaries such as the *Palandt* and the *Münchener Kommentar*. In France it is not especially common for judges to write in academic journals,[97] with the exception, however, of administrative law and constitutional law.[98] Some members of the *Conseil d'État* have indeed published leading treatises on French public law. In Italy, quite like in England, there seems to be an increasing tendency for judges to publish books[99] as well as articles.[100]

Not only do English judges publish books or articles and reviews in academic journals, but they also attend conferences organised by academics, or give lectures or seminars at universities.[101] In some cases it is a matter of a single lecture or a single seminar, in others it is a matter of an entire series of lectures. Some judges taught at universities right after having completed their degree, and before embarking on a career in legal practice, such as Beatson J and Cranston J, Buxton LJ and Elias LJ, Lord Collins, Lord Goff, Baroness Hale, Lord Hoffmann, Sir Robert Megarry, Lord Rodger and Lord Wright.[102] Others dedicate themselves to teaching once they have retired, such as Lord Hoffmann, who is giving seminars on 'Patents, Trade Marks and Allied Rights', at the University of Oxford. Thus,

---

[97] An exception is, for example, Pierre Sargos, former *Président de la chambre sociale de la Cour de cassation*.

[98] See, for instance, Guy Canivet member of the *Conseil Constitutionnel* and Bernard Stirn, member of the *Conseil d'État*, as well as former members of the *Conseil d'État* such as Macarel, Cormenin, Aucoc, Laferrière, Odent, Braiant and Errera. See J Rivero, 'Jurisprudence et doctrine dans l'élaboration du droit administrative' (1955) *Etudes et Documents, Conseil d'État* 27.

[99] See, eg, the numerous publications by Vincenzo Carbone, President of the *Corte di Cassazione*, by Luigi Rovelli, President of one of the chambers of the *Corte di Cassazione*, as well as by Massimo Scuffi and Massimo Dogliotti, who both serve as Consigliere of the *Corte di Cassazione*. See further the publications by Giacomo Oberto, member of the Court of Appeal of Turin, in the field of family law and Marco Rossetti, judge at the Tribunal in Rome, who has produced publications on the 'danno esistenziale'.

[100] eg, the articles in the law journal *Danno e responsabilità*.

[101] eg, in 2004 Lord Rodger gave the Blackstone Lecture in Oxford and in 2005 it was Lord Hoffmann's turn. Several judges have also delivered the prestigious Hamlyn Lectures or the Neill Lecture at Oxford University. As for the Sir David Williams Lectures in Cambridge, see above n 88. Another example is the yearly Presidential Address to the Holdsworth Club at Birmingham University, delivered by a senior judge.

[102] Lord Hoffmann was Stowell Civil Law Fellow at the University College of Oxford (from 1961 to 1973); Lord Goff was Fellow and Tutor at Lincoln College, Oxford (from 1951 to 1955) while Lord Rodger was a Junior Research Fellow at Balliol and a Fellow and Tutor in Law at New College, Oxford (from 1970 to 1972). Moreover, he taught Roman law in Oxford for 2 years; Lord Collins has been a Fellow of Wolfson College, Cambridge, since 1975.

Among present and former members of the Court of Appeal who have taught for a few years are: Kay LJ who was a Lecturer at the University of Hull from 1967 to 1972, and between 1972 and 1973 at the University of Manchester. He was then nominated Professor of Law at Keele University between 1973 and 1983. Lord Justice Hooper was Assistant Lecturer and Lecturer at the University of Newcastle upon Tyne from 1962–65. He then became Assistant and Associate Professor of the Law Faculty of the University of British Columbia from 1965 to 1968. Between 1969 and 1970 he was Professor Associé of the Université de Laval, and between 1971 and 1973 Professor of the Osgoode Hall Law School at York University; Buxton LJ was first a Lecturer and then a Fellow and Tutor in Law at Christ Church College, Oxford (1962–64 and 1964–73); Elias LJ was a Fellow of Pembroke College, Cambridge, (1973–84) and a Lecturer at the University of Cambridge, (1975–84); Sir Mark Potter was Assistant Supervisor, Legal Studies, at Girton, Gonville and Caius, Queens' and Sidney Sussex Colleges, 1961–68. The information is taken from *Who's Who* 2010.

some judges hold the position of Visiting Professors at English Universities.[103] This too is quite unusual in Italy. Despite judges being educated at universities, they are little involved in university teaching. They may be invited to give a lecture, but that is more the exception than the rule. In France, things are a little different, but that is principally true for administrative law, a field in which judges have always written and taught.[104] In Germany, some judges as well as practitioners teach as *Honorarprofessoren* and may give entire lecture series in their area of expertise. Others might give occasional lectures on specific topics, sometimes together with an academic. At the same time, some academics serve as part-time judges.

What is perhaps more unusual in the eyes of a continental observer is that in England, judges may take part in the selection process of professors to be appointed to prestigious chairs. This is something that would not normally happen in Italy, nor indeed in Germany. In France, it may occasionally happen that a member of the *Cour de Cassation* is part of the jury that appoints a professor. Furthermore, English judges are members of advisory boards of Law faculties[105] and can be involved in the activities of other research Institutions such as the Institute of European and Comparative Law in Oxford[106] or the Institute of Advanced Legal Studies[107] and the British Institute of Comparative law in London.[108] Notably, the British Institute of International and Comparative Law in London has recently established the Bingham Centre for the Rule of Law, which was presided over by Lord Bingham himself.

Moreover, English judges are also involved in the activities of the Society of Legal Scholars. As mentioned earlier, the Society is keen on maintaining a strong connection with the judiciary. Judges do not only attend the events organised by the Society, many are also honorary members and some of them have acted as President.[109] Besides taking part in initiatives promoted by academics, judges also invite academics to their events. For instance, as mentioned above, the Judicial Studies Board involves academics in the training of judges.[110]

---

[103] Baroness Hale is not only Chancellor of the University of Bristol but also Visiting Professor at King's College, London, while Lord Collins is a Visiting Professor at Queen Mary, University of London. And, as mentioned earlier, Lord Hoffmann is a Visiting Professor at the University of Oxford.

[104] In this sense, Bell, *French Legal Cultures* (n 10) 183–84.

[105] eg, the Board of the Law Faculty of the University of Oxford has an Advisory Council of which Lord Rodger is a member.

[106] Among the members of the Advisory Council of the Institute are Cranston J, Lord Hoffmann, Lord Mance, Lord Saville and Silber J.

[107] Lord Hope and Mummery LJ are members of the Advisory Council of the Institute.

[108] Lord Bingham was the President and Chairman of the British Institute of International and Comparative Law. Several Court of Appeal judges serve as members of the Advisory Council of the Institute.

[109] eg, in 1965–66 Robert Megarry acted as President of the Society of Public Teachers of Law, as the Society of Legal Scholars was then known. For a list of the honorary members of the Society, most of whom are judges, see www.legalscholars.ac.uk/about/honorary-members/index.cfm.

[110] Interestingly, the *Cour de Cassation* organises conferences and events for academics and practitioners. In this sense, Bell, *French Legal Cultures* (n 10) 147. The same is true of the Italian *Corte di Cassazione*. It would not seem, however, that the German *Bundesgerichtshof* organises conferences

So, all in all, in England academics and judges do not seem to belong to two distant, disconnected worlds. Although in the past certain judges such as Lord Diplock and Lord Denning did keep a close relationship with the academic world, the number of judges taking part in the dialogue today is visibly higher. In England, therefore, the risk of a growing disjunction between judges and academics, that took place in the US, does not seem to subsist.

### III  STILL NOT A PARTNERSHIP BETWEEN EQUALS

All this leads to an important question. Has the fact that judges are open to a dialogue with legal academics affected their authority in any way? Is their willingness to engage with academic literature a sign of weakness? In my view, the answer is negative. On the contrary, the fact that judges take academic legal writings into account and openly declare that they do is, I believe, an indication that English judges are confident in their role. If judges felt somehow weakened or threatened, they would probably not be that transparent in their dialogue. That does not imply that English judges have a patronising attitude, nor that they are merely polite and nice, but rather that their strength allows them to admit their limits, and to seek the assistance of academics. They know that they can benefit from it and that it is ultimately up to them to decide whether to take the academic argument into account, whether to adopt it and whether to cite it or not. Thus, they initiate the dialogue, conscious of the fact that they are in a powerful position.

At the same time, over the past 30 years or so, academics have gained a stronger position in relation to the other legal actors. Not only are they more numerous, they also have more to offer. They have changed the way they interpret their functions, no longer defining themselves merely as teachers—as was the case during the first half of the twentieth century—but almost foremost as researchers. Academics are also clearly more aware of their influence and the contribution they can have to the development of the law. Studies have appeared which analyse the relevance of citations of academic material in court and which focus on the level of influence academics have on the judiciary.[111] Furthermore, academics have also started to engage more critically with questions concerning their function and their methodology.[112] Be that as it may, while French, German

to which academics are specifically invited.

[111]  Duxbury, *Jurists and Judges* (n 63).

[112]  See, eg, F Cownie, *Legal Academics: Cultures and Identities* (Oxford, Hart Publishing, 2004) and BR Cheffins, 'Using Theory to Study Law: A Company Law Perspective' (1999) *Cambridge Law Journal* 197; idem, 'The Trajectory of (Corporate Law) Scholarship' (2004) *Cambridge Law Journal* 456. See, further, volume 50(6) of 1987 of the *Modern Law Review* 673–54 which is dedicated to issues of legal scholarship in the common law world. Quite interestingly also, at present, there is a taxonomy debate going on in the field of private law: G Samuel, 'English Private Law: Old and New Thinking in the Taxonomy Debate' (2004) 24 *Oxford Journal of Legal Studies* 335. As for the contribution of the late Peter Birks, see A Burrows and A Rodger, *Mapping the Law: Essays in Memory of Peter Birks* (Oxford, Oxford University Press, 2006).

and Italian legal scholars do conceive of themselves as a collective entity that represents a source of law, English legal academics still do not think of themselves in those terms. Thus, although the balance between the legal actors has changed in England, and despite the fact that English academics are in a much stronger position now than they were only 20 or 30 years ago, the relationship is still not a relationship between equals. In contrast to what we find in continental legal systems, academics in England are still in a weaker position and continue to be deferential towards the power of the judiciary.

There are several reasons for this. First, one should not forget that the relationship is to a certain extent mediated by practitioners. If counsel do not refer to academic work or omit to make a correct use of academic material in their skeleton arguments, it will be difficult to truly recognise academia's contribution to the relevant judgment. They bring academic material to the court's attention, although, as many of the cases cited above show, judges clearly do their own reading and research.[113] Furthermore, contrary to France or Italy, in England the law syllabus of universities is heavily influenced by the needs of the legal profession. It is the practising branch that establishes which law degrees receive recognition and which do not. As for Germany, the State examinations are basically organised by courts and examiners are usually judges, legal practitioners, notaries and civil servants. Second, unlike in Italy, France and Germany, an English university degree in law is still not a prerequisite in order to access the legal profession and become a judge.[114] On the continent it is necessary to have a university law degree in order to become a member of the practising profession, and judges are usually appointed straight after the end of their legal education.

To some degree, English academics therefore still do not have the opportunity to play all their cards and to explore their full potential in shaping the development of the law, especially considering that academics who are appointed as judges are still relatively few in number. When in July 2003 the House of Lords was presented with a Consultation Paper concerning constitutional reforms, and in particular, the Supreme Court, the Lords of Appeal in Ordinary were asked to consider the opportunity to facilitate the access of distinguished academics to the judiciary. The following was the response given by the Law Lords:

> Since we are of the firm opinion that merit should be the overriding criterion of appointment at all levels of the judiciary, we could not support any rule which precluded consideration of any candidate who was or might be worthy of appointment on grounds of merit. Our collective experience in the 3 UK jurisdictions does not, however, yield any example of a candidate who was considered deserving, or

---

[113] See n 27.

[114] 11 out of the 12 members of the Supreme Court have a law degree from a UK university (mostly Cambridge or Oxford). According to the Annual Statistical Report 2009 of the Law Society, in 2008–09 approximately 20% of those who enrolled did not have a law degree.

The report is available at www.lawsociety.org.uk/secure/file/183555/e:/teamsite-deployed/documents/templatedata/Publications/Research%20Publications/Documents/asr2009report.pdf.

possibly deserving, of appointment on grounds of merit and who was debarred from consideration for want of the requisite qualification. In practice, a number of legal practitioners have held academic appointments before turning to practice or accepting judicial appointment; and a number of academic lawyers with judicial ambitions recognise the value of familiarising themselves with the practice of the law and the conduct of trials to supplement their store of academic learning. We would ourselves regard a measure of experience (whether in practice or on the bench or both) as an all but essential qualification of trial judges, and while, on occasion, appeals may raise fairly abstract questions of law, this is not in our experience the norm, and we see special dangers in decisions made on appeal by judges who have never experienced the exacting reality of conducting a difficult case or presiding at a difficult trial.[115]

The judges did not therefore want to provide academics with a 'reserved lane'. According to the Law Lords, the selection process is to be based on merit and it is important to nominate people who have experience in practising the law. The current situation might however change, with the replacement of the system of secret soundings by one operated, independently of the executive, by a Judicial Appointments Commission.[116] Also, given that more and more academics seem to practise law, they have the practical experience that makes them eligible for appointment as judges.[117] In view of the creation of the new Supreme Court, for instance, some commentators suggested to widen the appointment pool so as to achieve a greater diversity by appointing senior legal academics.[118] After all, at least as far as constitutional courts are concerned, in several other legal systems, distinguished academics are appointed as judges.[119] Whether that will actually happen is uncertain. Also, those who act as judicial assistants to the members of the English Court of Appeal or the Supreme Court are not necessarily chosen, as they are in the US, from among the very best law graduates of English universities.[120]

---

[115] See www.parliament.uk/documents/upload/JudicialSCR071103.pdf. Members of the House of Lords were Lords Nicholls of Birkenhead, Hoffmann, Hope of Craighead, Hutton, Millett, Rodger of Earlsferry, Bingham of Cornhill, Steyn, Saville of Newdigate and Walker of Gestingthorpe.

[116] As created by ss 61 and 62, and schs 12 and 13, of the Constitutional Reform Act 2005. See the speech the Master of the Rolls, Lord Clarke of Stone-cum-Ebony gave on 22 September 2009, entitled 'Selecting Judges: Merit, Moral Courage, Judgment and Diversity'. His Lordship encourages barristers, solicitors, legal executives as well as academics to apply where they meet the statutory qualifications. See, in particular, page 23 of the speech.

[117] Academics have also been encouraged to apply for a judicial position by the 'Reporter', the Newsletter of the SLS, Spring 2009, at page 7.

[118] A Le Sueur and R Cornes, *The Future of the United Kingdom's Highest Courts*, 2001, 115. See also T Legg, 'Judges for the New Century' [2001] *Public Law* 62, 68. In an article published in the *Cambridge Law Journal*, Sir Sydney Kentridge QC said that: 'I must make it clear that I am certainly not against the appointment of academics to the bench. But I believe that they should come to judicial office by the same route as practising barristers or solicitors. Some academics have become recorders and in appropriate cases sit as deputy High Court judges. I hope and expect that some of these appointments will lead to a full-time judicial career, with every prospect of promotion on merit to higher courts.' (2003) 62 *Cambridge Law Journal* 55, 62–63.

[119] That is the case in France, Germany and Italy. Apparently, one of the arguments against the appointment of academics in England is the fear that they use their position in order to further their agendas regardless of the merits of cases. In this sense Le Sueur and Cornes *The Future* (n 118) 115.

[120] On the other hand, for now, the judicial assistants' roles are not as far-reaching as those of a Law Clerk in the US. See R Munday, 'Of Law Clerks and Judicial Assistants' (2007) 171 *Justice of the Peace* 455.

This means that, unlike in the US, in England the judiciary is not necessarily assisted by students trained in academic research, although they have to be qualified as solicitors or barristers.

Finally, it must be mentioned that the social prestige and status of legal academics in England is not the same as in other countries. In England, judges as well as members of the practising profession still have a social reputation that is not equalled by academics. This might partly explain why the payment legal scholars receive is not usually comparable to that of the legal profession,[121] nor the judiciary. Interestingly, in August 2008 *The Times* published a list of UK's most powerful and influential lawyers, at the top of which was Lord Bingham. Among the first 10 lawyers were four judges but no academic. Among the remaining 90 there were four (either full or part-time) academics. On 23 July 2009, *The Times* published a new list. This time there were five academics listed among the 100 most influential and powerful lawyers. Although it is true that such rankings should be viewed with caution, they do reveal who are commonly perceived as the most powerful lawyers in the country.

## III  CONCLUSIONS

To conclude, as Professor Birks said in his Mann Lecture, in England academics take part in the law-making process. As a matter of fact, academics are nowadays commonly acknowledged to have a certain degree of influence on judges[122] and the image of the English common law as a merely judge-made law is therefore progressively regarded as incomplete.[123] All in all, the role of legal scholarship and its impact on the judiciary can no longer be seen as a major factor that differentiates England from civil law countries or certain other common law jurisdictions.[124]

However, while in France and Italy, the dominant partner is the academic community, in England it is still the judge. Despite the fact that the citation practice of the French higher courts does not allow for citations of academic literature, judges are strongly influenced by the *doctrine*, which sets the tone. In Italy, too, academics are the stronger partner in the relationship. Not only have Italian academics a greater prestige than their judicial counterparts, they

---

[121] See, however, 'Gold standard reassessed', *Times Higher Education* (London, 15 May 2008): 'In the past decade, a seemingly inexorable decline in higher education funding that began in the late 1970s has been halted and arguably reversed. The salaries of academics are at last regaining the ground they lost to private-sector equivalents.' See also J Walker, A Vignoles, and M Collins, 'Higher education academic salaries in the UK' (2009) *Oxford Economic Papers Advance Access* (26 March 2009) 1–24.

[122] Duxbury, *Jurists and Judges* (n 63) and Braun, *Giudici e Accademia* (n 11).

[123] Birks, 'The Academic' (n 2) 399; T Weir (tr), K Zweigert and H Kötz, *An Introduction to Comparative Law*, 3rd edn (Oxford, Oxford University Press, 1998) 270.

[124] R Zimmermann, 'Der europäische Charakter des englischen Rechts. Historische Verbindungen zwischen civil law und common law' (1993) *Zeitschrift für Europäisches Privatrecht* 4, 7 ff; M Reimann, 'Die Erosion der klassischen Formen – Rechtskulturelle Wandlungen des Civil Law und Common Law im Europa des 19. und 20. Jahrhunderts' (2006) 28 *Zeitschrift für Neuere Rechtsgeschichte* 209, 221.

also dominate the scholarly debate. In Germany, however, the relationship seems to take place between equals.[125] Although traditionally legal scholars were predominant, in recent years the prestige of the judiciary has increased.[126]

Relationships are, of course, not static and change according to internal and external circumstances. One therefore wonders how things will develop in the future. Might the partnership between the two legal actors change? The number of legal academics in England has clearly increased over the years, and might grow still further. This might enhance their strength as a group and improve their confidence. One can already observe that the English academic community has acquired a new awareness of its functions and of the role it wants to play within the law-making process.[127] In this sense it is significant that last year's SLS's 2008 conference was entitled 'The Impact of Legal Scholarship'. Whether this means that English academics will start to think of themselves a collective entity in the same way that their French, German or Italian counterparts do, remains to be seen. After all, French academics only started to perceive themselves as an *ensemble* when they became aware of the influence and impact they had and when they wanted to impose themselves as a source of law.[128]

No doubt, the increase in the number of legal academics has an impact on the amount of literature produced. And one wonders whether the proliferation of law journals that has taken place since the 1990s, as well as of textbooks and monographs, will ultimately have an impact on the dialogue.[129] As mentioned earlier, judges have started dedicating entire sections to the analysis of the academic debate on a particular point and occasional references are made to the weight of academic authority.[130] Such sections might become more frequent and perhaps longer. In the future, this could affect the style of the judgment as well as its length. Also, it may well be the case that references will be made more frequently to the academic debate rather than to single pieces of literature.

At the same time, the new tendency, of the Civil Division of the Court of Appeal, to write composite judgments might also affect the dialogue.[131] Not only might it transform from a dialogue between individuals into a dialogue between the court (and not the single judge) and the single academic (or even the group as such), its transparency might be affected too.[132] We may no longer be able to

---

[125] See Vogenauer, 'Learning and Lawmaking' (n 7) 650–51.

[126] ibid 661–62.

[127] Cownie and Cocks, *A Great and Noble Occupation!* (n 81); W Twining, 'The SLS Centenary Lecture: Punching our weight? Legal scholarship and public understanding' (2009) 29 *Legal Studies* 519, 523.

[128] See Jestaz and Jamin, *La doctrine* (n 6).

[129] For an analysis of the development of legal journals in England see Braun, *Giudici e Accademia* (n 11) 187–95.

[130] See text to n 13.

[131] As mentioned earlier, the Criminal Division is required by statue to give a single judgment.

[132] R Munday, 'All for One, and One for All: The Rise to Prominence of the Composite Judgment in the Civil Division of the Court of Appeal' (2002) 61 *Cambridge Law Journal* 321; ibid, 'Judicial Configurations: Permutations of the Court and Properties of Judgment' (2002) 61 *Cambridge Law Journal* 612; ibid, 'Reasoning without Dissent; Dissenting without Reason' (2004) 168 *Justice of the Peace* 968, 991. Roderick Munday highlighted that in 2004 almost one in three judgments of the Court

ascertain which judge read the academic literature and found it convincing, as it is the case in France and Italy. Whether this practice will also affect judgments of the new Supreme Court is still unclear. However, if one looks at the judgments the court has pronounced since October 2009, a move away from seriatim judgments seems to be taking place, though, as yet, there is no consistent style to be detected.[133]

Be that as it may, the development of the relationship might also be influenced by other factors. Indeed, if more academics were to be elected to the bench and if law degrees were to become compulsory, the impact academics have on shaping the minds of practitioners and future judges, and ultimately on the development of the common law, could increase further.

of Appeal were authored in composite format. See also J Lee, 'A Defence of Concurring Speeches' [2009] *Public Law* 305. On composite judgments see also Lord Mance, 'The Common Law and Europe: Differences of Style or Substance and do they matter?', Holdsworth Club Presidential Address of 24 November 2006, page 7, and Arden LJ, 'The Form of Judgments in Common Law Jurisdictions: A Comparison' at www.judiciary.gov.uk/docs/speeches/amatter_of_style_bingham_conference.pdf.

[133] See, eg, *R v B* [2009] UKSC 12; *R v Horncastle* [2009] UKSC 14; *S-B (Children)* [2009] UKSC 17; *Re GB v RJB and GLB (In Re B (A Child))* [2009] UKSC 5; *Her Majesty's Treasury v Mohammed al-Ghabra (FC)* [2010] UKSC 1; *Re W (Children)* [2010] UKSC 12; *Agbaje v Akinnoye-Agbaje (FC)* [2010] UKSC 13; *British Airways plc v Ms Sally Williams* [2010] UKSC 16; *Office of Communications v The Information Commissioner* [2010] UKSC 3; *Norris v Government of the United States of America* [2010] UKSC 9.

# 12

# *Does Advocacy Matter in the Lords?*

## ALAN PATERSON

### I INTRODUCTION

D OES ADVOCACY MATTER in the final court of appeal? This
beguilingly naive question is a subset of a less discussed topic, namely,
the significance of the dialogue between counsel and Law Lords in
understanding judicial decision-making in the final court of appeal in the UK.
A whole career and almost 40 years ago,[1] I argued that the key to understanding
judicial decision-making in the House of Lords was the recognition that the Law
Lords' decisions were the product of a complex of social interactions, namely,
a series of dialogues between Law Lords and counsel, other courts, academics,
Parliament, the Executive as well as amongst the Law Lords themselves. The
dialogues were, and are, not all alike. Some were oral, some written, some
symbolic, some in real time, others historic. While some were sequential, others
went in parallel. Nor were the dialogues equally important for the outcome of
the cases. Some were always more significant than others, whilst others would
be particularly telling in some cases but not in others. Advocacy in the Lords
involved two of these dialogues—that between counsel and Law Lords (and vice
versa) and that between the Law Lords themselves. This chapter will focus on
the former dialogue,[2] and examine how it has changed over the last 40 years, but
scholars of the court neglect at their peril the significance of judicial advocacy by
Law Lords.

---

[1] A Paterson, *The Law Lords* (London, Macmillan, 1982).

[2] The original research conducted in the 1970s involved 15 interviews with current or former Law
Lords and 46 interviews with the counsel who had appeared in the leading cases in the 15 years prior
to the interviews. In 2008 and 2009, with the generous assistance of the Nuffield Foundation, which I
gratefully acknowledge, I conducted interviews with 22 current or former Law Lords or Justices, six
members of the Court of Appeal, nine leading counsel, six judicial assistants and two Principal Clerks
of the Judicial Office. I am most grateful to these individuals, without whom this research would not
have been possible.

## II  THE NATURE OF THE DIALOGUE
### BETWEEN COUNSEL AND LAW LORDS

A number of metaphors have been coined to describe the unique character of the exchanges which took place between counsel and Law Lords in the Appeal Committees[3] and Appellate Committees of the House of Lords,[4] ranging from 'an academic seminar'[5] or 'Oxbridge tutorial',[6] to 'an informed dialogue',[7] and 'a dialectic between Bench and Bar'[8] which resembles nothing so much as a 'conversation between gentlemen on a subject of mutual interest'.[9]

In truth, while these descriptions were certainly true of the court in the Bingham era, and remain so of the Supreme Court of today, in the 1930s, 1940s and the 1980s, there were times where the exchanges in the oral hearings were rather more robust than these adjectives might suggest. Lord Pannick QC[10] hinted as much in his valedictory column on the House in *The Times*[11] when he referred to its unique atmosphere as a mixture of academic seminar, comfortable club and all-in wrestling match.[12]

Lord Reid dominated the House 35 years ago because of his forensic skills, his length of service as a Law Lord and his ability to give a lead to his colleagues.[13] Lord Reid was in his element in the hearings, his interventions were legendary—courteous but devastating, for there was no malice in them, becoming part of the

---

[3] Oral hearings in Appeal Committees dealing primarily with petitions for leave to appeal grew progressively less common in the final years of the judicial House of Lords.

[4] The atmosphere was in part a product of the physical geography of the Committee Rooms in the Lords where the hearings took place, with its semicircular table(s) for the Law Lords and a large central lectern for counsel towering over the seated Law Lords, who wore no wigs and gowns but only lounge suits.

[5] Coined by a senior Law Lord.

[6] B Markesinis, 'Five Days in the House of Lords' (1995) 3 *Torts Law Journal* 169.

[7] Senior counsel Michael Beloff QC told me: 'I do regard the Lords as having a much more conversational and relaxed atmosphere than other courts . . . it is very much a dialogue exercise . . . Sometimes they allow you to go for a little while, but when that happens you begin to wonder a little bit if something's gone wrong.'

[8] A Law Lord.

[9] David Pannick QC in *The Times* (1 October 2009) observed that in the new building, counsel sit 'close enough to conduct a conversation designed to identify the right answers, or at least the best available answers, to difficult problems.'

[10] A veteran of 100 appearances in the House of Lords—the last of which was the final (and unscheduled) hearing in the Lords of a leave petition in the *JFS* case which took place on Friday 31 July, the day after the official end to judicial hearings in the court .

[11] *The Times* (London, 30 July 2009).

[12] The US Supreme Court in the last half-century, by contrast with the Bingham court, perhaps because of the severely curtailed periods of oral argument permitted there, has been described as 'designed as the Agincourt of the mind': L Baker, *Brandeis and Frankfurter, A Dual Biography* (New York, Harper & Row, 1984) 132.

[13] Paterson, *The Law Lords* (n 1) 72. As Lord Wilberforce in a tribute at his death observed: '[H]e has guided us with the influence of an equal in status, of a superior in wisdom, common sense, and where appropriate, imagination.' TB Smith, 'Reid, James Scott Cumberland, Baron Reid (1890–1975)' *Oxford Dictionary of National Biography*, (Oxford, Oxford University Press, 2004).

enduring folklore at the Bar.[14] The practically unlimited scope for oral arguments at that time (cases lasted three to four days on average, but could last for weeks)[15] entailed that the Law Lords in Reid's era relied far more on oral arguments than on counsel's submissions in the printed Case.[16] At that time, some Law Lords, including such heavyweights as Lords Denning, Radcliffe, Reid and Devlin, did not even read the printed Case, or if they did so, only skimmed it casually in advance of the oral argument. As Lord Devlin put it, 'I never used to read the printed Case. I would have done if I hadn't known it was going to be said all over again in oral argument.' Those Law Lords who did read in advance were regarded as something of a mixed blessing by their colleagues. Lord MacDermott, for example, told me that he had 'known some who've read their written material closely beforehand who have tended to push others into a line of thought too early.'

The point was made repeatedly to me in my original interviews that the advantage of a predominantly oral approach lay in the flexibility it gave to the arguments. Counsel were expected to respond to the thoughts expressed by the Court and to adjust their arguments accordingly. Frequently, a case would change course in mid-stream as a result of a point thrown up in the debate. At any rate, the Law Lords and counsel interviewed in the 1970s were strongly in favour of retaining the predominantly oral approach of the Lords—some even complained that counsel were putting too much effort into printed Cases.[17]

Curiously, within 10 years much had been transformed through the aegis of one man, Lord Diplock. As Lord Wilberforce wryly observed after Diplock's death:

> I think that as a general point you cannot really estimate a judge's influence without knowing from behind the scenes what influence he had on his colleagues . . . Lord Diplock possessed the quality of persuading his colleagues to the extreme . . . it almost got to the stage of a mesmeric quality . . . Lord Diplock was a very persuasive man. He was a man who got his way in almost everything.[18]

Counsel found Diplock even more problematic than his colleagues. It was not unusual for him to have made his mind up before the appeal began, and indeed it is alleged that he sometimes even wrote the judgment before the appeal began. The truth is that in the Appellate Committee, Diplock was a bully 'who really didn't have much time for advocacy', particularly if he thought it was off the point. His 'consciousness of his own ability made him dismissive of ideas at which his own fast brain had not arrived first' and he would 'mine the advocate's

---

[14] Lord Rodger, 'The form and language of judicial opinions' (2002) 118 *LQR* 226, 242.

[15] Between 1952 and 1968 25% of English appeals to the Lords lasted more than five days and 10% of them took seven days or more: L Blom Cooper and G Drewry, *Final Appeal* (Oxford, Clarendon Press, 1972) 235. As late as 1989 in the Tin Council case, *JH Rayner Ltd v Department of Trade and Industry & Ors* [1990] 2 AC 418, the oral argument lasted for 26 days.

[16] In contrast to the US Supreme Court who relied predominantly on the written briefs because of the 30-minute limit on oral hearings there.

[17] Paterson, *The Law Lords* (n 1) 38.

[18] In G Sturgess and P Chubb, *Judging the World* (Sydney, Butterworths, 1988) 275.

path with Socratic questions the answers to which would in due course, as he knew, destroy the case.'[19] Once,[20] he announced to counsel at the outset of the appeal that there was no point in argument since the House had only given leave to sort out the poor reasoning in the Court of Appeal's judgments, but the result of the case was not going to change. Counsel were effectively told to have a polite discussion, but not to argue the case. As Lord Hope told me:

> [When] Lord Diplock [presided] . . . the attitude was a good deal more brisk then. He didn't allow arguments to develop that he thought had nothing in them and he would sit on you at the very start of an appeal and really cut you short. It was very difficult to get through and his colleagues on the whole did seem to be pretty compliant and didn't really feel that they could speak up if he was saying there wasn't anything in the case, and then you found he wrote the judgment.

Lord Diplock, unlike the heavyweights of Reid's era, believed in reading the printed Case, and having read the Case he saw no reason why counsel should be allowed to say it all again in the oral hearing, just to suit his 'less industrious' colleagues, even if they were only seeking to avoid making their minds up too early. In consequence, when Diplock was in the chair, the length of the oral arguments came down. So too did the length of the printed Cases, following a stiffly worded injunction from Lord Diplock on behalf of the House in 1982 on the matter.[21]

After Lord Diplock, the Lords reverted to type with Lord Fraser in the chair. He was so courteous that he allowed oral argument to go for nine days over the meaning of two words in a statute, namely, 'ordinarily resident'.[22] Yet, Fraser's contemporaries Lords Brandon and Templeman (the latter being generally known to counsel under the soubriquet of Sid Vicious)[23] had nothing to learn from Diplock in terms of aggressive behaviour on the Bench. Generally when they sat together they would constantly snipe at one another, a blessed relief to counsel who when assailed by Brandon could be sure that Templeman would weigh in on his side, and vice versa. If either were rebuffed they would sulk. Lord Templeman raised a point in one oral argument that hadn't been argued in the court below and counsel said he'd like time to look at the authorities. When Lord Templeman observed that new authorities had to be lodged well in advance of the hearing, counsel retorted quite fairly that it was a new point so he didn't have the authorities to hand. Eventually counsel asked the presiding Law Lord if he might bring the authorities the following day. When this request was granted Lord Templeman put the cap on his pen and folded his arms in disgusted petulance. As a presider he was not much better. In one case the appellant had

---

[19] S Sedley and G Le Quesne, 'Diplock, (William John) Kenneth, Baron Diplock (1907–1985)' *Oxford Dictionary of National Biography*, (Oxford, Oxford University Press, 2006).
[20] *Antaios Compania Naviera SA v Salen Rederierna AB (The Antaios)* [1985] AC 191.
[21] See *MV Yorke Motors v Edwards* [1982] 1 All ER 1024, 1025j.
[22] *R v Barnet LBC ex p Shah* [1983] 2 AC 309.
[23] See M Beloff QC, 'The End of the Twentieth Century' in L Blom Cooper, B Dickson and G Drewry, *The Judicial House of Lords 1876-2009* (Oxford, Oxford University Press, 2009).

not been on his feet two minutes when Templeman handed both counsel a typed note from the Law Lords indicating that they saw no merit in the respondent's argument and did the appellant want to add anything.

If the reputation of the House at that time was not already damaged by the behaviour of some of its judicial members, it probably was by the debacle of the *Lonrho* contempt hearing.[24] Nor was the sight of the House shortly thereafter spending 26 days of argument on the Tin Council case[25] guaranteed to restore its reputation. After that case the Judicial Office began to ask for clearer estimates from counsel as to the possible duration of appeals.

As the 1990s wore on and Lord Browne-Wilkinson took over the chair, the atmosphere began to change and the oral hearings grew more relaxed again. Occasionally, even humour would creep in, something Lord Diplock would not have tolerated. Unfortunately, tensions returned in the aftermath of the *Pinochet* affair. It took the appointment of Lord Bingham to finally establish the conversational style of the Lords of 2009. A grateful counsel commented:

> The atmosphere that Lord Bingham has imposed through sheer force of personality rather than by actually saying anything is an atmosphere in which you have a very informed dialogue with the bench without there being any of the sort of the acrimony that one used to have.

Lord Bingham was a strong believer in the value of oral advocacy, but unlike Lord Diplock would never let his impatience with poor advocacy show in the courtroom. However, in one respect Lord Bingham did go along with Lord Diplock, namely in seeking to keep the work of the court moving on. It was during his time that counsel's estimates as to the amount of time they would need, came under real scrutiny and if the parties wanted more than two days of the House, a good case had to be made out. With time limits for hearings in place, Bingham took on the role of ensuring that counsel for either side did not overrun, causing problems either for the House or for their opponent. Lord Bingham had a way of saying 'Y–e–s', which would quicken if counsel failed to take the hint.

### III HOW HAS THE DIALOGUE BETWEEN COUNSEL AND LAW LORDS CHANGED?

In *The Law Lords*,[26] I concluded that counsel did not form a significant reference group for Law Lords but that nonetheless that they did have an influence (which was considerably greater than had been commonly recognised at the time) on the Law Lords' decisions, because of the dialogue which takes place between counsel and Law Lord in actual cases. This involved more than advocacy in its traditional

---

[24] *Re Lonrho Plc (Contempt Proceedings)* [1990] 2 AC 154. In all, the proceedings accounted for 13 judicial sitting days and costs in excess of £1,000,000, without much by tangible result except embarrassment for the Law Lords.

[25] *JH Rayner Ltd v Department of Trade and Industry & Ors* [1990] 2 AC 418.

[26] Paterson, *The Law Lords* (n 1) 31.

senses, to which we will return, but also the constraints that counsel could impose on the court's decision-making. These constraints included: counsel's influence on the selection and timing of appeals going to the Lords, their ability to constrain the points of law for decision by the court through concessions or simply a refusal to run certain arguments,[27] the shared understanding between Bench and Bar that the points of law which determine an appeal must be raised by, or at least put to, counsel and the understanding that counsel could not run points of law in the Lords which they had not run in a lower court.[28] It is clear from my interviews over the last two years that each of these constraints has lost some of its potency. In the last 30 years the caseload of the Lords has completely transformed.[29] First, in the type of cases which now predominate: tax, shipping and private law cases have declined, whilst public law and human rights cases have dramatically increased. Although in theory counsel and clients with a series of potential cases in the former categories might many years ago have sought to influence the order in which those cases came to the Lords,[30] the new areas do not lend themselves to even that unlikely scenario. Only the Crown has a sufficient number of HRA cases, and is often an intervener rather than a direct party.[31] Secondly, the House has gained far greater control of its caseload than it did 30 years ago. Now, 83 per cent of its cases come by leave of the House; then, it was 17 per cent.[32]

In the 1960s the position seems to have been reached that most Law Lords and counsel believed that decisions in appeals should only be reached on points of law that had been argued by counsel, whether originally raised by them or by the Law Lords.[33] Twenty years later whilst counsel remained strong in their belief that this should be the position, the Law Lords were less unanimous.[34] Nevertheless, there was a range of cases where the Law Lords expressed their regret or annoyance at being unable to deal with a point because of an earlier concession by counsel or a straight refusal by counsel to run an argument, for instance that a previous decision was wrongly decided. In this way counsel of

[27] Of course, the Law Lords have always possessed, and exercised, a considerable capacity to decline to hear argument from counsel.

[28] See Paterson, *The Law Lords* (n 1) ch 3.

[29] See S Shah and T Poole, 'The Impact of the Human Rights Act on the House of Lords' [2009] *Public Law* 347.

[30] This could have occurred in the *Three Rivers* litigation during the first decade of the 21st century, but there is nothing to indicate that it actually did.

[31] David Pannick told me: 'There may . . . be some tactical consideration by counsel as to which is the appropriate case to go to the Lords. Those decisions are then affected by non-scientific factors, for example, the personality issue that everybody wants their own case to go to the Lords. In any event the courts may not co-operate with any wish that you may have, other cases may be listed first, leave to appeal may be granted before your case can be considered. So it's very difficult to manipulate the system in that sense.'

[32] B Dickson, 'The processing of appeals in the House of Lords' (2007) 123 *Law Quarterly Review* 571, 572.

[33] See Paterson, *The Law Lords* (n 1) ch 3.

[34] With Lords Cross, Edmund-Davies, Gardiner, Guest and Pearson supporting it and Lords Diplock, Hailsham, Kilbrandon, Simon and Wilberforce more ambivalent on the point.

30 years ago could impose limitations on the creative decision-making by the House. Today, the expectation is subtly altered. Whilst the great majority of counsel and Law Lords believe that the Law Lords should not decide cases on points of law that have not been raised by, or at least put to, counsel, it is also clear that the Law Lords of today believe that it is sufficient for them to give counsel the opportunity to comment[35] on cases or points of law raised by the Law Lords following their own researches—or those of their judicial assistants—or subsequent decisions of the ECHR, which emerge after the hearing but before the judgments are delivered.[36] Should counsel choose for whatever reason not to take up the invitation, it was clear to me that many if not most of the Law Lords in the last decade or so would have been prepared to determine the appeal on the new point irrespective of the absence of argument by counsel, even if it included departing from one of their own precedents.[37]

Thirdly, as Blom-Cooper and Drewry argued in *Final Appeal*: 'It is an unwritten, but firm rule of the House not to consider arguments which have not been considered by the courts below. In only twelve cases [between 1952 and 1968] was this rule expressly waived.'[38]

Although this understanding appears more like a constraint on counsel's arguments (which it is), it is also a method by which counsel through concessions or through the arguments which they ran in the lower courts[39] can constrain the ground for decision in the final appeal court. However, even by the late 1970s Law Lords were indicating that the expectation was not a compelling argument. As Lord Cross put it:

> It is completely a matter of discretion . . . it rather depends on how good . . . [the Law Lords think . . . [the point is]. If they think there is not much in the point anyway, they probably say 'Oh, we couldn't listen to that it was not mentioned in the Case.' But if they think it is something that really goes to the root of the thing, if they think the whole thing would be rather a mess if they did not allow it to be argued, then they would probably allow it on terms as to costs.[40]

[35] Usually in writing, as in *Doherty (FC) (Appellant) and others v Birmingham City Council (Respondents)* [2008] UKHL 57, [2008] 3 WLR 636. Very occasionally, there will be a reconvened hearing, as in *Pepper v Hart* [1993] AC 593 and *Sempra Metals Ltd (formerly Metallgesellschaft Ltd) v Her Majesty's Commissioners of Inland Revenue and another* [2007] UKHL 34, [2008] 1 AC 561.

[36] As in the *Doherty* case, when *McCann v UK* [2008] LGR 474 was published after the oral argument in *Doherty* had been completed, but judgments had not been handed down.

[37] For a recent instance where the US Supreme Court did just this in a re-hearing at their own request to reconsider one of their own precedents, see *Citizens United v Federal Election Commission* (08-205).

[38] Blom-Cooper and Drewry (n 15) 247.

[39] David Pannick told me: 'I think if you're appearing for the Secretary of State or for some other public body your client and therefore you may have an interest in doing more than winning the case. You're concerned about the way in which the case is decided because of its implications for the future, indeed you may know albeit that it's not explored in argument that to have the case decided in a particular way may be very damaging to the interests of that Department of State for reasons that may simply be not known to the Law Lords or indeed not known to your opponent and therefore you may well have that in mind, you may therefore be seeking to nudge the Law Lords in a particular direction.'

[40] See also Lord Reid in *Kaye v Hosier and Dickinson* [1972] 1 All ER 121, 124.

Certainly I was left in little doubt from my recent interviews that today's Law Lords regard the issue in exactly the same pragmatic way as Lord Cross.

If counsel's ability to constrain decision-making in the final appeal court has declined in the last 40 years, what, if anything has happened to more traditional forms of advocacy? Here there have been major changes. Following the introduction of time constraints to oral advocacy the average length of oral hearings has dropped to two days or below, from an average of three to four days 40 years ago.[41] Despite the efforts of Lord Diplock, the size of the printed Cases and skeleton arguments has probably increased by a greater margin in the same period. Finally, in a small way, some of the Law Lords have begun to use their judicial assistants as sounding boards where previously they would have relied on counsel's arguments.

These changes in the forms of advocacy have in turn had a further consequence. In Lord Reid's era where the bench was cold or lukewarm at best the appellant was thought to have a significant advantage in the opportunity to set the legal and factual framework for the appeal. Anyone who has read the judgments of Lord Denning or Lord Atkin will know the importance of the way the facts are presented. As Lord Atkin's daughter recalled:[42]

> When he gave us the facts of a case and asked us what we thought about it, his way of presenting the problem was such that there was never any suggestion in our minds that the other side would have a leg to stand on.

Hardly surprising, then, that almost every counsel that I interviewed first time around considered that the appellant had an advantage from speaking first.[43] The Law Lords were evenly divided between those who thought it was an advantage, those who thought it was not, and those who said it depended on the case. Interestingly, the minority who paid more attention to the written materials were the ones who considered it was an advantage to speak first, almost as though they had developed a practice of reading the Case to neutralise the advantage they perceived the appellant to gain from going first.[44] Now, all of the Law Lords read the Cases and skeleton arguments in advance, with some discussing the appeals in advance with their judicial assistants. The resulting 'hot bench' means that nowadays few counsel or Law Lords consider that it is an advantage to be the appellant, and those that do, attribute this to the fact that the appellant has a right of reply which is denied the respondent.

Today's shorter oral hearings, hot benches and changed case type have also reduced the very limited potential which used to exist for counsel to tailor their arguments to the individual traits of the Law Lords sitting on a particular panel. Whilst it remains the case now as it was then that a proportion of all appeals turn

---

[41] Blom-Cooper and Drewry (n 15).
[42] Paterson, *The Law Lords* (n 1) 53.
[43] ibid 57.
[44] ibid 58.

on which five Law Lords actually sit on the Appellate Committee,[45] counsel's difficulty is that what appeals to one Law Lord might not appeal to the others.[46] As David Pannick observed, the old advocate's ploy of dangling an attractive fly before a chosen Law Lord is:

> unrealistic nowadays. It perhaps was an appropriate analogy at a time when. . .the Law Lords had done far less preparation and where perhaps the subject matter of the cases that came before them was far more esoteric, whereas nowadays the diet of the Appellate Committee, certainly in the cases that I'm dealing in, tends to be Human Rights Act, public law issues where any sort of attempt to dangle is likely to lead to your finger being bitten off.

That is not to say that counsel should not be sensitive to their audience—including what they have said in earlier cases. Moreover, there may be occasions when a focus on a specialist or a dominant Law Lord may be justified in the hope that (s)he will play a disproportionate part in the disposal of the appeal, but it remains a high-risk strategy.[47] This was graphically illustrated by one experienced counsel, who had consciously addressed the bulk of his arguments to the two Law Lords who he thought were going to be the most sympathetic and likely to swing a majority of the court his way, only to find that one of the two had dissented and the other had written a short concurring speech, leaving the Law Lords whom he had neglected to determine the outcome of the appeal.

Being sensitive to one's audience also means dealing with the points that are troubling the Law Lords when they arise. This, as Lord Bingham has observed, is almost a golden rule of appellate advocacy and reinforces the point that it is about dialogue rather than sequential monologues:

> Enter fully and readily into dialogue with any member of the tribunal who raises any point or question. When a judge asks a question or challenges any point in your argument—or makes a point in your favour—you have his or her attention. Any discussion of this kind involves an engagement, if not a meeting, of minds. It is your best opportunity to persuade. If you evade the question or duck the discussion you may find yourself addressing a tribunal of the deaf and mute.[48]

Counsel agreed:

> What you have to remember . . . with the House of Lords is . . . they are going to have a certain conception as to how things should work and if they ask you a question you

---

[45] There is no consensus as to what proportion of cases come into this category. Nowadays around 20% of all appeals involve a dissent, so perhaps the figure can be set at least at 20%. See Brice Dickson's essay 'Close Calls in the House of Lords' in this volume.

[46] Thirty years ago, counsel were not even told in advance which Law Lords would sit on their appeal. Even though counsel can now learn the make up of the panel some weeks in advance, it has not really changed the perceptions of counsel that seeking to target arguments at one or two Law Lords in a panel is a tricky and potentially dangerous tactic.

[47] The bench's counterpart to this—where a Law Lord feeds a line of questioning ostensibly to counsel but actually in the hope that it will impact on his companions, is relatively more commonplace. See Paterson, *The Law Lords* (n 1) ch 4.

[48] Lord Bingham, 'The Role of an Advocate in a Common Law System', lecture delivered at Gray's Inn, 6 October 2008.

should really treat it as both evidence to indicate what they're thinking but also an opportunity to try to respond to that way of thinking or to show how your conceptual framework can accommodate whatever concern [they were raising] . . . The most important element in the course of oral advocacy is to answer the tribunal's points convincingly. A fluent and compelling response to an adverse judicial intervention is the holy grail of oral advocacy.

Dealing properly with the Bench's questions is equally important in American appeal courts:

If you don't know the answer, admit it; the penalty for not having an answer at your fingertips is less severe than the penalty for trying to fake it, getting caught, and giving the court an opportunity to bat you around like a cat playing with a ball of yarn.[49]

Attempted evasion in an oral argument is a cardinal sin. No answer to an embarrassing point is better than an evasive one . . . Lack of candour in meeting a difficult point . . . goes far to destroying the effectiveness of a lawyer's argument, not merely as to the point . . . but often as to other points on which he should have the better of it. For if a lawyer loses the confidence of the court, he is apt to end up almost anywhere.[50]

## IV  HAVE THE QUALITIES OF GOOD APPELLATE ADVOCACY CHANGED?

If the dialogue between counsel and Law Lords has changed significantly in the last 40 years what impact has this had, if any, on what counts as good advocacy in the Lords? To answer this, we need first to look at what constitutes persuasive advocacy in the Lords, next to look at the qualities of robustness, courage and timekeeping, and finally to examine the rise in written advocacy.

### A  Persuasive advocacy

The object of appellate advocacy, oral or written, is persuasion. It is, however, an art rather than a science[51]—this means that different counsel when faced with the challenge of arguing a final appeal will adopt different routes. David Pannick QC and Jonathan Sumption QC were repeatedly identified by the Law Lords I interviewed as at the top of the profession, but their styles are quite different. As one leading counsel put it:

The function of the advocate is to comfort the tribunal by conveying to them the sense that his argument is credible. Putting it pejoratively, it is a con trick—in the sense that you need to win the confidence of the tribunal. There are many different ways

[49]  William J Boyce, quoted in A Scalia and B Garner, *Making Your Case: The Art of Persuading Judges* (Eagan MN, West Publishing, 2008) 193.

[50]  Justice JM Harlan II, 'The Role of Oral Argument' in DM O'Brien (ed), *Judges on Judging* (Washington DC, CQ Press, 2009).

[51]  See Lord Judge LCJ, 'Developments in Crown Court Advocacy' Kalisher Lecture delivered on 6 October 2009.

of doing that—through sheer intellectual superiority, through pedestrian diligence, through force of personality, through eloquence, sometimes even with humour—but the most important element in the course of oral advocacy is to answer the tribunal's points convincingly.

Whatever the differences in approach taken by those who appear in the tournament of champions which is the final appeal court, their ultimate goal is the same—to win (or lose)[52] in a way that assists their clients' interests. Moreover, each has in their own way to gain the trust[53] and confidence of the court. Here the leading performers undoubtedly have an advantage through the trust placed in them by the Law Lords:

> There are certain advocates who are given a lot of leeway because they are highly respected who I think actually get a slightly unfair advantage. (Law Lord)

One senior counsel added:

> However clever the Lords are they're not computers, they're human beings and you've got to make them want to decide in your favour, and that's what advocacy means, it's working out a way of making them feel comfortable coming with you. [54]

As we have seen, with hot benches, appellants have lost much of their ability to set the legal and factual framework for the appeal. However, there remains plenty scope for different styles of oral advocacy. The very best speak with an authority that makes them seductively dangerous to the court. A seeming simplicity can be equally beguiling, as Lord Walker told me, 'sometimes the most effective advocacy is quite brief and has at any rate a superficial appearance of simplicity although no doubt there's an awful lot of art that goes into that'. Equally dangerous are the advocates who appear so dispassionate in their presentation as to be more concerned with assisting the court come to the right answer than in winning the case. As one Law Lord observed, 'I think the really good debater is the one that makes you feel he's joining with you in seeking the right answer, whatever his point is.' Rather less common today is the seductive power of deliberately underselling one's case in the hope that the Law Lords will re-state it in a more powerful way. Lord Halsbury LC explained why he considered a little-known barrister was the best advocate that he had ever heard: 'Well, he had the great gift of always making it appear that he had a first class case being hopelessly ruined by a third class advocate'. [55]

Most respondents this time round were of the opinion that good appellate advocacy remains what it always was: being well prepared, succint, resilient,

---

[52] Leading counsel are well aware—as are their clients—that they cannot win every case. Where the case is likely to be lost their job is to minimise the damage to their client's interests.

[53] On the importance of trust in professionals, see Onora O'Neill's Reith Lectures, *A Question of Trust* (Cambridge, Cambridge University Press, 2002).

[54] Trust is primarily garnered through demonstrating excellence in advocacy skills including diligence. Curiously, trust is not dictated by whether one is on close personal terms with any of the Law Lords or not.

[55] See Paterson, *The Law Lords* (n 1) at 60 ff.

addressing the questions from the bench and only putting your good points. Dealing with your opponents' good points is a trickier art. As counsel put it:

> One of the skills of advocacy is, to traduce would be too strong a word, but not fairly to represent the argument that they are rejecting . . . you will use the arts of advocacy to belittle, so far as you can, the argument that you are addressing and if there are strong points in it you may be advised to try to attack them by stealth rather than full on.

Jonathan Crow QC added:

> In this context, one thing that I have learned . . . is that you can still win a case even if you cannot necessarily refute all of your opponent's arguments. Indeed, you can sometimes gain considerable credibility with the tribunal if you acknowledge that your opponent has got a good point on X to which you do not have a direct answer, so long as you can also persuade the tribunal that you have a better point on Y to which your opponent has no answer.

## B Robustness and resilience

One area where oral appellate advocacy has undoubtedly changed in the last 40 years is in the degree of robustness required of counsel. In the Diplock era, one route to success was to batter the Law Lords into submission. Gordon Pollock QC's astonishing success in the *Lonrho* case,[56] where after a day and half of dogged persistence he forced the whole panel of resistant Law Lords to recuse itself, has already entered the annals of the House.[57] The only way to deal with Lord Diplock was to take him on. As one Law Lord said to me, 'Hit the ball back to him as hard as possible in the hope of stunning his hand. It was the only way to stop him walking all over you.' Robustness and resilience are closely related virtues and the latter was also needed in earlier times. If Lord Reid was devastating in his ripostes, he lacked the 'dripping sarcasm'[58] of Lord Diplock or the sheer combativeness of Lords Bridge, Brandon and Templeman. On one such occasion where the senior had taken a terrific hammering from all three of them and his junior was then asked by Lord Bridge if he wished to add anything, the junior replied, 'Not without a helmet.' The Law Lords had the grace to laugh.[59] Resilience under fire to this degree was fortunately not an essential quality in the Lords in its final decade. Lord Bingham was determined that the court should eschew the excesses of the Diplock era, and even Law Lords who might have been tempted to stray were held in check by respect for Lord Bingham's authority.

---

[56] *Re Lonrho Plc (Contempt Proceedings)* [1990] 2 AC 154.

[57] Beloff (n 23) 235 describes Pollock as trading blows with Lord Ackner over the relevance of the fact that Ackner's father had been Tiny Rowland's dentist.

[58] Lord Rodger, 'Appreciation: The Hon Lord Davidson (1929–2009)' (2009) *SLT (News)* 157, 158.

[59] Certainly in the case of Brandon and Templeman, several of my respondents indicated that these particular Law Lords respected counsel who stood up to them.

This is not to say that some resilience[60] is no longer necessary. In both the UK and US Supreme Courts, the Bench continues to emphasise the significance of the Socratic dialogue, as we have seen.

## C Courage

Good appellate advocacy has always required courage. Robust resilience may no longer be required, but other forms of courage are needed. A recurring theme in American writings on appellate advocacy is the importance of 'going for the jugular', ie getting to the heart of the case by selecting and arguing its one or two controlling points. This is the best way, it is said, to 'capture the issue' and to 'stick that capture' into the minds of the judges. Unsurprisingly, counsel and Law Lords agreed with this, both in the original interviews and those of today:

> Good advocacy is what it always was, which is to identify the points that the court thinks are good. (Law Lord)
>
> I personally prefer the counsel who puts his best point and doesn't necessarily throw all his points at you. A good advocate uses discretion in his presentation. (Lord MacDermott)

However, as Sir Patrick Hastings KG observed, 'The ability to pick out the one real point of a case is not by itself enough; it is the courage required to seize upon that point to the exclusion of all others that is of real importance.' Great advocates of the past are said to have had this daring, eg Sir Walter Monckton QC and Lord Wilberforce when at the Bar when faced with eight points to choose from, are said to have picked the best one and abandoned the other seven to press it. One of today's Justices observed that Jonathan Sumption QC is a very good example of somebody who decides what the case is about and decides what points he wants to run, and runs them. Such role models are easier to admire than to copy, since it requires the judgment to select the best argument and the courage to stick with that choice. An excellent example of this occurred in an appeal where the respondent, feeling that he could not successfully defend the reasoning with which his clients had been successful in the Court of Appeal, sought leave at the outset of the appeal to run the case on an argument that had been abandoned in the court below. His opponent addressed the Committee for about an hour with a plenitude of authorities. However, in reply the respondent spoke for only two minutes, saying: 'It's a very short point and it's going to come up again so if you don't let me argue it on this appeal and you find against me on the first point, it will leave an unanswered question hanging that will make the case a pointless appeal.' He then promptly sat down, much to the surprise of all in the Committee Room. The Law Lords, nonplussed by the turn of events, eyed

---

[60] 'Counsel, it's a good thing you've got a lot of fallback arguments,' Chief Justice Roberts told one struggling attorney recently, 'because you fall back very quickly.' M Doyle, McClatchy Newspapers, www.mcclatchydc.com/2007/05/16/16193.

each other, concluded that nothing more need be said and let the respondent run the point.[61] Nonetheless, more risk-averse counsel will be attracted by David Pannick QC's observation that:

> I don't think that it can be good tactics *only* to go for the point that you think is your best point. It seems to me the right approach is to pursue all the good points, there may be more than one of them even if the second and third is not as good as the first.

Another senior counsel had his own take on the 'good points' thesis:

> As a client once said to me: 'Anyone can prepare their good points. What matters is how you deal with the bad ones.' There is much in this. Some advocates lose considerable credibility with the tribunal by banging on about a point that is not going to win them the case. Others lose credibility by giving up a tricky point too easily. This is a difficult judgment call because, on the one hand, you do not want to collapse with the first signs of judicial opposition but, on the other hand, you do not want to ruin your case by flogging away at a point they are not going to find in your favour. So one has to avoid both being pusillanimous and being stubborn—and the path between the two is a judgment that one often has to make literally on one's feet in the course of oral argument.

Lord Bingham on the other hand identified another form of courageous appellate advocacy to which he was attracted, namely the counsel who says:[62]

> My Lords, I have six propositions. They are the following. If any of these propositions is unsound, I must fail. But I submit that they are sound, and I shall now seek to make them good.

The attraction of this approach is in the clear road map which it provides to the court and the opportunity it affords to test the building blocks of counsel's argument for their consistency with principle and as to their consequences.

## D Timing

The reduction in the length of time allowed for advocacy, especially in complex cases, has entailed that counsel must acquire the timing skills of a *Today* presenter on Radio 4 to bring their argument to a close on time. Counsel have to give accurate estimates as to how long they will need for their argument without

---

[61] A similar story from an appeal court in the USA describes how the appellant 'took such a battering from the court that it was obvious to everyone the judgment below would be affirmed. Counsel for the respondent arose, bowed, and said, "If the Court please, I must apologize for an error in my brief. At page 32, second line from the bottom, the citation should be to 112 Federal Second and not to 112 Federal . . . Unless there are any questions, I will submit the respondent's case on the brief," and sat down. I have it on excellent authority that it was one of the most effective arguments ever heard by that court.' FB Wiener, 'Oral Advocacy' (1948) 62 *Harvard Law Review* 56, 59–60, quoted in A Scalia and B Garner, *Making Your Case: The Art of Persuading Judges* (Eagan MN, West Publishing, 2008).

[62] See n 48.

knowing how interventionist the Law Lords will be during the case.[63] Moreover, some opponents will leave their discussions as to the length of time needed for reply until the robing room. This can lead to what in other circumstances might be seen as gamesmanship, especially if the Presiding Law Lord allows one of the counsel to significantly overrun. Not the least of Lord Bingham's skills in the chair was his ability to manage timing issues in a fair and seemingly effortless fashion. As one experienced counsel remarked:

> Lord Bingham liked to be told in advance, usually in a letter, that I had spoken to the other counsel and that we had agreed a timetable . . . If you overran by over half-an-hour then certainly in Lord Bingham's case he would intervene very forcefully and tell you that you had to finish in the next five or ten minutes and he actually made out a timetable of his own if you had overrun.

One noticeable feature of the modern-day leaders in the final court is the speed of their delivery. It is markedly faster than that of their counterparts 20 to 30 years ago. As one observer noted:

> One of most extraordinary things about [leading counsel] is that they do it all at an enormous speed so quickly so that the slower members of the class as it were are still trying to work out what [counsel's] last point is or his last point but three is.

Finally, the reduction in time for oral argument is an added impetus to counsel to stick to the key points in the case. As David Pannick QC put it:

> You need to work hard to prepare the case because you know that you are not going to be able to take time developing the background and responding to the thoughts that judges may have as to background. You've got . . . to get to the heart of the case and that requires very different skills. It means that you have to be much more aggressive in focusing on the issues in the case.

### E Written advocacy

Above all, however, the last 30 years have seen the rise in importance of written advocacy. Whilst not identical to oral advocacy in its characteristics, there are nonetheless many more similarities than differences between the two art forms. Each of them is about persuasion—which, as Lord Bingham has noted, requires communication and communication requires the advocate to engage with the mind of the audience.[64] The views of counsel were remarkably consistent on this—pointing to the symbiotic relationship between the Case and the oral argument:

> It's essentially exactly the same as oral advocacy, it is having an eye for the winning point, it's not an eye for the clever point, it's an eye for the winning point . . . you've got

---

[63] See DN Pritt QC on this point in Paterson, *The Law Lords* (n 1) 68.

[64] Bingham (n 48). Lord Bingham's recipe for the good printed Case is a neutral and fully referenced statement of the facts, clarity of purpose, appropriate simplicity, sparing citation of authority, brevity and clarity of expression.

to find a way of making the judges want to come with you and I think a lot of it is, it's not just sort of cosmetics but it's finding a way of presenting your story in an attractive way, it's that simple. (Senior counsel)

In terms of what wins cases in the Supreme Court, oral advocacy on its own is not enough. Written advocacy matters every bit as much. If you have not at least started to win them round with your printed Case, you are very unlikely to finish the job on your feet. By 'written advocacy' I do not just mean persuasive writing. It is far more complex than that. The real skill in presenting a written argument is to identify the winning point [from amongst those available to you]. Any lawyer can think of legal arguments, but you do not win appeals by smothering the Court with mere arguments. What you need to do is to identify the point that matters. (Jonathan Crow QC)

If you know that the Law Lords are going to spend a substantial amount of time preparing, then it's in your interests to argue the Case more fully perhaps than you would otherwise do and also deal not just with the bare assertions, the strengths of your case but also try to anticipate the points against you and deal with them. On the oral side the consequence of the printed Case is that they will not accept in my experience you simply going through your printed Case because they have read the printed Case. You're expected to focus your oral argument on meeting the points made by your opponent in their printed Case. Obviously some elaboration of your side of the case is necessary, they won't sit and listen to the printed Case being read out. (David Pannick QC)

You might say, 'The steps in the argument go A, B, C. You've seen our written Case on A, we say our argument's very powerful, I'm not going to take up time developing that. B is more debatable and perhaps you'd take a little bit of time on that, but then you say the main point we say is C and I'm going to take my time on that' and so the written materials give you a certain degree of freedom then to concentrate on your oral advocacy on the pressure points and that means that you can be more reactive in the oral advocacy. (Mr Justice Sales)

One wants to reserve something quite deliberately for oral advocacy—as it were to take a forensic punch, to start off with something that captures their imagination immediately. Whereas, I would regard written advocacy as just a way of setting out as fully and as perhaps neutrally as possible the basic information they will need to have in order to determine the point or points of law and to identify what the issues are and clearly to set out what one's case about them is. But. . .my oral would not reflect my written. . .they would be two quite different exercises. (Michael Beloff QC)

What you're doing is taking the whole thing as read but saying the real key point is paragraph fifteen, this is why it matters, these are the cases that support it and then you go to the authorities and read them the passages and wrap it all up, so you just dwell on one or two key points under each section of the argument. Actually, you don't parrot each point as you go through, you just home in on what you think is the winning point under each heading. (Senior counsel)

However, the printed Case lacks a crucial element which is present in oral advocacy, namely flexibility. Almost invariably a case will develop in an unexpected direction, whether due to the line of questioning which emanates from the panel, or the answers provided by counsel. When writing the Case counsel can never cater for all the possible avenues along which the oral hearing may progress. As David Pannick QC put it:

> I don't think you can anticipate all the avenues not least because no case ever proceeds in a way that you can predict. . .it always goes off on byways that are unexpected. It may end up at a conclusion that you realised was very likely but it always travels along a route that is unexpected and that is inevitable. But the drafting of the written Case does require particular skills, because although it is longer than it ever was, it is still necessary to seek to be concise in the analysis of each particular point. Further, it is necessary to try to identify your arguments to anticipate as best you are able the arguments against you which is much more difficult if you are the Appellant than if you are the Respondent. If you are the Respondent you know what the printed arguments are against you and then you've got to deal with the arguments in the Court of Appeal below which are not necessarily the same arguments as your opponent is going to run, and that's difficult. There may also be cases that you're aware of that haven't been cited in the court below which either help you or hinder you and you've got to deal with those as well.

## V DOES ADVOCACY MATTER IN THE LORDS?

If the nature of the dialogue between Law Lords and counsel has changed in the last 35 years, and with it the qualities required of a good advocate, what impact, if any, have these developments had on the efficacy of advocacy in the Lords? Clearly advocacy can have an impact in a range of ways. As will be seen from the first four parts of this chapter, it may affect (1) the speed and efficacy of the decision-making process in the court, (2) the stress and enjoyment experienced by the decision-makers, (3) the cost of the decision-making process, and (4) the decision-makers' trust in and the reputation of, counsel. Whilst these are matters of some consequence, from the perspective of the client, the most significant issue is whether advocacy makes a difference to (5) the outcome of the case, or at the very least to (6) the quality of reasoning and therefore the appropriate development of the law.

Slightly to my surprise, a number of the counsel whom I interviewed this time round were sceptical as to how often in the Lords advocacy had a determinative effect on the eventual outcome of appeals. David Perry QC, when asked if advocacy made a difference in the Lords, replied:

> That's a very good question because in the vast majority of cases I think the answer to that is probably, No. I'd be very surprised if five Law Lords or sometimes seven or sometimes nine didn't, when they go away and analyse all the materials, come to their own conclusions and see that if they had been beguiled by what an advocate had said, if they didn't recognise that fact.

Michael Beloff QC was more optimistic:

> Yes, advocacy does matter; after all the very questions put (and discussion between the Law Lords) shows that they frequently start off with a completely open mind (in

sense of being undecided) and we would all give up if we thought we were merely there to make up numbers. Who would pay us if that were so. The reason why the route of ECJ and USASC has not been taken is because the Judges here believe in the value of oral advocacy.

Mr Justice Sales:

Yes. It's one of these difficult questions as to when advocacy matters anywhere in courts and it's always a little bit difficult to generalise but I think that it does matter in the Lords. Often in the Lords you are getting cases which are difficult, there isn't an obvious answer, that's how they tend to get up that far and so that's a factor which points in favour of advocacy making more of a difference. On the other hand you've got very strong-minded, very clever [judges] who are likely to have some quite strong views themselves, so that pulls in the other direction. So where does that balance out? I'd say perhaps in about thirty per cent of cases it makes a significant difference, very roughly.

Another experienced counsel drew a distinction between oral and written advocacy:

Not to the outcome, No . . . Having seen the Supreme Courts of other countries and seen the ECJ and the European Court of Human Rights as well, where in all of those jurisdictions the system is much more based on paper anyway but given the calibre and the intellect of the judges that we're talking about I'd be surprised if they're likely to be swayed all that much by the oral hearing; because they're not likely to hear much that they haven't already read about and thought about to some extent at least.

However, he did think that the printed Case could make a difference:

Yes, absolutely, I think written advocacy certainly does, so the quality of the printed Cases is undoubtedly important . . . I think that's your most important opportunity in effect to set out what you think the Law Lords' judgments in due course should look like.

Perhaps the most telling answer came from Jonathan Sumption QC:

I think that advocacy matters much more in perceiving what are likely to be regarded as the meritorious points, what are likely to be regarded as the direction the Lords will want to move in than in actually the analysis of case law or statutes . . . I don't think it ever makes the difference between success and failure but I think it makes a difference to the reasoning of a decision, which can be in the public interest . . . I have found myself quite often reformulating the way that the issue is argued, not fundamentally, it's not jettisoning the grounds below, but trying to suggest a completely different approach to the problem. I think that's part of the function of counsel and I think it's an exercise which can make a considerable difference to the quality of the reasoning. Most judges start from the answer and work backwards. The House of Lords do that even more often than other courts. I think that it is quite unusual to shift the majority of the House from an opinion that they have initially formed. It happens but it's not that common, what you can shift is the reasoning.

These relatively modest assessments by counsel of what advocacy can achieve in the Lords might, if they were the whole story, make clients wonder why they pay out sometimes in excess of £20,000 a day for the QC of their choice. True, if resources are not an issue, people going into a litigation with a lot at stake will always opt for the most formidable counsel they can get, almost as an insurance policy to get the benefit of any marginal edge that the best advocates can bring. Nonetheless it is an expensive insurance policy. Fortunately, the Law Lords were in general rather more positive as to the impact of good advocacy. All the Law Lords told me that they had changed their mind during the oral argument, and not that infrequently, in some cases. This was true 35 years ago and remains true today. Even in the US Supreme Court, where oral advocacy has been reduced to 30 minutes a side, it is thought that 'the best attorneys can still capture a swing vote in a close case and carry the day'.[65]

As Lord Hope told me:

> I find advocacy, good advocacy from some of the people we see immensely helpful and it helps you to think into a case. If you are writing a judgment it's much easier to write it after you've heard the oral argument than it could possibly be if you've just read about it. . . The oral presentation can alter your view quite dramatically as the hearing goes on. . .[it also] helps you both to probe more deeply into what the case is really about and to begin to test the argument with the contributions from people on either side of you.

Lord Bingham was characteristically balanced and concise as to whether advocacy matters: 'In some cases certainly, but not all', before going on to observe of oral advocacy:

> Sometimes undoubtedly. There are some cases where I think the truth is that by the time everybody has read two judgments below and two quite lengthy Cases they've formed a view one way or the other and they don't change it. But, I think there are quite a lot of cases in which people read one Case and they think that's very persuasive and then they read the other and they think that's very persuasive and so they do genuinely go into court with open minds looking to counsel to try and get an answer. Not only does it vary, as you would expect, from case to case but it varies from individual to individual because I think some people reach much firmer opinions early on than others do.

### A  Case studies in effective advocacy

Both counsel and Law Lords pointed to a wide range of cases in which the exercise of appellate advocacy skills by counsel had influenced the outcome or the reasoning within appeals.[66] From the 1970s came the *Johanna Oldendorff*,[67] one of the earliest exercises of the 1966 Practice Statement freedom to depart from an earlier precedent of the House. The respondents were sure that they would win,

---

[65]  The quote comes from a former clerk in the Supreme Court, Edward Lazarus, *Closed Chambers* (New York, Penguin Books, 1999) 35. See Dickson (n 46).

[66]  Space does not permit all of them to be discussed, including the occasions when counsel sees the structure of their argument—and sometimes part of its content—re-appear in the Law Lords' judgments. See Paterson, *The Law Lords* at 63.

[67]  *The Johanna Oldendorff; E L Oldendorff & Co GmbH v Tradax Export SA* [1973] 3 All ER 148.

but Robert MacCrindle QC persuaded the House 5:0 to reverse a long-standing decision of the House. Equally, Kemp Davidson QC achieved a major success in *McGhee v National Coal Board*,[68] such that for 'many years there was a feeling that Kemp had won too well—that he had pulled the wool over their Lordships' eyes', until the result was vindicated in *Fairchild v Glenhaven Funeral Services*.[69]

Gordon Pollock QC has scored a range of unlikely victories in the Lords. Most famous was probably the *Lonhro plc*[70] case, where he persuaded a resistant panel of five Law Lords in a contempt of court hearing to recuse themselves after a day and half of trench warfare. Equally notable was when he turned Lord Diplock, for what was perhaps the one and only time in the Lords, in a shipping case where the ship's master had the odd habit of preferring to navigate off charts that were at least 10 to 15 years old, leading to damage to a oil pipeline costing $25,000,000 to repair.[71]

The *Pinochet* litigation also threw up a notable piece of advocacy. One reason why *Pinochet (No 3)*[72] produced a much narrower ruling against General Pinochet than *Pinochet (No 1)*[73] was due to the fact that the senior who had led for Pinochet in *Pinochet (No 1)* was unavailable for some of *Pinochet (No 3)* and in his absence Clare Montgomery QC ran an argument which her leader had not run in *Pinochet (No 1)*. It was that argument that prevailed in the later case. As Jonathan Sumption QC told me,

> I regard that as a good example of a case in which advocacy made a considerable difference, not to the initial starting point of the tribunal, nor to the tribunal's propensity to carry a starting point through to the finish, but to the particular reasoning which can have a very considerable effect in the particular case as well as on the developments of law. That's a striking example of something that in my experience happens really quite frequently and the Lords is in the business of formulating general rules for long term application and very often their initial instincts about which way the case should go is very sensitive to the particular circumstances of the case. You offer them a way of doing what they want to do in the particular case which produces a more acceptable result in the long term and you've probably got the wind behind you.

Sumption himself is thought to have won over a majority in the House on a number of occasions. One of these was in the second *Shayler*[74] case, where he persuaded the House, contrary to its initial stance, that injunctions, once granted and then broken, must be contempt of court, otherwise it would lead to complete chaos in circumstances where the Law Lords took a different view of the merits.

[68]    *McGhee v National Coal Board* [1973] 1 WLR 1, 1973 SC (HL) 37.
[69]    *Fairchild v Glenhaven Funeral Services* [2002] UKHL 22, [2003] 1 AC 32. See Lord Rodger (n 58) 158.
[70]    *Lonrho* (n 24). Pollock also prevailed in a 3:2 appeal, *Alfred McAlpine Construction Ltd v Panatown Ltd* [2001] 1 AC 518 despite severe hostility at one stage from Lord Goff.
[71]    *Grand Champion Tankers Ltd v Norpipe A/S (The Marion)* [1984] AC 563.
[72]    *R v Bow Street Metropolitan Stipendiary Magistrate ex p Pinochet Ugarte (No 3)* [2000] 1 AC 147.
[73]    *R v Bow Street Metropolitan Stipendiary Magistrate ex p Pinochet Ugarte (No 1)* [2000] 1 AC 61.
[74]    *Attorney General v Punch Ltd and another* [2002] UKHL 50, [2003] 2 WLR 49.

Not to be outdone, David Pannick QC is believed to have won one appeal in the last three years in his reply alone, and to have assisted Lord Hoffmann in the remarkable turn around in the *ProLife* case[75] (on whether the BBC could censure the party election broadcast of the ProLife Alliance party). Counsel in my interviews were generally sceptical that appeals could be won on reply, but the Law Lords were less so and in addition to Pannick's success, counsel for the appellant is understood to have won the much debated *Doherty*[76] case with an argument raised in reply.

Other recent cases are thought to have been influenced by advocacy[77] but the most spectacular of these was undoubtedly in the Chagos Islands case.[78] This was an appeal where the Government's position was morally indefensible. Between 1965 and 1973 the British Government had ruthlessly (and deceitfully) expelled the indigenous inhabitants from the Chagos island to secure the principal island, Diego Garcia, as a military base for the United States of America. Under challenge, the Foreign Secretary announced in 2000 that the islanders would be permitted to return home to the islands, except Diego Garcia. However, the Government secretly reversed its policy in 2004, covertly passing orders removing the islanders' right of abode in the islands. The validity of the orders was challenged by Bancoult, who was successful before the Divisional Court and the Court of Appeal. The Secretary of State brought in new senior counsel and squeaked home in the Lords by a 3:2 margin, to the astonishment of many observers. The key was the advocacy adopted in the printed Case, where Jonathan Crow QC conceded all of the Government's bad behaviour in earlier times, but by redefining the merits successfully argued that the refusal to permit the re-settlement of islanders in 2004, whilst unpopular, was a rational policy for the Government to adopt.

## VI FACTORS WHICH MAKE A DIFFERENCE

What, if anything, can we distil from all this as to when counsel are more likely to make a difference with their advocacy? In the absence of a major multivariate study, any conclusions on this are necessarily tentative. Nonetheless, it would seem that the efficacy of the dialogues in which counsel engage depend on three principal factors: (1) the calibre and characteristics of those engaged in the debate, (2) the context and characteristics of the debates, and (3) the nature of

---

[75] *R v BBC ex p ProLife Alliance* [2003] UKHL 23, [2004] 1 AC 185. After several switches of mind during the hearing the original divide at the end of oral arguments was 4:1 to ProLife. It is believed that Lord Hoffmann won round a majority to his persuasion, since the final result was 4:1 to the BBC.

[76] *Doherty (FC) and others v Birmingham City Council* [2008] UKHL 57, [2008] 3 WLR 636.

[77] For example, *R (on the application of Mullen) v Secretary of State for the Home Department* [2004] UKHL 18, [2005] 1 AC 1, *A and others v Secretary of State for the Home Department* [2004] UKHL 56, [2005] 2 AC 68, and *Huang v Secretary of State for the Home Department, Kashmiri v Same* [2007] UKHL 11, [2007] 2 AC 167.

[78] *Bancoult v Secretary of State for Foreign and Commonwealth Affairs* [2008] UKHL 61, [2009] 1 AC 453.

the cases being argued—including their intrinsic merits. Although they will be analysed independently, in reality, like oral and written advocacy, the three factors interact with each other.

## A  The primary opponents

The first factor is undoubtedly the calibre of the debaters. As set out above, counsel with excellent appellate advocacy skills can undoubtedly have an impact on the quality of decision-making in the final court and sometimes on the outcome of the appeal. Equally important are the characteristics of the primary opponents in these debates—who are, of course, the Law Lords. As Lord Kilbrandon told me in the original interviews:[79] 'if you really want to know . . . the debate is really much more between counsel and the Bench than it is between opposing counsel'. Indeed, one of my original counsel described the dialogue between Bar and Bench as 'like a football game: you only play as well as the opponents let you—and by opponents I mean the tribunal'.[80] The quality of their intellect can be taken for granted although some are exceptionally fleet of thought in the oral arguments, eg Lords Reid, Diplock, Bingham and Hoffmann sometimes disconcerting their colleagues. When in the chair they were able to give a lead to their colleagues[81] and a steer to counsel which tended to have a significant effect on the course and length of the dialogue. Some presiders over the years, however, have been more silent or less directive, eg Lords Wilberforce, Radcliffe, Fraser, Keith, and Nicholls, affording counsel more influence in the direction of the dialogue. In truth, UK counsel find silence from the Bench particularly disconcerting, whether it is the House of Lords[82] eg Lord Walker,[83] or in Strasbourg or Luxembourg, since they are unable to gauge what is troubling the bench and consequently whether to alter course or not. The opposite challenge is little more palatable. As we have seen, the combativeness of certain Law Lords over the years, eg Lords Diplock, Brandon, Bridge and Templeman, required a degree of robustness in counsel if the latter was to contribute effectively to the nature, duration and outcome of the dialogue.

The open-mindedness of the Law Lords also impacts on the efficacy of the oral arguments. Although David Robertson[84] endeavoured valiantly to explain decisions in the Lords from the ideological preferences of the Law Lords taking

[79]  Paterson, *The Law Lords* (n 1) 50.

[80]  Paterson, *The Law Lords* (n 1) 51.

[81]  In *The Law Lords* (n 1) ch 4, I established that the Law Lords use their powers of intervention in the dialogue for the purposes of curtailment and focus, testing counsel's and their own propositions, clarification and to persuade their colleagues. These were still the primary purpose of Law Lords' interventions in 2009.

[82]  Paterson, *The Law Lords* (n 1) 70ff.

[83]  Lord Walker, whilst a much less regular intervener than most of his colleagues, is positively garrulous when compared with Justice Thomas on the US Supreme Court who, at the time of writing, has not asked a question during the oral hearings in that court since 22 February 2006.

[84]  D Robertson, *Judicial Discretion in the House of Lords* (Oxford, Clarendon Press, 1998).

part, most commentators on the Lords today have not found that a fruitful line of analysis to pursue. The easy identification of the swing voters on the US Supreme Court over years because of their centrist ideological position, eg Justices Powell, O'Connor and Kennedy, has no crossover to the House.[85] Moreover, even where Law Lords are not silent, it is not always easy even for experienced observers to tell from which direction their interventions are coming. Some make their positions pretty transparent in their interventions,[86] eg Lords Hoffmann, Steyn, Hobhouse and Carswell. Others, eg Lord Rodger, are thought occasionally to adopt the role of the devil's advocate.

Hot benches also influence both the length and content of the dialogue as we have seen. They may also impact on the open-mindedness of the Bench, as Lord Bingham noted earlier. Similarly, one senior counsel noted:

> Whether or not oral advocacy can change somebody's mind if it's already been made up, I think, probably depends upon the individual. Some Law Lords come into the hearing knowing what they think the answer is and they cannot be shaken. I think they've all read in advance and some of them are more sure of their own judgments than others.

In fact, Lord Diplock's reluctance to shift from his initial position gained from doing his homework thoroughly, affected his tolerance as presiding Law Lord to hear arguments and material which he felt was covered in the written material. Lord Bingham favoured greater open-mindedness at the start of hearings, and he was not alone. As one of today's leading counsel commented:

> You don't suddenly stand up in court with an adverse tribunal and persuade them round . . . when people ask the question does oral advocacy matter in the Lords, what they have in mind is a relatively . . .harsh concept of an adverse tribunal whom you then persuade. I think that that is probably not a situation that arises very often, partly because I don't think a majority come into court with their minds made up and partly because if you are in one of the rare situations where five or at least three have made their minds up I think it's very rare that one could actually persuade them to change their minds. I think that what happens in oral advocacy and why it does matter is that you come into a tribunal where maybe one is firmly of one view, maybe another is firmly of a different view and you've got three swing votes and they haven't made their minds up and you then do try and talk them through .

As Lord Hope told me:

> I try not to form preconceived views and I don't actually usually do so. I tend to keep an open mind before I go into a hearing and you sometimes say casually to yourself 'well, this looks a fairly straightforward case' one way or the other but by the time you get into the oral argument it may not seem nearly as straightforward as you thought it was.

---

[85] That is not to say that watchers of the House could not over the years predict with some considerable accuracy the likely position that would be taken by some Law Lords in certain types of case before the oral argument had begun.

[86] As one experienced counsel put it: 'I'd like to play poker against some of them more than I would against others because some of them simply don't have poker faces, they let you know exactly what they are thinking.'

## B  The calibre of the secondary opposition

The calibre of opposing counsel and the quality of their arguments inevitably has some impact on the development of the dialogue between Bench and Bar and on the efficacy of the advocacy of the initial counsel. This is true whether the opponent's advocacy is good or bad. The good opponent presents a constant threat to the success of one's advocacy. As one counsel put it: 'There are some barristers that one is concerned about who can turn any case round, others that you're less concerned about. So even with a strong case if I was going against [one of the greats] I'd be nervous.' However, even being a brilliant counsel is not enough. As another experienced counsel recalled:

> I was involved in a case against a senior counsel and I sat there for a day listening to a brilliant tutorial given by him with hardly any interruptions from the committee. This was on topic one. Then he came to deal with topic two; not his field. I could tell that the appeal was slipping away on topic one, because when your opponent starts quoting classic works of economic philosophy off the top of his head, and the Committee sit there absorbing it all, you know that all is lost. But when it came to topic two, it was quite interesting. There were some interventions, but then there came a point when the interventions stopped, as if to signal that the argument was not going anywhere. Sure enough, his arguments on topic one were accepted, and his arguments on topic two rejected.

What happens if the opponent is a weak advocate or has an off day? Can bad advocacy lose a case that should be won? Some Law Lords and counsel considered that it could. Rabinder Singh QC considered that an appeal could be lost in the printed Case, and others similarly noted that a bad printed Case could lose a case, or at least ensure that counsel was starting several steps behind when they come to the hearing. Often the Law Lords will make up for any deficiencies in the argument put by counsel, but Law Lords are human too, and confronted with an incoherent, convoluted and obscurely expressed Case, may not strive as hard as they might to find the killer point in dense materials,[87] especially if there are attractively packaged points put up by the good advocate on the other side. However, one counsel commented:

> I think it's easier to lose a case at the oral hearing because that's when they test the propositions and if the arguments don't stand up to scrutiny in the forum of debate as the House of Lords is then that's when it becomes clear that the argument is a bad one ... The printed Case may have been expressed in such an obscure way that they're not really sure about whether your argument is a good one or a bad one, but that becomes clear at the hearing.

---

[87] In one case the appellants produced five bound volumes of academic commentaries without comment or analysis. One of the Law Lords wearily replied, 'Well what are we supposed to do, take it on holiday with us and read it on the beach? What are you saying about them?' The respondents took the hint and presented an analysis of the commentaries including their content and the preponderance of the arguments therein.

Counsel do not improve their prospects by being rude to the Law Lords or ignoring Bingham's golden rule of advocacy by failing to answer the Law Lords' questions, as happened in one major appeal in the last five years. Such advocacy loses the trust (and the ear) of the tribunal. As Gordon Pollock QC told me:

> [T]ake Donald Nicholls: he disliked counsel who didn't answer his questions properly and whenever you appeared in front of him you had to be very, very careful if he asked you a question that you answered it . . . and you didn't try and give him an answer that skated round the problem. You either met it head on or basically in my view he shut off and he didn't take you seriously from then on . . . [H]e focused on usually the one point that might sink you . . . If he thought you were treating him properly on a proper intellectual basis then he would go along with you. If he thought that you were just flimflamming, away it went . . . Lord Oliver was exactly the same.

Equally, if counsel's arguments lack conviction this may undermine their efficacy in the dialogue. Whilst counsel are divided as to whether it is necessary to believe in the arguments that they put before the Lords some were of the opinion that if you could not convince yourself as to the merits of your arguments your voice and body language would be unlikely to convince the House.

The second factor to influence the quality of the dialogue and counsel's role in it lies in the context and characteristics of the debates themselves. The physical geography of the courtroom, counsel's proximity to the Law Lords, the conversational style encouraged by today's Law Lords,[88] the shift to shorter oral and more written advocacy all contribute to an atmosphere which has an impact on the successful use of the technical skills of advocacy.

## C  The merits of the case

The third, and by no means the least, factor which affects the success of advocacy skills is the intrinsic merits of the appeal itself. Taking first the moral merits. The majority of counsel and Law Lords today believe that even at the level of the House/Supreme Court, the perceived equities of an appeal are relevant and may significantly influence its outcome. Lord Bingham told me: 'I think they matter enormously. [If] it seems grossly unfair that a certain result is achieved, people are going to be much more receptive to any alternative solution.' A number of examples were cited in which an advocate's skill in boosting the justness of his side of the case had paid dividends.[89] Probably even more important for the outcome of the case are the perceived legal merits of the respective sides. In a significant proportion of the appeals, the balance of the respective legal arguments is such that even good advocacy is unlikely to secure a result and bad advocacy will be rectified by the Law Lords. I asked the Law Lords what proportion of appeals

---

[88]  The absence of a fixed lectern in the new Supreme Court courtrooms is understood to stem from a desire to enhance the 'conversational' atmosphere in hearings there.

[89]  eg, *EB (Kosovo) v Secretary of State for the Home Department* [2008] UKHL 41, [2008] 3 WLR 178.

set down for hearing before the House could at that stage go either way with a reasonable legal justification. Lord MacMillan had placed the proportion as close to 100 per cent, whilst Lord Reid felt it was nearer to 30 per cent. Today's Law Lords are similarly divided, with roughly a third saying 50 per cent or over, a third opting for 33 per cent and a third for below 33 per cent. Given that there was a dissent in 20 per cent of appeals in the last decade and a 3:2 split in 10 per cent of cases in that time, it would seem that the minimum proportion of cases for advocacy to make a difference in for any Law Lord would be 10 per cent, and for most it would be at least 33 per cent. Counsel, if anything, thought the proportion of appeals which could go either way at the outset, was somewhat higher.[90] Interestingly, one of them took account of all three factors listed above before reaching his figure:

> One would be the basic strength of your case . . . partly, again, it would be a function of your opposition and thirdly the Law Lords have track records. You get a sense of their general disposition towards particular sorts of argument and if you put those three together I'd say. . . [advocacy makes a difference in] something like fifty or sixty per cent of the time.

## VII CONCLUSION

We return now to the question of the significance of the dialogues which take place between counsel and Law Lords for understanding judicial decision-making in the final court of appeal in the UK. We have seen how the dialogues have changed over 40 years. Time limits on oral advocacy, a greater emphasis on written advocacy and a weakening of the ability of counsel to impose constraints on decision-making in the House, have altered the nature of oral advocacy and the dialogues between Bar and Bench. The dialectic may remain with the tribunal rather than the other side, but the form of the dialectic has changed. Nonetheless we have seen that counsel's advocacy continues to matter in the last days of the House as a final court, depending on the input from the tribunal, the opposition and the merits of the case.

As for the dialogue between Law Lords themselves, in Lord Bingham's time the Law Lords had little prior discussion inter se before appeals[91] and less discussion at lunch than 40 years ago. With hearings reduced in length by a half, the scope for dialogues between the Law Lords in the hearing phase had greatly reduced over time. True, the Law Lords continued to interact with each other in the oral hearings, though usually in the guise of questions apparently directed to counsel, and they retained the long-standing practice of meeting immediately the hearing was over to exchange their extempore views on the appeal. This conference,

---

[90] It is perhaps relevant to remember that for the last 30 years the average success rate for appeals in the Lords has been in the region of 45%.

[91] Unlike the Court of Appeal, the European Court of Justice and the European Court of Human Rights.

however, remained more a series of seriatim opinions with relatively little by way of debate except in the more significant or divided cases. In recent years, therefore, the character of the dialogue between Law Lords—judicial advocacy as it were—had shifted imperceptibly from oral to written with an increased emphasis on the early circulation of opinions.

What of the future? Some have argued[92] that on grounds of cost alone the way forward for the UK Supreme Court should be to impose even greater constraints on the length of oral arguments, as presently exists in the US and Canadian Supreme Courts, the European Court and the European Court of Human Rights. The loss in input from counsel could, they say, be rectified in part through the greater availability of judicial assistants which now exists in the Supreme Court.[93] However, few of the Law Lords and counsel that I interviewed this time round favoured such a move, which would have greater consequences for the dialogue between Bench and Bar than is often appreciated and with it to the quality of decision-making in the final court of appeal. Currently, ideas derived from the debates in the lower courts are developed in the printed Cases, refined during the oral exchanges between counsel and Law Lords, distilled in the draft written judgment of one or more of the Law Lords and polished through the circulation of opinions between the Law Lords. The dramatic curtailment of oral advocacy in the final court would reduce costs, but only at the expense of quality of oral advocacy,[94] and the loss of a nuanced refining process for ideas. Written advocacy and the input of largely inexperienced judicial assistants are unlikely to produce better judgments at the end of the day. Written advocacy lacks the flexibility of its oral counterpart and the Law Lords' use of judicial assistants as sounding boards is not an effective substitute for the rigorous testing of propositions which occurs in the forensic arena of the final court. The complex of parallel and interactive dialogues which are the hallmarks of current appeals would give way to sequential and one-dimensional dialogues. Not only would this presage the demise of the shared responsibility between Bench and Bar for the development of the law in the final court identified by Wetter,[95] it would see judicial advocacy surpassing counsel's advocacy in terms of significance in the decision-making process of Supreme Court.

[92] See eg R Gordon, 'The Relationship between the Bar and the House of Lords' in A Le Sueur (ed), *Building the UK's New Supreme Court* (Oxford, Oxford University Press, 2004). Lord Bingham raised the possibility unenthusiastically in his lecture on 'A New Supreme Court for the United Kingdom' delivered at The Constitution Unit on 1 May 2002.

[93] The number of judicial assistants has doubled from the four that existed in the final year of Lord Bingham.

[94] It is widely recognised that the general quality of oral advocacy in jurisdictions which severely limit the length of oral hearing is lower than that in jurisdictions such as the United Kingdom and Australia where oral advocacy in the final court is relatively untrammelled. See D Terris, C Romano and L Swigart, *The International Judge* (Oxford, Oxford University Press, 2007) 85. Nevertheless, there is an argument that greater case management by the Supreme Court at the Permissions phase could be used to regulate more precisely the length of hearing that is appropriate for a given appeal.

[95] G Wetter, *Styles of Appellate Judicial Decisons* (Leyden, AW Sythoff, 1960) 72.

# 13

# Close Calls in the House of Lords

BRICE DICKSON

## I INTRODUCTION

WHEN THE UNITED Kingdom's top court is deciding what are the legal rules and principles in accordance with which appeals should be decided, the judges sitting in that court, usually five in number, frequently disagree over what those rules and principles are, or what they mean in practice. Sometimes the disagreement is fairly marginal, with just a single judge expressing dissent on one or more points. On other occasions the disagreement is more marked, with at least two judges adopting a different position from that preferred by the judges in the majority. For the purposes of this chapter I am calling these wider disagreements 'close calls'. The question I am addressing is what do the rate and nature of these close calls tell us about the approaches of our most senior judges to their adjudicative role?

To attempt to answer that question I have looked at decisions taken by the Appellate Committee of the House of Lords between 1 January 2001 and 1 October 2009, the date on which the Appellate Committee was replaced by the United Kingdom's Supreme Court. During that period of almost nine years there were 54 cases where there were at least two dissenters,[1] including one where the split was 7:2[2] and another where it was 4:3.[3] These 54 cases represent 9.9 per cent of the 554 sets of judgments issued by the House during that period.

I abide by the assessments I have made elsewhere of the quality of the judgments issued by Law Lords since the mid-1990s,[4] and any comments made here about

---

[1] I have excluded from the list cases where there were two or more dissents but on different points (eg *EB (Kosovo) v Home Secretary* [2008] UKHL 41, [2009] 1 AC 1159), but have included cases where there were dissents on the same point even though the dissenters ultimately agreed with the majority as to whether the appeal should be allowed or dismissed (eg *Jordan v Lord Chancellor* [2007] UKHL 14, [2007] 2 AC 226).

[2] *AG's Reference No 2 of 2001* [2003] UKHL 68, [2004] 2 AC 72.

[3] *Rees v Darlington Memorial Hospital NHS Trust* [2003] UKHL 52, [2004] 1 AC 309.

[4] See, eg, 'Judicial activism in the House of Lords 1995-2007' in B Dickson (ed), *Judicial Activism in Common Law Supreme Courts* (Oxford, Oxford University Press, 2007) ch 9; 'A hard act to follow: the Bingham court 2000–8' in L Blom-Cooper, B Dickson and G Drewry (eds), *The Judicial House of Lords 1876–2009* (Oxford, Oxford University Press, 2009) 255–75.

the judgments I am discussing must be read in that wider context. The points I am making are not intended to denigrate the internal coherence of particular judgments, still less the integrity of particular judges. I should also stress that I am not arguing that dissent is undesirable per se. I agree wholeheartedly with Justice Kirby's writings about the importance of dissenting judgments[5] and I also support James Lee's advocacy of concurring speeches.[6] The simple point I am providing evidence for is that even at the very top level of our judiciary there are quite fundamental differences as to what rules or principles should prevail in our law. Usually the judges wrap their disagreements in polite language, but there can be no disguising the schisms that exist. The disagreements reveal quite a lot about the underlying judicial philosophy of particular judges and lend weight to the contention that the outcome of an appeal in the United Kingdom's highest court may well depend on which judges are selected to hear the appeal.

## II  THE RATE AND NATURE OF THE JOINT DISSENTS

The only judges who sat as Law Lords during the whole of the period 2001 to 2009 were Lords Hope and Scott. Lord Bingham sat for all but the last 12 months (and was the Senior Law Lord until Lord Phillips assumed that role in October 2008), while Lord Hoffmann sat for all but the last five months. Naturally it was those four judges who appeared most frequently in the list of 54 close calls: Lords Hope and Bingham sat in 25 of them, Lord Scott in 23, and Lord Hoffmann in 19. The number of dissenting judgments from those judges is also higher than for others, but not remarkably so. Lord Bingham joined in a dissent on 10 occasions, Lord Scott on nine, Lord Hope on seven and Lord Hoffmann on five. Some judges who sat for shorter periods were equally prone to join in a dissent: Lord Nicholls, despite retiring in 2007, joined in nine dissents; Lord Steyn retired in 2005 but had by then joined in seven dissents. Conversely, Lady Hale and Lord Mance, who did not join the Lords until 2004 and 2005 respectively, had by 2009 each notched up nine cases in which they had joined in dissents.

However no significant patterns of joint dissenting emerge. The most commonly dissenting couples were Lords Bingham and Steyn and Lords Scott and Mance, each of whom jointly dissented in four cases. Lords Bingham and Steyn usually voted the same way in all appeals: by my reckoning they sat together in 75 appeals during this period and disagreed on only six occasions, including in two close calls.[7] Likewise Lords Scott and Mance usually seemed to think alike:

⁵  M Kirby, 'The Importance of Dissent' (2005) speech available from www.michaelkirby.com.au, no 2030; and 'Judicial Dissent – Common Law and Civil Law Traditions' (2007) 123 *Law Quarterly Review* 379.

⁶  J Lee, 'A Defence of Concurring Speeches' [2009] *Public Law* 305.

⁷  *R (Munjaz) v Mersey Care NHS Trust* [2005] UKHL 58, [2006] 2 AC 148; *Rees v Darlington Memorial Hospital NHS Trust* (n 3) (Lord Steyn dissenting on both occasions).

they sat together in 33 cases and always voted the same way except twice.[8] The highest number of interpersonal disagreements in the period under review was eight—between the pairings of Lords Mance and Walker, Lords Hope and Scott, and Lords Bingham and Carswell. There were seven disagreements between Lords Hope and Hoffmann and also between Lady Hale and Lord Carswell. But most of these pairings did also agree in some of the close calls: Lords Hope and Scott agreed five times, Lords Hope and Hoffmann three times, and Lords Bingham and Carswell also three times. Lady Hale, however, agreed with Lord Carswell only twice, and Lords Mance and Walker never agreed. These levels of disagreement are interesting, but of themselves they do not allow us to draw firm conclusions about the judicial philosophies of the judges or their attitudes to particular colleagues. In the House of Lords there has been nothing approaching the predictable voting patterns that are discernible in the US Supreme Court[9] and, to a lesser extent, in the High Court of Australia.[10]

It is remarkable how many of the 54 close calls occurred in private law cases—contract law, shipping law, restitution law, defamation law, taxation law, even employment law.[11] There were 27 such cases (exactly 50%), 18 public law cases[12] and nine cases on criminal law or procedure. It would not appear that there is any greater unanimity amongst their Lordships in the private law field than in others. This would suggest that, whatever the reasons for differences of opinion between their Lordships, they are not linked to attitudes to the state or to what individuals should expect from state bodies. If there is activism as opposed to restraint, or liberalism as opposed to conservatism, these features seem to be on display regardless of the area of law in question.

What is most striking is the importance of the issues in respect of which close calls took place and the strength of feeling displayed by some of the Law Lords in relation to them. Time does not permit me to set out every instance of this importance and strength of feeling, so I have decided to focus on just three fields of law to illustrate the diversity of opinions. I will touch upon the eight cases in criminal law and procedure, the 10 cases in human rights law, and the 14 in tort law, proceeding largely in chronological order within each field. The full flavour of

---

[8]  *R (BAPIO Action Ltd) v Secretary of State for the Home Department* [2008] UKHL 27, [2008] 1 AC 1003; *Stone & Rolls Ltd v Moore Stephens* [2009] UKHL 39, [2009] 3 WLR 455.

[9]  See, eg, T Keck, *The Most Activist Supreme Court in History* (Chicago, University of Chicago Press, 2004).

[10]  See the annual analyses of High Court constitutional law cases by Andrew Lynch, published since 2004 in the *University of New South Wales Law Journal*.

[11]  In all three of its decisions involving the interpretation of regulations on work equipment the House was split 3:2: *R (Junttan Oy) v Bristol Magistrates* [2003] UKHL 55, [2004] 2 All ER 555; *Fytche v Wincanton Logistics* [2004] UKHL 31, [2004] 4 All ER 221; and *Smith v Northamptonshire County Council* [2009] UKHL 27, [2009] ICR 734.

[12]  Ten of these were applications for judicial review; four others were claims about human rights; I am also including a further case on inquests (*Jordan v Lord Chancellor*, n 1 above) and one on the election of the First and Deputy First Minister of Northern Ireland (*Robinson v Secretary of State for Northern Ireland* [2002] UKHL 32, [2002] NI 390).

the tensions between the judges is evident only when one examines the judgments in depth. Here I can merely hint at the intensity of feelings.

### III  CRIMINAL LAW

In recent years the House of Lords has not been known for its boldness or clarity in the field of criminal law,[13] perhaps because few judges appointed as Law Lords have had long experience of practising in that area. Judges who have been chief justices in their own jurisdiction—England and Wales, Scotland or Northern Ireland—are inevitably more expert at dealing with criminal appeals, but that does not seem to have helped the House as a whole to be more creative when adjudicating in such matters.

In *R (Wardle) v Crown Court at Leeds*[14] the Lords were asked whether dropping a charge of murder against a person on the last day of the 70-day time limit for keeping him in custody, and then charging him instead with manslaughter, triggered a new 70-day custody time limit. Lords Slynn, Hope and Clyde thought it did, but Lords Nicholls and Scott (both primarily Chancery lawyers) thought it did not. The majority also thought there was no violation of art 5(3) of the European Convention on Human Rights, while the dissenters thought there was. In the majority's view, if the current state of the law gave rise to concern over prosecutors' latitude to prolong periods of detention by charging detainees with new offences, that was a matter for Parliament to remedy.[15] Lord Nicholls, however, described the majority's interpretation of the relevant legislation[16] as 'frankly, absurd',[17] 'nothing short of a nonsense'[18] and 'irrational'.[19] In answer to Lord Nicholls' jibe about absurdity, Lord Slynn observed:

> I decline to dismiss as absurd the opinion of judges experienced in criminal law and procedure in the cases in the Divisional Court to which we have been referred and the views of the stipendiary magistrate, the Crown Court judge and the Divisional Court in the present case.[20]

Lord Scott was more measured than Lord Nicholls. He said the difficulties created by interpreting the regulations literally could not be overcome by 'a purposive reformulation of the statutory language',[21] but thought he was nevertheless entitled to give them the effect Parliament clearly intended them to have because a decision of the Law Lords on company law in 1969 had legitimised such an approach.[22]

---

[13]   JR Spencer, 'Criminal Law', in Blom-Cooper et al (n 4) 609–10.
[14]   *R (Wardle) v Crown Court at Leeds* [2001] UKHL 12, [2002] 1 AC 754.
[15]   ibid [26] (Lord Slynn), [100] (Lord Hope) and [110] (Lord Clyde).
[16]   Prosecution of Offences (Custody Time Limits) Regs 1987 regs 2(2) and 4.
[17]   *Wardle* (n 14) [39]. Also [44].
[18]   ibid [41].
[19]   ibid.
[20]   ibid [26].
[21]   ibid [142].
[22]   *DPP v Schildkamp* [1971] AC 1 (another 3:2 decision).

The basic reason for the dissents in *AG's Reference No 2 of 2001*[23] was simply that the two Scottish Law Lords, Lords Hope and Rodger, preferred to abide by the traditional Scottish approach of staying criminal proceedings if there had been an unreasonable delay in a trial, while the seven other Law Lords involved, all from England and Wales, preferred to be more flexible, only wanting to stay proceedings if there was no lesser remedy which would adequately vindicate the defendant's right to a fair trial. A decision by the Privy Council in a Scottish case on the same point[24] was expressly 'doubted' by the majority in the House of Lords.

How to deal with Parliament's clear intention was again the issue in *AG's Reference No 4 of 2002*,[25] where it was common ground that when enacting s 11(2) of the Terrorism Act 2000 Parliament intended to impose a *legal* burden of proof on an accused person to show that the organisation which he was accused of belonging to was not a proscribed organisation at the time he was a member and that he did not take part in any of its activities while it was proscribed. Lords Bingham, Steyn and Phillips, very boldly, held that the imposition of this burden on a defendant was not 'a proportionate and justifiable legislative response to an undoubted problem',[26] and that s 11(2) should therefore be read down, under s 3 of the Human Rights Act 1998, so as to impose merely an evidential burden. Lords Rodger and Carswell, dissenting, felt that Parliament's wording was perfectly fair, reasonable and proportionate.[27] At one level we see here a difference of opinion over what it is practicable for a defendant to demonstrate in a criminal trial. At another level we are conscious of a radical divide over the need to resort to s 3 of the 1998 Act.

Lords Rodger and Carswell again dissented in *R v Hayter*,[28] this time disagreeing with their brethren's view that the long-standing common law rule against allowing a confession by a defendant to be admitted as evidence in a joint criminal case against a co-defendant should be qualified. Lord Rodger said the majority's approach 'will, in effect, destroy one vital aspect of the common law rule which Parliament has so recently decided should be preserved'.[29] He added that there was no principled basis for making the change and that it 'is likely to have undesirable effects in practice'.[30] Lord Carswell was less forthright, but he did describe what the majority were doing as 'an impermissible breach of principle' and said that if the principle needed to be modified in the public interest, it was for Parliament to do so.[31] Lords Bingham, Steyn and Brown,

---

[23] *AG's Reference No 2 of 2001* [2003] UKHL 68, [2004] 2 AC 72.
[24] *R v HM Advocate* [2002] UKPC D3, [2004] 1 AC 462 (3:2, with Lords Hope, Clyde and Rodger in the majority and Lords Steyn and Walker in the minority).
[25] *AG's Reference No 4 of 2002* [2004] UKHL 43, [2005] 1 AC 264.
[26] ibid [50] (Lord Bingham). Lords Steyn and Phillips simply concurred with Lord Bingham.
[27] ibid [77] and [92] respectively.
[28] *R v Hayter* [2005] UKHL 6, [2005] 1 WLR 605.
[29] ibid [57].
[30] ibid.
[31] ibid [74].

however, were unmoved by such reasoning. They were prepared to step in to do something which Parliament had declined to do just a few years earlier. As in the previous case, Lords Bingham and Steyn were particularly keen to supplement Parliament's law-making in a way which, in their eyes, improved the law.

However in two of the appeals in *R v Abdroikov*[32] Lords Rodger and Carswell once more dissented, the issue being who should be allowed to sit on a jury. Consistent with their approach in the preceding two cases, they preferred to be faithful to what Parliament had recently enacted.[33] They held that the jurors in question (a police officer and an employee of the Crown Prosecution Service) could be considered to be impartial, but Lords Bingham and Mance, and Lady Hale, held that they could not. Echoing his words in *R v Hayter*, Lord Rodger said the majority's decision 'will drive a coach and horses through Parliament's legislation and will go far to reverse its reform of the law'.[34] The majority saw themselves as deducing the obvious from Parliament's words; Lady Hale said: 'There is no indication that Parliament intended to abrogate the common law and Convention rules upon what constitutes a fair trial'.[35]

In *R v Asfaw*[36] an Ethiopian woman who had stopped over in London for a few hours while en route to the USA, where she wanted to seek asylum, argued that she should not be prosecuted for presenting a false passport when boarding the plane to America, because under the Convention on the Status of Refugees she should be deemed to have immunity. That Convention listed offences for which applicants for asylum could claim immunity, but obtaining air transport services by deception was not one of them. Lords Rodger and Mance did not think the wording of the Convention (which in this respect was given force in the UK by the Immigration and Asylum Act 1999) could be stretched to cover this offence, but the majority did. Lord Bingham stressed that the Act had to be given a purposive interpretation, and Lord Hope stressed that to prosecute the appellant for attempting to leave (rather than enter) the country would be an abuse of process. But Lord Rodger was categorically opposed to such views, saying:

> I have come to the clear conclusion that the interpretation favoured by the appellant is not only *impossible* on the language, but is actually at odds with the scheme of the Convention and with its true humanitarian philosophy.[37]

Lord Phillips LCJ also held against the appellant at the Court of Appeal stage; had he been sitting in the Lords (as he sometimes did during his years as Master of the Rolls and then Lord Chief Justice) and had he replaced, say, Lord Carswell (the third judge in the majority), the decision in the House would presumably have been different.

---

[32] *R v Abdroikov* [2007] UKHL 37, [2007] 1 WLR 2679.
[33] Here, in the Criminal Justice Act 2003.
[34] *Abdroikov* (n 32) [43].
[35] ibid [46].
[36] *R v Asfaw* [2008] UKHL 31, [2008] 1 AC 1061.
[37] ibid [84] (emphasis added).

In *R v G*[38] the issue was whether it was a breach of a 15-year-old boy's right to a private life to prosecute him for rape whenever the prosecution knew that the alleged victim had supposedly 'consented' to the sexual intercourse (even though she was only 12). For the majority, Lord Hoffmann said: 'Prosecutorial policy and sentencing do not fall under Article 8 . . . This case is another example of the regrettable tendency to try to convert the whole system of justice into questions of human rights.'[39] Lady Hale did not mince her words either: 'Every male has a choice about where he puts his penis'[40] and:

> Parliament has very recently decided that ['rape'] is the correct label to apply to the activity [in this case]. In my view this does not engage the Article 8 rights of the defendant at all, but if it does, it is entirely justified.[41]

Lord Mance agreed. Lord Hope (dissenting, along with Lord Carswell) rejected Lord Hoffmann's proposition that the Convention rights have nothing to do with prosecutorial policy.[42] He agreed with all that Lady Hale had to say 'about the dangers of under age sexual activity',[43] but he went on to hold that it was a breach of the 15-year-old boy's art 8 rights to continue to prosecute him for rape even after the girl had admitted that she had consented to the intercourse. Lord Carswell simply concurred with Lord Hope,[44] perhaps somewhat surprisingly, given his reputation for preferring a narrow view of the scope of Convention rights.

In *R v Islam*[45] Lords Walker and Neuberger dissented on whether the black market value of a consignment of heroin could be taken as its 'market value' for the purposes of a confiscation order being made against an importer of the drug. Lord Walker said that because he was dissenting it would be inappropriate to set out his reasons at length,[46] but he did say that judges had to give the same meaning to the same words occurring in different parts of an Act.[47] Lord Neuberger thought that to take 'market value' as including black market value would lead to the court condoning an illegal act. These attitudes were diametrically opposed to those displayed by Lords Hope and Mance, and Lady Hale. In their view the difference in meaning within the Act occurred because the contexts were different. The judgments of Lords Hope, Mance and Neuberger do all refer to the others' points of view, but there is no disguising the fundamental difference between them. Lords Walker and Neuberger did not want to dignify the illegality committed with any value at all, whereas the majority did (despite the fact that the defendant in question never actually sold any of the heroin in

---

[38] *R v G* [2008] UKHL 37, [2009] 1 AC 93.
[39] ibid [10].
[40] ibid [46].
[41] ibid [54].
[42] ibid [34].
[43] ibid [36].
[44] ibid [61].
[45] *R v Islam* [2009] UKHL 30, [2009] 1 AC 1076.
[46] ibid [19].
[47] Here, the Proceeds of Crime Act 2002.

question because it was seized by customs officials before he could take delivery of it). From a lawyer's point of view, what was at stake was an issue of statutory interpretation. From a justice point of view what was at stake was the fairness of a penalty. The heroin was valued at £71,000 and Mr Islam was subjected to a confiscation order of more than £400,000.

Let me now sum up these criminal cases. We see some judges (Lords Walker, Neuberger, and especially Rodger and Carswell) adopting a rather restrained approach in that they preferred to let changes to the law be brought about by Parliament rather than making the changes themselves, and they adopted a more literal approach to the interpretation of legislation than that favoured by their fellow judges. But one cannot be categorical here, because such 'conservative' opinions were not displayed by the same judges in other cases where one might have expected them to occur. Lord Carswell, for example, joined Lords Bingham and Hope in upholding the Refugee Convention rights of one defendant and joined Lord Hope in upholding the European Convention rights of a young man charged with rape. On the basis of this brief survey of cases, it would be improper to label particular judges as consistently, or even predominantly, pro-prosecution or pro-defence in criminal cases. The difference in judicial philosophy relates more to the preparedness of the judges to go beyond what Parliament has stated to be the law. Some, in this sense, are much more activist than others.

## IV  HUMAN RIGHTS LAW

This dichotomy between those in favour of judicial restraint and those in favour of judicial activism is also apparent in the field of human rights law, though again the picture is complicated by the fact that judges first and foremost pay attention to the wording of the legislation they have to interpret.

In *R v Kansal (No 2)*[48] the Appellate Committee had to decide if, four months earlier, a differently constituted Committee had made a mistake when ruling that a person who had been convicted of a crime before the Human Rights Act came into force could not rely upon his or her Convention rights in an appeal occurring after it came into force.[49] Lords Lloyd, Steyn and Hope held that a mistake had been made, but that the law should not be changed because (a) the previous ruling was very recent, (b) it represented an arguable point of view, (c) it was not unworkable, and (d) it related to a legislative provision that was merely transitional.[50] Lords Slynn and Hutton dissented, but on the ground that the earlier decision was correct. Theirs was an even more conservative view than that of the majority.

---

[48]  *R v Kansal (No 2)* [2001] UKHL 62, [2002] 2 AC 69. One might have expected a bench of seven judges to hear this case.

[49]  *R v Lambert* [2001] UKHL 37, [2002] 2 AC 545.

[50]  Human Rights Act 1998 s 22(4).

In *Harrow LBC v Qazi*[51] a housing authority evicted a man from his council home because the tenancy had been brought to an end by the man's wife, who had served a valid notice to quit. The man argued that this interfered with his right to respect for his home under art 8 of the European Convention. Lords Hope, Millett and Scott said it did not, because the housing authority had an unqualified right to immediate possession of the house under domestic contract and property law, but Lords Bingham and Steyn said that there was an interference and that the case should be sent back to the county court for a decision on whether it was justifiable or not.[52] The dispute here, then, was about the priority that should be given to human rights arguments in cases coming before British courts, not about the ultimate outcome of the case. Lord Steyn thought the majority's approach 'empties Article 8(1) of any or virtually any meaningful content',[53] and he feared that it would not withstand European scrutiny.[54] Interestingly, in a later case dealing with the same issue[55] the House managed to reach a unanimous conclusion which was something of a midway position between those of the majority and minority in *Qazi*.

In *R (Razgar) v Secretary of State for the Home Department*[56] Lord Walker and Lady Hale dissented when holding that it would not be a breach of art 8 of the European Convention to return an Iraqi asylum seeker to Germany, even though there was evidence that he could well suffer mental health problems if that were to occur. Their Lordships in the majority (Lords Bingham, Steyn and Carswell) preferred to send the case back to an immigration adjudicator for a decision on the strength of the psychiatric evidence. Perhaps uncharacteristically, Lady Hale said:

> [T]his is a field in which harsh decisions sometimes have to be made. People have to be returned to situations which we would find appalling. The United Kingdom is not required to keep people here who have no right to be here unless to expel them would be a breach of its international obligations. It does the cause of human rights no favours to stretch those obligations further than they can properly go.[57]

Article 8 of the European Convention was again at issue in *R (Munjaz) v Mersey Care NHS Trust*,[58] where the close call related to whether the 'seclusion' of psychiatric patients detained in mental hospitals was a breach of the patients' right to respect for their private and family life. This time Lord Bingham joined

---

[51] *Harrow LBC v Qazi* [2003] UKHL 43, [2004] 1 AC 983.
[52] In a later case, Lord Bingham said that he and Lord Steyn certainly thought that Mr Qazi was most unlikely to win even if his case was remitted to the county court: *Lambeth LBC v Kay* [2006] UKHL 10, [2006] 2 AC 465 [23].
[53] ibid [27]. Lord Hope tried to reassure him on the first point: [81]–[82].
[54] In fact Mr Qazi did lodge an application in Strasbourg but it was declared inadmissible: see Lord Bingham's remarks in *Kay* (n 52) [23].
[55] *Lambeth LBC v Kay* (n 52). Lords Hope, Scott and Bingham again sat in this case.
[56] *R (Razgar) v Secretary of State for the Home Department* [2004] UKHL 27, [2004] 2 AC 368.
[57] ibid [65].
[58] *R (Munjaz) v Mersey Care NHS Trust* [2005] UKHL 58, [2006] 2 AC 148.

Lords Hope and Scott in holding that it was not, with Lords Steyn and Brown dissenting. Lord Steyn was again quite forceful when stating his opinion:

> Compared to the judgment of the Court of Appeal the judgment of the majority of the House permits a lowering of the protection offered by the law to mentally disordered persons. If that is the law, so be it. . .For my part, the decision today is a set-back for a modern and just mental-health law.[59]

Lord Brown was less blunt, but he did conclude that in order to comply with Strasbourg's requirement that any interference with art 8(1) had to be 'in accordance with law', the Secretary of State's Code of Practice had to be treated as a document which could not be departed from, as Ashworth Hospital had sought to do in this case. The dissenters upheld the unanimous opinion of the Court of Appeal, which comprised one judge (Hale LJ) who had become a Lord of Appeal by the time the case reached the Lords and another (Lord Phillips MR) who would later be appointed Senior Law Lord. Had either of them been sitting with Lords Steyn and Brown in the House, this decision too would have gone the other way.

In *R (Roberts) v Parole Board*[60] the dispute was over the scope of art 6 of the European Convention, in particular whether a prisoner's right to procedural fairness had been violated when the Parole Board, in determining whether to release the prisoner on licence, took account of an informant's information that was not revealed to the prisoner but only to a specially appointed advocate acting on his behalf. Lords Woolf CJ, Rodger and Carswell held that the prisoner's right had not been breached, but Lords Bingham and Steyn, as in *Qazi*, disagreed. The majority said that the meaning of procedural fairness differed depending on the nature of the decision being taken. Lord Bingham was more fundamentalist in his support for basic rights:

> It is in my opinion contrary to legal principle and good democratic practice to read [a power to depart from the ordinary rules of procedural fairness] into a statute which contains no hint whatever that parliament intended or even contemplated such a departure.[61]

Lord Steyn was equally unbending in his support for the prisoner's right to a fair hearing.[62] Lord Woolf was 'acutely concerned' that Lord Steyn's conclusions were so dramatically different from his, but attributed it to the fact that Lord Steyn was focusing on the position of the prisoner, whereas Lord Woolf considered it essential to focus as well on the problem faced by the Parole Board in having to protect the safety of the public and the rights of the prisoner.[63] There can be little doubt that the fact that there were three chief justices sitting in this case (Lords Rodger

---

[59]  ibid [48].

[60]  *R (Roberts) v Parole Board* [2005] UKHL 45, [2005] 2 AC 738.

[61]  ibid [30].

[62]  'If the decision of the Parole Board is upheld in the present case, it may well augur an open-ended process of piling exception upon exception by judicial decision outflanking Parliamentary scrutiny': ibid [92].

[63]  ibid [79] and [81]. Lord Rodger regarded these observations 'as being of great force': ibid [111].

and Carswell having held that position, or its equivalent, in Scotland and Northern Ireland respectively) made it almost inevitable that the appeal would be dismissed. If, on the other hand, Lord Brown or Lady Hale had been asked to sit alongside Lords Bingham and Steyn, it is likely that the appeal would have been allowed

*R (Hurst) v London Northern District Coroner*[64] revealed differences between Lords Bingham, Rodger and Brown on the one hand and Lady Hale and Lord Mance on the other. The majority ruled that inquests into deaths occurring before the Human Rights Act came into force did not have to comply with art 2 of the European Convention, while the dissenters held that the coroner was still at liberty (though not obliged) to take into account the UK's international obligations under the Convention. Lady Hale pointed out that, while it might not be possible for a coroner's inquest to reach a verdict of 'unlawful killing caused or contributed to by police neglect', there was still a useful purpose to be served in resuming the inquest here. Lord Mance went so far as to admit that he found it unattractive that the country's international obligations, even fundamental ones, were merely discretionary.

Lady Hale was again on the side of Convention rights in *YL v Birmingham City Council*,[65] though this time she was joined in her dissent by Lord Bingham, while Lord Mance joined the majority (with Lords Scott and Neuberger) in holding that a company providing care and accommodation was not exercising an inherently public function and so residents placed in the company's home under arrangements made with a local authority that was paying for their care could not claim Convention rights against the company. The majority's decision meant that people cared for in homes run by the local authority itself could claim Convention rights but people cared for in private homes, even though paid for by the same local authority, could not. Their reasoning turned on distinguishing between the arranging of care and the providing of care. Lady Hale, on the other hand, said that her (alternative) conclusion was 'inexorable'.[66] But of course it too would have led to an anomaly in that some people in a care home would have been granted Convention rights but other people in the same home would not.[67]

In *Somerville v Scottish Ministers*,[68] the issue was whether petitioners who wanted to argue that a member of the Scottish Executive had breached the Human Rights Act had to bring their claim within the one-year limitation period specified in that Act.[69] Lords Hope, Rodger and Walker thought they did not; Lords Scott and Mance thought they did. The latter is the more conservative position, because it limits the availability of remedies for alleged breaches of human rights, but Lords Scott and Mance reached it because they felt so compelled by the wording

---

[64] *R (Hurst) v London Northern District Coroner* [2007] UKHL 13, [2007] 2 AC 189.

[65] *YL v Birmingham City Council* [2007] UKHL 27, [2008] 1 AC 95.

[66] ibid [73].

[67] And this seems to be the result of the government's reaction to the House's decision: the Health and Social Care Act 2008 s 145, extends the definition of public function to embrace those bodies running homes in so far as they care for people under payments made by local authorities.

[68] *Somerville v Scottish Ministers* [2007] UKHL 44, [2007] 1 WLR 2734.

[69] s 7(5).

of s 100(3) of the Scotland Act 1998. Lord Scott admitted to having had 'an embarrassing number of changes of mind'[70] before deciding that Parliament could not have intended to create, without expressly saying so, an entirely new cause of action in damages.[71] Lord Mance was more confident in his conclusions.[72] Two members of the majority, however, did not see much difficulty in imputing an intention to Parliament.[73] The 'swing voter' was Lord Walker, whose relatively short judgment hinges on his assertion that the way in which Lords Scott and Mance wanted to interpret s 100(3) caused even greater difficulties than the way in which Lords Hope and Rodger wanted to interpret it.[74] He was perhaps subconsciously influenced by the fact that this was a Scottish appeal and the views of the two Scottish Law Lords were therefore all the more significant.

A year earlier it was Lords Hoffmann and Carswell who were in the minority whenever the majority comprised Lords Bingham and Brown and Lady Hale. This was in *Secretary of State for the Home Department v JJ*,[75] where the issue was whether the restrictions placed on men who had been issued with 'control orders' under the Prevention of Terrorism Act 2005 amounted to 'deprivation of liberty' and not just to 'restrictions on freedom of movement' for the purposes of art 5 of the European Convention. The majority held that they did, the minority held that they did not. Both sides found support for their conclusions in the European Court's judgment in *Guzzardi v Italy*.[76] What tipped the scales was each judge's conception of acceptable state practice, especially in light of the ongoing threat of terrorism.

Finally, in *R (Bancoult) v Secretary of State for Foreign and Commonwealth Affairs (No 2)*[77] what was at issue was the legality of the British Indian Ocean Territory (Constitution) Order 2004, in so far as it removed from the people who lived on the Chagos Islands in the Indian Ocean the right of abode there. Lords Hoffmann, Rodger and Carswell held that the Order was legal, but Lords Bingham and Mance held it was not. The same split occurred in relation to whether the British government's decision to reimpose immigration controls and prevent resettlement on the islands was an abuse of power, unreasonable or contrary to legitimate expectations. Lord Hoffmann was of the view that, in a ceded (as opposed to a settled) colony: 'The Crown has plenary legislative authority. It can make or unmake the law of the land . . . [T]he right of abode is a creature of the law. The law gives it and the law may take it away'.[78] Lord Rodger

---

[70] *Somerville* (n 68) [78].

[71] ibid.

[72] 'The correct analysis is a nuanced analysis which recognises the different functions of the [Scotland Act and Human Rights Act] . . . [C]laims for damages for conduct incompatible with Convention rights belong to the context of the Human Rights Act': ibid [193].

[73] ibid [31]–[35] (Lord Hope); [115] and [122]–[132] (Lord Rodger).

[74] ibid [166].

[75] *Secretary of State for the Home Department v JJ* [2007] UKHL 45, [2008] 1 WLR 385.

[76] *Guzzardi v Italy* (1980) 3 EHRR 533.

[77] *R (Bancoult) v Secretary of State for Foreign and Commonwealth Affairs (No 2)* [2008] UKHL 61, [2009] 1 AC 453.

[78] ibid [44]–[45]. Lords Hoffmann and Rodger ([98]) both admitted they had been influenced by a

agreed, pointing out that the legality of the 2004 Order meant that there was no breach of chapter 29 of Magna Carta (assuming it applied to BIOT), which provides that 'No freeman shall be . . . disseised of his freehold, or liberties, or free customs, or be outlawed, or exiled . . . but by lawful judgment of his peers, or by the law of the land'.[79] Lord Carswell's judgment expresses agreement with Lords Hoffmann and Rodger. Lord Bingham, on the other hand, thought that there *was* legal authority for saying that people 'belonging' to the BIOT had a right of abode there, and Lord Mance thought that the distinction between settled and ceded colonies applied only to local private law, not to constitutional questions such as the extent of the Crown's prerogative.[80] The case illustrates in stark form the difference in approach between, on the one hand, Law Lords who decide cases strictly by authority, however regretfully,[81] and, on the other, those who are prepared to look at old authorities in the light of more recent legal developments.

In the human rights field, then, we see from the nine close calls summarised above that there is a similar rift to that which appears in the criminal cases. Lords Rodger and Carswell maintained their conservative position in that they were reluctant to extend the reach of the Human Rights Act, except when Lord Rodger was considering the peculiar devolution settlement for Scotland. For their part, Lord Hoffmann displayed his conservatism in *JJ* and *Bancoult*, while Lord Scott did so in *Qazi*, *Munjaz*, *YL* and *Somerville*. On the other hand, Lord Steyn and Lady Hale staunchly upheld human rights in the three close calls they appeared in. Lords Bingham, Brown and Mance mostly tended to favour an expansive approach to human rights, but each of them adopted a more conservative position at times (Lord Bingham in *Munjaz* and *Hurst*, Lord Brown in *Hurst*, Lord Mance in *YL* and *Somerville*). Such widespread unpredictability makes it hard to label all judges as tending to harbour preconceptions in this field.

## V  TORT LAW

The range of issues covered by the law of torts is vast, and conservatism in this field can manifest itself in a variety of ways. Most frequently it takes the form of denying the claimant what he or she is asking for, or of ensuring that the conditions necessary for liability to exist in the first place are onerous to meet. In *Three Rivers DC v Bank of England (No 3)*,[82] for example, the argument centred on whether depositors in the failed Bank of Credit and Commerce International should be permitted to proceed with their claim against the Bank of England for the tort of misfeasance in public office. Lords Steyn, Hope and Hutton felt that they should, because they had raised an arguable case, but Lords Hobhouse and

---

paper written by Professor John Finnis for the Oxford Law Faculty.
[79]  ibid [77] and [117].
[80]  ibid [155].
[81]  See in particular Lord Carswell: ibid [136].
[82]  *Three Rivers DC v Bank of England (No 3)* [2001] UKHL 16, [2003] 2 AC 1.

Millett disagreed, largely on the basis that '[t]here is no point in allowing claims to proceed which have no real prospect of success'.[83] As things turned out, the litigation did ultimately fail, thereby vindicating the minority's position.[84] Theirs was a more pragmatic stand, with no big issue of principle at stake. The case bears comparison with *Ashley v Chief Constable of Sussex Police*,[85] where Lords Bingham, Scott and Rodger allowed a claim for assault and battery to proceed to trial even though the police had already conceded liability in negligence and false imprisonment and no further damages would be recoverable. Lords Carswell and Neuberger thought this would be an abuse of the process of the court, with Lord Carswell approving the views of judges in the courts below to the effect that 'civil courts exist to award compensation, not to conduct public inquiries. Nor is it their function to provide explanations'.[86]

The existence of a right to sue was also at stake in the fascinating case of *Cullen v Chief Constable of the RUC*,[87] where the claimant asked for compensation when he suffered an infringement of his right to access a solicitor while he was in police custody. Lords Hutton, Millett and Rodger dismissed the claimant's appeal, but Lords Bingham and Steyn (in a jointly composed dissent) were in favour of granting compensation. The majority viewed the wrong that had been done as the breach of a public law right, a 'quasi-constitutional right' in Lord Millett's words,[88] the remedy for which should be judicial review. But for Lords Bingham and Steyn there were practical difficulties with judicial review which could not be adequately answered.[89] They also observed that the fact that the majority was prepared to allow compensation to be awarded if 'harm' had been suffered significantly undermined the principle underlying the majority's reasoning.[90]

In *Mirvahedy v Henley*,[91] Lords Nicholls, Hobhouse and Walker upheld the Court of Appeal in ruling that the owners of a frightened horse were strictly liable for the injuries it caused when it ran across a road and collided with a car. Lords Slynn and Scott interpreted the Animals Act 1971 differently, concluding that if Parliament had intended to extend strict liability to situations where a non-dangerous animal causes injury by behaving in a way which it does not generally do but which is normal at particular times (eg when it is frightened), it could have expressly said so. The case is pre-eminently one which turns on attitudes to statutory interpretation, with both the majority and the minority finding clues in the history and wording of the Act to support their preferred reading of it. The

---

[83] ibid [159]. See too [175], and also [193] (Lord Millett).
[84] J Randall, 'It looks Bleak for Deloitte as judge says case was a load of Pollock', *Daily Telegraph* (London, 14 April 2006).
[85] *Ashley v Chief Constable of Sussex Police* [2008] UKHL 25, [2008] 1 AC 962.
[86] ibid [81]. See too Lord Neuberger [131].
[87] *Cullen v Chief Constable of the RUC* [2003] UKHL 39, [2003] 1 WLR 1763.
[88] ibid [67] and [71].
[89] ibid [20].
[90] ibid [19].
[91] *Mirvahedy v Henley* [2003] UKHL 16, [2003] 2 AC 491.

majority adopted a more literal interpretation, with the minority focusing on the Act's overall scheme and purpose.

*Rees v Darlington Memorial Hospital NHS Trust*[92] was the first of three close calls in medical negligence cases during 2001–09, this time a 4:3 decision. None of the seven judges wanted to overrule the House's earlier decision that able-bodied parents could not recover compensation for the costs of bringing up a healthy child born after negligent sterilisation advice,[93] but Lords Bingham, Nicholls, Millett and Scott nevertheless agreed to make a 'conventional' award of £15,000 to mark the wrong done to the parent in such cases, while Lords Steyn and Hope preferred to leave the law completely untouched and Lord Hutton distinguished the earlier authority and would have awarded full recovery because the parent in this case was disabled. There is some irony here, in that we find an activist judge such as Lord Steyn criticising a conservative judge such as Lord Millett for going too far in developing the law. Lord Steyn said:

> I regard the idea of a conventional award in the present case as contrary to principle. It is a novel procedure for judges to create such a remedy. There are limits to permissible judicial creativity for judges. In my view the majority have strayed into forbidden territory. . .If such a rule is to be created it must be done by Parliament.[94]

Lord Hope, too, was rather shocked at his colleagues' boldness:

> The lack of any consistent ratio in support of the proposition in the speeches of the majority is disturbing . . . The issue is, as Lord Steyn says, hugely controversial and I agree with him that its creation . . . ought to have been left, preferably with the benefit of a report by the Law Commissions, to Parliament.[95]

In the second of the medical negligence cases, *Chester v Afshar*,[96] their Lordships were again creative, this time establishing a special rule on causation. The majority held that a patient who has not been warned about the dangers of an operation does not have to prove that she would never have had the operation if she had been warned; she only has to prove that she would not have had the operation at that time. *Gregg v Scott*,[97] the third case, was obviously a very difficult one for their Lordships because seven months elapsed between the hearing of the appeal and the issuing of the judgments, which then spread over 227 paragraphs. The claimant asked for damages for the reduction in his chances of survival following the delay in diagnosing his non-Hodgkin's lymphoma (his chances of surviving 10 years were apparently reduced from 42 per cent to 25 per cent). Lords Hoffmann and Phillips and Lady Hale agreed with the trial judge and the majority of the Court of Appeal (Simon Brown and Mance LJJ—both future

---

[92] *Rees v Darlington Memorial Hospital NHS Trust* [2003] UKHL 52, [2004] 1 AC 309.
[93] *McFarlane v Tayside Health Board* [2000] 2 AC 59.
[94] *Rees* (n 92) [46].
[95] ibid [74] and [77].
[96] *Chester v Afshar* [2004] UKHL 41, [2005] 1 AC 134. Lords Steyn, Hope and Walker were in the majority; Lords Bingham and Hoffmann dissented.
[97] *Gregg v Scott* [2005] UKHL 2, [2005] 2 AC 176.

Law Lords) that such a loss was not recoverable, but Lords Nicholls and Hope disagreed. Lord Nicholls said the case revealed different perceptions of what constitutes injustice in a common type of medical negligence case. He thought that not to give a remedy just because the claimant's initial chances of surviving for 10 years were not higher than 50 per cent was 'irrational and indefensible'[98] and 'would make no sort of sense'.[99] Yet to Lord Hoffmann, what the dissenters were proposing:

> would be so radical a change in our law as to amount to a legislative act. It would have enormous consequences for insurance companies and the National Health Service. . .I think that any such change should be left to Parliament.[100]

He also felt that the minority's view was inconsistent with previous House of Lords authority. Lord Phillips (Master of the Rolls at the time) reached his conclusion by questioning the statistical analysis relied on in the court below. He did not think that the injustice identified by Lords Nicholls and Hope was as 'cogent' as they suggested, nor that it justified the proposed change to the law.[101] Apparently ignoring *Chester v Afshar*, he added:

> it seems to me that there is a danger, if special tests of causation are developed piecemeal to deal with perceived injustices in particular fact situations, that the coherence of our common law will be destroyed.[102]

Both Lords Hope and Hoffmann reached consistent decisions in *Chester v Afshar* and *Gregg v Scott*, though Lord Hope was in the minority in the former and in the majority in the latter while Lord Hoffmann played the reverse roles. Lord Hope was in favour of the claimant recovering in both cases, while Lord Hoffmann was against it in both cases. Lord Walker joined Lord Hope in the majority in *Chester v Afshar*, which suggests that if he had sat in *Gregg v Scott*, in place, say, of Lord Phillips MR, that case might have been decided differently.

The rule that defendants must take their victims as they find them was again at issue in *Lagden v O'Connor*,[103] where an impecunious claimant, whose car had been negligently damaged by the defendant and who could not afford to pay ordinary commercial car hire charges for a replacement car and had to enter into an ultimately more expensive agreement with a credit hire company, sought recovery of the extra expenditure. Lords Nicholls, Slynn and Hope were in favour of allowing recovery, but Lords Scott and Walker were not. The dissenters thought it was inappropriate to create an exception to a principle that had fairly recently been confirmed by the House,[104] with Lord Scott adding that making a distinction

---

[98] ibid [3].
[99] ibid [4]. Lord Hope agreed, saying ([92]) that he would not have written at such length had the result of the appeal been clear to him at the time, which suggests that at least one of his colleagues had prevaricated over the result.
[100] ibid [90].
[101] ibid [171].
[102] ibid [173].
[103] *Lagden v O'Connor* [2003] UKHL 64, [2004] 1 AC 1067.
[104] *Dimond v Lovell* [2002] 1 AC 834.

between impecunious and non-impecunious claimants would do a disservice to the law by unnecessarily complicating it on a conceptually imprecise basis.[105] Lord Walker thought the proposed modification of the law was 'dangerously open-ended'.[106]

In the well-known case of *Campbell v MGN*[107] Lords Nicholls and Hoffmann teamed up to dissent, as against Lords Hope and Carswell and Lady Hale. They did not think that the *Mirror's* disclosure of Naomi Campbell's attendance at Narcotics Anonymous, the details of her treatment there, or a photograph of her leaving meetings, was sufficiently intrusive to amount to a breach of her rights to confidence, given that she herself had already admitted that she was a drug addict and was receiving treatment for her addiction.[108] Lord Phillips MR heard the case in the Court of Appeal and adopted the same position as the two dissenting Law Lords. *Polanski v Condé Nast*[109] further illustrates a sharp difference of opinion as to what makes an undeserving claimant, though again the claimant won. Roman Polanski wanted to pursue libel proceedings in England but did not wish to go there in person because, being a fugitive from justice in the United States, he feared being arrested and extradited. He therefore applied to give his evidence by video conference link from France, where he lived. Lords Nicholls and Hope, and Lady Hale, held that he should be allowed to do so, but Lords Slynn and Carswell dissented. Obviously the dissenters were swayed by their conception of public policy. Lord Slynn, for example, said that:

> to accede to a request like the present, whose avowed sole aim is to avoid his being extradited, in the absence of other overriding considerations compelling the grant of the application, is contrary to public or judicial policy.[110]

This is yet another case where one of the Court of Appeal judges who held the same view as the two dissenting judges in the Lords, Simon Brown LJ, was later promoted to the Lords.

Lady Hale and Lord Carswell were again on opposite sides of the argument over access to justice in *Seal v Chief Constable of South Wales Police*,[111] where Lords Bingham, Carswell and Brown held that it would not be a breach of the common law, nor of art 6 of the European Convention on Human Rights, to deny someone the right to sue the police under the Mental Health Act 1983 for the statutory tort of unlawfully removing him to a place of safety, simply because he had not first sought the leave of the High Court to issue proceedings, as required by the Act. Lady Hale, standing up as ever for the rights of the vulnerable, declared

---

[105] *Lagden* (n 103) [86]–[88].

[106] ibid [104].

[107] *Campbell v MGN* [2004] UKHL 22, [2004] 2 AC 457.

[108] *cf* Lord Hoffmann's views on art 8 in the criminal case of *R v G*, discussed at text to n 38. Lord Nicholls also dissented on the breach of confidence point (this time joining Lord Walker) in *OBG v Allan* [2007] UKHL 21, [2008] 1 AC 1.

[109] *Polanski v Condé Nast* [2005] UKHL 10, [2005] 1 WLR 637.

[110] ibid [50]. See too Lord Carswell: [93].

[111] *Seal v Chief Constable of South Wales Police* [2007] UKHL 31, [2007] 1 WLR 1910.

that '[a]ccess to the courts is one of the most fundamental principles of the rule of law upon which our democracy is based'.[112] Lord Woolf agreed, on the basis that 'Parliament certainly did not make it clear that civil proceedings commenced without leave . . . were to be a nullity'.[113] His implication was that, if Parliament has not expressly prohibited something, the conduct must still be permissible under the common law.

But Lady Hale was not so keen on granting access to justice to trading companies. In *Jameel v Wall Street Journal*[114] a company sought to sue for libel without having to prove special damage. Lords Bingham, Hope and Scott held that it could do so, but Lord Hoffmann and Lady Hale thought it could not. Lord Hoffmann was very brief on the point, saying that 'a commercial company has no soul and its reputation is no more than a commercial asset, something attached to its trading name, which brings in customers'.[115] Lady Hale had regard to the decision by the European Court of Human Rights in the so-called McLibel case[116] and warned that the majority's view 'may have a disproportionately chilling effect upon freedom of speech'.[117] She thought that a change to the rule 'would achieve a proper balance between the right of a company to protect its reputation and the right of the press and the public to be critical of it'.[118]

In *OBG Ltd v Allan*,[119] which comprised three separate appeals, two Law Lords dissented in the first two of them. In the first, Lord Nicholls and Lady Hale jointly disagreed that it would be too drastic a reshaping of the law to extend liability for conversion to interference with contracts, with Lady Hale being particularly keen to see such an extension made.[120] In the second, Lords Nicholls and Walker disagreed that a confidential secret existed in relation to photographs of a wedding even after the 'authorised' photographs had been published. In this appeal the minority were supportive of a unanimous Court of Appeal comprising three judges all of whom later became Law Lords.[121]

Finally, in *Stone & Rolls Ltd v Moore Stephens*[122] auditors tried to rely on the defence of *ex turpi causa non oritur actio* when they were sued by what was in effect a one-person company for not having detected massive fraud on the part of that person. Lords Phillips, Walker and Brown held that the defence was available, but Lords Scott and Mance disagreed. Given that the company in question was in liquidation (having had to pay very large sums to the victims of the fraud), Lord Scott emphasised that if the auditors had to pay damages, these would not benefit the fraudulent owner of the company, only the company's creditors.

---

[112]  ibid [55].
[113]  ibid [35]. Lord Woolf was sitting as a retired senior judge.
[114]  *Jameel v Wall Street Journal* [2006] UKHL 44, [2007] 1 WLR 359.
[115]  ibid [91].
[116]  *Steel and Morris v UK* (2005) 41 EHRR 403.
[117]  *Jameel* (n 114) [158].
[118]  ibid.
[119]  *OBG Ltd v Allan* (n 108).
[120]  ibid [309]–[317].
[121]  Lord Phillips of Worth Matravers MR, and Clarke and Neuberger LJJ.
[122]  *Stone & Rolls Ltd v Moore Stephens* [2009] UKHL 39, [2009] 3 WLR 455.

This led him to say: 'The wielding of a rule of public policy in circumstances where public policy is not engaged constitutes, in my respectful opinion, bad jurisprudence.'[123] For his part Lord Mance said: 'The contrary result espoused by the majority of your Lordships will weaken the value of an audit and diminish auditors' exposure in relation to precisely those companies most vulnerable to management fraud.'[124]

To sum up the tort cases, the most outstanding feature is probably the reluctance of Lord Hoffmann to expand the scope of tortious liability (whether for libel, medical negligence, interference with contracts, or breach of confidence), but Lords Brown and Carswell also displayed a mainly restrained approach, with the exception of Lord Carswell's support for Naomi Campbell. Lord Steyn and Lady Hale were more often in favour of expanding liability than of contracting it, and Lord Bingham even more so. Lords Nicholls and Hope were the most activist in this field, with one or other of them being on the less conservative side of the divide in all but three of the 14 cases here reviewed. There were fundamental differences over central questions of private law: when can someone evade having to pay compensation just because he or she, or a third party, has acted illegally, when can access to justice be denied for purely procedural reasons, and when can professionals be sued even though the harm suffered is only indirectly linked to their action or inaction? There were also strong differences of opinion over the exact scope of three developing torts—breach of confidence, misfeasance in public office and interference with contracts.

## VI CONCLUSIONS

On the basis of such a brief survey it is difficult to draw definite conclusions. I will nevertheless plant some seeds for consideration. The first is that the differences of opinion uncovered by this study are not at all confined to questions of statutory interpretation, with some judges preferring a more literal approach and others a more purposive one. There are many instances of differences on some crucial common law issues, such as the extent of the abuse of process and *ex turpi causa* doctrines,[125] the recoverability of damages for lost chances,[126] and the availability of interest on claims for money paid by mistake.[127]

The second is that, while a Law Lord rarely displays any real animosity towards a colleague, sometimes the language used is rather strong, indicating that the judge cannot understand how anyone could have come to an alternative

---

[123] ibid [123].

[124] ibid [276]. Lord Mance put detailed consideration of overseas authority into an annex to his judgment, just as he put into an appendix in *R v Asfaw* (n 36) an analysis by the UN High Commissioner for Refugees of relevant meetings leading up to the 1951 Convention.

[125] *Polanski v Conde Nast Publications* (n 109) and *Stone & Rolls Ltd v Moore Stephens* (n 122) respectively.

[126] *Gregg v Scott* (n 97).

[127] *Sempra Metals Ltd v Inland Revenue Commissioners* [2007] UKHL 34, [2008] 1 AC 561.

conclusion to the one he or she prefers. Frequently, forceful declarations by judge X are not prefaced by detailed consideration of all the reasons given by judge Y for an alternative position, so the impression is created (no doubt misleadingly) that judge Y's judgment was not fully scrutinised before judge X finalised his or her judgment or that judge X simply had no answer to judge Y's reasoning, other than mere assertion of a different way of looking at things. Some Law Lords are more conscientious than others at cross-referring to colleagues' opinions.

The third conclusion is that the outcome of an appeal in our highest court can sometimes depend on which judges are sitting to hear the appeal. Many have long suspected this to be the case, even though the official position must be that it is not. It is perfectly possible, of course, that it is the quality of the advocacy they are presented with which ultimately persuades judges to adopt certain views, not their predisposition to do so. The fact remains that in several of the close calls the two dissenting judges were agreeing with a judgment in the Court of Appeal by one or more judges who were later promoted to the Lords. This is surely an argument for our top court always sitting en banc, like the US and Canadian Supreme Courts, or at least for deploying a nine-judge bench more frequently than occurs at present.[128] If such a step is not taken, the suspicion that the appeal system has a distinctly aleatory aspect to it, with the outcome depending on which judges happen to be selected to hear the case, will only grow and fester.

---

[128] The first modern nine-judge case was *AG's Reference (No 2 of 2001)* (n 23). There have been seven other such cases since then, including three decisions by the new Supreme Court. The first nine-judge decision of the Supreme Court saw a 5:4 split on one issue, with nine separate speeches: *R (on the application of E) v Governing Body of JFS* [2009] UKSC 15, [2010] 2 WLR 153. The second decision saw a 6:3 split, again with nine separate speeches: *R (Smith) v Oxfordshire Assistant Deputy Coroner* [2010] UKSC 29, [2010] 3 WLR 223.

# Index